WHITE HOUSE, INC.

THE TRUMP FORTUNE

(Estimates as of March 1, 2020)

ASSET	VALUE	DEBT	TRUMP'S STAKE	TRUMP'S EQUITY
555 California St. (San Francisco)	$2.3 billion	$548 million	30%	$517 million
1290 Ave. of the Americas (NYC)	$2.5 billion	$950 million	30%	$457 million
40 Wall St. (NYC)	$471 million	$141 million	100%	$330 million
Trump Tower (NYC)	$330 million	$100 million	100%	$230 million
6 East 57th St. (NYC)	$211 million	$0	100%	$211 million
Ten U.S. golf clubs	$210 million	$18 million	100%	$192 million
Mar-a-Lago (Palm Beach, Fla.)	$170 million	$0	100%	$170 million
Trump Park Ave. (NYC)	$173 million	$10 million	100%	$163 million
Cash	$160 million	$0	100%	$160 million
Trump National Doral Miami	$209 million	$125 million	100%	$84 million
Hotel management and licensing	$80 million	$0	Various	$80 million
Scotland and Ireland golf clubs	$79 million	$0	100%	$79 million
Trump Int'l Hotel Las Vegas	$136 million	$0	50%	$68 million
Trump Tower penthouse (NYC)	$52 million	$0	100%	$52 million
Trump Parc East (NYC)	$30 million	$0	100%	$30 million
Winery (Charlottesville, Va.)	$30 million	$0	100%	$30 million
Estate (Bedford, N.Y.)	$30 million	$0	100%	$30 million
Two airplanes and two helicopters	$27 million	$0	100%	$27 million
Palm Beach, Fla., houses	$36 million	$11 million	100%	$25 million
Trump Plaza (NYC)	$37 million	$13 million	100%	$24 million
Trump World Tower (NYC)	$24 million	$0	100%	$24 million
Trump Int'l Hotel Washington, D.C.	$200 million	$170 million	77.5%	$23 million
Caribbean estate (St. Martin)	$13 million	$0	100%	$13 million
Undeveloped lots in California	$12 million	$0	100%	$12 million
Trump Parc (NYC)	$11 million	$0	100%	$11 million
Trump Int'l Hotel & Tower (NYC)	$14 million	$6.5 million	100%	$7.5 million
Trump Int'l Hotel & Tower Chicago	$96 million	$95 million	100%	$1 million
Virginia homes	$1.5 million	$0	100%	$1.5 million
Product licensing	$500,000	$0	100%	$500,000

Total assets (attributable to Trump): $4.2 billion
Total debt (attributable to Trump): $1.1 billion

NET WORTH: $3.1 billion

Source: Dan Alexander for *Forbes*

THE MULTIBILLION-DOLLAR PRESIDENCY

Donald Trump elected to donate his $400,000 annual salary as president. He doesn't need the government check. By the time Trump's first two years in office were over, his businesses had already collected an estimated $1.2 billion in revenue. That put the president on pace to haul in $2.4 billion of revenue by the end of his first term and $4.9 billion by the end of his potential second term. Here, for the first time ever, is a look at all the money flowing into the president's business.

ASSET	2017-2018 REVENUE (EST.)	ON PACE TO HIT AFTER ONE TERM IN OFFICE	ON PACE TO HIT AFTER TWO TERMS IN OFFICE
U.S. golf clubs	$216 million	$432 million	$864 million
Trump National Doral Miami	$151 million	$301 million	$603 million
1290 Ave. of the Americas (NYC)	$108 million	$217 million	$433 million
40 Wall St. (NYC)	$84 million	$168 million	$336 million
Trump Int'l Hotel Washington, D.C.	$81 million	$163 million	$325 million
Real estate management and licensing	$81 million	$162 million	$324 million
Scotland and Ireland golf clubs	$80 million	$159 million	$318 million
555 California St. (San Francisco)	$78 million	$156 million	$311 million
Trump Int'l Hotel & Tower Chicago	$72 million	$144 million	$288 million
Trump Tower (NYC)	$69 million	$137 million	$275 million
Mar-a-Lago (Palm Beach, Fla.)	$48 million	$96 million	$191 million
6 East 57th St. (NYC)	$26 million	$52 million	$104 million
Trump Int'l Hotel Las Vegas	$26 million	$52 million	$104 million
Other	$25 million	$50 million	$100 million
Skating rink and carousel (NYC)	$19 million	$37 million	$75 million
Restaurants	$8 million	$16 million	$33 million
Trump Park Avenue (NYC)	$8 million	$16 million	$32 million
Trump Plaza (NYC)	$5 million	$11 million	$21 million
Trump Int'l Hotel & Tower (NYC)	$5 million	$9 million	$18 million
Real estate brokerage	$4 million	$8 million	$16 million
Trump Parc East (NYC)	$4 million	$8 million	$16 million
Trump World Tower (NYC)	$2 million	$5 million	$9 million
Trump Parc (NYC)	$1 million	$2 million	$5 million
TOTAL	$1.2 billion	$2.4 billion	$4.9 billion

Note: For buildings in which Donald Trump holds a stake of less than 100%, estimates represent revenue attributable to the president.

PRESIDENTIAL PROFITS (2017)

In 2017, President Trump hauled in an estimated $150 million of profit from operations at his various businesses. A serious haul, even though an estimated $42 million of it covered interest payments. Below, a first-of-its-kind look into how the president's properties fared during his first year in office.

PROPERTY	EST. PROFIT FROM OPERATIONS	EST. INTEREST EXPENSE
1290 Ave. of the Americas (NYC)	$28 million	$10 million
U.S. golf clubs	$22 million	$600,000
40 Wall St. (NYC)	$20 million	$6 million
555 California St. (San Francisco)	$20 million	$9 million
Trump Tower (NYC)	$14 million	$4.2 million
Hotel management and licensing	$12 million	$0
6 East 57th St. (NYC)	$11 million	$50,000
Mar-a-Lago (Palm Beach, Fla.)	$6 million	$0
Trump National Doral Miami	$4.3 million	$4 million
Trump Int'l Hotel Washington, D.C.	$4 million	$4.4 million
Trump Park Avenue (NYC)	$3.1 million	$400,000
Trump Int'l Hotel Las Vegas	$2.6 million	$900,000
Trump Int'l Hotel & Tower (Chicago)	$2.5 million	$1.6 million
Trump Plaza (NYC)	$1.7 million	$600,000
Spring Creek Towers (NYC)	$1.4 million	$800,000
Winery (Charlottesville, Va.)	$1 million	$0
Trump World Tower (NYC)	$1 million	$0
Trump Int'l Hotel & Tower (NYC)	$900,000	$300,000
Trump Parc East (NYC)	$600,000	$0
Product licensing	$500,000	$0
Trump Parc (NYC)	$500,000	$0
Palm Beach, Fla., houses	$0	$5,000
Estate (Westchester County, N.Y.)	$0	$250,000
Trump Int'l Golf Links (Scotland)	- $1.7 million	$0
Trump Int'l Golf Links (Ireland)	- $2.1 million	$0
Trump Turnberry (Scotland)	- $4 million	$0
TOTAL	$150 million	$42 million

Note: For buildings in which Donald Trump holds a stake of less than 100%, estimates represent profits attributable to the president.

PRESIDENTIAL PROFITS (2018)

By Trump's second year in office, his last name was more famous than ever. That wasn't necessarily a good thing for his business. Fewer people paid him less money to license the Trump brand for products and properties. But Trump got a boost from two buildings without his name on them: 1290 Avenue of the Americas, in New York City, and 555 California Street, in San Francisco. His business also managed to juice profits at Doral even though revenues stayed relatively flat.

PROPERTY	EST. PROFIT FROM OPERATIONS	EST. INTEREST EXPENSE
1290 Ave. of the Americas (NYC)	$32 million	$10 million
555 California St. (San Francisco)	$23 million	$9 million
40 Wall St. (NYC)	$21 million	$6 million
U.S. golf clubs	$21 million	$600,000
Trump Tower (NYC)	$15 million	$4.2 million
6 East 57th St. (NYC)	$11 million	$0
Trump National Doral Miami	$10 million	$5 million
Hotel management and licensing	$8 million	$0
Trump Int'l Hotel Las Vegas	$6 million	$200,000
Mar-a-Lago (Palm Beach, Fla.)	$5 million	$0
Trump Int'l Hotel Washington, D.C.	$4 million	$6 million
Trump Park Avenue (NYC)	$3.1 million	$350,000
Trump Plaza (NYC)	$1.7 million	$500,000
Trump World Tower (NYC)	$1 million	$0
Winery (Charlottesville, Va.)	$1 million	$0
Trump Int'l Hotel & Tower (Chicago)	$900,000	$2 million
Trump Int'l Hotel & Tower (NYC)	$800,000	$300,000
Trump Parc East (NYC)	$700,000	$0
Spring Creek Towers (NYC)	$500,000	$350,000
Trump Parc (NYC)	$500,000	$0
Palm Beach, Fla., houses	$200,000	$250,000
Product licensing	$100,000	$0
Estate (Westchester County, N.Y.)	$0	$250,000
Trump Int'l Golf Links (Scotland)	- $1.4 million	$0
Trump Int'l Golf Links (Ireland)	- $1.7 million	$0
Trump Turnberry (Scotland)	- $3.5 million	$0
TOTAL	$161 million	$43 million

Note: For buildings in which Donald Trump holds a stake of less than 100%, estimates represent profits attributable to the president.

WHITE HOUSE, INC.

HOW DONALD TRUMP TURNED
THE PRESIDENCY INTO
A BUSINESS

Dan Alexander

PORTFOLIO | PENGUIN

PORTFOLIO / PENGUIN
An imprint of Penguin Random House LLC
penguinrandomhouse.com

Most Portfolio books are available at a discount when purchased in quantity for sales promotions or
corporate use. Special editions, which include personalized covers, excerpts, and corporate imprints, can be
created when purchased in large quantities. For more information, please call (212) 572-2232 or e-mail
specialmarkets@penguinrandomhouse.com. Your local bookstore can also assist with discounted
bulk purchases using the Penguin Random House corporate Business-to-Business program.
For assistance in locating a participating retailer, e-mail B2B@penguinrandomhouse.com.

Library of Congress Cataloging-in-Publication Control Number: 2020936891 (print)

ISBN 9780593188521 (hardcover)
ISBN 9780593188538 (ebook)

Printed in the United States of America
1 3 5 7 9 10 8 6 4 2

BOOK DESIGN BY MEIGHAN CAVANAUGH

While the author has made every effort to provide accurate telephone numbers,
internet addresses, and other contact information at the time of publication, neither
the publisher nor the author assumes any responsibility for errors or for changes that occur
after publication. Further, the publisher does not have any control over and does not
assume any responsibility for author or third-party websites or their content.

To my wife, Kate, the kindest person in the world

And to Mrs. Boone, my high school journalism teacher

CONTENTS

Author's Note   *xiii*

Prologue   *1*

1. Art of the Self-Deal
THE RISE OF DONALD TRUMP   *9*

2. Moscow Money
TRUMP, PUTIN, AND THE
2016 PRESIDENTIAL ELECTION   *31*

3. The Takeover
INAUGURATING AMERICA'S
BILLIONAIRE IN CHIEF   *55*

4. Presidential Palace
INSIDE TRUMP'S
OTHER WASHINGTON, D.C., HOME   *73*

5. Bad Lie

THE TRUTH BEHIND TRUMP'S GOLF GAME *95*

6. All the President's Tenants

INSIDE TRUMP'S TOWERS *117*

7. Cashing In

THE BUSINESS BEHIND TRUMP'S
500-PLUS HOMES *137*

8. All in the Family

"NEPOTISM IS KIND OF A
FACTOR OF LIFE" *153*

9. Like Father, Like Son-in-Law

JARED KUSHNER'S WORLD OF CONFLICTS *169*

10. Fill the Swamp

TRUMP'S TEAM *185*

11. 2020 Money

CAMPAIGN CASH AND CORONAVIRUS COSTS *205*

Appendix *215*
Acknowledgments *221*
Notes *225*

AUTHOR'S NOTE

At a time when journalism is under fire, I believe it is important for reporters to show their work. To that end, I have included an unusual number of endnotes throughout the book. As you will see, this account is based primarily upon documents, buttressed by interviews. It includes hundreds of financial figures. All estimates for the value of assets are as of March 1, 2020, unless otherwise indicated. Outside fact-checkers spent months reviewing every line of the book. The White House received a detailed list of questions before publication. A spokesperson responded, "These are all questions for Trump Org." The Trump Organization did not respond to requests for comment.

Prologue

I n the heart of San Francisco's Financial District, a few blocks from the Transamerica Pyramid Center that defines the city's skyline, sits a 52-story tower, the kind you might find in any major city. Its name, 555 California Street, is as forgettable as its appearance, all brown and black and boring. Inside, a team of security guards watches over the elevator banks in the lobby, checking IDs. They are protecting more than just office space.

To get past them and into the heart of the building, I signed up for a desk in a coworking space on the 49th floor before arriving. Once there, I ride down to a different floor, the 43rd, and walk off the elevator. Before me stands a pristine office with shiny concrete floors, subdued gray couches, empty chairs, and a sign that spells out "Qatar Investment Authority Advisory (USA) Inc." and, in smaller type, "A subsidiary of the Qatar Investment Authority." Nothing inside the place looks as if it has been touched. There is a marble welcome desk but no one to welcome visitors. On top of the counter rests a plant that looks like it has been dead for months.

I rap my knuckles on the glass doors to see if anyone is inside. No one answers, even though it's the middle of the afternoon. The next day, in the morning, I return to the same scene. Again I knock. And again no one answers.

Why would anyone, much less an entity that serves as an arm of the Qatari government, bother outfitting an empty office in an expensive San Francisco skyscraper? Well, consider who owns the building. The lobby features signs for Vornado Realty Trust, the publicly traded firm, with innumerable shareholders, that has a 70% stake in the tower.[1] The other 30% belongs to a single man: Donald J. Trump, the president of the United States.[2] His interest here is worth an estimated $517 million after debt—making it the most valuable asset in his entire portfolio. It's worth more than twice as much as Trump Tower, six times as much as Trump's Doral golf resort in Miami, 17 times as much as his hotel in Washington, D.C.[3]

The amount Qatar pays in rent remains a mystery. Odds are it adds up to a sum most billionaires not named Trump would hardly notice. According to a Vornado document, the office is just 5,557 square feet.[4] If the Qataris are paying the average rate in the building, that would amount to $450,000 a year, and Trump's 30% would total $135,000.[5]

The money does not flow directly. Instead, it appears to go from the U.S. subsidiary[6] of the Qatar Investment Authority, a sovereign wealth fund, to HWA 555 Owners LLC. According to filings Trump sent to federal ethics officials, the Donald J. Trump Revocable Trust owns 30% of HWA 555 Owners LLC.[7] And that trust, according to documents the Trump Organization submitted to authorities in Washington, D.C., was set up "to hold assets for the exclusive benefit of Donald J. Trump."[8] Trump, in other words, personally holds 30% of the space the Qataris are leasing. Strip away the layers and it boils down to just the sort of arrangement the founding fathers feared. A foreign government, it seems, has been secretly paying the president of the United States for more than a year. Yet, with so many other scandals brewing, this one has managed to go entirely undetected—until now.

IN ORDER TO understand why Qatar might want to funnel cash to the president, it's important to first understand U.S.-Qatari relations. A peninsula hanging off Saudi Arabia, smaller than the state of Connecticut,[9] Qatar has played an outsize role in global politics for one reason: money.[10] There are 77% more natural gas reserves sitting under[11] Qatar than under the entire United States, helping make Qatar, on a per capita basis,[12] the second-richest nation on earth.

Although Qatar doesn't share many American values—monarchs rule[13] the country, and its labor abuses are legendary[14]—it has long been an ally of the United States. Qatari troops fought alongside Americans in the Gulf War. Afterward, the tiny nation spent more than $8 billion on a military base hosting American troops near[15] Doha, the Qatari capital, which has been a key center for operations in Afghanistan and Syria.[16]

America has other allies in the region, of course, including Saudi Arabia[17] and the United Arab Emirates.[18] But for years, the allies have been sparring among themselves. In 2014, Saudi Arabia, the United Arab Emirates, and Bahrain pulled their ambassadors from Qatar, accusing the country of backing terrorists.[19] In May 2017, Trump took his first trip overseas as president,[20] visiting Saudi Arabia, a nation that had recently pumped more than $270,000[21] into the Trump International Hotel. In early June, the Saudis and several other Middle Eastern nations collectively cut off diplomatic ties with Qatar.[22] Saudi Arabia also shut down its border with its neighbor, turning Qatar into a virtual island.[23]

President Trump left little doubt about whose side he was on in the dispute. "During my recent trip to the Middle East I stated that there can no longer be funding of Radical Ideology," he tweeted in June 2017. "Leaders pointed to Qatar—look!"[24]

Qatar denied the charges and worked to defend its reputation,[25] shelling out hundreds of thousands of dollars to lobbyists to vouch for the embattled nation in Washington.[26] The Qataris also[27] struck deals with American companies like Boeing and Raytheon. And, in a move that managed to evade detection, they figured out how to rent space inside Trump's most valuable property, apparently directing money to the president of the United States.

THE QATARIS FINISHED outfitting their new office space on the 43rd floor sometime after February 2018, when the Saudi dispute was still raging, according to someone who worked inside the skyscraper.[28] In August 2018, Trump's partner Vornado filed a document with San Francisco officials about work being done on the premises, describing the Qatar Investment Authority Advisory (USA) Inc. as a "lessee."[29] Construction crews built out an office, complete with intricate white latticework in the entryway. After the hammers stopped banging, however, the space went unusually quiet.

"I never saw a single person enter the office other than construction," the person who worked in the building explained in a text message. "I travel a lot so could have missed it but definitely saw people in other offices.

"Always thought it was strange," the source added.[30]

Also strange: the lobby's long list of tenants made no mention of the Qatar Investment Authority. The website for the Qatar Investment Authority listed an office in New York,[31] but it didn't say anything about one in San Francisco.

When asked about this deal and others, a spokesperson for the White House replied in an email, "These are all questions for Trump Org. Not the White House."[32] For its part, the Trump Organization did not respond to a long list of questions. Spokespeople for Vornado and the Qatar Investment Authority declined to comment.[33] It's unclear what, if anything, goes on inside the space that the Qatar Investment Authority is leasing. Regardless, the arrangement may be a violation of the U.S. Constitution, which forbids presidents from accepting "emoluments"—compensation—from foreign governments.[34] The president's legal team has previously argued that when a foreign government pays the president at his Washington, D.C., hotel, it's legal, because the trade constitutes a "value-for-value exchange"[35]— Trump gets money, and the officials get a place to stay. In the San Francisco office tower, however, it's harder to make that case. Trump apparently still receives the money, and the Qatar Investment Authority gets an empty office space that it does not seem to need.

Close to the time[36] that workers were renovating the 43rd floor, the president's attitude toward the Gulf nation changed. In April 2018, Trump welcomed Sheikh Tamim bin Hamad Al-Thani, the ruler of Qatar,[37] to the Oval Office. On this visit, the U.S. president commended Qatar for fighting against terrorism funding.[38]

A year later, Al-Thani returned to Washington. This time, Trump was ready with a welcome party inside, of all places, the Treasury Department's Cash Room,[39] which once stored America's gold, silver, and dollar bills.[40] Steven Mnuchin, secretary of the Treasury, kicked off the dinner with a toast. "This room," he said, "is a fitting tribute to the economic and security partnership between our two nations."[41]

Encircling the tables, adorned with royal-blue cloths, sat 40-odd business leaders,[42] about a third of whom held personal fortunes of over $1 billion.[43] Some of the names on the guest list were the sort of people you might expect at a function like this—corporate titans with cash-fueled relationships in Qatar. Dennis Muilenburg, then the CEO of Boeing, was selling five 777 Freighters to Qatar's national airline. Raytheon CEO Thomas Kennedy was ready to ship off a couple of missile systems. Chevron Phillips Chemical CEO Mark Lashier was teaming up with the Qataris on a new petrochemicals complex.[44]

But there were other businessmen there with a more unorthodox connection to Qatar. Their businesses helped link the Qatari government to the president's own family. Billionaire[45] Bruce Flatt of Brookfield Asset Management was there.[46] Brookfield's real estate arm, Brookfield Property Partners, invested in a fund that paid $1.3 billion to lease[47] 666 Fifth Avenue, a troubled Manhattan skyscraper owned by the family of Trump's son-in-law, Jared Kushner. The largest outside shareholder[48] in Brookfield Property Partners is the Qatar Investment Authority. Also on the guest list:[49] Vornado CEO Steven Roth, Trump's partner in the San Francisco tower where the Qatar Investment Authority had leased office space.

Given the business ties, Flatt and Roth had reason to recognize a few faces among the official Qatari delegation. The CEO of the Qatar Investment Authority, Mansoor bin Ebrahim Al-Mahmoud, was there. As was the chairman, Sheikh Mohammed bin Abdulrahman Al-Thani, and two other directors, Saad Sherida Al-Kaabi and Ali Shareef Al-Emadi.[50] In all, more than one-third[51] of the Qatar Investment Authority's board of directors had assembled inside the Cash Room.

President Trump stood up to give remarks. "I have to say that the investments that you make in the United States," he told his guests, "are very much appreciated."[52]

DONALD TRUMP NEVER REALLY got out of business. Sure, he delegated day-to-day responsibilities to his sons Eric and Don Jr. upon taking office. Every business owner hands over work to subordinates, especially when they get preoccupied with other interests. But President Trump did not sell his companies. Nor did he give them away. He remains the owner of over 100 different entities,[53] which, taken together, make up the Trump Organization, one of the most unusual businesses in America.

Inside that business lie hundreds of secrets that, thanks to lax disclosure laws and a president uninterested in transparency, have remained buried throughout Trump's tenure in the White House. Among the mysteries: Who is paying the president? What are the revenues and profits of his companies? Which of his businesses are under distress, and which are thriving? How much is Trump gaining—or losing—on the presidency? This book cracks open the shell corporations, unearths new documents, and exposes hundreds of millions of dollars flowing between President Trump and entities around the world. It lasers in on a five-year period, from the beginning of Trump's campaign in 2015 to the ramp-up of his reelection campaign in 2020, offering the most complete financial investigation of President Trump's business ever published.

It also investigates Trump's associates. The president's disregard for norms set the tone at the top of the federal government, sparking a trickle-down ethics crisis with no precedent in modern American history. Trump appointed a cadre of tycoons who had long been a part of his inner circle—including Jared Kushner, Ivanka Trump, and Wilbur Ross—to some of the most powerful positions in America. With the president as their guide, they proceeded to bust through barriers meant to separate their financial holdings from their government roles.

All this could have been prevented. Before Donald Trump took office, most people figured he would divest his assets and assume the presidency with clean hands. Instead, he held on to everything— the office buildings, residential units, golf courses, personal mansions, licensing ventures, private planes[54]—and opened it all up to years of conflicts and consequences. What happens to a multibillion-dollar business when its leader ascends to the presidency of the United States? And what happens to American democracy when the nation's leader is a conflict-ridden businessman? No one knew at the time Trump took office, because no one had ever tried such a thing. But Trump took the risk, launching an experiment that has unfolded over the past few years, with results that his business has hidden from the public.

Midway through Trump's first term, the president's businesses had hauled in an estimated $1.2 billion in revenue and produced roughly $311 million in profits from operations. The entities paying that money included political groups, powerful corporations, the U.S. government, and foreign nations. Despite an influx of new customers, however, Trump was worth less[55] three years into his tenure than he was at the time he took office. His name became more powerful than it ever was—but it also became more polarizing. For every Qatari leader looking to pay Trump a few hundred thousand dollars, there are a few million critics uninterested in paying him anything. Trump's decision to keep hold of his business empire proved to be a bad bet that poisoned his properties and, more important, his presidency.

1

Art of the Self-Deal

THE RISE OF DONALD TRUMP

D onald Trump sits in his New York City office, behind an oversize desk cluttered with magazines. Almost all of them feature him on the cover. It's September 21, 2015, and Trump has surged to an early lead in the Republican primaries.[1] But while everyone else is talking about his budding candidacy, Trump wants to talk about money. His own money.

The annual Forbes 400 list of America's richest people is days from hitting the press, and Trump is slated to appear with a net worth of roughly $4 billion.[2] "You're so low, it's ridiculous," he tells three *Forbes* journalists, Randall Lane, Kerry Dolan, and Chase Peterson-Withorn. "I mean, I don't care. You're not going to put this, so it doesn't matter. I'm worth much more than $10 billion.[3]

"I like Steve Forbes, but it may be because he ran for president," Trump says at one point, referring to the former Republican candidate who now serves as honorary editor in chief of the magazine[4] but has no role in deciding where Trump ranks on the list. "He spent most of his money on running for president, and he failed—to put it mildly. He got zero percent of the vote. I have almost 40 percent of the vote, and I've spent nothing."

Not quite nothing, but close to it. Trump, who has invested just $1.9 million in his campaign so far,[5] doesn't need TV ads, yard signs, or campaign buttons to attract attention. He never has. For years, Trump has been his own spokesperson and, when coverage hasn't gone his way, his own attack dog. "You're going to look bad," he says. "And look, all I can say is *Forbes* is a bankrupt magazine that doesn't know what they're talking about, okay. That's all I'm going to say. Because it's embarrassing to me."

It's hard to think of anyone else in the world who would be embarrassed by a $4 billion fortune, but Donald Trump is one of a kind. Which is why, on this September day, in the midst of one of the most hectic campaigns in American history, he has cleared his schedule to offer *Forbes* an asset-by-asset breakdown of his personal fortune. So what if, as Lane notes in a subsequent story, Trump has a call with Stephen Colbert's show at the same time? "We'll call him back." Or if rival candidate Scott Walker drops out mid-conversation? "See if you can get his one vote."

Trump jumps into the numbers, lobbying for a richer valuation on his most famous skyscraper, Trump Tower, which *Forbes* has pegged at roughly $470 million. He points to the Crown Building, a stately, terraced edifice on the other side of Fifth Avenue that sold for $1.8 billion five months earlier.[6] "This is bigger," he says, even though the space he owns is actually 25% smaller.[7]

Trump Tower is making annual profits of "$80, $90 million this year," he tells the *Forbes* staffers. Less than 30 seconds later the profits are up to "$89, $90 million net." In fact, Trump Tower is on pace to make about $15 million in 2015.[8] Plenty of money, to be sure, but a long way from $90 million.

Whatever. Trump brings up 40 Wall Street, a skyscraper in Lower Manhattan.[9] "It's a 78-story building," he says of the 63-story building. "It's fully rented," he adds, even though documents show that 5% remained vacant as of a few months ago.[10] "We're going to make $64 million," he boasts, "after debt service." He is actually going to make $11.9 million—before debt service.[11] "If I wanted to sell 40 Wall Street, I'd get $750 [million] for it tomorrow," Trump says, failing to mention that his lender ran the numbers on that exact same hypothetical three months earlier and came up with an estimate $210 million short of Trump's figure.[12]

He addresses his liquid assets. "About three years ago," he says, "when the market was low, I said, 'You know what? I'll buy stock.' For the first time in my life. I never bought a stock in my life." Except he has. Lots of times. He bragged about his stock trades in his 1987 best-seller *Trump: The Art of the Deal*.[13] He bought roughly 27% of a department store chain named Alexander's in the late 1980s[14] and eventually got a seat on the company's board. In the 1990s and 2000s, he owned more than 35% of the shares in a publicly traded casino company, which he created and named after himself.[15]

"We have $793 million in cash," Trump says, apparently unaware that just a year before this, his executives welcomed a *Forbes* reporter into his offices to show documents detailing $307 million.[16] Asked how he added nearly $500 million in one year, Trump points to the sale of his interest in the Miss Universe competition, which brought in an estimated $15 million.[17] Can he provide any additional evidence? "Yeah, I guess we could," he says, then never does.

His phone rings. "Ivanka, my little Ivanka," he says, asking his eldest daughter to come say hello. Nine minutes later, she walks through the door: "Hiiii!"

"I was on a construction call with the Doral folks," she tells her father, conveniently segueing into a discussion of how much the Miami golf resort is worth. "*Forbes* actually did a very nice profile on that project." The magazine now has it down for $119 million. "That's a joke," Ivanka counters, noting that the reporter who wrote the story a couple of years earlier, which appeared in the lifestyle spinoff of *Forbes*, suggested a much higher figure. She has a point. The earlier story did in fact say the land at Doral was worth "close to $1 billion."[18]

But it's not. That reporter had apparently fallen for Trump math. Ivanka explains that a 12-acre property sold for $40 million, or $3.3 million an acre, which would suggest that the 800-acre Doral is surely worth upward of $1 billion. The *Forbes* staffers inside Trump's office on this day, however, are not falling for the same trick. They are professional number crunchers, each of whom has spent years figuring out the fortunes of billionaires. They understand that Trump purchased the property three years ago, for just $150 million.[19] A renovation has not made the place six times as valuable. A valuation the Trump Organization will later show the magazine predicts Doral would be worth $433 million once all the work is done. Then there are the liabilities. "We have like no debt on it," Ivanka says, ignoring two Deutsche Bank loans totaling $125 million.[20]

Allen Weisselberg, chief financial officer of the Trump Organization, gets in on the game too, talking up the value of the Mar-a-Lago club. "There was a sale—here's the article that was in the *Palm Beach Daily News*," he says, grabbing a printed article about a nearby property that he claims includes 8.8 acres. "It was a combined sale for $116.1 million. Not our property, another property in Palm Beach. But they don't have half of what we have on our property.[21]

"We have about 19 acres—you do the multiplication," Weisselberg says. Plus, Trump invested $14 million to build the grand ballroom, another $4 million to install cabanas near the water, and $700,000 to add a tennis facility, he says. "Total of $267 [million]."

But Trump's estate cannot be subdivided into lots for mega-mansions. It's a mere trophy for a rich guy, not a potential gold mine for a developer. The result? Mar-a-Lago is worth about $100 million less than what Weisselberg is claiming.[22]

Amid this onslaught, Trump turns on the charm, asking if his visitors would like to see his penthouse.[23] "I don't show this to anybody— I've never brought *Forbes* up here." Other than that time, 15 years earlier, when a *Forbes* photographer went there, as Lane later points out.[24] *Architectural Digest* got its own tour, back in 1985.[25] *People* would, too, for a cover story that would hit newsstands in less than two weeks.[26] And *60 Minutes* would, for an interview airing that Sunday.[27] So would, well, never mind.

"This is the best apartment ever built, they say," Trump says, gazing out at the sweeping views of Manhattan. "They just sold the one over here for $225 [million]," he adds, nodding to another apartment on the skyline. "You have this marked down at $90 [million]." How many square feet is it? "Thirty-three thousand, plus the roof," Trump says. "The roof is like 15 or something—15,000." So 48,000 total, in Trump's mind.

A few minutes after opening the doors to his palace, Trump has to get back to running for president. "Call me if you want—feel free," he says. "And I promise I won't say it's a horrible, bankrupt . . ." Everyone laughs, and Trump marches on his way. *Forbes* ends up estimating the penthouse is 30,000 square feet and juices the valuation to $100 million.[28]

A year and a half later,[29] however, one of the reporters standing with Trump today, Peterson-Withorn, will take a closer look at property records. They'll show that Trump's penthouse is in fact only 11,000 square feet. In other words, it's worth $65 million or so—about a quarter of the figures Trump has been throwing around, and 35% less than what *Forbes* published.[30] It's tough to catch every lie, something Trump knows well.

A former Trump lawyer named Thomas Wells once noticed that every time a new story mentioned Trump's penthouse, there seemed to be a different number of rooms. In one article, it would have eight. In another, 16. Then 20, even 30. Wells later recalled that he finally asked Trump directly: How many rooms did his apartment really have? His response: "However many they will print."[31]

DONALD TRUMP IS a lot of things. He's a tough negotiator. He's a sweet-talker. He beats around the bush. He cuts through the crap. He's unfathomably rich. And inexplicably cheap. But in order to really understand our 45th president, you have to start with the man who gave him his name, Fred Trump, who originally developed the Trump way of doing business, showing his son how to profit from politics and manipulate the media. A portrait of Donald Trump's father sits in the Oval Office,[32] just behind the Resolute Desk, constantly peering over the president's shoulder.

Unlike Donald Trump, Fred was a self-made man. When he was 12 years old, his own father died during the 1918 Spanish influenza epidemic, according to Gwenda Blair, who chronicled the first family's history in her book *The Trumps: Three Generations of Builders and a President*. Fred stayed in school long enough to get his high school diploma, then with his mother formed a construction company, E. Trump & Son, when he was still too young to start one on his own. He worked long hours and built a collection of homes on the edge of New York City.[33] By the time Franklin D. Roosevelt took office in 1933, promising a New Deal for America,[34] Fred Trump was 27 years old and in exactly the right industry to forge a fortune.

The foundation for Fred Trump's business empire was a government program. In 1934, FDR led an effort to create the Federal Housing Administration, which put the government's guarantee behind home loans, allowing banks to take greater risks.[35] If borrowers couldn't pay everything back, Uncle Sam would cover the losses. Cash flooded into the housing market, much of it going to builders like Fred Trump. By 1943 he had constructed at least 2,000 homes in Brooklyn, enough to make him a millionaire.

World War II provided additional opportunities, especially when soldiers started coming home. To ensure there were enough places for them to live, the government helped builders secure financing. In turn, developers had to limit rents based on their estimated costs of construction. If they didn't anticipate spending much to build a place, they couldn't charge much to rent it out. Fred Trump's projected costs, however, did not match his actual costs. At one housing complex in Brooklyn, he got a $16 million loan, allegedly $4 million more than he actually needed to build the project. He held on to the extra cash and apparently used the inflated estimates to justify charging America's veterans more in rent. Never officially accused of a crime, he nonetheless got a tongue-lashing on Capitol Hill.[36]

What made Fred Trump so successful, in addition to his relentless work ethic, was a knack for pushing the limits of the law. In 1960, the state of New York created a new program, also meant to jolt the housing industry.[37] Like FDR's initiatives, the New York program involved builders estimating how much projects would cost. It then allowed them to take a percentage of that cost as a builder's fee, as Blair explains. Fred Trump submitted a bulked-up estimate, claiming his work would cost $8 million more than it actually did, thereby increasing his fee by $600,000.

He made more money from another scheme. Fred Trump got financing from the state, then used his funds to pay contractors for various expenses on his projects. One of the contractors was the Boro Equipment Company. Boro had exceptionally high prices, charging many times the market rate for dump trucks, backhoes, bulldozers, and so on. But the typically frugal Trump did business with Boro anyway. Why? Because he owned the company.[38]

On January 27, 1966, 12 years after facing the U.S. Senate Committee on Banking and Currency for questionable estimates that produced big gains,[39] Fred Trump appeared before the New York State Investigation Commission for similar shenanigans. One commissioner wondered how to stop Trump from exploiting the government in the future: "Is there any way of preventing a man who does business in that way from getting another contract from the state?"[40]

WHEN DONALD TRUMP was three years old, his father gave him and his siblings an unusual gift. Not trucks or trains or dolls, but a piece of land—40 acres near the Brooklyn waterfront. There wasn't much the kids could do with this new gift, if they even knew it had been given to them. But Fred Trump, who bought the parcel for about $180,000, had a plan.[41] Around 1949, he began building 1,860 apartments on the land.[42] Since the plot technically belonged to his kids, he then paid them rent of $60,000 a year.[43] By turning his children into his landlords, Fred Trump had opened up a spigot that would rain cash on his heirs for decades while avoiding the gift and estate taxes that usually accompany such transfers of wealth.

Thus, Donald Trump was collecting an estimated $1,000 a month from his father as a three-year-old.[44] Donald turned out to be a troublesome kid. When he was in second grade, he punched his teacher in the face, "because I didn't think he knew anything about music," Trump explained in *The Art of the Deal*. Six years later, his father effectively kicked him out of the house, sending him to a military boarding school.

"I was a good enough student at the academy," Trump said years later, "although I can't say I ever worked very hard. I was lucky that it came relatively easily to me, because I was never all that interested in schoolwork. I understood early on that the whole academic thing was only a preliminary to the main event—which was going to be whatever I did after I graduated from college."[45]

What he did, after getting a degree at the University of Pennsylvania,[46] was go home to the father who had sent him away years earlier. In 1972, when Donald Trump was in his midtwenties, Fred Trump introduced him to the wonders of public financing. Together they created a company to buy a senior-living facility in East Orange, New Jersey. The state contributed $7.8 million in financing, Fred Trump invested nearly $900,000, and Donald Trump put up nothing. He got a 25% stake anyway.

The younger Trump then followed his father's playbook to siphon more money from the project, creating a second company, which he owned outright. The father-son venture proceeded to pay the son-only venture to manage the building, handing over as much as $4,000 a month. Never mind that the only people managing anything were Fred Trump's employees. Donald Trump got the payout, along with additional money by doing things like renting air-conditioning units. There was a $25,000 "consulting" fee as well, which had no clear purpose. No purpose, that is, other than shifting more money tax-free. Annual gifts of $6,000[47] around Christmastime helped, too.

In 1973, at age 27, Donald Trump got his first taste of the limelight, though not for glamorous reasons. The U.S. Department of Justice sued him, his father, and their business for allegedly discriminating against black people.[48] The younger Trump called the claims "ridiculous," but the evidence was damning. According to FBI files, a rental agent at the Trump family's Shore Haven Apartments said that the neighborhood was safe and clean, "in part because it was controlled by the Mafia, but also because there are no blacks in the immediate area."

One of Fred Trump's rental supervisors explained that the lack of diversity was intentional. "Fred Trump told me not to rent to blacks," he informed an FBI agent. "He also wanted me to get rid of the blacks that were in the building."[49]

The Trumps' lawyers advised settling. But hanging out in a swanky New York City joint called Le Club, young Donald Trump met a man named Roy Cohn.[50] Cohn had made his name working alongside the infamous senator Joseph McCarthy, but he made his career as an attorney for big businessmen and reputed mobsters.[51]

"I don't like lawyers," Trump told Cohn. "I think all they do is delay deals, instead of making deals, and every answer they give you is no, and they are always looking to settle instead of fights."

"Is this just an academic conversation?" Cohn asked.

"No, it's not academic at all," Trump said. "It so happens that the government has just filed suit against our company and many others, under the Civil Rights Act, saying that we discriminated against blacks in some of our housing developments."

"My view is tell them to go to hell," Cohn replied.[52]

That was Trump's view as well. Together, he and Cohn cooked up a $100 million countersuit against the Justice Department,[53] which a judge promptly dismissed, according to news reports from the time. The Trumps then settled, promising to change their company practices but not admitting wrongdoing. From a legal standpoint, they ended up exactly where the attorneys had advised them to go from the start. But from a reputational standpoint, the Trumps landed in a better spot, having pushed a counternarrative. They weren't racist; the Department of Justice was just overzealous.

In the mid-1970s, Donald Trump got his second chance in the spotlight, this time with a flashy new real estate deal. Fred Trump had made his money in the outer boroughs of New York City, but Donald Trump wanted to make his in the center of it all. So while still in his twenties, he proposed fixing up a struggling hotel next to Grand Central Terminal.[54] Fred Trump lent him money and served as a backstop.[55]

It must have provided some comfort that his son's deal embraced a familiar formula, squeezing profits from politics. In early 1975, the city of New York adopted something called the Business Investment Incentive Policy, designed to give businesspeople tax breaks for making dramatic investments.[56] Donald Trump made it clear that he would fix up the hotel only if he got $50 million or so in incentives.[57]

He faced opposition, including from three New York legislators who held a news conference to protest the plan.[58] But it's hard to outshine a guy like Donald Trump, who crashed the event, reminded everyone that the hotel would continue to decay if he did not get his tax breaks, and ultimately won.[59] Not even 30 years old, he had a deal to replace the Commodore Hotel with the Grand Hyatt New York. It was, by any measure, an impressive achievement—even for a young man with a rich father.

It would have been a more impressive accomplishment, of course, if Trump had done it all on his own. So he began spinning a myth, one he fine-tuned over the ensuing decades, that he was a self-made man with a golden touch. "He is tall, lean and blond, with dazzling white teeth, and he looks ever so much like Robert Redford," began a 1976 profile in *The New York Times*. "He rides around town in a chauffeured silver Cadillac with his initials, DJT, on the plates. He dates slinky fashion models, belongs to the most elegant clubs and, at only 30 years of age, estimates that he is worth 'more than $200 million.'"[60]

Trump's net worth became a part of his persona, a marker of his success. In 1982, he got a chance to independently validate the figure when *Forbes* launched its inaugural list of the richest people in America.[61] Trump invited reporter Jonathan Greenberg to his office on Fifth Avenue, where he told him he had just purchased a property at the bottom of Central Park for $13 million.[62] As if on cue, a broker called Trump, offering $100 million for the building. Trump turned it down.

Most tycoons did not want to be on the *Forbes* list. Trump was an exception. How had he gained $87 million on that Central Park property? He hadn't. Trump purchased the building for $65 million, all of it borrowed.[63] The $100 million offer, Greenberg suspected, was a ruse. So was Trump's claim that he already owned 80% of the family fortune. Greenberg fell for that one,[64] at least in part. *Forbes* ended up attributing 50% of the Trump family empire to Donald Trump, a share worth an estimated $100 million,[65] enough to qualify him for a spot on the ranking.

Trump's true net worth at the time was closer to zero.[66] In addition to the property near Central Park and a partial stake in the Grand Hyatt New York, he owned bits of his father's outer-borough buildings, an unfinished project on Fifth Avenue, a Mercedes-Benz, and about $400,000 in cash, according to an October 1981 report with the New Jersey Casino Control Commission. He also owed his father $7.5 million, money he was using to help make payments on a $35 million line of credit with Chase Manhattan Bank.[67]

To help with his mythmaking, Trump brought in outside help. One day, Greenberg was working at his desk when his phone rang. He picked up the receiver. "This is Roy—Roy Cohn," the person on the other end of the line told him. "You can't quote me. But Donny tells me you're putting together this list of rich people. He says you've got him down for just $200 million. That's way too low, way too low. Listen, I'm Donny's personal lawyer, but he said I could talk to you about this. I am sitting here looking at his current bank statement. It shows he's got more than $500 million in liquid assets, just cash. That's just Donald, nothing to do with Fred, and it's just cash."[68]

Two years later, Greenberg got a call from another person at the Trump Organization, John Barron. "I'd like to talk to you off the record, if I can," Barron said, explaining that the financial arrangement between Fred Trump and his son Donald had changed. "You can really use Donald Trump now, and you can just consolidate it." Asked whether the money had been transferred for tax purposes, Barron confirmed, "Correct. Correct. That's correct."[69] In 1985, *Forbes* removed Fred Trump from the list and attributed the entire family fortune, estimated at more than $600 million, to Donald Trump alone.[70]

There was just one problem: John Barron wasn't a real person. He was an alter ego Trump used to dupe people on the phone. Trump wasn't worth $600 million. At 39, he had begun to break out on his own, but his father remained firmly in control of the family fortune.[71] Even the idea of using a fake persona apparently came from Fred Trump. Donald's father had been known for employing a similar trick, making calls as "Mr. Green."[72]

HAVING ESTABLISHED A reputation as one of America's richest business tycoons, Donald Trump went on a spending spree, with money he didn't have. At first the strategy worked. Leveraging funds from his father and a $130 million loan from five banks, he built Trump Tower, a dazzling skyscraper on Fifth Avenue.[73] Celebrities like Johnny Carson and Steven Spielberg got places alongside Trump,[74] who kept the penthouse for himself and still generated a reported $275 million from condo sales.[75] The commercial space rented to high-end retailers like Harry Winston and Cartier.[76] Trump got a $100 million tax break, too[77]—not that he really needed it. "We got the highest rents ever, anywhere," says Barbara Res, a former Trump executive who helped build the place. "I mean, it was just amazing what he was getting for a square foot."[78]

Emboldened, Trump chased after more deals. He bought a second-tier professional football team, the New Jersey Generals, for $7 million in 1983.[79] He picked up a 282-foot yacht that had once belonged to a

Saudi arms dealer, handing over roughly $30 million.[80] He doled out so much money to politicians that a 1986 report listing big political donors in New York City put him and his father at the top of the list.[81] He purchased Mar-a-Lago for about $10 million.[82] Eastern Airlines Shuttle cost him another $365 million.[83] He sold $675 million in bonds to finance big ambitions in Atlantic City,[84] where his parents had reportedly honeymooned.[85] The jewel in his debt-fueled empire, however, was the Plaza Hotel, a $407 million vanity project that even Trump admitted made little sense.[86]

"I haven't purchased a building," he explained in an advertisement celebrating the deal. "I have purchased a masterpiece—the Mona Lisa. For the first time in my life, I have knowingly made a deal which was not economic—for I can never justify the price I paid, no matter how successful the Plaza becomes."[87]

The problem with throwing around other people's money is that eventually they expect you to pay it back. By 1990, Trump was short on cash. He had amassed $3.4 billion of debt on an estimated $3.6 billion in assets. To cover payments on his Atlantic City bonds, he borrowed $20 million from banks. Shortly thereafter, he borrowed another $45 million. The situation got so dire that, after examining Trump's financial picture, one New Jersey regulator concluded, "The possibility of a complete financial collapse of the Trump Organization is not out of the question."[88]

Desperate, Trump made a move toward a pile of assets he had always counted on—his father's. In 1990, Donald sent Fred, then 85 years old, a paper the elder Trump had never seen before, according to *The New York Times*. The document would have changed Fred's will, protecting Donald's inheritance from his creditors while also strengthening his grip on his father's estate. Fearing the document could allow his son to risk the family fortune amid his efforts to save his own, Fred Trump ordered up a new document, removing Donald's singular control of his estate.[89]

At the same time, he worked to bail out his son. Fred sent one of his lawyers to Atlantic City, where Donald had an interest payment coming due. To provide some liquidity for his son's casino operation, Fred's lawyer went to a blackjack table and bought 670 gray chips, worth $5,000 apiece, or $3.35 million in total. He had no intention of playing cards. The lawyer instead slipped the chips into a small case.[90] The next day, Fred Trump wired another $150,000, and his lawyer got another 30 chips. In effect, Fred Trump had given his son a loan of $3.5 million. "In 13 years of casino gaming in Atlantic City," a member of the New Jersey Casino Control Commission remarked at the time, "this transaction is probably the most unique singular action that has ever taken place, out of tens of billions of dollars that have been moved around Atlantic City one way or another."[91]

The unusual transactions didn't stop there. In 1992, the Trump family created a new company called All County Building Supply & Maintenance, according to *The New York Times*. All County was a purchasing agent for Fred Trump's apartments, which bought supplies and materials. Or at least that's the way it appeared. But in fact, All County was not really buying supplies—it was merely marking up the cost of already negotiated deals. And since All County's owners were Fred Trump's heirs, the young Trumps earned a tidy profit without doing much of anything.[92] Boiled down, All County was a sophisticated way of transferring millions of dollars, free of estate or gift taxes.

Fred Trump's largesse could only help his son so much. In July 1991, seven months after Fred bought chips at one casino, another casino declared bankruptcy. One of the largest creditors for the Trump Taj Mahal was an insurance company represented by a bankruptcy specialist named Wilbur Ross.[93] Along with bondholder Carl Icahn, Ross decided to treat Trump more kindly than unpaid creditors sometimes do. Rather than wipe out Trump, Ross and Icahn backed a plan that left him with 50% of the casino.[94] It was a stroke of luck for

Trump—one he never forgot. Shortly after he was elected president, Trump announced roles in the new administration for Icahn and Ross.

IN JUNE OF 1995,[95] Donald Trump showed up ready to make a splash at the New York Stock Exchange. Wearing a blue suit and a red power tie, with his second wife, Marla Maples, hanging on his arm, he was in full comeback mode, ready to launch a public company. "This is such a big day for us,"[96] Trump said, basking in the thought of his new corporation, Trump Hotels & Casino Resorts, trading on the world's most important stock exchange. Plenty of others agreed, and they shelled out a total of $140 million that day for a piece of the Donald.[97]

At 48 years old, Trump was new to running a public company. He had spent his whole life helming private businesses, with one clear objective: adding to his own personal fortune. Now he was legally required to look out for others. As the head of a public enterprise, he was presumably in charge of thousands of people's personal savings—some of whom invested directly, while others bought in through vehicles like mutual funds or pensions. If Trump made money, so would, say, teachers in Iowa and nurses in Arizona. If he lost money, they did, too. Like any partnership, this one came with a certain set of expectations.

But Trump, as his investors soon found out, did not seem to care about those expectations. At the start, Trump Hotels & Casino Resorts—with the ticker symbol DJT[98]—owned one gambling haven in Atlantic City.[99] Trump owned another two outside of the public company, including the Trump Taj Mahal, which was drowning in debt. In April 1996, Trump's public company purchased the Taj Mahal in a deal that valued Trump's 50% interest at $40.5 million.[100] His debt problems were now other people's debt problems.

There was more money for Trump. As part of the deal, the public company also handed over $61 million in cash and stock to buy land that Trump owned, paying about 19 times as much as it cost to lease that land annually.[101] Two months later, in June 1996,[102] Trump Hotels & Casino Resorts announced it was buying Trump's third Atlantic City casino for roughly $500 million. Richard Sokol, an analyst familiar with the stock, estimated the property was actually worth about $100 million less.[103] By that math, Trump, who owned 100% of the private casino[104] and about 25% of the public company,[105] had taken $75 million of shareholder money for himself. Investors fled, sending shares spiraling 37%.[106]

In less than one year, Donald Trump had shifted more than $175 million from a publicly traded company into his own private holdings. The deals bolstered his personal balance sheet, but they ruined the company's. Trump Hotels & Casino Resorts suddenly owed 47% more interest per year than it produced in operating profit.[107]

With the company reeling and investors out millions of dollars, Trump proceeded to drain the business of what little cash remained. In 1996, the year he torpedoed the company's balance sheet, Trump collected a $1 million salary and a $5 million bonus.[108] As an extra reward, the company also forgave a $3 million personal loan.[109] From 1995 to 2004, Trump took home a collective $17 million in salary and bonuses.[110]

In addition, he racked up another $3.9 million in expense reimbursements, according to an analysis of documents filed with the Securities and Exchange Commission.[111] The company shelled out $13 million to do things like rent space in Trump Tower, use Trump's personal airplane, and take high rollers to Trump's other properties.[112] When, after all this self-dealing, Trump still found himself strapped for cash, he treated the company like his personal piggy bank, taking out an $11 million loan in mid-1998, then borrowing another $13.5 million in October.[113]

Then there were the fees. A "services agreement" paid a Trump-owned company $1.3 million in 1995. What Trump did to earn that money was not entirely clear. The agreement itself specified that his company was "not required to devote any prescribed time" to its responsibilities in order to collect the fee.[114] Trump got another slice of money based on the performance of Trump Marina, one of the three Atlantic City casinos. According to that arrangement, if the company underperformed, Trump had to pay the funds back "promptly."[115] It did underperform, and he never paid the money back, instead forcing the company to credit the absconded funds against later earnings. In the 10 years after Trump Hotels & Casino Resorts went public, Trump got a total of $15 million in fees.

Add up the cash payments—salaries, rents, fees, and so on—and Donald Trump made roughly $50 million from 1995 to 2004, on top of the more than $175 million he moved from the public company to his private holdings through dealmaking. Meanwhile, thanks to crippling interest payments, the company lost $647 million.[116] In 2004, Trump Hotels & Casino Resorts declared bankruptcy.[117] The investors who had trusted in Trump got crushed.

IN ORDER TO understand how anyone could have let this happen, it helps to look at the company's board of directors. The job of any board is to make sure everyone is acting in the best interests of the enterprise. But the board of Trump Hotels & Casino Resorts only had five members, including Trump and one of his employees.[118] Two of the other directors, who were supposed to be independent, had previously served on the boards of Trump entities. The last one had been a senior vice president at Chase Manhattan Bank, one of Trump's preferred lenders early in his career.[119]

No surprise, then, that the group responsible for reining in Trump's excesses instead let them multiply. After the board signed off on the roughly $500 million purchase of Trump's Castle casino, the one that amounted to an estimated $75 million heist, a group of shareholders sued. Trump fought them in court for five years before finally agreeing to settle without admitting wrongdoing.

The settlement offered some level of justice. Trump had to hand over half of his interest in the Miss Universe competition to the company. Oh well. By forcing his own investors to tangle with him in court for a half decade, Trump bought himself enough time to allow the rest of his business empire to recover. When he finally settled, in 2001, *Forbes* estimated he was worth $1.4 billion more than he had been when he took the money in the first place.[120]

The settlement also called for changes to the board of directors. The company had to install a special committee, made up of only outside board members, to approve every significant transaction it did with Trump. The company also added a new director, Robert McGuire, a former federal prosecutor who had also been head of the New York City Police Department.

Even McGuire, however, had financial ties to Trump, which do not appear to have been previously reported. In his spare time, McGuire served as president of the Police Athletic League,[121] a nonprofit that runs summer camps and after-school programs for kids.[122] Donald Trump happened to sit on the board of directors for the charity.[123] The year McGuire joined the board of Trump's casino company, Trump's charitable foundation donated $25,000 to the Police Athletic League.[124] The money kept flowing year after year, adding up to more than $800,000 from 2001 to 2014.[125] Over that span, the Police Athletic League, McGuire's pet cause, received more money from the Donald J. Trump Foundation than any other charity. Attempts to reach McGuire proved unsuccessful.

It seems unlikely that Trump made the donations to the Police Athletic League *solely* to corrupt the newest board member at his casino company. After all, Trump already sat on the board of the charity the year McGuire became a director for the casino company. Nonetheless, Trump's donations to the charity certainly raise the question of whether his generosity had something to do with his business interests, especially given the history of the Donald J. Trump Foundation.

As David Fahrenthold of *The Washington Post* first documented, Trump operated his nonprofit foundation as if it were an arm of his for-profit business. With foundation dollars, he settled a lawsuit, fixed up a fountain outside a Trump hotel,[126] purchased portraits of himself, and donated to a political group tied to a Florida attorney general at a time when she was weighing whether or not to investigate one of his businesses.[127] He apparently even employed his foundation in a scheme that shifted money from his son's kids-cancer charity to his own business.[128]

In 2007, Donald Trump stopped donating much of his own cash to the foundation and instead collected the majority from outsiders. Billionaire WWE cofounder Vince McMahon and his wife, Linda, gave $4 million that year, almost all the money in the foundation. Trump, who later named Linda to his cabinet, then took those funds and doled them out as if they were his own. By 2009 he was not donating *anything* to the foundation but only giving away other people's money and claiming the credit for himself.[129]

TRUMP'S CRITICS LIKE to say that he is not a billionaire and that all the money he has came from his father. They are wrong. The truth is, Trump received at least $413 million in today's dollars from his father, according to *The New York Times,* which won a Pulitzer Prize for its investigation of tens of thousands of pages of Fred Trump's financial documents.[130] If he had simply taken that money and invested in the

S&P 500, Donald Trump would have been worth $2 billion by March 1, 2020.[131]

Instead, Trump was worth an estimated $3.1 billion, making him one of the few billionaire heirs to actually outperform the market over the course of his life.[132] The bulk of his gains come from just three deals. First, there's Trump Tower, his 1983 home run where, even after he sold off everything but the commercial space and penthouse, Trump's assets are still worth an estimated $282 million net of debt. Second, there's 40 Wall Street, which Trump bought and fixed up for a reported $35 million.[133] It's now worth an estimated $329 million after debt. Most important, there's his 30% interests in two skyscrapers—1290 Avenue of the Americas, in New York, and 555 California Street, in San Francisco—that Trump did not want but his business partners forced him to take in 2006 as part of a complicated exchange. The value of Trump's interests in those buildings has since shot up an estimated $895 million.[134]

Trump might not own any of those today if he had not escaped his debt nightmare of the 1990s. But he did, cutting deals with creditors and heaving piles of debt onto investors in his public company while managing to extract big money for himself. Look at the history of Donald Trump's fortune and it tells a different tale than he does. Trump is not much of an innovator, nor a corporate leader, nor even a negotiator. But he does have a talent, inherited from his father, for skirting the rules and siphoning money, especially by moving funds from one entity he controls into another.

On June 16, 2015, Donald Trump launched a campaign to put himself in control of the biggest entity on the planet, the United States of America. "Ladies and gentlemen," he announced in the marble-lined atrium of Trump Tower. "I am officially running for president."[135]

2

Moscow Money

TRUMP, PUTIN, AND THE 2016
PRESIDENTIAL ELECTION

It's October 28, 2015, and 14 million people are tuned in to the third Republican presidential debate.[1] "Mr. Trump, let's talk a little bit about bankruptcies," says moderator Becky Quick, training her gaze on the billionaire at center stage. "Your Atlantic City casinos filed for bankruptcy four times. In fact, Fitch, the ratings agency, even said they were serial filers for all of this. You said you did great with Atlantic City—and you did."

Trump purses his lips and grabs hold of the podium. "But some of the individuals," Quick continues, "the bondholders, some of the contractors who worked for you, didn't fare so well. Bankruptcy is a broken promise. Why should the voters believe the promises that you're telling them right now?"

Well, Trump explains, lots of rich people use bankruptcy protection at one point or another. "I've used [bankruptcy] to my advantage as a businessman—for my family, for myself." He shrugs. "Hundreds of companies I've opened—I've used it three times, maybe four times. Came out great, but I guess I'm supposed to come out great. That's what I could do for the country."[2] It's an effective answer, one that leaves viewers with the impression that Trump is ready to give up his life in business and employ his rough-and-tumble tactics on behalf of the American people.

But the truth is that Donald Trump is not yet ready to give up his business. As he stands onstage answering questions before millions of people, his associates are secretly pursuing a business deal in Russia, one that opens his campaign up to unprecedented conflicts of interest. Just hours before the debate, Trump's lawyer received an email with a letter of intent, laying out a plan for a soaring skyscraper named Trump Moscow.[3]

Doing such a deal would make Trump a decent chunk of change—an estimated $35 million up front and about $2.6 million in yearly fees if everything went well—but it would also expose his business to the whims of Russian officials. "You will need a lot of governmental approval for all the projects in Moscow," explains Anna Shepeleva, director of research in the Moscow office of real estate firm CBRE.[4] Most politicians would never consider putting themselves in such a position, dependent on a foreign adversary for financial favors at a time when they are running for office in the United States. But Trump is not like most politicians. At his core, he is a businessman. While he wanted the U.S. presidency, he also wanted a Russian tower. So when he got the chance to look at the document from the developer in Russia, he flipped to the signature page, grabbed a thick pen, and affixed his famous name to the agreement.[5]

IT WAS THE CULMINATION of a decades-long effort to build in Russia. "The idea got off the ground after I sat next to the Soviet ambassador, Yuri Dubinin, at a luncheon held by Leonard Lauder, a great businessman who is the son of Estee Lauder," Trump wrote in his 1987 book. "Dubinin's daughter, it turned out, had read about Trump Tower and knew all about it. One thing led to another, and now I'm talking about building a large luxury hotel across the street from the Kremlin, in partnership with the Soviet government."[6]

That plan fell through, as did several later attempts.[7] In 2013, Trump finally got a deal in Russia. It was not for a building, but for a beauty pageant. A Russian billionaire named Aras Agalarov and his pop-star son Emin decided to host the Miss Universe competition in Moscow.[8] Trump, part owner of the pageant, boarded a plane and invited Vladimir Putin to meet him at the event.[9] The Russian president apparently turned down the invitation.[10]

It was quite a show anyway. Techno beats pulsed through the concert hall as 86 women pranced onstage, put their hands on their hips, flashed diamond smiles, and screamed the names of their home countries. Miss Venezuela walked away with the tiara, but Trump walked away with the money, an estimated $3 million.[11]

He kept his eye on a bigger prize. "I had a great weekend with you and your family," Trump tweeted at Aras Agalarov. "You have done a FAN-TASTIC job. TRUMP TOWER-MOSCOW is next."[12] Indeed, the very next month, the Trumps and the Agalarovs signed a preliminary agreement to turn Trump's dream of a tower in Russia into a reality.[13]

The terms of the deal, as outlined in Robert Mueller's report on Russian interference in the 2016 election, were straightforward. It called for 800 apartments, with 3.5% of all sales going to the Trump Organization.[14] At the time, luxury apartments were selling for as much as $8.3 million in pricy parts of Moscow.[15] But according to Emin Agalarov, the Trump project would have commanded far less, since it would have been a half hour outside of the city's center and only partially finished at the time of the sale.[16] Still, Emin says, Trump would have made about $17.5 million in all.[17]

Ivanka Trump traveled to Moscow two months later, in February 2014.[18] "We spent some time in my office," Emin explained in an email. "I showed her the plans for the future, and we looked at the site of construction zone from my window."[19]

Around the same time, 500 miles to the southwest and far out of view from Agalarov's window, crowds filled Independence Square in Kiev, Ukraine. They were protesting Ukrainian leader Viktor Yanukovych, a pro-Russian politician who had risen to power with help from an American consultant named Paul Manafort. Politics provided both men with a life of luxury. The Ukrainian president took up residence in an opulent mansion with a garageful of antique cars and a personal zoo.[20] Manafort, meanwhile, earned more than $60 million and laundered enough of it back to the United States to make purchases of $1.4 million at a clothing store and another $1 million with a rug merchant.[21]

As allegations of corruption arose, protesters turned out en masse, hurling Molotov cocktails. The government allegedly responded with sniper fire. The United States sided with the protesters, while Putin backed the president. On February 22, 2014, as the demonstrations spiraled out of control, the Russian leader reportedly held a late-night council to help Yanukovych flee his country. At the end of the meeting, Putin issued an order to his bleary-eyed deputies: "We must start working on returning Crimea"—a territory the Soviets had ceded to Ukraine in 1954—"to Russia."[22]

Unmarked soldiers soon showed up at airports, military bases, and government buildings in Crimea, according to reports.[23] By the time everyone realized they were working with the Russian government, Putin was already in control. A referendum followed, and Russia claimed Crimea.[24]

World leaders cried foul. The presidents of the European Council and the European Commission issued a joint statement, calling the move "illegal and illegitimate."[25] David Cameron of the United Kingdom declared, "Russia has acted in flagrant breach of international law."[26] And Vice President Joe Biden derided the action as "nothing more than a land grab."[27] Not wanting to spark a violent confrontation out of a mostly bloodless takeover, however, the United States responded with weapons of economics rather than war. On March 17, President Obama announced sanctions against the Russians.[28] Three days later, he targeted Putin personally, leveling additional measures against four oligarchs in his "inner circle."[29]

The sanctions added to the troubles of the Russian economy, already facing a devastating fall in oil prices. Russia's oligarchs—many of whom got rich by grabbing assets when the Soviet Union collapsed and stayed rich by making peace with Putin[30]—lost billions of dollars.[31] The Russian recession crippled Moscow's property market, slashing the price of residential real estate by 35% in dollar terms.[32] Emin Agalarov estimates that Trump's potential payout from his Moscow partnership would have been cut in half. And that's if the project even happened at all, which seemed increasingly unlikely. Agalarov says, "It was fizzling out from the start."[33]

The fallout rippled through the global economy, also hitting Trump closer to home. At the start of 2014, Trump owned 47 luxury condos in New York City, worth an estimated $270 million, according to a review of property records.[34] Russians had been buying units like his all over Manhattan for years, helping drive up prices. But that largely stopped after the sanctions set in. Donald Trump acknowledged the situation in December 2014. In an onstage interview in Washington, D.C., with fellow billionaire David Rubenstein, Trump predicted that the latest condo developments in New York City would fail. He offered a single explanation: "I mean, Russia has been taken out of it over the last year, as you know. Russia is gone. And a lot of these Russians that were buying these apartments are no longer buying apartments, and they've got bigger problems."[35]

Their problems might explain why Russia was so interested in up-ending American politics. In the summer of 2014, as the sanctions set in, four Russians filed applications to get inside the United States, claiming on the forms that they were just friends on a vacation. In fact, they were secret operatives, working for an organization intent on waging "information warfare" against the United States.[36] The mission was to sow chaos in the 2016 presidential election.

They allegedly traveled across the country, to California, Nevada, New Mexico, Texas, Colorado, Illinois, Michigan, Louisiana, and New York, gathering information as they went.[37] Their organization created accounts on Facebook and Twitter that promoted views across the political spectrum. There was an immigration group called "Secured Borders," a Black Lives Matter group called "Blacktivist," and a religious group named "United Muslims of America."[38] According to an indictment later filed as part of Robert Mueller's probe into Russian interference, they criticized establishment candidates like Marco Rubio, Ted Cruz, and Hillary Clinton, while hailing the revolutionaries—Bernie Sanders and Donald Trump.[39]

Spewing hate online is a quick way to gain an audience, and before long, the Russian accounts had hundreds of thousands of followers. To fund the efforts, companies controlled by a Russian oligarch connected to Putin allegedly shelled out more than $1.25 million a month. It was enough to employ hundreds of content creators and computer professionals,[40] as well as to purchase more than 3,500 ads on Facebook for roughly $100,000. The return on those investments was staggering. Facebook ultimately said the Russian accounts reached at least 29 million people, and maybe as many as 126 million[41]—or nearly 40% of the U.S. population.

As with the Crimean takeover, it wasn't until it was all over that anyone got a full sense of what had happened. The Trump campaign did not create Russia's disinformation factory, but it unknowingly promoted it. In fact, the Russian accounts got cited or retweeted by Trump advisers Kellyanne Conway, Brad Parscale, and Michael Flynn. Trump's children Eric and Don Jr. spread the propaganda, too, as did Donald Trump himself.[42]

MEANWHILE, TRUMP pressed ahead with another secret operation, to erect a different skyscraper in Moscow.[43] Yes, the Agalarov plan had fizzled out, but after Trump announced that he was running for president, other opportunists jumped in.

Among them: Giorgi Rtskhiladze, who had once made money moving American products like computers into Moscow and cigarettes into the former Soviet republic of Georgia. Eventually Rtskhiladze decided to import Trump as well, with a deal for a Trump tower in Batumi, Georgia—giving the Trump Organization a toehold in the former Soviet Union.[44] But as Trump's presidential campaign heated up, Rtskhiladze got involved with a new potential Trump project, this time in Russia. On September 22, 2015—one day after the Trump Tower meeting with *Forbes* staffers—Trump's lawyer, Michael Cohen, sent Rtskhiladze a design study for the new building. "I look forward to your reply about this spectacular project in Moscow," Cohen wrote.[45]

Rtskhiladze, who had previously traveled to the former Soviet Union with Cohen,[46] passed along the message to one of his friends in Moscow,[47] who he said had initially asked him to reach out to the Trump Organization about a potential deal.[48] "If we could organize the meeting in New York at the highest level of the Russian government and Mr. Trump," Rtskhiladze told his friend, "this project would definitely receive worldwide attention."[49] He didn't know how right he was.

But ultimately, Cohen decided to move forward with a third deal-maker, not the Agalarovs or Rtskhiladze but Felix Sater. Sater had also previously worked with the Trump Organization and he had deep ties inside Russia. Born in Moscow and raised in Brooklyn, Sater was once a Wall Street whiz kid. That chapter of his life ended when he got angry at a bar, grabbed a margarita glass, and smashed it into another man's face. Convicted of assault, he was sent to prison for 15 months.[50] When he got out, he had a family to feed and no way to get a job on Wall Street again, so he found a different way of making money. Sater got caught up in a Mafia-tied pump-and-dump scheme, and in 1998 he pled guilty to racketeering.[51]

He avoided a second stint in prison by cooperating with federal investigators, supplying information on Italian mobsters, North Korea's nuclear program, and Osama bin Laden's hideout. Meanwhile, he hustled for real estate deals and wound up working with the Trump Organization in Arizona, Florida, and New York.[52] For a time, he even occupied an office on the 26th floor of Trump Tower, not far from the desk of Donald Trump.[53]

To Sater, the 2016 presidential campaign was just another opportunity to make money off the Trump name, acting as a middleman between his contacts in Russia and the Trump Organization in New York. "Let me ask you a question," he says. "Who fucking thought he was going to get elected?"[54] Apparently not even Trump. "He thought he was going to lose," says one of the president's business partners and best friends, billionaire Phil Ruffin.[55] But even if he did lose, Trump had the sense that a presidential run could help his business, given his position in the polls. "I'm at 33 and the next highest is at 11," he said in September 2015, three months after entering the race. "You know, in a certain way, that's brand value."[56]

Within days of that September 2015 statement, Cohen and Sater were exchanging drafts of the document Trump ultimately signed. The first version described lucrative terms—1.8 million square feet of residential condos, with at least 5% of all sales going to Donald Trump.[57] Assuming they sold for as much as other high-end units in Moscow,

Trump could have reaped $110 million.[58] By the time he actually signed it, the artist of the deal had gotten whittled down to a possible $35 million or so up front,[59] plus a couple million in annual fees. Despite the diminished potential payout, however, Trump stayed involved. "To be clear," Cohen later testified before Congress, "Mr. Trump knew of and directed the Trump Moscow negotiations throughout the campaign."[60] Sater, who worked through Cohen, says he had no doubt that Trump knew all about the plans: "Every. Single. Word."[61] With the boss's support, they got to work trying to pull together the pieces.

First, the land. "Meeting with Andrey Molchanov on Wednesday to do Trump Moscow on his site," Sater emailed Cohen on October 9, 2015. "Best, biggest site in Moscow."[62] Also one of the most perilous. Andrey Molchanov, who studied in St. Petersburg,[63] had gotten rich after reportedly buying a city-owned construction company[64] the year he graduated from college.[65] At the time, Vladimir Putin was working inside city hall in St. Petersburg.[66] As Putin ascended in politics, Molchanov ascended in business, receiving financing, contracts, and special treatment from the Russian government.[67] Meanwhile, Molchanov's stepfather reportedly served as vice governor of the local region,[68] where he was, according to a confidential U.S. diplomatic cable, "widely rumored to be corrupt."

Second, the financing. "[Andrey Kostin], who is Putin's top finance guy and CEO of 2nd-largest bank in Russia is on board and has indicated he would finance Trump Moscow," Sater emailed Cohen three days later. "This is major for us, not only the financing aspect but Kostin's position in Russia, extremely powerful and respected. Now all we need is Putin on board and we are golden."[69] Sater did not mention that Kostin's bank, VTB, had been sanctioned by the U.S. government in response to the Crimea takeover.[70] Nor did he mention that he had not really secured Kostin's blessing, having only heard through an emissary that representatives of the bank would be interested in looking at the deal.[71] VTB, for its part, says it never held negotiations related to Trump Moscow.[72]

Third, the marketing. In hopes of luring rich Russians (and boosting the prices they would pay), Sater says he was hoping to give away the penthouse to Vladimir Putin.[73] He claims he would have built whatever the Russian president wanted. "It didn't matter," he says. "Oh, you're only approving a 100-story building? Hey, Vladimir, if you approve 120 stories, we'll give you the top two."[74]

Fourth, the partners. Officially, Trump's local partner was a second-tier developer named Andrey Rozov.[75] Unofficially, Sater was trying to bring on two of Vladimir Putin's closest cronies, Arkady and Boris Rotenberg.[76] Together, the two brothers made up 50% of the four "inner circle" oligarchs the Obama administration had sanctioned in response to the Crimea takeover.[77] The Rotenbergs, according to Sater's plan, would have put up the real money for Trump Moscow. "We would have gone to them and asked them for four or five hundred million dollars, cash," Sater says.[78] On November 3, 2015—shortly after Cohen sent back the letter of intent with Donald Trump's signature on it—Sater was on board a plane to the Bahamas to meet up with Rozov and a business partner of the Rotenbergs. Between hanging out and soaking up the sun, Sater talked up the project to the Rotenbergs' partner, whose name he refuses to divulge.

The real estate deal and Trump's campaign got muddled into one bizarre mix of politics and business. In Sater's view, Putin's approval would benefit Trump in both arenas. Just as he was about to kick off his time in the Bahamas, Sater emailed Cohen to suggest he get a clip of Obama criticizing the strength of the Republican field, in hopes that it would somehow set Trump apart. "Michael, we can own this story," Sater wrote in an email. "Donald doesn't stare down. He negotiates and understands the economic issues and Putin only wants to deal with a pragmatic leader, and a successful businessman is a good candidate for someone who knows how to negotiate. Business, politics, whatever it all is the same for someone who knows how to deal."[79]

SATER IS PRONE TO big talk. The reality is that he never secured a plot of land,[80] he didn't have the financing lined up, the Rotenbergs never signed on to the deal,[81] and Putin wasn't exactly picking out furniture for his new penthouse.[82] By December, Cohen was getting skeptical. "No response from Russia?" he texted Sater, who assured him that an invitation to the former Soviet country was coming soon.[83]

It wasn't the answer Cohen wanted to hear. "The second I get back to NYC," he texted, "I am on my own and will demand that you cease from all conversation regarding this project, and I will send a termination letter regarding the [letter of intent]. I will not let you fuck with my job and playing point person. I still have no numbers from anyone who is allegedly involved in this deal other than the fact I will have whatever invite I need within 48 hours. Not you or anyone you know will embarrass me in front of Mr. T when he asks me what is happening."

"I'm not going to argue with you—what's the point," Sater told Cohen. "As they say in politics, if you want a friend, buy a dog. I guess they are right. Except I'm not in politics. I'm just a hard-headed Russian kid from Brooklyn."

The next day, Sater said he found an invitation from Russia in his spam folder. "Michael, this is through Putin's administration, and nothing gets done there without approval from the top," he texted. "The meetings in Moscow will be with ministers—in U.S., that's cabinet level, and with Putin's top administration people. This most likely will include Dmitry Peskov, Putin's press secretary, to discuss goals, meeting agenda and meeting time between Putin and Trump."

The invitation came on official letterhead—not from Kostin's VTB Bank, as Cohen was expecting, but from a financial institution named Genbank,[84] which was later taken over by Bank Rossiya,[85] which the U.S. Treasury Department describes as the "personal bank for senior officials of the Russian Federation."[86]

Cohen was not impressed. "First it was a government invite, then VTB and then some third-rate bank," he texted Sater. "It's like being invited by Independence Savings Bank. Let me do this on my own. After almost two months of waiting, you send me some bullshit letter from a third-tier bank, and you think I'm going to walk into the boss' office and tell him I'm going there for this? Tell them no thank you, and I will take it from here."

"Michael, a lot of work has been done, and it's not a 3rd-rate anything. You are going to be meeting VTB chairman and a minister and Putin's press secretary. If you want to wait till the 12th, you will get the invite from VTB directly. This was done to speed up the process."

"I'm calling bullshit again," Cohen responded. "Let me do this on my own."

"People went all the way to the boss for this, and using them as disposable scumbags is not a way to operate. Please don't do this, Michael."

"We're done. Enough. I told you last week that you thinking you are running point in this is inaccurate. You are putting my job in jeopardy and making me look incompetent. I gave you two months and the best you send me is some bullshit fucking garbage invite by some no-name clerk at a third-tier bank. So I am telling you enough as of right now. Enough! I will handle this myself. They are not disposable scumbags. They are no one, and not a single person I know knows of this bank, and each of the people I have asked does real business in Moscow. Do you think I'm a moron? Do not call or speak to another person regarding MY project."[87]

Two weeks later, Cohen sent an email directly to Putin's press secretary, according to the Mueller report. "Dear Mr. Peskov," it began. "Over the past few months, I have been working with a company based in Russia regarding the development of a Trump Tower-Moscow project in Moscow City. Without getting into lengthy specifics, the communication between our two sides has stalled. As this project is too important, I am hereby requesting your assistance. I respectfully request someone, preferably you, contact me so that I might discuss the specifics as well as arranging meetings with the appropriate individuals. I thank you in advance for your assistance and look forward to hearing from you soon." Just like that, the Russian government had documentary evidence that Donald Trump was pursuing a business deal in Russia—while the American people remained in the dark. It was the kind of material that might allow Putin to exert leverage over Trump.

And the Russian leader was about to get even more. Six days after he sent the email, on January 20, 2016, Michael Cohen had a call with Elena Poliakova, Peskov's assistant. She peppered him with questions and took notes. Cohen, either unaware or unbothered by the fact that he was giving the Russian government potentially compromising information, walked away impressed. He told Trump about the phone call, remarking that he wished the Trump Organization had assistants as good as the Kremlin's.[88]

The very next day, Sater got back in touch. "Call me when you have a few minutes to chat," he texted Cohen. "It's about Putin. They called today."

With the Kremlin involved, Sater and Cohen made up—and got to work arranging travel plans. "I had a chat with Moscow," Sater texted on May 4, 2016, two and a half months before the Republican National Convention, in Cleveland. "ASSUMING the trip does happen, the question is before or after the convention."

"My trip before Cleveland," Cohen responded. "Trump once he becomes the nominee after the convention."

"Got it, I'm on it," Sater said. The next day, he followed up. "Peskov would like to invite you as his guest to the St. Petersburg Forum, which is Russia's Davos. It's June 16–19. He wants to meet there with you and possibly introduce you to either Putin or [Russian prime minister Dmitry] Medvedev, as they are not sure if one or both will be there. This is perfect. The entire business class of Russia will be there as well."

"Works for me," said Cohen.

Sater set the stage for Trump's attorney. "Not only will you sit with No. 1 or No. 2, but the whole biz community is there. I'll be running around setting nice $100 mill deals. And you will come back and the whole campaign team can kiss your ass. Keep this very, very close to the vest, otherwise half a dozen idiots will try to jump on your coat-tails. If it goes great, you are a hero. If it doesn't, all you did was go to an economic forum to check out business. Bro, this is why you got me working in the shadows. I will make sure you are clean as a whistle either way."

On June 13, Sater sent Cohen an invitation to the St. Petersburg International Economic Forum, which was set to begin three days later.[89] Cohen seemed excited about the trip until, suddenly, something changed.[90] He arranged to meet Sater and explained that he couldn't go to Russia after all.[91] But he did not tell his boss upstairs that the project was over, since there was a chance it could be revived in the final months of the campaign.[92]

JUST AS SATER was trying to arrange business meetings in Russia, a representative for Emin Agalarov, whose version of a Trump Tower in Moscow had sputtered out more than a year earlier, got back in touch about a different kind of meeting. "Emin just called and asked me to contact you with something very interesting," the representative told Donald Trump Jr. in an email. "The crown prosecutor of Russia met with his father Aras this morning and in their meeting offered to provide the Trump campaign with some official documents and information that would incriminate Hillary and her dealings with Russia and would be very useful to your father. This is obviously very high level and sensitive information but is part of Russia and its government's support for Mr. Trump—helped along by Aras and Emin."

The president's son responded minutes later. "If it's what you say, I love it, especially later in the summer."[93]

It remains unclear whether Donald Trump knew about this particular meeting. Michael Cohen, however, had his suspicions. "I remembered being in a room with Mr. Trump, probably in early June of 2016, when something peculiar happened," he later testified before Congress. "Don Trump Jr. came into the room and walked behind his father's desk, which in and of itself was unusual. People didn't just walk behind Mr. Trump's desk to talk to him. And I recall Don Jr. leaning over to his father and speaking in a low voice, which I could clearly hear, and saying, 'The meeting is all set,' and I remember Mr. Trump saying, 'Okay, good. Let me know.' What struck me as I looked back and thought about the exchange between Don Jr. and his father was, first, that Mr. Trump had frequently told me and others that his son Don Jr. had the worst judgment of anyone in the world. And also that Don Jr. would never set up any meeting of significance alone, and certainly not without checking with his father. I also knew that nothing went on in Trump world, especially the campaign, without Mr. Trump's knowledge and approval."[94]

For his part, Don Jr. said he never told his father. He did, however, tell his brother-in-law, Jared Kushner, and Paul Manafort, who had moved on from propping up a corrupt Ukrainian politician and was now heading Donald Trump's electoral machine. On June 9, 2016, Trump Jr., Manafort, and Kushner all gathered inside Trump Tower to meet with a Russian attorney, her translator, and two of Agalarov's representatives who had previously worked with the Trumps on the beauty pageant and the stalled deal. The Russian lawyer, who had maintained ties to the Kremlin, claimed that the billionaire Ziff family had dodged taxes and laundered money in the United States and Russia, and that the Ziffs had funneled money to the Hillary Clinton campaign or Democratic National Committee.

Don Jr. asked how the money could be traced to Clinton. The lawyer said she could not track the money once it entered the United States, and instead changed topics to something called the Magnitsky Act, an obscure 2012 law that enabled the United States to levy sanctions against Russian officials. This, it seemed, is what the lawyer really wanted to talk about. Bored, Kushner emailed his assistants, asking them to call him mid-meeting so that he would have an excuse to walk out. Don Jr. explained that he couldn't help the Russian lawyer, since his father was not yet in power. The meeting ended after about 20 minutes.

The only person who might have gotten anything out of this bizarre encounter was Vladimir Putin. No, the Russian president did not get Trump insiders to agree to alter the Magnitsky Act. But if the Agalarovs passed on their emails to the Kremlin—a representative did not respond to inquiries about whether they did—then Putin would have had even more compromising material on Trump. He also would have had confirmation that the Trump family would "love it" if a hostile foreign power were to dig up dirt on Clinton. Good news for Putin, since his government had already done so.

In July 2016, Republican insiders worked on revisions to the party platform ahead of the Republican National Convention.[95] They started with the platform from 2012, when the Republican nominee was Mitt Romney, who at the time was derided for naming Russia as America's biggest foe. Trump, on the other hand, had praised Putin time and time again: "Putin has been a very strong leader for Russia"[96]; "He's making minced meat out of our president"[97]; "He said Donald Trump is a genius."[98]

One delegate proposed amending the platform to offer support for "providing lethal defensive weapons to Ukraine's armed forces." A Trump campaign official, who had been instructed to be a mostly passive observer in the platform discussions, nonetheless decided to tweak the language on that particular amendment, replacing it with a watered-down pledge for "appropriate assistance." The Trump campaign official later told special counsel Robert Mueller's investigators that was the only change he remembered the campaign requesting.[99]

On June 14, 2016, news broke that Russia had compromised the computer network of the Democratic National Committee.[100] And on July 22, 2016, document database website WikiLeaks began releasing thousands of internal emails.[101] They were damning. Party leadership, which was supposed to be neutral in the Democratic primary, had ripped Bernie Sanders in private emails. "He isn't going to be president," said DNC chairwoman Debbie Wasserman Schultz in one message.[102] Two days after the emails came out, she announced her resignation.[103]

On July 27, 2016, Trump strode out to a podium at Trump National Doral, his Miami golf resort. One reporter posed a question about whether Trump was going to tell Putin to stay out of American politics. "What do I have to get involved with Putin for?" Trump said, turning his palms up in disbelief. "I have nothing to do with Putin. I've never spoken to him. I don't know anything about him, other than he will respect me. He doesn't respect our president. And if it is

Russia—which it's probably not, nobody knows who it is—but if it is Russia, it's really bad for a different reason. Because it shows how little respect they have for our country, when they would hack into a major party and get everything. But it would be interesting to see. I will tell you this: Russia, if you're listening, I hope you're able to find the 30,000 emails that are missing."[104]

Apparently, the Russians were listening. Within about five hours, officers inside Russia's military intelligence agency began targeting Clinton's personal office for the first time, according to the Mueller report.[105]

On October 7, 2016, a month before the election, *The Washington Post* published a 2005 video of the Republican nominee bragging about his behavior with women. "You know, I'm automatically attracted to beautiful—I just start kissing them," Trump says in the video. "It's like a magnet, just kiss. I don't even wait. And when you're a star, they let you do it. You can do anything. Grab 'em by the pussy. You can do anything."[106]

Dozens of Republicans denounced their party's nominee. Even Trump's own running mate, Mike Pence, stopped answering Trump's phone calls, according to *The New Yorker*.[107] But in the darkest hour of President Trump's campaign, Putin was there for him. Not even an hour after the release of the tape, another batch of Russia-hacked emails went public on WikiLeaks, exposing internal emails from Clinton campaign chairman John Podesta. They were even more damaging, revealing embarrassing lines from speeches Clinton had given to Wall Street banks and showing her campaign received advance notice about a CNN town hall question.

For Trump, the counterpunch from WikiLeaks surely helped, but it didn't solve all concerns. There were rumors among Trump's associates that additional tapes existed—not in the hands of a news organization but in the hands of Russians. Trump had done something compromising, the rumor went, and people connected to the Agalarovs—who brought Trump to Russia for the 2013 Miss Universe contest—had it all on tape.

Nine days before the 2016 election, Giorgi Rtskhiladze, who had corresponded with Cohen about one of the Trump Moscow proposals that stalled out quickly, resurfaced. "Stopped flow of some tapes from Russia but not sure if there's anything else," he texted Cohen. "Just so you know." Rtskhiladze later said he heard the tapes were fake, but he did not mention that to Cohen, who told Trump about the supposed tapes.[108] Even if the tapes did not exist, it's hard to imagine that the conversation did not leave Trump wondering whether Putin held yet one more thing over his head.

IN THE WEE hours of the morning on November 9, 2016, Hillary Clinton called Donald Trump to congratulate him on becoming the 45th president of the United States. Shortly thereafter, Trump's press secretary, Hope Hicks, got a call from a Washington, D.C., number, according to the Mueller report. She picked it up but could not make sense of what the person on the other end of the line was saying. Hicks did, however, catch the words "Putin call." She told whoever it was to send her an email.

The next day, she received a message purportedly from Vladimir Putin, offering Trump congratulations on the victory. "Can you look into this?" Hicks said in a message to Jared Kushner. "Don't want to get duped but don't want to blow off Putin!" She eventually concluded that the message was worth passing along, and five days later, the Russian president was on the phone with Trump and his aides, including future national security adviser Michael Flynn.[109]

The Trump-Putin relationship faced an early hurdle in December 2016, when outgoing president Barack Obama announced a new round of sanctions to punish Russia for its interference in the elections.[110] The Russian ambassador to the United States, Sergey Kislyak, texted Flynn. "Can you kindly call me back at your convenience?"

Flynn was vacationing in the Dominican Republic at the time, a sea away from most of Trump's advisers, who were stationed with the president inside Mar-a-Lago, in Palm Beach, Florida. He called K. T. McFarland, who was set to serve as Flynn's deputy in the new administration.[111] Flynn got the message that the Mar-a-Lago crowd did not want the Russians to escalate things any further.[112]

He hung up, dialed Kislyak,[113] and asked him to play it cool.[114] The next day, Putin announced that Russia would not retaliate against the Obama sanctions.[115] "Great move on delay (by V. Putin)," Trump tweeted. "I always knew he was very smart!"[116]

Two weeks later, *The Washington Post* revealed Flynn's phone call with Kislyak.[117] Flynn asked McFarland to call the paper and deny what had happened, according to the Mueller report. She followed those orders—knowing that what she said was not true as she said it. Flynn later lied to Vice President Mike Pence about the call as well, and on January 24, 2017, Flynn lied to the FBI—committing a federal crime by doing so. The whole time, of course, the Russian government knew the truth, which meant that America's national security adviser was compromised.

After Flynn's lies finally fell apart the next month, he was asked to resign. He walked into the Oval Office and gave Trump a hug. "We'll give you a good recommendation," the president said. "You're a good guy. We'll take care of you."[118] Flynn ended up pleading guilty to lying to the FBI.[119] But he later sought to withdraw that plea,[120] and in an unusual move, Trump's Department of Justice asked a court to dismiss the case, despite the fact that Flynn had already admitted to the crime.

Trump's associates started spinning the Russia story almost as soon as it emerged. Two days after Flynn resigned, Trump friend Phil Ruffin sat inside the first-floor restaurant of the Trump International Hotel, holding a newspaper packed front-to-back with Russia.[121] "This stuff about him having financial investments all over Russia—that's just pure crap," Ruffin said. "I went to Russia with him. We took my airplane. We were having lunch with one of the oligarchs there. No business was discussed."[122]

The next month, on March 20, 2017, FBI director James Comey walked into the Longworth House Office Building, past clicking cameras, and took a seat before the House Intelligence Committee. Wearing a gold-striped tie and plenty of hair gel, he briefly thanked his hosts, then shifted in his seat. "As you know, our practice is not to confirm the existence of ongoing investigations, especially those investigations that involve classified matters. But in unusual circumstances, where it is in the public interest, it may be appropriate to do so, as Justice Department policies recognize. This is one of those circumstances.

"I have been authorized by the Department of Justice to confirm that the FBI, as part of our counterintelligence mission, is investigating the Russian government's efforts to interfere in the 2016 presidential election. And that includes investigating the nature of any links between individuals associated with the Trump campaign and the Russian government—and whether there was any coordination between the campaign and Russia's efforts."[123]

That announcement set Washington ablaze, and a month and a half later Comey was back before Congress, this time facing the Senate Judiciary Committee, which was probing for answers. Senator Richard Blumenthal asked Comey, "Potentially the president of the United States could be a target of your ongoing investigation into the Trump campaign's involvement with Russian interference in our election, correct?"[124]

Comey put his hands up and winced. "I just worry—I don't want to answer that because that seems to me unfair speculation. We will follow the evidence."

President Trump was not happy. Eating dinner at one of his New Jersey clubs the following Friday, alongside his son-in-law Jared Kushner and policy adviser Stephen Miller, he announced that he wanted to dismiss the FBI director. As Trump drafted a termination letter on the spot, Miller took notes, according to the Mueller report. "Dear Director Comey," the letter began, "While I greatly appreciate your informing me, on three separate occasions, that I am not under investigation concerning the fabricated and politically motivated allegations of a Trump-Russia relationship . . ."[125]

The following Tuesday, May 9, 2017, Comey was standing in an FBI office in Los Angeles when he saw news of his firing flash across a television. Comey thought someone was pulling a prank on him by messing with the TV monitor. But then he got an email from his assistant, which included a scanned letter from the president of the United States.[126] It was true: he was gone.

One day later, Trump met in the Oval Office with Russia's ambassador and foreign minister. "I just fired the head of the FBI," he told them, according to the Mueller report. "He was crazy, a real nut job. I faced great pressure because of Russia. That's taken off."[127] In fact, it was not.

A week later, in the very same room, Trump sat with top White House lawyer Don McGahn, Attorney General Jeff Sessions, and Sessions's chief of staff, Jody Hunt, who was taking notes. In the middle of the meeting, according to those notes, Sessions got a phone call. He stood up, walked by the presidential seal on the carpet, and left the office.

Deputy Attorney General Rod Rosenstein was on the line. He told Sessions about Robert Mueller's appointment as special counsel, charged with investigating efforts to influence the 2016 election. Sessions, a slight, 70-year-old man who had served as Alabama's senator for 20 years before joining the Trump cabinet three months earlier, walked back into the Oval Office and delivered the news to his boss.

Trump slumped back in his chair. "Oh my God," he said, letting it sink in. "This is terrible. This is the end of my Presidency. I'm fucked."[128]

3

The Takeover

INAUGURATING AMERICA'S BILLIONAIRE IN CHIEF

On January 11, 2017, just nine days before taking office, Donald Trump hosted his first news conference as president-elect. A crowd of reporters gathered inside Trump Tower, next to a bank of elevators. Future White House power players Steve Bannon and Kellyanne Conway, Jared Kushner and Stephen Miller milled about. When the elevator doors finally opened, out walked Donald Trump himself.[1]

He had a stern look on his face, which made sense, given the circumstances. The previous day, *BuzzFeed News* had released the infamous Steele dossier, a report prepared by former British intelligence officer Christopher Steele alleging a vast conspiracy between the Trump campaign and Russia.[2] At the time, there were few answers—but plenty of questions. Had the Russians really hacked the 2016 elections? Did the Kremlin actually have business ties to the incoming president? And did Putin truly hold compromising information on Trump?

Incoming press secretary Sean Spicer took the microphone first. "It is frankly outrageous and highly irresponsible for a left-wing blog that was openly hostile to the president-elect's campaign to drop highly salacious and flat-out false information on the internet just days before he takes the oath of office."

Vice President–elect Mike Pence stepped up next. "The irresponsible decision of a few news organizations to run with a false and unsubstantiated report, when most news organizations resisted the temptation to propagate this fake news, can only be attributed to media bias, an attempt to demean the president-elect."[3]

They had a point. The dossier was certainly salacious and undoubtedly unverified. It said Michael Cohen had held a secret meeting in Prague,[4] a city he had never visited.[5] And it claimed, apparently without solid evidence, that Trump had once paid prostitutes to defile a Moscow hotel room where the Obamas had slept, by performing a "'golden showers' (urination) show in front of him."[6] Spicer and Pence responded like most politicians would—they went into spin mode. They ignored damning facts, pointed out false claims, and made the strongest statements they possibly could while generally staying within the boundaries of the truth.

Donald Trump took a different approach. "I have no deals that could happen in Russia," he said, "because we've stayed away."[7] To Trump, the line between spinning and lying never mattered all that much. Life was a series of sales pitches: He was self-made! He would save Atlantic City! He was one of the best bets on Wall Street! None of it was true, but all of it was convincing, at least to enough people that Trump got what he wanted. Now, days before taking the Oval Office, he was focused on his latest pitch: that his business was going to be independent from his presidency.

That was the original point of the press conference, before the dossier hijacked the news cycle. "I will be holding a major news conference in New York City with my children," Trump tweeted in November 2016, "to discuss the fact that I will be leaving my great business in total in order to fully focus on running the country in order to MAKE AMERICA GREAT AGAIN! While I am not mandated to do this under the law, I feel it is visually important, as President, to in no way have a conflict of interest with my various businesses. Hence, legal documents are being crafted which take me completely out of business operations. The Presidency is a far more important task!"[8]

By lying about his dealings in Russia, Trump was trying to stay on message. But his potential conflicts of interest went well beyond Moscow. He also had loans from banks facing regulatory oversight.[9] Deals with federal contractors.[10] Payments from foreign countries.[11] Even two separate leases with the U.S. government.[12]

Never before had someone assumed the presidency with such a large business, reaching into so many different areas. Federal law gives most officials no choice but to get rid of conflict-prone assets upon entering the government. For everyone in the executive branch, it is a crime to take official actions on specific issues that will clearly affect personal holdings.[13] Everyone, that is, besides the president and the vice president, who are exempt from the statute. Trump's predecessors acted like the rule applied to them anyway. Jimmy Carter put his peanut farm in a blind trust.[14] Ronald Reagan, Bill Clinton, and both George Bushes did the same with their investments.[15] Barack Obama invested his into benign index funds.[16]

Other laws do apply to the president, like the U.S. Constitution. It bans receiving "emoluments" from foreign governments without the consent of Congress.[17] But the precise definition of an emolument—a payment or benefit—is somewhat murky. Does money flowing through a private business like Trump's count as an emolument? Ethics experts said yes.[18] Trump's legal team said no.[19]

That was enough for the president-elect to make his decision.

"What I'm going to be doing," he announced from the podium inside Trump Tower, "is my two sons, who are right here, Don and Eric, are going to be running the company. They are going to be running it in a very professional manner."[20] Rather than sell his business, he was merely putting his heirs in charge, something a lot of tycoons do when they reach their seventies.

Watching the announcement on a TV in his office, Walter Shaub, the top ethics official in the executive branch, felt his heart sink. He had tried, without success, to get Trump's team to engage on ethics matters for weeks. "When we heard there was going to be this press conference, ever the optimist, there was a small part of me that dared to hope somebody had gotten through to him and he was going to do the right thing, Shaub says. Instead, the president revealed his plan to delegate rather than divest. Shaub decided to speak out, assuming it would cost him his position.[21] "Stepping back from running his business is meaningless from a conflicts-of-interest perspective," he said in a speech at the Brookings Institution that day. "The presidency is a full-time job, and he would've had to step back anyway."[22]

Donald Trump had left little doubt about who was ultimately in charge of his business. "I hope, at the end of eight years, I'll come back and say, 'Oh, you did a good job,'" he said at the close of the press conference, his sons looking on. "Otherwise, if they do a bad job, I'll say, 'You're fired.'"[23] And with that, the billionaire in chief walked offstage.

MORE THAN TWO centuries earlier, Alexander Hamilton pondered what might happen if an American president were too focused on money. "An avaricious man might be tempted to betray the interests of the state to the acquisition of wealth," he wrote in *Federalist* no. 75. "An ambitious man might make his own aggrandizement, by the aid of a foreign power, the price of his treachery to his constituents."[24]

Foreign powers were eager to influence the United States in revolutionary times, just as they are today. In 1785, King Louis XVI of France gave Benjamin Franklin 408 diamonds, set in a snuffbox, as a gift upon his departure from the embassy in Paris.[25] America's original constitution, the Articles of Confederation, prohibited presents from foreign heads of state.[26] But Franklin got special permission from Congress to keep the diamonds anyway.[27]

Two years later, he and his fellow revolutionaries convened inside Philadelphia's Independence Hall for the Constitutional Convention. They tore up the Articles of Confederation and crafted a new founding document. One rule that stayed on the books? The emoluments clause. "No person," the new constitution reiterated, "holding any office of profit or trust under [the United States], shall, without the consent of Congress, accept of any present, emolument, office or title, of any kind whatever, from any king, prince or foreign state."[28]

Following rules is harder than making them. Four years after the Constitutional Convention, Thomas Jefferson received a snuffbox of his own from the French court. Rather than hand it back or ask Congress if he could hold on to it, Jefferson came up with a secret plan, detailed in Zephyr Teachout's *Corruption in America*. He instructed one of his aides to extract the diamonds, sell them, then place the proceeds in his personal account. He used the money to pay off embassy debts.[29]

How much does a box of diamonds distort someone's thinking? It's impossible to know. Franklin and Jefferson themselves probably could not answer that question. But their actions leave room to wonder whether the gifts impacted their view of the world. When the masses rose up against King Louis in 1789, Jefferson initially expressed his support for the people,[30] which made sense, given that the French Revolution had echoes of the American Revolution. But years later,

Jefferson seemed to change his mind, concluding that France was not in fact prepared for the transition from "despotism to freedom."[31]

America's next generation of leaders had to contend with a different type of corruption, one of their own making. After taking office in 1829, Andrew Jackson decided to reward his supporters by doling out government jobs.[32] It was a questionable governing model, but a successful political one. For the next half century or so, that's how America functioned. Voters offered support, financial and otherwise, and politicians repaid them with jobs.[33] Eventually, unqualified officials filled the ranks of every department, and the federal government turned into a giant spoils system.[34]

President James Garfield got elected in 1880 and quickly fell victim to the sort of jealousies that such a system could produce. A man named Charles Guiteau expected an appointment, but it never came. So Guiteau went to a Washington, D.C., train station on July 2, 1881, clutching an ivory-handled pistol.[35] When Garfield walked into the building, Guiteau approached from behind, raised the gun, and fired two bullets into the president.[36] Garfield collapsed on the floor and died 79 days later.[37] The murder inspired reform. In 1883, Chester Arthur, who had been Garfield's vice president, signed the Pendleton Act, which in essence required certain government jobs to go to people who actually knew what they were doing.[38]

That helped end the spoils system, but it spawned a new problem. Since politicians were unable to raise big money from job seekers, they needed a new source of campaign funds.[39] In stepped America's business titans. In 1896, William McKinley's campaign manager, a wealthy railroad industrialist named Mark Hanna, leaned on his fellow members of the upper crust.[40] Andrew Carnegie, John D. Rockefeller, and J. P. Morgan handed over at least $250,000 apiece,[41] totaling the equivalent of almost $23 million today. The McKinley campaign printed 200 million pamphlets[42] and spent five times as much money as the campaign of his competitor, William Jennings Bryan.[43] On November 3, 1896, Americans went to the polls, and McKinley emerged the victor, with 51% of the vote to Bryan's 46%.[44] A week later, Hanna walked into the Republican Club of New York City and the room burst into applause. "If I have succeeded," he told the crowd, "it is because I brought the business interests under the one banner."[45]

One of the people sitting in the room that night was the president of New York's board of police commissioners, a 38-year-old named Teddy Roosevelt.[46] Five years later, after Roosevelt made his name fighting in the Spanish-American War, he became McKinley's vice president.[47] When another assassin killed McKinley, in 1901, Roosevelt turned into the 26th president of the United States of America.

Big political change often happens when the leader of one party crosses his base and embraces an opposing viewpoint. That's what Roosevelt did, going after the very same monopolists who had propelled his party to power. He signed the nation's first major campaign finance law, banning corporations from making political donations.[48] Additional legislation soon followed, capping the amount candidates could spend on House and Senate races.[49] The influence of the tycoons began to fade. "The first requisite of successful self-government," Roosevelt declared, "is unflinching enforcement of the law and the cutting out of corruption."[50]

The framework Roosevelt championed endured for nearly seventy years, when Richard Nixon's downfall sparked a new wave of legislation.[51] Congress created the Federal Election Commission, an agency that tracks how campaigns handle their money,[52] as well as the Office of Government Ethics, which reviews how officials invest their personal funds.[53]

When Gerald Ford took over as president in 1974, he appointed former New York governor Nelson Rockefeller to the vice presidency. Although Rockefeller never stood for election as vice president and only served in the office for two years, his financial arrangement is the closest parallel we have to Donald Trump's situation. Like Trump, he was exempt, as vice president, from the conflict-of-interest statute.[54] And, like Trump, he brought an enormous fortune with him into office.[55]

Rockefeller held far less power than Trump. His fortune, worth $218 million (equal to $1.1 billion today), stemmed from the work of his grandfather, oil baron John D. Rockefeller Sr.[56] By the time Nelson Rockefeller was tapped to be vice president, he still held interests with serious potential for conflicts, including a $28 million stake in Exxon (equivalent to $146 million today) and $20 million in IBM ($103 million today).[57] Since both companies were so enormous, Rockefeller's stakes offered no level of control. Nonetheless, his wealth caused a stir in Washington, even among his fellow Republicans. "The whole subject is not whether he has millions of dollars," said conservative senator Barry Goldwater. "It's whether or not he's used these millions of dollars to buy power."[58]

In response, Rockefeller opened his books to Congress, sharing seven years' worth of income tax returns. He testified on Capitol Hill, explaining that he wanted to be sure everyone got a full picture of his finances. He promised to put his holdings into a blind trust. And in the end, he leaned on his reputation, forged through decades of public service. "The abstract questions about private wealth and the power of the presidency come from finally to a direct personal question about my being in the line of succession: Am I the kind of man who would use his wealth improperly in public office?" Rockefeller said. "Or, more generally and more importantly, would my family background somehow limit and blind me, so that I would not be able to see and serve the general good of all Americans? I think the answer is no."[59]

Since Rockefeller left office, billionaires have figured out a multitude of ways to circumvent the law and pour money into politics. For decades, as *New Yorker* journalist Jane Mayer describes in the book *Dark Money,* industrial barons David and Charles Koch funneled money into right-leaning think tanks, advocacy groups, and conservatively minded university programs. Much of the cash traveled through private foundations, providing an additional benefit beyond influence. According to the tax code, the Kochs could write off their donations as charitable expenditures, saving millions of dollars per year.

Michigan tycoon Richard DeVos, who cofounded multilevel marketing giant Amway, also gave away big sums. Working around campaign laws that limited the amount a donor could give to an individual candidate, DeVos and his family made big gifts to broad causes. These sorts of donations, known as "soft money," came under scrutiny in the 1990s, because they allowed people like DeVos to gain the sort of influence that Teddy Roosevelt and others had so carefully tried to weed out at the beginning of the century.[60] DeVos's daughter-in-law, Betsy, decided to publicly defend her family's practices in a tongue-in-cheek op-ed published in *Roll Call.* "I know a little something about soft money, as my family is the largest single contributor of soft money to the national Republican party," she wrote in 1997.

"I have decided," she added, "to stop taking offense at the suggestion that we are buying influence. Now I simply concede the point. They are right. We do expect some things in return. We expect to foster a conservative governing philosophy consisting of limited government and respect for traditional American virtues. We expect a return on our investment; we expect a good and honest government. Furthermore, we expect the Republican party to use the money to promote these policies, and yes, to win elections. People like us must surely be stopped."

Hoping to strike another blow to campaign finance restrictions, the DeVos family donated to a little-known nonprofit called the James Madison Center for Free Speech. Led by a lawyer named James Bopp, the James Madison Center helped fight campaign finance restrictions around the country through litigation.[61]

In 2009, one of Bopp's clients, a nonprofit named Citizens United, faced off against the Federal Election Commission in the U.S. Supreme Court.[62] Amid the 2008 campaign, Citizens United released a movie denouncing Hillary Clinton, which it feared would lead to punishment because of campaign-finance rules. The nonprofit took the matter to court, saying it should be able to market the film. And in 2010, the Supreme Court agreed. In addition, the court rejected limits on how much corporations could spend in elections.[63]

"We had a 10-year plan to take all this down," Bopp told *The New York Times* shortly afterward. "And if we do it right, I think we can pretty well dismantle the entire regulatory regime that is called campaign finance law."[64]

Citizens United, combined with a subsequent ruling, allowed companies and individuals to put unlimited sums into federal elections.[65] The Roosevelt-era reforms, which had lasted roughly 100 years, disappeared. The Gilded Age was back, and this time there were even more tycoons, with more money. In the 2010 election, held ten months after the *Citizens United* ruling, $93 million flowed into so-called super PACs, groups that allow donors to pump endless sums into elections.[66]

Today, $93 million seems rather quaint. Ten individuals—six of whom tend to support Democrats and four of whom usually give to Republicans—collectively invested more than $1 billion into the American political system from 2010 to 2018, according to an analysis of data released by the Center for Responsive Politics.[67] Then the 2020 election began. In a matter of months, Michael Bloomberg shelled out more than $1 billion promoting his own campaign and bashing President Trump.[68] Tom Steyer spent $317 million doing the same.[69] Even the people at the center of the arms race agree it makes no sense. "The corporations have bought our government,"[70] cried Steyer, who has personally pumped more than a half billion dollars into the political system since 2010.[71] "I'm against very wealthy people attempting to or influencing elections,"[72] added Sheldon Adelson, the biggest donor on the right.[73]

Rather than view the problem as a barrier, candidate Donald Trump spotted opportunity. Since he was so rich, he reasoned, his own piles of cash would shield him from the influence of other big-money interests. "I don't need anybody's money," he said on June 16, 2015, the first day of his campaign. "I'm using my own money. I'm not using the lobbyists. I'm not using donors. I don't care. I'm really rich."[74]

It was a message Trump carried all the way to the White House. "Today we are not merely transferring power from one administration to another, or from one party to another—but we are transferring power from Washington, D.C., and giving it back to you, the people," he said in his inaugural address. "For too long, a small group in our nation's capital has reaped the rewards of government while the people have borne the cost. . . . That all changes starting right here, and right now, because this moment is your moment. It belongs to you."[75]

To figure out who was really going to hold power during the Trump administration, however, all you needed to do was look at the people with the best seats at the inauguration, sitting onstage with the president. There was Adelson, a casino king worth an estimated $30 billion. Next to him was Linda McMahon of WWE, former bankroller of Donald Trump's foundation and soon-to-be head of his Small Business Administration. A few seats down from her was Woody Johnson, owner of the New York Jets and future ambassador to the United Kingdom. Three billionaires—investor Carl Icahn, New England Patriots owner Robert Kraft, and Las Vegas legend Steve Wynn—had spots in his same row. Oil tycoon Harold Hamm, tech titan Peter

Thiel, and real estate mogul Steven Roth—all billionaires—sat one row behind them.[76]

Betsy DeVos, the same person who admitted that she expected a return on her political investments, was there, too, poised to become the next secretary of education. Her net worth, including assets held by her husband and children, stood at an estimated $2 billion, making DeVos the richest appointee to a historically rich cabinet.[77] Other members included Secretary of Commerce Wilbur Ross ($600 million), Treasury Secretary Steven Mnuchin ($400 million), and Secretary of State Rex Tillerson ($325 million).[78]

Positioned along the aisle, with one of the clearest views of the president, sat Tom Barrack, executive chairman of investment firm Colony Capital and an old friend of Trump's. Back in 1988, while working for Texas billionaire Robert Bass, Barrack had sold Trump the Plaza Hotel for roughly $407 million,[79] in that deal that Trump admitted made no financial sense. Three decades later, Barrack agreed to serve as chairman of the 58th Presidential Inaugural Committee, the organization that would pay for events at Trump's inauguration.

Barrack had not lost his touch for squeezing money out of rich guys. He got more than 25 billionaires to pony up funds, raising $107 million in total.[80] "They all want to kiss the rear of whoever wins the election," says Richard Painter, who kept a close eye on inaugural fund money while serving as George W. Bush's chief ethics counsel. The money coming in can raise suspicions, as can the money going out, especially if it goes to people in the government. "It's a potential problem that every decent ethics lawyer knows is a huge issue," adds Painter. "The problem with Trump [is] they never really had an ethics lawyer."[81]

Coal billionaire Chris Cline donated $1 million to the inaugural festivities. Obama-era policies had been harming the coal industry for years, but Trump promised to shake things up. A trust connected to fellow coal magnate Joseph Craft III pitched in another $1 million. Craft's wife, Kelly, ended up getting nominated to be ambassador to Canada, then later promoted to U.S. ambassador to the United Nations.[82]

Another $250,000 came from Kelcy Warren, cofounder of pipeline giant Energy Transfer.[83] His company's Dakota Access pipeline had been thrown into limbo thanks to a fight with the Standing Rock Sioux Tribe. Trump was ready, as one of his first acts in office, to write a presidential memorandum expediting approval of the project.[84] Shares of Energy Transfer, therefore, jumped 17% the day after the election, boosting Warren's personal fortune an estimated $440 million.[85] Why wouldn't he chip in $250,000, or 0.06% of that haul, to celebrate?

Three brokerage tycoons—Thomas Peterffy of Interactive Brokers, Marlene Ricketts of TD Ameritrade, and Charles Schwab of, well, Charles Schwab—pitched in as well.[86] Rising interest rates and hope of deregulation helped push stock in the three firms up by more than 10% before Trump even took office, boosting their families' fortunes by an estimated $1.1 billion (Peterffy),[87] $700 million (Ricketts),[88] and $1.3 billion (Schwab).[89] As an extra touch, Trump picked another member of the Ricketts family, Todd, to be deputy secretary of commerce. Ricketts later withdrew his name, with a spokesperson citing potential conflicts of interest.[90]

It's not easy to spend $107 million on a celebration that lasts just a few days, but with these kinds of guests, the money disappeared quickly. On January 17, 2017, Barrack[91] had a dinner inside the Andrew W. Mellon Auditorium in Washington, D.C.[92] A stream of black cars rolled up, depositing men in tuxes and women in ballroom gowns. The guest list included at least 19 billionaires, as well as congressional leaders like Mitch McConnell and Kevin McCarthy, plus ministers from the United Arab Emirates, Qatar, and Saudi Arabia.[93] The setting suited the clientele. Attendees walked into a space with marble floors, gold finishes, and soaring columns made of crushed clamshells.[94]

Such scenes played out around the capital all week, often roped off to the public. Behind the barricades surrounding the Trump International Hotel, for instance, Trump's foreign business partners got to spend time together. On a couch below a giant American flag, Indonesian billionaire Hary Tanoesoedibjo texted fellow billionaire Hussain Sajwani of Dubai. Eventually they met up, and the two developers of far-flung Trump properties snapped a photo together in the lobby of the recently opened Trump building, just down Pennsylvania Avenue from the White House.

Joo Kim Tiah, Trump's partner on a hotel in Vancouver, also booked a room there—though he might have had second thoughts about his selection, given the raucous celebration unfolding downstairs. He had an early flight the next morning and finally had to ask the hotel staff if they realized what time it was. "I'm sorry, Mr. Tiah, we can't turn the music down," a worker responded. "This is once in a lifetime."[95]

No question about that. The man staying in the presidential suite, after all, was the president-elect himself. Not far away, his friend, business partner, and fellow billionaire Phil Ruffin took up quarters in another room, paying $18,000 a night. "We had a great suite," Ruffin says. "It wasn't worth $18,000 a night."[96]

Bills like that added up quickly. Documents for the Trump hotel showed revenues in January 2017 hit $6 million, 99% above internal expectations.[97] That allowed the business to turn a one-month profit of $1.6 million, when it had been expecting to lose $600,000. In addition to all the money coming directly from billionaire buddies, $1.5 million reportedly flowed from the 58th Presidential Inaugural Committee, headed by Barrack.[98] That suggests that at least 25% of the revenue that Trump's hotel generated in January 2017—his first month in office—came from the president's own political donors, many of whom were big businessmen and some of whom were just everyday supporters trying to help out with the inauguration.

All of this could have been legal if the inaugural fund paid fair market rates. But it's not clear that it did. Stephanie Winston Wolkoff, one of Melania Trump's associates, who was helping to organize the inaugural festivities, sounded the alarm.[99] "I wanted to follow up on our conversation and express my concern," she emailed one of Barrack's top deputies, according to correspondence revealed by ProPublica and WNYC. "These events are in [President-elect Trump's] honor at his hotel and one of them is for family and close friends. Please take into consideration that when this is audited, it will become public knowledge."[100]

ONE MONTH AFTER the inauguration, I sit across from one of the men in charge of the president's business, Eric Trump, just down the hall from his brother, Don Jr., at Trump Tower. The man who built the building, Donald Trump, is gone. Sort of.

"My father and I are very close," Eric tells me. "I talk to him a lot. We're pretty inseparable. We were before. We worked together every day for the last 10, 12 years, and he's a big part of my life. At the same time, every time I turn on the TV—including, I can actually bet you right now that if I turn on the TV, let's just see if I'm right—I will bet you that he will be on that screen in some way, shape, or form. Let's see if I'm right. Minus if it's a commercial." Eric picks up the remote and points it toward a small screen in the corner of his office. It lights up, showing a reporter talking straight into the camera: "A hearing in federal court today could allow hundreds of people who were deported under President Trump's original—"

"There we go," Eric says, powering the TV off. "So I won the bet, right? So anyway, I see him up there all day, every day. And I also realize how big of a magnitude the decisions he makes and the things he has on his plate. So, you know, I also minimize fluff calls that you might otherwise have, because I understand that time is a resource, and that resource is important, especially when you've got the biggest job in the world."

But, Eric emphasizes, his father has set out some clear rules to distance his presidency from his business. First, he has promised not to talk with his sons about it. "There is kind of a clear separation of church and state that we maintain, and I am deadly serious about that exercise," Eric says. "I do not talk about the government with him, and he does not talk about the business with us. And that's kind of a steadfast pact that we made, and it's something that we honor. We took the structure of the business very, very seriously. We took the separation of church and state very, very seriously. Not that he had to, because, quite frankly, the president doesn't have conflicts, but because it was the right thing to do. I'm very sensitive to it, and it's something that we adhere to." Less than ten seconds later, however, Eric contradicts himself, conceding that he will in fact update his father on the business. "Yeah, on the bottom line, profitability reports and stuff like that. But you know, that's about it." How often will those reports be? Every quarter? "Depending, yeah, depending." Could be more, could be less? "Yeah, probably quarterly."

Second, Eric notes, his father has promised to donate all profits from foreign dignitaries to the U.S. Treasury, a way of blunting criticism that he was violating the emoluments clause. "You take the profits and you give that away," says Eric. Sounds simple, but it's not. If the Trump Organization is counting its "profits" as the money left after paying off debt, for example, then Trump could still be getting richer from the foreign payments. When asked about how the business plans to calculate "profits," Eric Trump refuses to answer. "I don't know," he says. "The [accountants] have to figure out how it works." Given that his father is already in office at this point, one would assume that such things had already been figured out. Eric insists that profits—however they are measured—are pulled from all Trump properties.[101] But a handful of days ago, Phil Ruffin, who owns a 50% share of the Trump International Hotel in Las Vegas,[102] told me foreign dignitaries would not be treated any differently at that property. "They have to pay like everybody else." Pressed on whether they would then take out profits from those payments, Ruffin dismissed the idea. "They're not going to do that."[103]

Third, the president has committed to doing no new foreign deals while in office. "We've strictly said that we weren't going to do deals overseas," says Eric. "And we're not."[104] But they will, selling $3.2 million of land in the Dominican Republic one year later.[105] The president will reach other deals with foreigners; he'll just do it on U.S. soil. The Trump Organization will end up selling a Las Vegas condo, for instance, to a man named Yu Zhang, who will list his address on the deed as "Taiyuan City, China."[106] The president will also sell his $13.5 million mansion[107] in Beverly Hills to a company connected to Tanoesoedibjo, the tycoon from Indonesia who was texting inside the Trump hotel during the inauguration.[108] And then there's the lease with the Qataris.

Over the next three years, it will become clear that the plan the Trumps originally laid out is not the real plan. The real plan is for the president to talk finances with his family. The real plan is to collect money from foreign nations. The real plan is to keep striking new deals, with foreigners and Americans who have interests before the government. The real plan is to funnel political money into the Trump Organization. Donald Trump's real plan, in other words, is to turn the presidency into a business.

4

Presidential Palace

INSIDE TRUMP'S OTHER WASHINGTON, D.C., HOME

I t's December 8, 2019, at the Trump International Hotel in Washington, D.C., and the lobby is appropriately decked out for the holidays. A Christmas tree, 30 feet tall or so, stands in the middle of the room, wrapped in ribbon, adorned with golden balls. Chandeliers dangle from steel beams arching over the room—crystal earrings to complement the rest of the scene. Customers mill about below, sipping $10 beers and $20 glasses of wine while their eyes wander the room.

I'm seated in the corner, on the bottom floor of BLT Prime, the lobby restaurant, long known as the only D.C. establishment where President Trump has ever dined out.[1] A waiter comes by to check in. "You're going to see someone tonight," he says, taking in the atmosphere. "The Presidential Ballroom is booked tonight. You never know who you're going to see walking around. I've seen the president 10 times since I've been here."[2]

If he doesn't show up, it seems likely a crowd of his lieutenants will. After all, the person who booked the Presidential Ballroom for tonight is none other than Attorney General William Barr.[3] Jonathan O'Connell and David Fahrenthold of *The Washington Post* got ahold of the contract for the event, which showed that it would probably provide at least $30,000 in revenue for Trump's hotel.[4] O'Connell is here, too. He paces over to BLT and peers inside to see if he recognizes anyone. I spot him and introduce myself. We make small talk and wonder who else is going to show up for the party.

There are plenty of people all dressed up—in evening dresses and power suits—but none of them are cabinet members. Outside is a group of middle-aged women who came for the festivities, but they are clearly uninvited guests. "Shame!" they yell at cars pulling up to the entrance. "You're complicit!" "Your grandchildren will be ashamed one day!" There are just enough of them to hold up the letters they fashioned for the occasion, which spell out "Disbar Barr" on lighted placards. Not exactly the most heartwarming Christmas lights, but they make a statement. So do the passersby. One car honks in support, and the ladies let out a cheer. A pedestrian, meanwhile, shouts, "Four more years!"

"In prison!" one of the protesters counters.

A few feet away stands a hotel security guard, dressed in a black suit and red tie. He's a young guy, barely old enough to grow facial hair. I ask him about his job. The protesters—who appear at least twice his age—mock him as he's answering. "I'm working hard," he says. "It's hostile, you know. Everybody is doing their job, you know. At least, I have a family to look after. I have a job, you know. That's what I think about." He tells me that previous protesters came into the hotel and destroyed property, then pulls up a YouTube video appearing to show just that. "A lot of people are getting employed here, you know," he says.

Since the ballroom is set aside from the lobby—and I still haven't seen the attorney general—I start wondering whether Barr entered through a more discreet entrance. I walk around to the back of the hotel and find a couple of workers on a smoke break. "There is no party tonight at the ballroom," one of them tells me. I head back into the hotel and ask a couple of waiters in the lounge. They tell me they aren't sure whether there is a party or not. The hallway that leads to the ballroom includes a sign forbidding anyone but hotel employees from walking farther. Confused, I spot the security guard who had been standing outside and ask whether there is, in fact, a party in the Presidential Ballroom after all. "We cannot let anyone know what's going on," he tells me. "We've got to keep it private. That's our policy."

The official policy at the president's hotel is to not disclose who is there. Confusion seems to be the point. Hoping to make sense of what's going on as the night is winding down, I station myself outside of the hotel, with a view of the doors closest to the Presidential Ballroom, expecting to see a parade of well-dressed officials pouring out. They never come. Finally, I walk up to the doors—this set does not include a sign forbidding people from entering—and notice that one is ajar. I walk inside and head to the Presidential Ballroom.

An interior door opens into an immaculate space, with gold-accented walls and another set of crystal chandeliers. The room is entirely empty. Chairs are stacked on top of one another, and the place looks perfectly clean, as if no one has been inside all day. I come across a worker on the way out, who seems confused about what a random wanderer is doing near the Presidential Ballroom. He tells me there has been no one in the space tonight: "Should be empty."

Turns out, Barr's party got called off,[5] rescheduled for another night, presumably when journalists and protesters wouldn't be staking out the place. And so, on a Sunday night in the heart of the holiday season, the president's ballroom sits vacant.

Ask most people who follow the news about President Trump's Washington, D.C., hotel, and they'll tell you it's a cash cow—or at least was before the coronavirus crisis—hauling in money from influence seekers. The truth, as this night shows, is more complicated. Just because you turn the presidency into a business doesn't mean you turn it into a good business. Protesters aren't great for any hotel. Nor are stressed-out staff members. A close examination of the president's cash-flow situation at his hotel in Washington, which has remained shrouded in secrecy throughout his presidency, suggests a more troubled financial picture than was previously understood. The truth, it seems, is that the presidency made the Trump hotel less of a cash cow and more of a money pit.

Donald Trump has always been just as likely to blow money on hotels as make money on them. Take his reported $407 million purchase of New York's Plaza Hotel in 1988[6]—"not economic," as Trump admitted at the time.[7] Four years later, the hotel, burdened by the hefty debt load Trump took on at the place, reportedly filed for bankruptcy.[8]

Familiar territory for Trump. His first corporate bankruptcy came in 1991,[9] after he sold $675 million[10] in junk bonds to finish construction of a lavish hotel and casino, the Trump Taj Mahal, complete with onion domes and waitresses outfitted in Indian costumes. A year after opening, the Trump Taj Mahal filed for bankruptcy.[11] In 1992, two other Atlantic City hotel-casinos, Trump's Castle[12] and Trump Plaza,[13] exited bankruptcy. Then there was Trump's public company, which combined[14] the three Atlantic City properties. Trump Hotels & Casino Resorts declared bankruptcy in 2004,[15] changed its name[16] to Trump Entertainment Resorts, then filed for bankruptcy once more in 2009.[17] In total, that adds up to six bankruptcies, all involving hotels.

Scarred by his near collapse, Trump pursued new methods of building. He created skyscrapers that serve as part hotel, part condo complex, where investors can buy units as second homes and, when they aren't in town, leave Trump to manage them as hotel rooms. The condo-hotel model worked in New York[18] and Vegas[19] but proved unsuccessful in Chicago. Trump also began charging other developers to use his name on their buildings or run operations on their behalf.[20] Several of Trump's licensing and management ventures failed.[21] His partners and investors were left to deal with the consequences, while Trump walked away unscathed after pocketing varying fees. Such projects spread the Trump name to Panama,[22] Hawaii, Toronto, and Vancouver.[23] With little risk involved, they also served as perfect training grounds for the Trump kids, Don Jr., Eric, and Ivanka, who flew around the globe working the deals. "I think it's more my siblings' baby than it is his," Don Jr. said in a 2016 deposition, when asked about his father's involvement in the hotel ventures. "He gets involved more in the deals where we have heavy equity investments, as opposed to where we are a hotel manager and operator."[24]

Deals such as the Washington, D.C., hotel.[25] Ivanka initially spotted the opportunity.[26] Built between 1892 and 1899,[27] the Trump hotel, formerly the Old Post Office Building,[28] is a magnificent structure, the second-tallest in D.C., behind only the Washington Monument.[29] In 2011, the federal government, which had been operating the building and losing millions of dollars annually on it,[30] solicited offers from private operators interested in redeveloping the place.[31] Ten companies threw their names into the ring, including Hilton,[32] but the Trumps won the bid.[33] They committed to invest $200 million to convert the building into a hotel as part of a lease agreement with the federal government.[34] After doing a series of licensing and operating deals, Trump was back in the hotel game as a big-time equity holder, and once again he was throwing around serious money.

The project turned into a full family affair. Ivanka worked with D.C. officials.[35] Don Jr. handled the leasing. Eric pitched in as well, though his role was less clear.[36] Each of the three kids took a 7.5% stake,[37] making the hotel the most consequential Trump Organization asset in their personal portfolios.[38] It was still obvious who the boss was—Donald Trump took the other 77.5% for himself.[39] "I'm very much involved in the details," he said in a 2016 deposition of his own. "I was involved in the design of the building and the room sizes and the entrances and the lobby and the marble and the bathrooms and the fixtures and the bars. A lot of things. I mean, you know, I'm involved very much with the hotel. The important projects I get very much involved."[40]

That involvement came with a unique set of risks. When Trump announced he was running for president, for example, he famously opened with a string of controversial comments. "When Mexico sends its people, they're not sending their best," he told a crowd assembled inside Trump Tower, adding, "They're sending people that have lots of problems, and they're bringing those problems with us. They're bringing drugs. They're bringing crime. They're rapists. And some, I assume, are good people."[41]

Trump's business partners fled. Macy's, which had sold Trump-branded shirts and cologne, ended its partnership. So did mattress maker Serta.[42] Univision refused to air Miss USA, one of Trump's beauty pageants.[43] The fallout extended to the Washington hotel, where Spanish chef José Andrés was planning to open a new restaurant.[44] "Getting crushed over DJT comments about Latinos and Mexicans," one of Andrés's staffers, Kimberly Grant, wrote in an email to Ivanka. "Need your help."

The candidate's daughter forwarded the message to an executive in the Trump Organization, David Orowitz, who responded, "Ugh, this is not surprising and would expect that this will not be the last we hear of it." He also offered up a suggestion. "At least for formal, prepared speeches, can someone vet going forward?"[45]

These were early days, when not even everyone inside Trump's company understood how unscripted he would be as a politician. Andrés pulled out, and shortly thereafter, fellow chef Geoffrey Zakarian, who was preparing to create a second restaurant inside the hotel, followed suit.[46]

Around the same time, Trump's hotel managers began looking for people to hire. They found a wellspring of workers through, of all things, a program that helped asylum seekers find work in the United States.[47] "They were fantastic employees and looking for work," says Merrick Dresnin, who headed up human resources for the hotel in 2016 and 2017. "That's basically how we found a lot of great guest-service folks."[48]

The dissonance between candidate Trump's rhetoric and businessman Trump's actions was not lost on the workers inside the hotel. "There were a lot of immigrants," says Beatrice Dumitrache, who moved from Romania and got a job in the United States at Trump's hotel. "To me, it did not seem okay compared to how Trump always says we need to build the wall."[49]

On October 26, 2016, the Trump family took a detour on the campaign trail and visited their new hotel for a grand opening. "Two years ago, when we promised the city of D.C. that Trump would be coming to Pennsylvania Avenue in 2016, we had no idea what we were foreshadowing," said Ivanka Trump. "This is an important moment for our family and our company, and it wouldn't be possible without the hard work and support of this visionary man. So without further ado, let me introduce my father, Donald J. Trump."

The Republican nominee for president took the microphone. "We have built one of the great real estate companies of the world," Trump said. "But it seems very insignificant compared to what we're doing now, and as soon as we're finished cutting the ribbon, I'm off to North Carolina, New Hampshire, and back down to Florida." The D.C. hotel, in all its splendor, served as the perfect backdrop for the presidential campaign. "Today is a metaphor for what we can accomplish for this country," Trump said. "Same kind of thing. This building is a historical landmark, a true American original. It had all of the ingredients of greatness, but it had been neglected and left to deteriorate for many, many decades."[50]

Thirteen days later, while Trump watched the results roll in near his home in New York, a sea of supporters packed the lobby of his Washington hotel. One of Trump's hotel managers, who asked not to be named because he signed a confidentiality agreement with the business, went to bed at midnight—exhausted. The party was nowhere near done. "When I woke up at 4 a.m. or 3 a.m., I turned on the TV," recalled the manager. "I said, 'Oh my gosh. Life is going to change.'"[51]

WASHINGTON, D.C., is full of monuments to presidents, but none quite like the Trump hotel. Never before has an American president pre-built a place for his admirers, opened it right around the time he took office, then charged attendees to enjoy the space while he served in office. A bottle of chardonnay from the Trump winery in Virginia goes for $68. A seafood platter called the Trump tower, which includes a one-pound lobster and a dozen oysters and clams, runs $120. Non-Trump-themed items are just as pricy. An order of the lobster mac and cheese costs $35, and a hamburger goes for $26. The only free thing on the menu? The ever-present cocktail of money and power, which anyone can absorb simply by peering around the lobby.

From the moment Donald Trump won the election, his presidency has complicated things at the hotel. For starters, there's the lease itself, written in clunky legal language, which appears to prohibit elected officials from being a part of the deal. "No member or delegate to Congress, or elected official of the government of the United States," one provision begins, "shall be admitted to any share or part of this lease, or to any benefit that may arise therefrom; provided, however, that this provision shall not be construed as extending to any person who may be a shareholder or other beneficial owner of any publicly held corporation or other entity."

Shortly after the election, lawyers inside the General Services Administration started talking about whether Trump would be violating the lease from the start of his presidency. Eleven days after the inauguration, on January 31, 2017, Don Jr. and Eric met with GSA officials. An officer inside the agency, Kevin Terry, pushed for the president to divest. That did not happen.

Instead the Trump team argued that there was no issue with the lease, for two main reasons. First, Trump had signed on to the agreement before becoming president. Second, he held his interest through an entity, not directly. The Trump Organization asked the GSA for a certificate saying it was in compliance with the lease. And on March 23, 2017, the agency issued one.

How could Trump be in compliance with the lease when he had retained his interest in the hotel? And what about the fact that he was accepting foreign money there, potentially in violation of the U.S. Constitution? The GSA launched an internal investigation. After conducting more than two dozen interviews and reviewing over 10,000 documents during a 16-month inquiry, the investigators determined that no one had improperly pressured the GSA, but the agency had screwed up. Its lawyers agreed that the president might be violating America's founding charter, but they decided to ignore the issue. Their negligence was costly, according to the investigators, leaving an unresolved controversy hanging over the country. "GSA, like all government agencies," the report stated, "has an obligation to uphold and enforce the Constitution."[52]

In the meantime, lawsuits had piled up—from competitors,[53] congressmen,[54] and local governments[55]—all alleging that Trump was violating the Constitution. Three years into Trump's presidency, the litigation was still working its way through the courts.[56] America's justice system moves slowly, something Donald Trump knows well from years of battling lawsuits in business.

To stem criticism that the president was violating the Constitution by accepting foreign money, Trump's legal team claimed he would give the U.S. Treasury all hotel profits from foreign governments.[57] After initially declining to detail how, exactly, the business would calculate such profits, the Trump Organization eventually submitted its methodology to the House Oversight Committee,[58] conceding that it was not really trying to track all foreign government money. "To fully and completely identify all patronage at our properties by customer type is impractical in the service industry," explained a Trump Organization document, "and putting forth a policy that requires all guests to identify themselves would impede upon personal privacy and diminish the guest experience of our brand. It is not the intention nor design of this policy for our properties to attempt to identify individual travelers who have not specifically identified themselves as being a representative of a foreign government entity on foreign government business."[59]

The policy, in other words, was "don't ask, don't tell." As long as foreign officials did not identify themselves as representatives of another country, they could go ahead and pay the president. For the year of 2017, the Trump Organization donated $151,470 to the U.S. Treasury,[60] and the following year the president's business reportedly upped the donation to $191,538.[61] That would be real money to a small company, but not much for the D.C. hotel, for which it represented roughly 0.3% of revenues.[62]

THE FIRST SIGN that Donald Trump is coming to the hotel on any given night is often the dogs sniffing around[63] in the afternoon. "Oh, and the management are all stressed out," explains a waiter inside the hotel.[64] At some point, the hotel goes on lockdown, thinning out the crowd, according to Beatrice Dumitrache, who served as a hostess at the hotel from 2017 to 2018.[65]

When the president walks in, his entourage in tow, everyone erupts in applause. He heads to BLT Prime, passing through a lobby full of supporters.[66] "He actually talks a lot," says someone who works at the restaurant.[67] Trump tends to eat upstairs, where he can enjoy the splendor of his hotel lobby, shimmering chandeliers and all.[68] "You know," says the staffer, "one of the last things I heard him say was—he stood right there and he yelled, 'Don't worry, we're going to get that wall built!'"[69] Once seated, Trump is known to order pure Americana: steak[70] followed by apple pie.[71]

"People got really, really excited," says Michel Rivera, who worked behind the bar at the hotel. "And people got really, really drunk afterward. So it was like a celebration. Every single time he came in, we were like, 'Well, we are going to make money tonight.'" People who usually stayed for one or two rounds of drinks—a sensible choice, given the prices on the menu—instead might stick around for four or five. "I felt like I was in a nightclub the days that he was there,"[72] says Rivera.

Trump visited his hotel more than two dozen times during his first three years as president, according to NBC News.[73] He's not the only one traveling back and forth between the hotel and the White House. Three top officials—Treasury secretary Steven Mnuchin, small business administrator Linda McMahon, and National Economic Council director Gary Cohn—all reportedly took up residence in the building as the Trump administration was settling into D.C.[74] The president's personal lawyer, Rudy Giuliani, and his onetime press secretary, Sarah Huckabee Sanders, stopped by enough that the staff got to know them.[75] "They were regulars," says Dumitrache. "They would come once a week, I would say."[76]

Lesser Trumpers followed. Congressmen,[77] campaign surrogates,[78] Fox News personalities.[79] Most of these visits would have gone unnoticed if not for the tireless efforts of Zach Everson, a travel journalist who wrote a few stories about the hotel, then got obsessed with the place. Everson scours Instagram and Twitter day after day to see who has stopped by the Trump hotel. He publishes his findings in a newsletter, *1100 Pennsylvania*.[80] As of February 2020, Everson had spotted more than two dozen Trump cabinet members at the hotel, along with 32 of the 53 Republicans serving in the Senate and countless members of the House of Representatives.[81]

The politicians don't always pick up their own tabs. The Beltway is awash in political money, which donors from all over the country funnel into campaigns. Over the past few years, Trump acolytes have refunneled thousands of those dollars to the president via his hotel. While some members of the House Oversight Committee were actively examining the hotel,[82] its highest-ranking Republican, Jim Jordan of Ohio, spent more than $20,000 of campaign funds[83] on food and drink there, according to Federal Election Commission filings.[84] Mark Meadows, another Republican on the committee, whom Trump later tapped to be his chief of staff, distributed more than $10,000[85] of campaign money at the hotel and BLT Prime.[86] Congressman Greg Pence, the brother of Vice President Mike Pence,[87] shelled out more than $40,000 of campaign donor money[88] at the Trump hotel.[89] The Republican National Committee spent over $400,000[90] there. In total, the president's hotel collected more than $2.6 million from campaigns and committees during Trump's first three years in office.[91]

"It's such an unbelievable shock to the system," says Walter Shaub, the ethics official who spoke out against Trump's financial arrangement from the get-go. "I think with the onslaught of daily crises and scandals and norm breaches, we forget how extraordinary it is that the president has this hotel, and how atrocious it is that members of Con-

gress who are supposed to be conducting oversight have had fundrais-
ers there and spent campaign money there."

There's an old Washington, D.C., myth that in the mid-1800s,
President Ulysses S. Grant lit up enough cigars in the lobby of the
Willard Hotel that influence peddlers began hanging around there to
push him on one issue or another, prompting Grant to coin the term
"lobbyist."[92] Two centuries later, the number of lobbyists has multi-
plied,[93] and today the president has his own lobby. No surprise that
lobbyists like to hang around there. There is even, reportedly, a regular
gathering of them,[94] dubbed Trump First Tuesdays.

Then there were the foreign officials, whose visits put Trump at risk
of violating the Constitution. The prime minister of Malaysia stopped
by while in town to visit the president.[95] The government of Kuwait
hosted its independence day celebration at the Trump hotel.[96] So did
the Philippines.[97] The leader of Romania visited, according to Dumitrache.[98] A Russian ambassador did, too.[99] And a top aide of the Ukrainian president.[100] The Saudi government spent at least $270,000,
according to federal disclosures.[101] In all, Everson counted representatives of 31 foreign governments who had visited the Trump hotel as of
February 2020.[102]

"We had to be on our perfect behavior when that was happening,"
says Dumitrache, noting that dignitaries from one country or another
visited at least once a month. "They would print us a piece of paper,
showing us which country it is, where exactly they are staying, what is
the reason [for] their visit. So if the person would make contact with
us, we would know exactly what to say to them." The reasons for the
stays varied, according to Dumitrache. There were officials there for
summits, others for embassy visits, some for meetings with Trump.

"They just told us to treat them as VIPs because that's what they
were," Dumitrache says. "One day I told one of my managers, I said,
'Right, but we're a five-star hotel. Isn't everybody supposed to be

treated as a VIP, even if they don't spend the money that a VIP does?'
And they said, 'Yeah, but when it's someone like that, you have to treat
them extra special.'"[103]

BUSINESS WASN'T WHAT IT SEEMED. By law, officials serving in the
executive branch must list the "income" that their assets produce in a
financial disclosure report.[104] For officeholders with stocks and bonds,
it's a simple task that amounts to listing dividends, interest, and capital gains.[105] The rules for real estate assets are more complicated.
Filers can list "rent"—in other words, revenue—under the column labeled "income amount." But *revenue* and *income* suggest very different
things. Presented with a form asking for both rent[106] (a big number)
and income (generally a much smaller number), Trump listed the big
one. In 2017, the first full year his D.C. hotel was open to the public
(and the first year Trump served as president), he disclosed $40.4 mil-
lion of revenue at the property. That figure ticked up slightly the next
year, to $40.8 million.[107]

Reporting on the disclosures, several reporters referred to those
numbers as "income" instead of revenue, creating the false impression
that Trump was personally pocketing $40 million a year at his other
palace on Pennsylvania Avenue. "Trump made $40.8 million last year
from a hotel," shouted one headline.[108] "The president's income from
his company's hotel in Washington, D.C., topped $40 million last year,"
began another story.[109]

Some outlets, like *The Wall Street Journal, The Washington Post,*
and *The New York Times,* were more careful to distinguish between
revenues and profits.[110] But even those newspapers appear to have
made a different mistake (which I also previously made at *Forbes*).[111] A
closer examination of the federal guidelines shows that officials holding real estate can list the amount of rent attributable to them person-

ally, rather than the total amount produced by the property.[112] In other words, even though Trump lists hotel revenue of $40.8 million on his disclosure, that's not necessarily the total revenue of the hotel. It could just as easily be 77.5% of the total revenue, proportionate to Trump's personal interest in the property.

Ivanka Trump listed $3,952,480 of hotel revenue on her filing, from her 7.5% share of the revenue.[113] Ivanka's disclosure points to $52,699,733 in revenue, which matches her father's figure—if he disclosed only his 77.5% share of the revenue. That suggests the true revenue of the hotel is a number never previously reported: $52.7 million.

If figuring out the revenue at Trump's hotel is challenging, pinning down its profits is nearly impossible. But there are clues. Under the Trump Organization's lease with the federal government, it submits detailed financial information—including profits—to the General Services Administration, which is supposed to keep those filings confidential.[114] In August 2017, however, the GSA accidentally published four months of financial data on its website, which *The Washington Post* then downloaded. After the GSA realized its mistake and removed the documents, the *Post* released them publicly.[115]

Most of the coverage at the time focused on the fact that the Trump Organization had blown past its projections for the hotel, hauling in $18.1 million of revenue during the first four months of 2017, 49% above expectations. In addition, the hotel had produced a profit—measured as earnings before interest, taxes, depreciation, and amortization—of $2 million, when it was projected to instead lose $2.1 million.[116] It seemed like another indication that Trump was profiting from the presidency.

What virtually everyone, including me, failed to absorb at the time was that $2 million of profit on $18.1 million in revenue is not all that much money. It suggests a profit margin of just 11%—well below the industry average.[117] "That seems low for a hotel, for sure," says Dan Wasiolek, a hospitality analyst at investment research firm Morningstar.

"You know, I would have expected that it would be closer to 20%."[118] Even more troubling for the hotel: that underperformance occurred as Trump was first taking office, a time when the property was receiving more buzz than any hotel in U.S. history.

There are more bad signs. In 2019, the Trump Organization put together another document, this time for potential investors interested in purchasing the hotel. The pitch, reviewed by CNN, included the sort of rosy projections one might expect from a company known for its salesmanship. The Trump Organization projected that revenues would jump to $67.7 million in 2020, which, assuming 2018 revenues were $52.7 million, would represent a 28% increase in two years. It also predicted that, when that happened, the hotel would throw off $6 million of annual profits—measured as earnings before interest, taxes, depreciation, and amortization, minus the cost of updates.[119] The numbers suggest that, even in an optimistic scenario, the hotel would be running a profit margin of only 9%—even lower than the already unimpressive 11% the hotel produced in early 2017.

Those glimpses give us enough information to reasonably estimate— for the first time—how much money the president has actually made from his D.C. hotel while serving in the White House. Odds are, the profit margins in early 2017 (11%) and those reported on the investor pitch (9%) are higher than the average margins over the past few years. In a good scenario, the Trump Organization might have maintained that performance and turned a bit less than 10% of its revenue into profits each year. That would mean that the hotel produced annual earnings of $5.1 million in 2017 and $5.2 million in 2018, for a total of $10.3 million.[120] If the hotel instead ended up with, say, an 8% margin, that would suggest $4.2 million of annual pre-tax, pre-interest profit each year, or $8.4 million total.

One of the few people who has seen the real numbers for the hotel is Brian Friedman, a Washington investor who once offered to buy the place for $175 million from the Trumps. In order to view the books, Friedman signed confidentiality documents saying he would not share the data. But I ran my estimate of roughly $5 million in earnings before interest, taxes, depreciation, and amortization by him anyway, to gauge his reaction. "Does that sound in the range?" I asked.

"That sounds in the range," he replied.[121]

Five million sounds like a lot of money. Until you consider that those profits are before accounting for interest, taxes, depreciation, or amortization. Take just the interest. The Trump Organization borrowed $170 million from Deutsche Bank to renovate the property.[122] There is no evidence that Trump has paid down any of the principal on that loan, though it's possible he has. That makes it difficult to pinpoint exactly how much he is paying in interest, especially since Trump has a variable interest rate on the property. But let's say the Trump Organization still owes $170 million and paid something like 3.35% in 2017, which would have made it one of the president's cheaper loans.[123] On $170 million of debt, 3.35% interest adds up to $5.7 million in annual payments. Poof—there goes the possible $5.1 million in profits for that year. In 2018, much to the chagrin of the president, interest rates increased,[124] likely boosting his company's expenses.[125] An analysis of the president's financial disclosure report and interest-rate benchmarks suggests the Trump Organization paid something close to 4.2% interest on the hotel loan during his second year in office, or about $7 million. Enough to bury the estimated $5.2 million in earnings.

It's impossible to be certain without seeing the official numbers, but it sure seems likely that the president is actually losing money on the D.C. hotel—the property that most people have assumed is such a big moneymaker. "He spent a ridiculous amount of money—a hell of a lot more than I thought he was going to spend," says Friedman. "It's real

INDEBTED IN D.C.

Before Donald Trump became president, Deutsche Bank handed him $170 million to turn Washington, D.C.'s Old Post Office Building into the Trump International Hotel. In exchange, Trump promised to pay that money back to the German bank, along with interest. A close look at the property's performance, however, suggests the hotel might not be profitable enough to keep up with those interest payments.

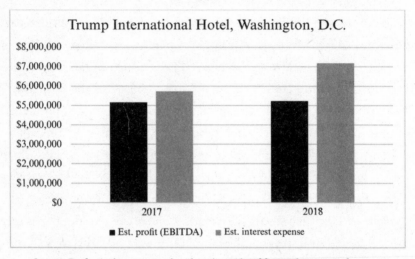

Sources: Profit: Author estimates based on 4 months of financials, reports of investor sales pitch, conversation with prospective buyer. Interest: Author estimates based on analysis of Federal Reserve data, Trump's financial disclosure reports

money, and he did it. Now, did he do it effectively? Obviously not, because the numbers are what the numbers are."[126]

THE TRUMP ORGANIZATION first said that it was open to selling the hotel in October 2019.[127] There's a lot for potential investors to like, if they can get over the poor financials. "The bones are great," says Friedman, standing atop the perfectly polished floors just outside of the perfectly appointed lobby on a perfectly crisp January afternoon. "Even, like, people talk shit about the chandeliers. They know nothing. They know nothing. Those chandeliers are millions of dollars."[128]

It's a shame more people aren't around to enjoy them. The doors next to Friedman, with beautiful marble columns on either side, which open out onto Pennsylvania Avenue—one of the most famous streets in America—are completely closed off. A sign warns that an alarm will sound if anyone opens them. Outside stands a string of metal barricades keeping out tourists who might otherwise wander up to the door. None of these blockades used to be here, but, according to a waiter at the hotel, the Trump Organization shut down most of the entrances after protesters stormed the place.[129]

To a non-Trump owner, that spells opportunity. "I mean, this is it," Friedman says. "This was all supposed to be, like, retail." Indeed. This is steps from where Geoffrey Zakarian, the celebrity chef, was supposed to rent space and within eyeshot of where José Andrés was supposed to have his restaurant. "I would bring all of that back," says Friedman. Including José Andrés. "I would have him invest," Friedman claims. "He's going to be a partner." Peering out over the mostly vacant lobby, Friedman envisions a space with professionals typing away on laptops near fast-casual restaurants like Sweetgreen. Friedman says he wouldn't need to change much on the upper floors—"the rooms are awesome"—but he would add art.[130] "You go to the Four Seasons and there's Warhols on the wall," he says.[131] "You go to my hotels and there's art everywhere. There's no art. Trump has no style."[132]

What the Trumps lack in style, they make up for in ambition. Hence the reported $500 million[133] they are hoping to fetch for the hotel. If that actually happened, they could pay off the $170 million Deutsche Bank loan, and the president would walk away with $256 million in cash. Ivanka, Don Jr., and Eric would pocket $25 million apiece before taxes. But that scenario is unlikely. The truth is, this hotel—as nice as it is—is not worth a half billion dollars. "Five hundred [million] is not going to happen,"[134] says Michael Bellisario, a hotel analyst who works for Baird, an investment bank. Bill Moyer, a Washington, D.C., hotel broker who likes to frequent the property every two weeks or so, agrees that no one is likely to pay that much. "I don't think they're going to get the kind of pricing that they were just throwing out."[135] Wasiolek, the hospitality analyst for Morningstar, thinks a buyer might plunk down $240 million for the place if they were extremely aggressive. "Boy, I mean, that seems to be an upper limit, though."[136]

There are two primary ways to figure out what a hotel is worth. The first is by applying a multiple to its profits, the earnings before interest, taxes, depreciation, and amortization. Doing so allows potential investors to see how long it might take them to earn back their money. The nicer the hotel is, the more likely they are to wait a longer amount of time. For a super luxury property like Trump's, someone might be expected to pay, say, 20 times the cash stream. If it's throwing off $10 million a year, for example, there's a good chance someone would pay $200 million for the place. But Trump's pre-tax, pre-interest profits appear to be more like $5 million. At that level, Trump is asking an estimated 100 times the annual profits. A more realistic seller might ask, say, $100 million for a property that's producing $5 million a year.

Given its grandeur, however, it's unlikely the Trump hotel is worth only $100 million, which brings us to the second way of valuing a hotel. Investors often apply a price to each room and multiply that figure by the number of rooms. If you throw out the income approach and look just at the second method, it's possible to justify more than $1 million per room for Trump's hotel. Valuing something is an art rather than a science, and seven hospitality experts offered estimates of anywhere from $500,000 to $1.2 million a room for Trump's property, after being told about its low profit margins. The average was $761,000. Since the place has 263 hotel rooms, that would suggest it's worth $200 million. That seems to be a fair valuation that takes into account both the income and the price per room. It also comes to $300 million less than what the Trump Organization was asking.[137]

Standing outside a boxy Mercedes SUV parked across from the hotel, Friedman admits that he doesn't think his bid for the property will be successful. The problem: he figures Trump's hotel should be valued similarly to the Mayflower Hotel, which has 581 rooms and which, he says, went for $175 million. He's skeptical that the Trump family would sell for something like that. "It could go for some crazy, fuck-you number, because that does happen with real estate," he says at another point. "This is a diamond."[138]

Trump knows something about paying stupid money in ego-fueled purchases. Remember the Plaza Hotel? But today, Wall Street isn't shelling out money like it was in the late 1980s, meaning the most likely purchaser would be a well-established hotel company or a deep-pocketed tycoon[139] in the mood for a vanity project. It would be one heck of a way to curry favor with Trump. A $26 hamburger or $400 hotel reservation might not get the president's attention, but adding a couple hundred million to his bottom line undoubtedly would. "It could be some Saudi sheikh or someone from Iran or something,"[140] says Moyer, the D.C. hotel broker. Adds Bellisario, one of the hotel analysts, "You don't know what two billionaire brothers in London, or some sultan of Brunei, wants to buy a property."[141] Especially when the seller is the president of the United States.

5

Bad Lie

THE TRUTH BEHIND TRUMP'S GOLF GAME

Two and a half months after becoming president, Donald Trump sat inside his exclusive Palm Beach club, Mar-a-Lago, alongside Chinese ruler Xi Jinping, with the lights dimmed low.[1] It was a first date, of sorts, between the leaders of the two most powerful countries on the planet.[2] Trump was eager to make an impression.

Positioned between his wife, Melania, whose red dress matched his own red tie, and the president of China,[3] Trump turned to Xi as they were eating chocolate cake and let him in on a little secret. "Mr. President, let me explain something to you," Trump said. "We've just fired 59 missiles."[4] The rockets were already in the air, flying toward Syria as a message to Bashar al-Assad, the dictator who had recently used chemical weapons against his own people.[5] Commerce secretary Wilbur Ross later termed the rocket show "after-dinner entertainment," joking, "The thing was, it didn't cost the president anything to have that entertainment."[6]

Trump transformed Mar-a-Lago into a one-of-a-kind club, where members could get a glimpse of history along with their dinner. It was a perk that Trump, who took to calling the place the "Winter White House,"[7] could never have never imagined when he purchased the property, in 1985, for roughly $10 million.[8]

Quite an investment. When Trump filed his first financial disclosure report as a presidential candidate, he revealed that revenue at Mar-a-Lago was $15.6 million in 2014 and part of 2015. That number nearly doubled, to $29.8 million on the next year's report, before peaking at $37.3 million the following year.[9] "It's had a very positive impact," Trump said in a 2016 deposition, when asked about the effect of the campaign on his business. "The manager told me recently, he said, 'Boy, it is actually the best year we've ever had at Mar-a-Lago.' And I was looking at the numbers. I said, 'What do you attribute this to?' He said, 'The campaign.'"[10]

The presidency provided additional opportunities. After the election, word spread that Mar-a-Lago was doubling its membership fee from $100,000 to $200,000.[11] Trump reportedly asked four[12] club members to serve as ambassadors—to Ireland, Austria, South Africa, and the Dominican Republic—while designating another regular at the club, billionaire Isaac Perlmutter,[13] unofficial ruler[14] of Veterans Affairs. There's no doubt that the presidency added a little shine to Trump's trophy. Today, Mar-a-Lago is probably worth some $170 million, about $20 million[15] more than before Trump took office and $160 million more than when he bought the place. A spokesperson for the Trump Organization argues, in predictable fashion, that it's worth "closer to $500 million."[16]

On the surface, Mar-a-Lago seems to symbolize the Trump era, a place as prestigious as it is polarizing. To Trump supporters, it's a symbol of the president's business acumen. To his detractors, like former federal ethics chief Walter Shaub, it's "an embarrassing cash grab."[17] But all the focus on Mar-a-Lago distracts from what's going on at Trump's much larger portfolio of golf clubs and resorts.

While Mar-a-Lago generated $23 million[18] of revenue in 2018, according to the president's financial disclosure report, his 15 other clubs[19] and resorts received $224 million combined. Taken together, Trump's clubs and resorts brought in an estimated 25%[20] more revenue than the president's commercial real estate portfolio and nearly five times as much as his D.C. hotel.[21] It's an up-and-down business, though, because all that revenue comes with enormous expenses.

A closer look at income statements from Trump's golf clubs and resorts—including some that have never been reported on until now—sheds new light on how much profit the president actually manages to squeeze out of those properties. The documents make it clear that, despite Trump's success at Mar-a-Lago, his overall portfolio of courses and clubs is taking a beating. The same problems troubling the D.C. hotel—including struggles with security[22] and a brand that repels as many people as it attracts—have also infected Trump's clubhouses. Call it the price of the presidency.

GOLFERS OFTEN LEARN the rules of the game from their fathers, first in the backyard, then on the range, then on the course. Not Trump. He played golf only once with his dad, who was more focused on business than leisure. The younger Trump really got into the sport in college, knocking the ball around with a handful of buddies at a public course not far from the University of Pennsylvania. He ended up joining a legendary club 20 miles north of Midtown Manhattan called Winged Foot. "Golf is an amazing sport for business," Trump explained in a 2014 interview, adding, "You sort of learn about people's honesty on the course. You know—do they move the ball around?"[23]

It's not difficult to cheat in golf, as anyone who has ever played a round knows. It's a game of honor; there are no referees. According to people who have played with Trump, he doesn't have much of it. "We clearly saw him hook a ball into a lake at Trump National in Jersey," recalled the actor Samuel L. Jackson in a late-night interview in early 2016. "And his caddie told him he found it."[24] Trump thus avoided a one-stroke penalty. Another actor, Anthony Anderson, described something similar in a different late-night interview a month later. "I'm not going to say Trump cheats," Anderson explained. "His caddie cheats for him."[25]

When you own the course, you can play by your own rules. Trump's first club, minutes from Mar-a-Lago in West Palm Beach, Florida, opened in 1999. That seemed like a good time to invest in golf, as Tiger Woods was dominating the game and captivating a new generation of golfers. But as with investing in any asset class, how much money someone makes in the golf business largely depends on how much they pay to get involved. Trump claimed his first course cost $40 million.[26] If so, it was a terrible investment. Today that course, which generated $12.3 million of revenue in 2018,[27] is probably worth about $25 million.[28] So Trump apparently poured $15 million down the drain.

Undeterred, he kept spending. In 2002, the Trump Organization reportedly shelled out $35 million[29] or so for an estate once owned by the car tycoon John DeLorean, before turning it into a 36-hole masterpiece, Trump National Golf Club in Bedminster, New Jersey.[30] That same year, Trump paid a reported $27 million[31] for a course outside Los Angeles. He dropped another $28 million[32] on a club in Colts Neck, New Jersey. "Colts Neck is a lead weight around his neck," says someone close to the president's golf business, adding, "The aesthetics of the course were nothing special, but they were Donald's style. Big, open, surrounded by ostentatious money."[33] Not enough of that money made its way into the club. By 2018, Trump's course in Colts Neck was taking in just $6.8 million of annual revenue.[34] It is now likely worth about half of what Trump paid for it.[35]

The Great Recession wreaked havoc on the golf industry. Fewer people were willing to pay to duff balls around manicured lawns all day. In a case of unfortunate timing, Tiger Woods crashed an SUV outside of his Florida mansion in November 2009.[36] Eventually his personal problems, which included marital infidelity[37] and issues with prescription drug use,[38] came spilling out into the open, derailing his career—and disrupting the golf industry. The number of people hitting the links dropped 19% from 2005 to 2019, the most recent year on record, according to the National Golf Foundation. Bad news for anyone in the golf business. Given that Trump's courses are all privately held, it's hard to get a complete view of how all this affected his portfolio, but golf revenues at his club near Los Angeles dropped 32% from 2007 to 2009 and had still not fully recovered 10 years later, according to city records.[39]

In the downturn, however, Trump smelled opportunity. In December 2008, he called up Jeff Woolson, a golf course broker at real estate firm CBRE. "He was looking for things to steal," recalls Woolson. Eventually Trump found what he was looking for. He paid $13 million in 2009 for a course outside Washington, D.C.,[40] which is now worth about twice that amount. He scooped up a troubled club in Jupiter, Florida, for $5 million, plus the assumption of liabilities.[41] He also got a course near Charlotte, North Carolina, for $6 million[42] and reportedly put another $10 million into renovations;[43] it's now worth roughly $25 million.[44] "Donald Trump is an excellent distressed golf buyer," says the source close to his golf business. "That is what he has done best in his life. That is where he has bought properties for dimes or quarters or whatever—change on the dollar—and put some money in and built up the memberships and offered very good service, very good amenities, and done reasonably well with those clubs."[45]

By 2012, Trump had built up a portfolio of 10 traditional U.S. golf clubs,[46] a mix of bad investments and decent ones. One thing they all had in common? He named every one of them after himself.

TRUMP ARRIVES AT his courses by car,[47] or in some cases, helicopter. "Somebody would meet [him] there with a golf cart," says George Schwab, who served as a top manager at the Trump National Golf Club outside Washington, D.C., from October 2015 to May 2016. "His own golf cart. Nobody was allowed to touch the golf cart unless he was there." One day, Trump wanted to inspect the club's new tennis center. "We would call this the Taj Mahal, because there is no tennis facility in the world that looks like this place," says Schwab.

Trump was not impressed. "What the hell is this?" he said upon seeing the place, according to Schwab. "Why are these trees only 15 feet tall? I asked for 20-feet-tall trees. And why is this this color?"

One of Trump's underlings brought him a collection of swatches. "You'd say, 'Well, Mr. Trump, tell us what color you want and we'll make sure the next time you're here, it's the color you asked for,'" recalls Schwab. "So he would circle it, sign it.

"Next week, two weeks, three weeks later, we would all make the changes," Schwab goes on. "And he'd come back and start screaming and yelling and swearing at everybody and firing everybody and not paying the [subcontractors] because the trees weren't 30 feet tall. 'Well, you asked for 20 feet tall. First you asked for 15, we gave you 15. Then you asked for 20, then we gave you 20. And now you're pissed off because they're not 30 feet tall.'

"And then he said, 'Well the color is not right,'" Schwab recalls.

"'Well, Mr. Trump, here is the swatch. You circled it. You signed it. This is exactly the color.' But he would never take responsibility for any of these decisions. He would just yell and scream and fire, and then we would have to all scramble to do something different the next week. And that's over and over and over and over again."

Schwab had worked at other clubs, but he says Trump's was different. "You know, I was working with clubs that have boards. So there were multiple people that were involved. And you always had some semblance of reasonable people that are kind of keeping the other board members in line. So you had 12 board members, and you had two or three rogue ones. And the other seven or eight would keep them in line." That's not how it worked at Trump's place. "One guy was just going crazy all the time."[48]

Not all of Trump's former employees remember him the same way—even inside his own clubs, the president can be polarizing. "There was no yelling, no swearing, calling people names or anything," says a different top manager at the club, who did not feel comfortable speaking on the record. "It was always very cordial."[49]

Some of the people working at Trump's clubs were undocumented immigrants, as *The Washington Post* and *The New York Times* have detailed extensively.[50] That didn't mean Trump was pinching pennies. "He puts so much money that didn't have a return on investment into these clubs," says Schwab, adding, "Just the amount of money that goes into the fluff is unbelievable. That always impressed me quite a bit. It's not a good business. But he likes his gold and he likes his fountains."[51]

There is no question that Trump's properties are nice. "You walk in and the places are in fantastic condition," says Matthew Galvin, CEO of Morningstar Golf and Hospitality. "There's no tattered carpeting and paint coming off the walls and golf carts that are dying halfway through the round, which happens to everybody else in the industry.

He really spends money." Which is not to say Trump always gets that money back. "I think I have higher return requirements than he probably does."[52]

Some rich guys buy yachts, and others blow money on golf clubs. To Trump, the clubs serve as playgrounds as much as businesses—something Schwab witnessed firsthand. One of his responsibilities was to maintain a personal property that Trump owns[53] next to the golf club. Everything had to be just the way Trump wanted it. A full tube of toothpaste needed to be sitting in the bathroom at all times. Trump liked to use it only once, according to Schwab, and when he was done he threw it in a corner. Even though there was a garbage can nearby.

He did not hang his clothes up, electing to toss them in the corner as well, according to Schwab. "Stuff just went flying all over the place," he says. Trump insisted on a big bottle of mouthwash. He used it only once, then never wanted to see it again. The same applied to his toothbrush.[54] Then there was the hand sanitizer—critical for a famously germophobic man.[55] "There was a specific hand sanitizer that was industrial strength," Schwab says. "It was the kind of stuff that you would clean equipment with—not your hands."

The pantry had its own set of requirements. Among them: "a cupboard full of chips and Cokes," says Schwab. "At the time, he was experimenting with Dr Pepper. He wanted quite a bit of that. Then all of a sudden he didn't want a Dr Pepper anymore."[56] The other top manager, however, says he doesn't remember anything like what Schwab describes, insisting that Trump's house was actually "meticulous" and the president once experimented with Mountain Dew.[57]

As for alcohol, Trump doesn't drink.[58] He does own a winery, though, so inside the club, Schwab says, he wanted copious amounts of his own wine. "They make you buy all this wine from their winery. And I can't sell it, so I had to pour it off as banquet wine. I had to pour it off as kitchen wine. I had to do whatever I could to get it out of my inventory. And that always annoyed me as well. I had to buy all this freaking wine. It's not good wine, either. It's not good wine at all. So nobody would ever buy it. But I had to buy cases and cases of it."[59]

A third former employee, Ian Gillule, recalls Trump's micromanaging extending to the price that individual members paid to join his clubs. "There are people who joined on the same day at the Trump clubs that paid different prices," says Gillule, who used to serve as membership and marketing director at Trump National Golf Club in Westchester County, New York. "It was almost like a spinning wheel. There was a group of people that were from a club in Westchester that were let in for no initiation fee, when we were bringing in 25 to 30 people at between $100,000 to $150,000 a year for an initiation fee."

Trump acted as king, much to the chagrin of Gillule. "To play god and wave a wand over certain groups of people and say, 'Well, you don't have to pay,' while other people are paying for the same product, that doesn't sit well with me."[60]

DONALD TRUMP HAS always had big ambitions. So, in 2012, he took a major step toward transforming his hodgepodge of golf courses into a legitimate golf empire, buying a property in Miami named Doral,[61] which sits on 800 acres,[62] includes 643 guest rooms, and generates almost as much revenue as Trump's other 10 U.S. golf courses combined. "The only reason we were able to buy it for the price we were is that they needed cash," says Ivanka Trump, who worked on the deal, in an interview with *Forbes* three years later.

"Desperately," her father emphasizes.

"They told us that if we couldn't have a contract in five days, they were going to lose claim of the bankruptcy case," Ivanka goes on, adding, "So we basically stole it."

"We bought it for $150 [million], right?" Donald asks.

"A hundred and fifty, yeah," his daughter responds.

The elder Trump says that the price was originally higher—$175 million. "Before closing, I went to them. I said, 'This place is a shithouse. You got to cut the price—'"

"We had a contract," Ivanka says.

"They were dying to make a deal," Donald explains. "They had to make a deal quickly. We had a signed contract at $175. They cut $25 million off the price."[63]

Forget honoring your word—empire building, at least in Trumpland, requires cunning. One month after buying Doral, Donald Trump marched down a cart path in Aberdeen, Scotland, home to another new golf course, flanked by a pair of bagpipers wearing kilts and trailed by his children.[64] The Trumps were there, in the land from which Donald's mother had emigrated, to inaugurate the Trump International Golf Links, Scotland, their first golf property outside of the United States. Attired in a red fleece with a red ballcap, Donald stepped up to the tee as a crowd of photographers clicked away. He wound back, then whipped his driver forward, smacking the ball so cleanly that he barely bothered to watch where it went.

"I think Trump International Golf Links will go down, and already is going down, as the greatest golf course anywhere in the world," Trump later proclaimed in a promotional video. "I'm honored to have it as part of my legacy."

In early 2014, Trump added another European property,[65] buying a golf course and hotel in County Clare, Ireland, called Doonbeg Golf Club and spending nearly $20 million on the venture by the end of the year. In June 2014, he made an even larger investment, shelling out $66 million for Turnberry, a course on the west coast of Scotland whose history was as rich as its finances were poor. The place had hosted four British Open tournaments, but the year before Trump bought it, Turnberry had lost $10.6 million.[66]

Hoping to make winners of these four properties—Doral, Aberdeen, Doonbeg, and Turnberry—Trump poured in massive amounts of cash. At Doral, he spent $150 million on the purchase and claimed he put another $150 million into renovations.[67] In Aberdeen, he shelled out roughly $70 million.[68] At Doonbeg, he burned more than $30 million. And at Turnberry, Trump spent $66 million to acquire the property and $74 million renovating it[69]—lengthening the championship course, re-imagining a famous lighthouse, and unveiling a new ballroom.[70] Add it all up and the total comes to more than $500 million—enough to qual-ify as one of the biggest spending sprees in golf history. It could not have come at a riskier time.

ELEVEN MONTHS AFTER Donald Trump became president, in De-cember 2017, a tax specialist representing his business walked into a drab government building in Miami and took a place at an L-shaped table.[71] Alongside her sat two representatives from the Miami-Dade County Appraiser's Office, which had assessed the president's[72] Doral resort at a value that the Trump Organization claimed was too high.[73] This would have been just another mundane tax hearing if it didn't involve the president of the United States.

"Do you solemnly swear or affirm the testimony you are about to give is the truth, the whole truth, and nothing but the truth?" asked the magistrate officiating the proceeding, according to a video of the hearing obtained through a public records request.

"Yes, I do," replied Trump's representative, Jessica Vachiratev-anurak, her right hand held in the air.

A half hour later, after the local officials had presented their case, it was Vachiratevanurak's turn to testify. "Before I dive into the package, I do want to just note I met with representatives at the property."

"At the property?" asked the magistrate, seeming intrigued.

"Yes," Trump's representative responded. "I met with the director of finance, as well as the director of development for all of the Trump Organization. And they mentioned that throughout 2016, because of the political climate, that there have been severe ramifications of the things that were said during campaigning, the comments that were made."[74]

Among the ramifications referenced: the Professional Golfers' Association had announced in 2016 that it was moving the World Golf Championships tournament from Doral to Mexico, of all places, after struggling to secure sponsors.[75] "Donald Trump is a brand, a big brand, and when you're asking a company to invest millions of dollars in branding a tournament and they're going to share that brand with the host, it's a difficult conversation," PGA Tour commissioner Tim Finchem explained, according to ESPN. In the golf world, the move became something of a joke. "Quite ironic that we're going to Mexico after being at Doral," Rory McIlroy, one of the biggest stars in the game, reportedly said. "We just jump over the wall."[76] But Trump wasn't laughing. The property was traditionally packed during the tournament,[77] producing a rush of revenue for the real estate mogul. "Losing that event killed Doral," says Joel Paige, a resort operator who had managed Doral under previous ownership.[78]

Fallout from Trump's campaign extended beyond the PGA move. "There have been a multitude of charities who throw annual events at the property, and they have canceled, because, they say, 'We can't, in good conscience, be associated with this name,'" explained the Trump Organization representative in the tax hearing. The Trump brand, once an asset, had become a liability—and not just at Doral. "His name is actually being removed from the Trump SoHo hotel," added the representative. "It was a property that was being regularly frequented by, you know, NBA stars and NFL stars, and now they're quoted in this article as saying, 'I'm not going there. I'm not going to support this brand.' So there have been severe ramifications of the comments that were made throughout the campaigning process and since. The property was definitely impacted by that, and you'll see in the financials that there is a significant drop in revenue from last year to this year, and it reflects that."[79]

Indeed. From 2015 to 2016, as Trump morphed from a fame-seeking businessman from New York to the president-elect of the United States, revenues at Doral dropped 5% to $87.5 million, according to documents the Trump Organization filed with Miami-Dade County officials. Profits (as measured by earnings before interest, taxes, depreciation, and amortization) fell 10%[80] to $12.4 million. In May 2016, a top executive at Doral explained to a room of golf course appraisers, who happened to be at the property for an industry gathering, that the campaign was damaging the resort's business, according to three people who were there. "At the time there was a lot of talk about comments that Trump had made," says Jeff Dugas, one of the people in the room. "Nobody was extremely surprised."

Things got worse after Trump won. Doral lost 100,000 booked room nights following the election, according to someone familiar with the resort.[81] For a 643-room resort, 100,000 reservations amounts to five months of fully booked business. Revenues plunged to $75.4 million in 2017, Trump's first year in the White House. Since the resort prides itself on exceptional service, cutting costs isn't easy. So profits took an even steeper dive than sales, dropping 66%[82] to just $4.3 million. Customers, many of whom hailed from historically liberal-leaning areas like New York City, just weren't coming like they used to.

The dreariness continued in 2018, when revenues barely budged, hitting $76 million.[83] The busy season, which traditionally started in about September, now did not begin until November, according to Matias Magarinos, who worked as a server at a restaurant on the property from October 2018 to August 2019. In the quieter times, according to

Magarinos, there were roughly 100 people in the 643-room resort, on average. "It's bad," he says. Not the experience, but the business. "It was very well run," says Magarinos. "I think they just had the bad luck of their owner becoming president."[84]

At Trump's big properties in Scotland and Ireland, business was just as bleak. After purchasing Turnberry for $66 million in 2014, Trump dumped $63 million into renovations over the next two years, while he was running for president, according to documents filed with British authorities.[85] In 2017, when the place reopened for its first full year of operations under the Trump banner, just as its owner was settling into the White House, sales ticked up slightly to $20.6 million. A fancier club, however, meant bigger expenses, so Turnberry lost $4 million in 2017, more than twice as much as it had the year Trump bought the property. He bled another $3.5 million in 2018.[86] Six years after buying Turnberry, the president has yet to record an annual profit at the legendary club.[87]

Similar troubles plagued Doonbeg, the Irish golf course and resort that Trump picked up around the same time as Turnberry. He threw $9.2 million[88] at the property during the two years he campaigned for president, according to documents filed with the Irish government. Revenues grew, but not enough to make the place profitable. By the end of 2018, the most recent year on record, the Trump Organization's cumulative losses on the property totaled $12 million.[89]

Then there was Aberdeen, the Scottish club that Trump labeled the greatest golf course anywhere in the world. Even before Trump got into politics, it was struggling, and the losses continued to mount during the presidential campaign.[90] Sales dropped 12% in 2016,[91] then another 3% the following year. The Trump Organization, meanwhile, set out offerings[92] like corporate and international memberships, which would presumably generate additional revenue, while also allowing another way for people to discreetly pay the president of the United States through his offshore club. But that wasn't enough to rescue the business. The president's property slashed its workforce 17% from 2016 to 2018—and still failed to turn a profit.[93] By the end of that period, total losses since the year the Trump Organization opened the golf course amounted to $14.1 million.[94]

Eager to make some money, the Trump Organization laid out plans to build an entire village in Aberdeen, including 500 homes, new retail, and even an equestrian center.[95] Selling all that inventory would seemingly violate the president's pledge to do no new foreign deals while in office.[96] But apparently that did not trouble the Trumps.[97] They had bigger issues to worry about, like how to turn around their roughly $500 million wager on four golf properties that, in 2017 and 2018, lost an estimated $450,000 collectively.[98]

THE PRESIDENCY DOES have its benefits, such as the helicopters. No longer does Trump have to arrive at his courses with just one measly aircraft. Now there's a parade of them, according to someone who has witnessed the scene in Bedminster. First comes the Black Hawk helicopter, circling the area. Two Sikorsky choppers follow, painted marine green, with UNITED STATES OF AMERICA on their tails. As they descend, the action at the club comes to a virtual standstill. Golfers crane their necks to watch, and guests in the clubhouse peer out the windows for a glimpse. When the helicopters get close enough that wind whips around the club, people gather near the parking lot, just off the bistro, that doubles as a helipad. The landing skids touch down, the blades slow, and out walks the most powerful man in the country, ready to greet his customers. "He's incredibly engaging, because this is where he's most comfortable," says the witness. "His oxygen is adulation. And he clearly thrives on it, and he gets it at these clubs."[99]

By March 2020, roughly three years after Trump took office, he had

IN THE ROUGH

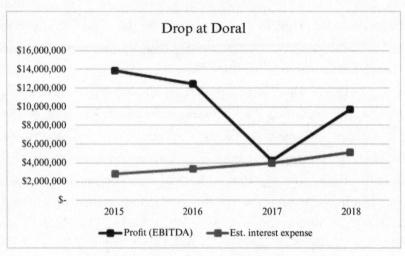

Drop at Doral

Sources: Profit: Miami-Dade County public records. Interest:
Trump's financial disclosure reports, Federal Reserve data, author estimates

Trump invested hundreds of millions in golf properties in Miami and Europe shortly before entering politics. Bad timing. Customers fled Doral, the president's most important golf property. Most of the operating profits in recent years appear to have been wiped out by interest expenses. Meanwhile, the president's courses in Europe are hemorrhaging money.

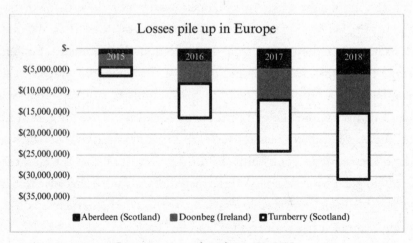

Losses pile up in Europe

Bars represent cumulative losses since 2015.
Sources: Ireland's Companies Registration Office and Great Britain's Companies House

already spent 245 days at his golf courses, according to NBC News.[100] The visits were always a show. Doug Rutherford, who worked at Trump's course in Jupiter, Florida, remembers when the president showed up with Japanese prime minister Shinzo Abe. "There were just people everywhere trying to see him," says Rutherford, "I guess to be able to say, 'Oh, I saw the president and I got to shake his hand.'"[101]

Who exactly gets access to the president at his clubs is largely a mystery. No complete list of Trump's golf club members exists in the public record. Federal disclosures don't require the president to reveal who is paying him through his clubs. Journalists have not figured out any systematic way to track the money flowing into the businesses, and there is no one obsessing over every movement at the properties, the way Zach Everson does at the president's Washington hotel. In 2017, reporters at *USA Today* used data from a golf handicap tracking system and social media posts to get a glimpse of some of the people frequenting the president's clubs. They found at least 50 business leaders whose companies had received federal contracts, along with a handful of lobbyists and lawyers representing clients like the government of South Korea and the kingdom of Saudi Arabia.[102]

Unlike most customers at Trump's clubs, political campaigns do leave a paper trail. In 2017, a pro-Trump congressional candidate named Omar Navarro spent nearly $8,000[103] at Trump's Los Angeles–area club while mounting an unsuccessful[104] bid to replace California representative Maxine Waters. The campaign[105] of a different long-shot congressional contender, Daryl Kipnis of New Jersey, also hosted a fundraiser at Trump National in Bedminster and shelled out another $8,000, one-third of his campaign's entire budget.[106] Not all the politicians at Trump's clubs are pretenders. A political action committee supporting former New Jersey representative Thomas MacArthur, who served in Congress from 2015 to 2019, also rented Trump's Bedminster property, funneling $15,000 to the president's business.[107] Then there was the

Republican National Committee. From 2017 to 2019, as Doral's business was struggling, the RNC provided a boost, spending $860,000 at the place. It spent another $289,000 at Mar-a-Lago.[108] The Trump Victory committee,[109] a joint fundraising effort between the president's reelection campaign and the RNC, tossed another $345,000 in Mar-a-Lago's coffers.[110] In all, politicians and their operatives disclosed spending $1.8 million[111] of campaign-donor money at Trump's golf properties and clubs during his first three years in office.

The president got more money from taxpayers. A nonprofit group named Property of the People filed Freedom of Information Act (FOIA) requests and lawsuits to dig up receipts of government spending at Trump properties. They found that the Department of Defense spent more than $60,000 at Trump International Golf Club in Palm Beach over a four-month stretch. The Department of Homeland Security spent $56,000 at Doral in May 2017.[112] Vice President Mike Pence visited his boss's property in Doonbeg, Ireland. Pence's chief of staff explained to reporters that Trump had suggested Pence stay there,[113] though the president later claimed he had nothing to do with the decision: "People like my product—what can I tell you?"[114] The Secret Service, which follows Pence and Trump virtually everywhere they go—including the president's golf courses—spent $254,000 at Trump properties in just the first five months after the inauguration.[115] The Secret Service has not released a full accounting of all the money it has spent at Trump's properties since he took office,[116] but assuming the spending continues at the same rate through the end of Trump's first term, it will wind up paying $2.4 million to the president's private business by January 2021.[117]

"It's just a flagrant exploitation of the limited Secret Service funds," says Virginia Canter, a longtime government ethics official who served in the White House during the Clinton and Obama administrations. "The federal government is subsidizing those businesses."[118]

Trump's smaller clubs don't need much taxpayer help, since they seem to be faring better than the president's mega-properties, according to a trove of documents, most of which have not been previously reported. From 2014 to 2018, revenues at Trump's course in Westchester jumped 29%, according to an analysis of records released in a lawsuit.[119] At the Trump club outside Los Angeles, golf revenue[120] grew 26% from 2015 to 2019, according to local tax documents. At the president's course in Jupiter, Florida, sales inched up 3% from 2015 to 2018, according to a review of papers filed with tax authorities.[121] Even in Democrat-filled New York City, where Trump operates a course that he does not own,[122] business finally began to recover in 2019 after three straight years of declines, according to filings obtained through FOIA requests.[123] All good news for the Trump Organization, to be sure, but not enough to make up for its troubles in Miami and Europe.

ONE NIGHT AT the White House, Donald Trump sat in the dining room with acting chief of staff Mick Mulvaney and some members of the administration's advance team, which scouts locations for events. The conversation centered on where to host the 2020 G7 summit, the annual meeting of world leaders scheduled to take place in the United States in June. The advance team suggested about a dozen possibilities. Trump then offered up his own idea: "What about Doral?"[124]

With that, the advance team headed to Florida to see if the president's struggling golf resort could host one of the most important summits in the world. According to Mulvaney, the scouts liked what they saw. "Mick, you're not going to believe this," Mulvaney said one of them told him, "but it's almost like they built this facility to host this type of event."

The president certainly seemed to think so. A reporter attending the 2019 G7 summit, set on the Atlantic coast of France, had asked

Trump if he anticipated hosting the following year's gathering at his own property. "We haven't made a final decision," Trump said, before launching into a full-throated sales pitch, with German chancellor Angela Merkel sitting next to him, expressionless. "It's a great place. It's got tremendous acreage. Many hundreds of acres. So we can handle whatever happens. It's really—people are really liking it. Plus, it has buildings that have 50 to 70 units in them, so each delegation can have its own building. So you'd have the seven various delegations, and they could have their own building." So would the reporters, Trump pointed out. "They could have buildings for the press. It's very big. Great conference facility. So we're thinking about it. They love the location of the hotel, and they also like the fact that it's right next to the airport, for convenience. And it's Miami. Doral. Miami. So it's a great area."[125]

In some ways, the president was right. "You couldn't have picked a better place to hold that thing," says Joel Paige, who ran Doral before Trump bought it. You certainly could have picked a better season for it. Miami can be stiflingly hot in the summer, which helps explain why the occupancy drops in those months, according to the Trump Organization's own records.[126] But the Trump administration didn't seem bothered by that. Or the fact that, as Paige puts it, "politically, it just was stupid."

In October 2019, Mulvaney walked into the White House briefing room and made it official. "We're going to announce today that we're going to do the 46th G7 Summit on June 10th through June 12th at the Trump National Doral facility in Miami, Florida."[127] Trump is exempt from the conflict-of-interest statute as president, but he is subject to the domestic emoluments clause of the Constitution, which bars the president from receiving any government compensation other than his salary.[128]

But Mulvaney insisted that the event would produce no profit for the president. He also claimed Doral would be cheaper than the other options, but he could not explain exactly how the math might work. "I don't have the numbers in terms of the cost," he said. Nor did he want to get into the details of how the White House came to its decision. "I don't talk about how this place runs on the inside," he added. "So if you ask us—if you want to see our paper on how we did this, the answer is: absolutely not."

At the very least, the G7 offered Doral a marketing opportunity, noted one reporter in the briefing room. "I've heard that before," Mulvaney responded, adding, "Everybody asks the question: Is it not a huge marketing opportunity? I would simply ask you all to consider the possibility that Donald Trump's brand is probably strong enough as it is and he doesn't need any more help on that."[129] Mulvaney did not mention that the Trump brand was, in fact, wreaking havoc on Doral's finances, as the Trump Organization's own representative had explained in sworn testimony.

The backlash was immediate, from Republicans and Democrats. On Saturday, two days after the announcement, the uproar had still not quieted down. Trump connected with Mulvaney to discuss a response.[130] The reality: there were no good options. So at 9:18 p.m., the president did something he almost never does: he backed down. "I thought I was doing something very good for our Country by using Trump National Doral, in Miami, for hosting the G-7 Leaders," he tweeted, launching into yet another sales pitch about how great his property is. "It is big, grand, on hundreds of acres, next to MIAMI INTERNATIONAL AIRPORT, has tremendous ballrooms & meeting rooms, and each delegation would have its own 50 to 70 unit building. Would set up better than other alternatives. I announced that I would be willing to do it at NO PROFIT or if legally permissible, at ZERO COST TO THE USA. But, as usual, the Hostile Media & their Democrat Partners went CRAZY! Therefore, based on both Media & Democrat Crazed and Irrational Hostility, we will no longer consider Trump National Doral, Miami as the host site for the G-7 in 2020."[131]

The president's supporters sighed in relief. "He had no choice," said Chris Christie, the former New Jersey governor who had championed Trump on the campaign trail. "It shouldn't have been done in the first place. And it's a good move to get out of it and get that out of the papers and off the news."[132]

The morning after Trump's announcement, Mulvaney appeared on Fox, where Chris Wallace conducted a typically tough interview. "Why did he cave?" asked Wallace.

"He was honestly surprised at the level of pushback," explained Mulvaney. "At the end of the day, you know, he still considers himself to be in the hospitality business."[133]

6

All the President's Tenants

INSIDE TRUMP'S TOWERS

For evidence that the president of the United States is violating the American Constitution,[1] all you need to do is walk onto the 20th floor of Trump Tower. It doesn't seem that difficult at first. The security outside the building, wearing helmets on their heads, pistols on their hips, and rifles across their chests, will wave you inside. So will the Secret Service agents checking bags. But in order to get upstairs, there's a third level of security: a man in a business suit standing behind a podium. If you don't have an appointment or an employee badge, good luck getting past him.

He's there to protect the office of the Trump Organization, sure, but he's also guarding a presidential secret—one that has been reported on[2] periodically but, amid so many other stories, always seems to be forgotten. Past the guard and up the elevators, on the 20th floor of Trump Tower, sits an office for the Industrial and Commercial Bank of China,[3] which is majority-owned[4] by the Chinese government. It is through this space that China, by way of its state-owned bank,[5] pays rent to the president of the United States. Of all the foreign government payments that spark allegations that Trump is violating the Constitution's emoluments clause, none involve more money than this one.

According to a 2012 debt prospectus filed with the Securities and Exchange Commission, the Chinese bank paid $1.9 million of rent a year, as part of a lease that was set to run out on October 31, 2019.[6] The timing of that expiration, which landed in the middle of Trump's first term in office, apparently put the president's two eldest sons, Eric and Don Jr., in a position to negotiate with the Chinese over how much money they would pay President Trump—while President Trump simultaneously negotiated[7] with China as part of his massive trade war.

Like a lot of what goes on inside the Trump family business, the details of those lease negotiations remain murky. They may not have happened at all. Donald Trump claimed, during his 2015 interview with *Forbes,* that the Chinese had "just extended their lease for another 10 years." But Trump was on a lying spree that day—seconds later,[8] he declared that Trump Tower's profits were five times higher than they actually were[9]—so it's hard to know whether he was telling the truth about the rental agreement.

There's plenty of evidence suggesting he was not. For starters, Eric Trump later said the lease included an option for two *five*-year extensions, without mentioning the possibility of a 10-year one.[10] Besides, why would a tenant sign a 10-year renewal in 2015 if its agreement did not expire until 2019? In 2018, the bank inked a new deal to rent 99,000 square feet of space in a different skyscraper a handful of blocks away.[11] Since the bank's new space was about five times larger than its old office, it seemed likely that the Chinese would be moving out of Trump Tower.

Instead, they stayed, for some reason electing to maintain two offices in Midtown Manhattan. Representatives of the Industrial and

Commercial Bank of China did not respond to a half dozen requests for comment. In January 2019, Bloomberg News reported that the bank was merely downsizing its space in Trump Tower, citing "people with knowledge of the matter."[12] If they did downsize, it doesn't seem to have been by much. "They are keeping a couple of floors," Eric Trump conceded onstage at a business conference weeks before the original lease was scheduled to expire.[13] According to the Trump Organization's own marketing materials, the floors inside Trump Tower contain roughly 15,000 square feet.[14] So by keeping "a couple of floors," the Chinese bank was apparently staying in most—if not all—of its previously occupied 20,000 square feet. These days, it's unclear exactly how much the China-owned bank is paying the president. If the rent is the same as it was before, then Trump will collect $7.8 million[15] from the bank by the end of his first term in office.

That appears to be enough money to disprove the Trumps' claim that they are handing over all their profits from foreign governments to the U.S. Treasury. In 2017 and 2018, the Trump Organization donated a reported $343,000[16] in profits from foreign governments.[17] Over those same two years, however, the Trump Organization collected roughly $3.9 million[18] in rent from the Chinese bank. The rent comes with some[19] expenses—profit margins at Trump Tower are an estimated 42%. That suggests profits from the deal with the Chinese would add up to about $1.64 million in 2017 and 2018. The Chinese government owns at least 70% of the bank, but even if you count only 70% of those profits as coming from a foreign government, you still end up with $1.2 million. In other words, more than three times as much as the Trump Organization's donations to the Treasury. And that $1.2 million figure is before accounting for any of the foreign money flowing through Trump hotels in D.C. and elsewhere.

The president's hotel in Washington, D.C., and his clubs around the world get plenty of attention. But the most important part of

Trump's business is actually his commercial real estate portfolio. Trump's office buildings, retail spaces, and assorted garages constitute 61% of the president's net worth, adding up to $1.9 billion altogether. That's more than five times as much as the president's golf business, which generates huge revenues but comes with smaller profit margins. And it's over 10 times as much as his hotel empire, burdened by big expenses and significant debt.[20] The commercial properties, with massive margins and relatively light leverage, are Trump's true money-makers.

WHERE THAT MONEY comes from, however, has remained something of a mystery. By law, the president has to disclose every company that pays him, but he does not have to reveal who, in turn, pays those companies.[21] That means that Trump, who holds his commercial properties through a web of entities, does not have to disclose who his tenants are—for example, the Qataris in their empty office at 555 California Street. It's a massive loophole in federal disclosure laws, one that allows the president to accept money from entities all over the world without ever having to tell federal ethics officials who is paying him. Anticipating concerns about conflicts of interest, the Trump Organization set up an ethics plan before the president took office. One of its key tenets: an adviser would review any new deals that came about while Trump served as president. The attorneys who helped put together this plan made it seem like an airtight arrangement. "Written approval of the ethics advisor is required for all actions, deals, and transactions that could potentially raise ethics or conflict-of-interest concerns," they wrote in a white paper.[22]

But that wasn't what happened. According to Trump Organization chief legal officer Alan Garten, Trump's business did not review potential tenants in buildings where Trump held a minority stake.[23] That opened up a massive breach in the ethics pledge, because Trump's two most valuable assets are minority stakes in office buildings: his 30% ownership of 1290 Avenue of the Americas and 555 California Street.[24] "We have no involvement or approval rights over the selection of any of the tenants in those buildings and play no role in the negotiation of any of their leases,"[25] Garten explained in an email.

Trump's 30%[26] share of the rent in the two office towers amounts to an estimated $99 million[27] annually, or roughly 52%[28] of the commercial rent flowing into the Trump Organization. In other words, despite pre-inauguration promises, half of the money flowing through the president's commercial real estate portfolio does not appear to have gone through any internal vetting process.

It didn't go through an external one, either, since neither the Trump Organization nor the White House would release a list of the president's tenants.[29] In early 2018, my former *Forbes* colleague Matt Drange and I started gathering data on who paid the president rent. Some companies were easy to find, like the ones renting space in storefronts at street level. Offices posed more of a challenge, since law firms and investment shops don't typically plaster their names on the sides of their buildings. At 40 Wall Street, another colleague, Deniz Çam, found a directory of tenants, which was later removed. Eventually we tracked about 75% of the money flowing into the president's coffers from tenants across the country.[30]

A good start, but not a comprehensive review. While writing this book, I dug in again, returning to the properties, speaking with tenants, and hunting for additional documents. The biggest breakthrough came in October 2019, when I happened upon a digital book revealing virtually all of the tenants inside Trump's two hardest-to-access towers, which also happen to be the most important properties, 1290 Avenue of the Americas and 555 California Street. The book had been published on a website called FlipHTML5, which helps companies create digital books, by a user named VNO—the three-letter ticker for Vornado, Trump's partner in both buildings. I sent the book to Vornado representatives to verify its authenticity; they declined to comment.[31] But after corroborating much of its information with calls to tenants and visits to the properties, I used it to help construct a new list of Trump's tenants—the most complete look at who pays rent to the president ever published. (See page 215.) The Trump Organization did not respond to an offer to review the data. The rent estimates are intentionally conservative, which helps explain why the total adds up to 93% of the roughly $191 million that the president generates in annual rent. By the time Trump finishes his first term in office, he will have collected about $750 million from more than 150 different tenants.

It's hard to fault the companies for the conflicts of interest this creates. Most are just trying to find places to do business. Many rented the locations before their landlord became president. Two said they did not even realize they were renting from the president until *Forbes* informed them that they were.[32] Instead, the blame lies squarely with the president. By hanging on to his portfolio, he put dozens of companies in the awkward position of asking the federal government for favors while paying the president huge sums of money.

It's an ethical nightmare. Four foreign government entities—from China, Qatar, India, and the United Arab Emirates—have rented space in Trump's buildings while he's served as president. At least 35 tenants[33] lobbied the federal government on policy issues. Twenty of those[34] pitched the White House or the president personally. Thirty or more[35] tenants collected more than $8 billion in federal government contracts from 2018 to 2019 alone.[36] At least 17[37] faced federal investigations on matters including fraud,[38] money laundering,[39] and corruption.[40] Add it all up and Trump's tenant relationships create one of the most significant potential conflicts of interest in American history.

. . .

Two floors above the Chinese bank,[41] the Abu Dhabi Tourism and Culture Authority, a registered foreign agent[42] based in the United Arab Emirates, once had an office. An archived screenshot of the authority's website shows that it listed its address as 725 Fifth Avenue—Trump Tower—on January 27, 2017,[43] one week after Donald Trump's inauguration. The next available archived screenshot, captured in May 2017,[44] lists an address at a new space down the street.

On the 46th floor[45] of San Francisco's 555 California Street, in which the president holds an estimated $517 million stake,[46] the Bank of India rented 3,800 square feet or so[47] for some time. Like the Chinese bank, the Bank of India is also state-owned.[48] Assuming[49] the Indians paid market rates, they likely handed over about $100,000 a year to the president. The bank, which did not respond to requests for comment, eventually moved out. When I visited the California skyscraper in December 2019, the Bank of India was no longer there. The Qatar Investment Authority, however, had moved in, on the 43rd floor of the skyscraper.[50] Its lease appears to have started in 2018, in the middle of Trump's first term in office.[51] Needless to say, it was yet another violation of the Trump Organization's promise to do "no new foreign deals whatsoever" during Trump's tenure in office.[52]

These sorts of relationships, involving money from overseas, are especially alarming to ethics experts. "Congress should be going through the records of the Trump Organization and finding out about any and all contractual commitments, borrowing, and everything else from overseas," says Richard Painter, President George W. Bush's chief ethics lawyer. "Where would we have been in World War II if Franklin Roosevelt had various side deals with Germany?"[53]

It's not such a far-fetched hypothetical. On the 10th floor[54] of 1290 Avenue of the Americas sit the offices of HQ Capital, an investment manager[55] for the descendants of Harald Quandt, a German industrialist whose mother married Nazi propagandist Joseph Goebbels in a wedding where Adolf Hitler reportedly served[56] as best man. It's unclear where exactly Harald Quandt's descendants invest their wealth these days, or how U.S. policy might affect their holdings. A different branch[57] of the Quandt family owns a multibillion-dollar[58] stake in BMW, the auto manufacturer at the center of Trump's trade negotiations with the European Union.

Clearer potential conflicts loomed elsewhere overseas. Santander Bank lobbied Congress on a tax agreement with Spain,[59] its home country, while renting a corner retail location in 1290 Avenue of the Americas for an estimated $1.8 million a year.[60] Axa Equitable Holdings, which paid an estimated $44 million annually[61] to lease space inside 1290 Avenue of the Americas, explained in an annual report that it had to disclose the Iran-connected business of its affiliates to the Securities and Exchange Commission, which in turn was required to send notice to the president of the United States. According to the annual report, the president then had to judge whether or not to impose sanctions.[62] Even though, in this case, the company involved happened to be paying him millions of dollars in annual rent.

Then there were law firms who served as tenants while lobbying on behalf of various foreign clients, including some with disastrous reputations. Jones Day helped Huawei, the Chinese technology company that Trump labeled a national security risk,[63] with issues before the White House[64] while also paying the president an estimated $1.5 million a year.[65] Venable LLP, a firm renting space[66] inside 1290 Avenue of the Americas for an estimated $12.2 million[67] a year, lobbied[68] the Treasury Department and Congress on behalf of Russian state-controlled bank[69] Sberbank, weighing in[70] on bills designed to expose corruption around the Kremlin and combat Russian interference in elections. A spokesperson for Venable suggested that connecting its rent payments to its

SECRET SKYSCRAPERS

Trump's best-performing properties are 30% stakes in two anonymously named skyscrapers, 555 California Street in San Francisco, and 1290 Avenue of the Americas in New York City. While the Trump brand has weighed down other parts of the president's portfolio, rents in these two skyscrapers have soared. Credit Steven Roth, CEO of Vornado Realty Trust, the firm that owns the other 70% of the properties and manages them on a day-to-day basis. After winning the election, Trump named Roth to his quickly scrapped infrastructure council.

Sources: Financial reports released by Trump's partner, Vornado Realty Trust

Source: Financial reports released by Trump's partner, Vornado Realty Trust

lobbying efforts requires "an incredible leap of logic."[71] Fair enough. But it's still remarkable that a Trump tenant was apparently pushing Vladimir Putin's agenda in Washington. And because of lax disclosure laws that leave the details of these transactions secret, it took until now, more than three years into Donald Trump's presidency, for anyone to notice.

TRUMP'S AGREEMENTS WITH American companies proved just as problematic. One month after taking office, the president hosted a group of retail CEOs at the White House.[72] He took a seat at a long table, flanked by administration officials and leaders of eight businesses from around the country. To Trump's right sat billionaire[73] Stefano Pessina of Walgreens Boots Alliance, a pharmacy giant that served as the largest tenant inside 40 Wall Street,[74] Trump's tower in the Financial District of New York City. The company paid about $3.2 million a year for retail and office space.

Pessina had come a long way to get to this point. Born in Milan,[75] he became a nuclear engineer before getting involved in his family's struggling pharmaceutical[76] business. He proceeded to go on a shopping spree, buying up a reported 1,500 competitors[77] throughout Europe to create a European giant called Alliance UniChem. In 2006, Alliance UniChem merged with Boots Group of Great Britain in a blockbuster deal, termed the largest leveraged buyout in European history.[78] Eight years later, Pessina began combining Alliance Boots with Walgreens, putting himself in position to become a drugstore giant on both sides of the Atlantic.[79] But that wasn't enough. In October 2015, Deerfield, Ill.–based Walgreens Boots Alliance unveiled plans to acquire Rite Aid for $9.4 billion.

In order to prevent buyout barons from creating monopolies, the Federal Trade Commission analyzes mergers and determines whether they will limit competition. Regulators in the Obama administration had studied the Walgreens–Rite Aid merger for more than a year, but they had not reached a conclusion by the time President Trump took over.[80] That left the decision up to an administration whose president was collecting millions of dollars a year from one of the parties asking for approval.

"Good morning, retailers," Trump said. "One of my favorite subjects—retailing."[81] The president launched into a brief speech touting how his administration planned to help the business community by cutting both taxes and regulations. It seemed as if Trump was particularly aware of the issues Walgreens Boots Alliance was having with federal regulators, which made sense, since the pharmacy chain was lobbying the White House on "competition policy issues," according to disclosures its representatives filed with the government.[82] The president gestured in the direction of Pessina. "You have a very, very big regulatory problem," he said. "And we're going to take care of that."[83]

Seven months later, the Federal Trade Commission cleared the way for a trimmed-down $4.4 billion[84] version of the Rite Aid takeover. The approval process was unusual. The FTC typically has five commissioners who weigh in on such things. But at the time, there were only two,[85] in part because Trump had been slow to nominate commissioners. One of the two commissioners disagreed with the move, saying it could limit competition and increase drug prices.[86] The other, who served as acting chairman,[87] disagreed, which was enough to let the deal move forward. A few months later, the president announced his plan to nominate[88] the commissioner who'd sided with Walgreens Boots Alliance, Maureen Ohlhausen, to serve as a federal judge.

It's difficult to know whether Trump's business ties to Walgreens Boots Alliance affected any of this. A spokesperson for the pharmacy chain claims that the lobbying on "competition policy issues" did not have to do with the Rite Aid merger.[89] Ohlhausen says Trump's relationship with Walgreens Boots Alliance had no impact on her analysis. "No one at the White House, including the president, ever made his or her opinion on this or any other pending merger known to me."[90] But President Trump has offered his opinion on mergers before other parts of the government. He lamented the FCC's refusal to approve a Sinclair Broadcast-Tribune Media merger, calling the move "disgraceful." And he said he was "not going to get involved in litigation" related to a potential AT&T–Time Warner combination but then declared it "a deal that's not good for the country."[91] They create additional concerns in cases where Trump has a business connection, leaving the American public to wonder whether companies paying the president get special treatment.

Also questionable: the president's interactions with Wall Street. Two weeks after his inauguration, Trump welcomed to the White House CEO Jamie Dimon, whose company, JPMorgan Chase, pays the president an estimated $2.5 million a year.[92] Trump expressed his excitement at hearing Dimon's thoughts on Dodd-Frank, the landmark legislation intended to rein in the excesses that led to the Great Recession. "There's nobody better to tell me about Dodd-Frank than Jamie, so you're going to tell me about it," Trump said to Dimon at the time. "We expect to be cutting a lot out of Dodd-Frank because, frankly, I have so many people, friends of mine that have nice businesses that can't borrow money. They just can't get any money because the banks just won't let them borrow because of the rules and regulations in Dodd-Frank."[93]

The regulations that govern Wall Street go beyond Dodd-Frank. For example, in 2015 Barack Obama suggested[94] a rule requiring retirement advisers to prioritize their clients' financial interests over their own. Sounds simple. For financial firms, however, it posed a challenge, since many of their businesses generate revenue by steering clients toward products with big fees, which may not be best for clients. One of Trump's tenants,[95] Morgan Stanley, lobbied on[96] the rule, taking its case straight to the Executive Office of the President—the official name for Trump and the team that surrounds him. The Trump administration issued a review of the rule and postponed its implementation.[97] Ultimately, the intervention proved unnecessary. The rule fell apart[98] in the courts, allowing financial planners to continue giving questionable financial advice. The Trump administration did, ultimately, end up implementing a different rule[99] to try to protect investors from bad advice. A different tenant, JPMorgan Chase, weighed in[100] on that regulation.

The administration also went easy on Trump tenants convicted of committing crimes. Before Trump took office, three of his tenants, JPMorgan, UBS, and Barclays, pled guilty to manipulating interest and foreign exchange rates. The Trump administration issued waiver extensions to all three banks, as well as Trump's lender, Deutsche Bank, allowing them to avoid part of their punishments.[101]

The potential conflicts reached into other industries as well, with tenants of all types pushing the president on issues big and small, in directions Trump favored and opposed. Columbia University lobbied on fetal tissue research[102]—a controversial topic for pro-life advocates—while handing an estimated $2.1 million to the president every year.[103] Nike lobbied the White House on international trade[104] while paying Trump an estimated $13 million[105] annually. Blockchain business Ripple Labs weighed in on financial regulations[106] while handing Trump roughly $1.2 million a year.[107] Even the Girl Scouts, whose New York City council leases space inside 40 Wall Street[108] for $600,000 a year,[109] lobbied the White House on designating June 2017 "Great Outdoors Month,"[110] which President Trump ultimately did.[111]

MILLIONS FLOWED FROM tenants to Trump, and billions passed from the Trump administration to the president's tenants. In 2017,

TROUBLE AT HOME

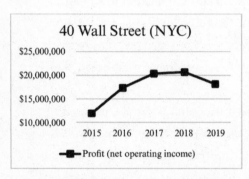

40 Wall Street (NYC)

Source: SEC filings submitted by Trump's lenders

Trump Tower (NYC)

Source: SEC filings submitted by Trump's lenders

As Donald Trump's political star was rising, his New York City real estate empire was fading. Profits at Trump Tower, Trump Plaza, and Trump International Hotel & Tower all dropped from 2015 (the year Trump declared his candidacy) to 2019 (when he was settled into the White House). Business was better at 40 Wall Street, a skyscraper where Trump had previously lured tenants with discounts. Profits eventually climbed, but they still failed to reach the expectations of Trump's lenders.

Trump Plaza (NYC)

Source: SEC filings submitted by Trump's lenders, author estimate (2019)

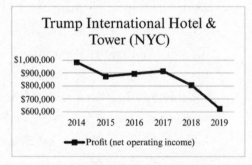

Trump International Hotel & Tower (NYC)

Source: SEC filings submitted by Trump's lenders, author estimate (2016)

Secretary of Defense James Mattis, a decorated general who served in three wars, traveled to Seattle and Silicon Valley, homes to the largest technology companies in the world.[112] Since biblical times, innovation has decided who won and lost battles. David killed Goliath with a sling, the Greeks conquered Persia with catapults, the Europeans took America with guns, and the United States ended World War II with atomic bombs. Mattis returned to Washington convinced that data, cybersecurity, and machine learning would shape the next era of warfare, and he was determined to keep America from falling behind.

So he kicked off an effort to put military data onto a centralized cloud, which would allow soldiers to access more information faster, including in the middle of combat. It was a monumental task, one the U.S. government wasn't going to handle internally, so the Department of Defense came up with a contract to offer an outside company the chance to do the work—and receive up to $10 billion for doing so.[113]

One of Trump's tenants, Microsoft, which pays an estimated $3.2 million[114] a year to rent space inside 555 California Street, put in a bid. From the start, Microsoft seemed like a long shot. Amazon, which had previously won a cloud computing contract from the Central Intelligence Agency,[115] was the clear favorite—so much so that a third bidder, Oracle, formally complained that the contracting process was biased in Amazon's favor.[116] Senator Marco Rubio expressed a similar concern: "They put out a contract that only one company in the world could possibly win, and that was Amazon."[117]

But Amazon faced an unexpected adversary: the commander in chief. According to a book by Guy Snodgrass, who served as Mattis's speechwriter, Trump called the secretary of defense in the summer of 2018 and told him to "screw Amazon" out of competing for the deal. Mattis relayed that message to his colleagues, according to Snodgrass.

"We're not going to do that," the former speechwriter recalled Mattis telling them. "This will be done by the book, both legally and ethically."[118] For his part, Mattis later said he didn't remember that happening. "I don't recall anyone trying to direct me what to do with the JEDI contract, and that includes the president," he told investigators. "I knew he probably wouldn't like it much if Amazon won, but that frankly wasn't my concern as long as we did it right."[119]

In December 2018, Mattis announced that he was resigning for unrelated reasons, fed up with Trump's worldview.[120] A handful of months after that, Trump told reporters that he had been getting a lot of complaints about Amazon and the Department of Defense. "It's a very big contract," the president said, noting that Microsoft, Oracle, and IBM were raising issues. "Great companies are complaining about it. So we're going to take a look at it. We'll take a very strong look at it."[121]

Five days later, the U.S. Senate confirmed Mattis's replacement, Mark Esper. Barely one week after Esper became the 27th secretary of defense, he told reporters that he would be personally reviewing the details of the contract.[122] Then, in October 2019, he changed tack, announcing, through a spokesperson, that he had recused himself from matters related to the deal.[123] Three days later, the Department of Defense announced that it had picked an unlikely winner—Microsoft, a Trump tenant.[124]

Everything about the process raised red flags, including Trump's decision to weigh in. Presidents usually stay out of such decisions,[125] and although a Pentagon official insisted that the people picking the contractor had done so through an independent process,[126] it's hard to imagine that they missed the public statements of the president. In April 2020, an inspector general issued a report concluding that the officials who picked Microsoft did so without pressure from the top brass inside the Department of Defense. But the inspector general's office also said it could not complete a full investigation because attorneys inside the administration had told witnesses not to answer questions about their communications with the White House.[127]

Most of the commentary surrounding the contract suggested that Trump's antagonism toward Amazon stemmed from the fact that Jeff Bezos, the CEO of Amazon, also owns *The Washington Post,* which had reported aggressively on the Trump campaign and administration. That's probably true. But Trump's possible reasons for favoring Microsoft, which declined to comment for this book,[128] go beyond newspaper articles. Not only did Microsoft pay Trump, but Amazon was costing him. The president owns 125,000[129] square feet of retail space near Fifth Avenue in New York City—America's most famous shopping corridor, which has long drawn crowds eager to peruse the aisles at dozens of retailers within walking distance of one another. Amazon challenged all that by creating a convenient online marketplace. As more shoppers go online, fewer go to places like Donald Trump's buildings, and this drives down rents and real estate values. During Trump's first year in office, in fact, this effect helped shave an estimated $400 million off the president's net worth.[130]

Microsoft, which will pay Trump an estimated $3.8 million in rent by the time he finishes his first term, has benefited from other government contracts as well. Back in 2015, the computer giant had $284 million worth of work with the federal government. That increased to $342 million in 2016, while President Obama was wrapping up his tenure in the Oval Office. It then swelled to $355 million in 2017 and $472 million in 2018. Even before securing the Defense Department's cloud computing contract, Microsoft was on pace to receive more than $1.5 billion in contracts from the federal government while its landlord served in office.[131]

The software giant was not a unique case. Trump tenant Columbia University secured nearly $900 million[132] in federal contracts in 2019. ICF, a consulting firm, saw its contracting business surpass $500 million in 2018,[133] while its landlord served as president. McKinsey, which leases 54,000 square feet of office space in 555 California Street,[134] boosted its government contracts 60% from 2016 to 2019.[135] In fairness, not everyone picked up additional revenue. Wells Fargo's $520 million in contracts from 2015 began drying up in 2016,[136] the year the Consumer Financial Protection Bureau fined the bank $100 million for secretly opening accounts customers did not need.[137] By 2019, Wells Fargo's federal government business was next to nothing, according to a database that details federal spending.[138] But the amount of money still flowing between Trump, his administration, and his tenants is staggering. In total, federal contractors appear poised to pay the president more than $200 million[139] in rent by the end of his first term in office. And those same contractors[140] will likely collect more than $10 billion in taxpayer dollars.

It would be easy to brush all this aside if Trump's tenants all had sterling reputations and had never been accused of using money to buy influence. But that's not the case. More than a dozen Trump tenants faced known federal investigations while their landlord was in office. Inside 40 Wall Street alone, at least six tenants faced[141] federal scrutiny. Among them: an engineering firm listed on a debt prospectus[142] filed with the Securities and Exchange Commission as the third-highest-paying tenant inside the building, responsible for $2.2 million in annual rent. In 2018, the Manhattan District Attorney's Office indicted the firm and its CEO as part of a corruption scheme related to New York City contracts.[143] The CEO ended up pleading guilty to first-degree bribery.[144] Today, a rebranded version of the firm, dubbed Atane, is still afloat with a slightly smaller lease, paying $1.3 million a year to rent in the president's building.[145]

Even Trump's blue-chip tenants have had issues. Walgreens Boots Alliance, JPMorgan Chase, Santander Bank, Morgan Stanley, Bank of America, Wells Fargo, and Goldman Sachs all paid the president rent while the federal government investigated their businesses. Capital One, which leased the corner space in Trump Park Avenue, faced an anti-money-laundering investigation.[146] So did UBS, which leases space in 555 California Street.[147]

Barclays, which once paid an estimated $2.4 million annually to rent space in 555 California Street,[148] handed over[149] $6 million in 2019 to settle charges that it had violated the Foreign Corrupt Practices Act by giving jobs to relatives of government officials in Asia in order to curry favor. In July 2019, at the same time that Microsoft was vying for the Defense Department's cloud computing contract,[150] the software giant paid $25 million to settle allegations that its subsidiaries in Hungary, Saudi Arabia, and Thailand had violated the Foreign Corrupt Practices Act, funneling money and gifts to government officials.[151]

Twenty-first Century Fox, the former parent company of Fox News, paid Trump a small sum for engineering space that appears to be connected to an antenna on top of Trump International Hotel & Tower, in New York City.[152] Despite all the attention paid to Trump's cozy relationship with Fox, the deal has flown almost entirely under the radar. Before CNN watchers get too enraged, however, it's worth noting that the Trump Organization has a similar agreement with that channel for use of an antenna atop the Trump International Hotel in Washington, D.C.[153]

If it's hard to keep up with all of this, that's the point. There is simply too much money flowing between the federal government, President Trump, and private entities to investigate every deal—or the motivations behind it. Federal ethics officials do not even know who the president's tenants are, much less what they pay or why they pay it. So the money keeps flowing.

7

Cashing In

THE BUSINESS BEHIND TRUMP'S
500-PLUS HOMES

December 2016 was a busy time for Donald Trump. Holed up inside Trump Tower, with protesters downstairs and security guarding the doors, the president-elect played host to a parade of political heavyweights. Rick Perry,[1] Rex Tillerson,[2] and Wilbur Ross,[3] all members of the incoming cabinet, stopped by. So did Paul Ryan,[4] Speaker of the House. Mitch McConnell,[5] Senate majority leader, followed not long after. America's most prominent business tycoons came, too. Amazon's Jeff Bezos, Google's Larry Page, Apple's Tim Cook. Trump assured them they could call whenever they'd like. "We have no formal chain of command around here."

Amid the chaos, the Trump Organization continued to function as a real estate business. Its executives, including the Trump children, split their time between political matters and business affairs. On December 14, 2016, for example, Don Jr., Eric, and Ivanka joined a meeting with members of the incoming administration and tech leaders from the

West Coast.[6] The same day, the Trump Organization, which Don Jr. and Eric were about to take over, reached a deal to sell a Park Avenue penthouse that Ivanka Trump once called home.[7] Daddy Trump still owned the property, so the proceeds of the sale went to him.[8]

All this money and all this power proved irresistible to influence peddlers such as Angela Chen,[9] the woman buying the penthouse. Chen runs a business called Global Alliance Associates, which boasts on its website that it uses connections to high-ranking government officials to help companies expand into China: "Influential relationships with key decisionmakers are imperative to enter the Chinese market and are the pillars upon which any sustainable business operation is based."[10]

No wonder, then, that Chen was willing to hand over $15.9 million for the apartment.[11] On a price-per-square-foot basis, it was the highest price anyone had paid for a unit in the building since 2004, according to an analysis of property records. Never mind that Trump sold an almost identical apartment for $1.8 million less than a year earlier. And never mind that prices in Trump Park Avenue were trending down, not up. Chen paid anyway, at a rate 79% higher than what the next 11 buyers in the building coughed up.[12]

The presidency now came with a price tag. By hanging on to his assortment of residential properties, Trump ensured that people with enough money to buy a condo or plot of land could pay him huge sums while he served in Washington. During his first three years in the nation's capital, the Trump Organization struck about 125 separate deals, yielding $117 million for the president.[13]

CASH IS CORE to any operating business. And yet, it was the first component of Trump's empire to feel the effect of his move into politics. The same year he declared his campaign for president, Trump left

DEALMAKER IN CHIEF

When Donald Trump ascended to the presidency, he didn't stop doing deals. In fact, with his children acting as his emissaries, the president of the United States sold more than 120 properties in the three years after Inauguration Day, collecting well over $100 million.[537]

ASSET	PROCEEDS
Four percent stake in Spring Creek Towers (NYC)	$33 million (est.)
Eleven oceanside lots (Rancho Palos Verdes, Calif.)	$23 million
One hundred Trump International Hotel Las Vegas units	$16.9 million
Penthouse in Trump Park Avenue (NYC)	$15.9 million
Mansion (Beverly Hills, Calif.)	$13.5 million
Three condos in Trump Parc East (NYC)	$7.5 million
Warehouse (North Charleston, S.C.)	$4.1 million
Land (Dominican Republic)	$3.2 million
Parking in Trump International Hotel & Tower Chicago	$300,000 (est.)
Residential real estate (Norfolk, Va.)	$150,000

TOTAL PROCEEDS: $117 million

The Apprentice, a reality television show that shaped the New York real estate player into an international icon. Federal Communications Commission regulations require all presidential candidates to receive equal airtime on non-news programs, which meant that if Trump wanted to comply with federal rules, he couldn't continue hosting his own non-news program.

It was a significant blow. According to a press release later issued by the Trump campaign, the candidate had received a total of $214 million from *The Apprentice* between 2004 and 2015, or an average of $19 million a year[14]—more money than Trump Tower produces in annual net operating income.[15] In another hit to Trump's cash supply, some of his product licensing partners severed ties with him in the wake of controversial comments on the campaign trail, likely costing Trump more than $1 million a year.[16]

Trump's forays into television and licensing were unusual for a real estate developer, and they came with big benefits. Chief among them: neither business line included significant expenses. Being a TV star takes time, sure. But it doesn't take a big capital investment up front, like building a hotel, fixing up a golf course, or purchasing a skyscraper. Licensing deals usually require a couple of site visits, a handful of lawyers, and a famous name, but they don't come with big costs like construction or maintenance.

Once those two cash streams slowed down to a trickle, Trump was left with his operating businesses, which involve major expenses. A review of documents from Trump's lenders, local officials, overseas regulators, and the Trump Organization itself suggests that the president's properties threw off an estimated $150 million of pre-tax, pre-interest income in 2017, the first year he sat in the White House. The next year, that figure hit an estimated $161 million. Two years, $311 million. (For a full property-by-property breakdown, see pages iv–v.)

The amount of money that actually landed in President Trump's pocket, however, was much smaller. The $311 million number does not include debt payments. During Trump's first two years in the White House, he spent an estimated $47 million paying down the principal on more than $1 billion of loans.[17] In 2017, he also spent an estimated $42 million on interest.[18] That figure increased to $43 million in 2018.[19] The reason interest went up, even while the Trump Organization was paying down its debt, is that the Federal Reserve raised interest rates, helping increase the cost of the president's estimated $300 million of variable-interest debt. For every percentage point that Trump's interest rates increase, the president owes an estimated $3 million in additional money to his banks per year.[20]

That might help explain why Trump, in defiance of precedent,[21] has so brazenly pushed the Federal Reserve to lower interest rates. "The Fed rate, over a fairly short period of time, should be reduced by at least 100 basis points," Trump tweeted on August 19, 2019.[22] Four days later, Trump was fuming. "As usual, the Fed did NOTHING!"[23] The president didn't let up the next month, tweeting that "the Fed should lower rates" while wondering how Fed chairman Jerome Powell, whom Trump had appointed, could see the world differently. "Where did I find this guy Jerome?" the president wondered aloud to his 64 million followers. "Oh well, you can't win them all!"[24] The president struck a less charitable note a few days later. "The USA should always be paying the lowest rate," he said. "It is only the naivete of Jay Powell and the Federal Reserve that doesn't allow us to do what other countries are already doing. A once in a lifetime opportunity that we are missing because of 'Boneheads.'"[25] The Fed, he insisted, was holding back the stock market. Trump did not mention that higher rates were also personally costing him a few million.

Take out all those debt payments, and the president's operating business probably supplied more like $180 million in pre-tax profits in 2017 and 2018. Real money, to be sure, but not a huge cushion for someone living a billionaire lifestyle—with six personal mansions, two private airplanes, and a propensity to pour piles of cash into golf properties.[26] Good thing Trump had one more stream of cash outside of his operating business—the constant supply of residential real estate going to the highest bidder.

SELLING PROPERTY WAS nothing new for Trump. He had been doing so, on a massive scale, since the early 1980s. That was when he built Trump Tower, offering six floors of luxury shopping, breathtaking views of Central Park, and a 60-foot indoor waterfall, luring buyers to 263 pricey condos. Modesty was not one of its features. Before the whole place even opened, Trump took out an advertisement in *Forbes*, declaring his creation "the most successful real estate development of recent times."[27]

Hype sells. Johnny Carson, Steven Spielberg, and Michael Jackson all became neighbors of Trump, who made the top unit his home.[28] He claimed the building cost $150 million to construct and that the apartments would provide $268 million in profits, which he would split with his partner Equitable Life.[29]

From the early days, there were rumors about the origins of that money, and whether some it may have come from illicit industries. "Once the money enters the banking stream through shady banks, it is indistinguishable from other money," explained a 1986 story in *Forbes*. "Fully one-third the apartments in Manhattan's super expensive condominium Trump Tower are owned by foreign corporations, mostly from Panama and the Netherlands Antilles. Yet no one would argue that even one of these apartments is owned by a drug dealer. That's the point: you don't know, and not knowing, there is not much the authorities can do."[30]

Trump never seemed particularly bothered by this sort of thing. Why would he be? Federal law requires banks to run sophisticated programs to detect money laundering, but it demands less of real estate professionals.[31] So Trump just kept on building. He opened Trump International Hotel & Tower, on the southwest corner of Central Park, in 1997. Four years later, he unveiled Trump World Tower on the East Side of Manhattan. Then came Trump Park Avenue, carved out of the old Delmonico Hotel, on 59th Street and Park Avenue.[32]

In the mid-2000s, when *The Apprentice* turned Trump into an international star, he began expanding outside of New York City, building new towers in Chicago and Las Vegas. Both projects opened right around the time the global economy was spiraling into crisis. The Chicago deal turned into a mess. Trump defaulted on his debt,[33] negotiated a discount from his lenders,[34] and ended up holding 177 unsold units, according to a review of property records.[35]

In Vegas, Trump and his business partner, billionaire Phil Ruffin, talked about filing for bankruptcy but never did. "He and a tax lawyer and myself got on the phone," Ruffin recalls. "And the tax lawyer said, 'Look, guys, if you declare bankruptcy, you guys get to charge off $500 million between you.'"[36] A $500 million loss would allow both men, 50-50 partners, to write off $250 million, which would save them roughly $100 million or so. "Don said, 'No, no, no. This is not Atlantic City. This is Las Vegas. We'll sell it. It'll sell out.'"[37]

Not quickly, it wouldn't. By the time Trump was elected president in 2016, eight years after the stock market collapsed, he and Ruffin still owned about 400 units in the building, worth roughly $170 million, according to an analysis of property records. In addition, Trump held the 177 in Chicago, plus 37 apartments[38] scattered about New York

City. Then there were 34 residential lots[39] next to a golf course near Los Angeles, along with six trophy properties in Florida, California, New York, and the Caribbean.[40] Add everything up and the incoming president owned nearly $500 million in residential real estate—much of it for sale.[41]

NOT EVERYONE WAS interested in buying. On the Caribbean island of St. Martin stands a pristine white palace, with a lawn cut like a fairway and a swimming pool overlooking the sea. To figure out who owns the place, all you have to do is look at the two front doors, which feature twin Trump family crests, in gold.

Shortly after Donald Trump took office, reports began to emerge that he was trying to sell the waterfront estate.[42] He had a big price in mind: $28 million. Local real estate brokers thought the property was worth more like $13 million.[43] By asking for so much money, the president was essentially inviting anyone to slip him $15 million or so in exchange for . . . well, that wasn't clear. Trump eventually conceded that he was hoping for too much and slashed the asking price 40% to a more modest, but still optimistic, $16.9 million.[44]

"I heard Donald Trump's villa is for sale," a Chinese billionaire told his real estate broker one day in 2018, digging into a salad over lunch at a nearby marina.

"Yes, it is," replied the broker, Mario Molinari. "Let me phone and see if I can get an appointment."

When no one picked up, Molinari threw out another idea. "Let's go drive up to the property and see if we can get in, if there's someone around there."

The billionaire, whose name Molinari refuses to divulge, agreed. So they hopped into Molinari's Kia Sportage, outfitted with a Century 21 sign on the door, and took a quick drive to the estate. When

CONDOS CRASHING

After Trump declared his candidacy for president, the value of condos in Trump Tower, measured on a per-square-foot basis, plummeted. Guess not too many people in liberal-leaning New York liked the idea of being Trump's neighbor. Things weren't much better a few blocks away at Trump Park Avenue, where Ivanka Trump and Jared Kushner keep an apartment.

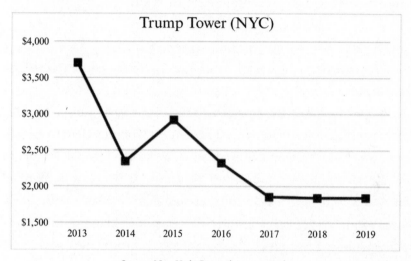

Source: New York City real estate records

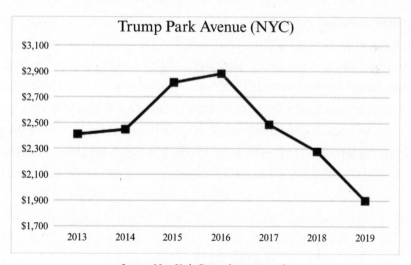

Source: New York City real estate records

they arrived, Trump's property manager was standing outside. She had bad news. "You can't see it today, because you need to get prescreened," she told her visitors, according to Molinari.

The Chinese billionaire, presumably annoyed by all the fuss, piped up from the passenger seat. "This is Trump's house here?" he asked the property manager, knowing full well that it was.

"Yes," she told him.

"It's too small for me," the billionaire sniffed.

With that they drove off.[45] As of June 2020, the house was still on the market.

St. Martin wasn't the only place Trump was having trouble selling property. Take New York City. There may be no president in American history more unpopular in his hometown than Donald Trump. In the 2016 election, he captured just 10% of the ballots cast in Manhattan and 21% of the votes in the outer boroughs.[46] Makes sense, then, that most buyers—with a few notable exceptions like Angela Chen—wanted nothing to do with the apartments in Trump buildings.

Other than Chen's, the president has not sold a single apartment in Trump Park Avenue since he took office, despite putting several on the market.[47] Other owners in the building have sold units—at steep discounts. The average price per square foot of condos trading in the building plummeted 32% from 2015, the year Trump launched his presidential campaign, to 2019, his third year in office.[48] Meanwhile, the value of luxury apartments across Manhattan actually climbed 15%.[49]

Similar trends played out inside Trump Tower. Prices fell every year from 2015 to 2018 before ticking up a hair in 2019. By that point, the damage was clear; the average price per square foot for Trump Tower condos was 37% lower than it had been in 2015, according to a review of property records.[50] It's less clear how exactly that might affect the value of President Trump's penthouse, the only residential unit he's known to hold in the building today. Dripping in gold, with marble pillars and crystal chandeliers, it's a place fit for a king. "The Louis XIV décor is extremely specific, appealing to a very limited audience," explains New York City broker Christine Miller Martin. "However, the location and views are breathtaking. I would expect the apartment to appeal to a wealthy foreign buyer, most likely from the Middle East or Russia."[51] With those types of potential customers, the presidency may actually boost the value of the penthouse.

In other Trump projects, virtually everyone was making money. Shortly after the inauguration, Ruffin spoke over the phone, exuding confidence about the Las Vegas tower. "There is no falloff in business," he said. "The Trump name is still strong."[52] Certainly stronger in Vegas than in New York. Trump won 42% of the 2016 vote in Clark County, which includes Sin City.[53] That wasn't enough to defeat Hillary Clinton, but it was more than twice the percentage Trump took in his hometown. He also won every other county in Nevada,[54] except one along the California state line, where he lost by just 1%.[55]

During Trump's first three years in office, he and Ruffin hauled in $34 million selling 100 condo-hotel units in Vegas, according to an analysis of property records—enough to make the tower Trump's most active real estate project by far. Prices in the building surged 15% from 2015 to 2019. Since the Vegas market remained relatively flat during that time, the increase seems to have as much to do with the big gold TRUMP on top of the building as anything else.

The tower in Las Vegas includes more than 1,200 units, most of which are virtual clones of one another. By the time Trump took office, he and Ruffin had sold about two-thirds of the units and still owned roughly 400 others. Before they offloaded those, however, some of their previous buyers had decided to resell their units. That meant Trump was competing against prior customers to sell the same product. It also meant the Vegas tower turned into a perfect experiment to see how much buyers would pay a random seller versus the president of the United States. Before Trump became the Republican nominee for president, there was little difference. But after July 2016, when he won the nomination, Trump sold his units for an average of 21% more than everyone else in the building, according to a review of property records.

Condos in other locales got similar presidential premiums. Angela Chen's Park Avenue penthouse provides one example. Two Trump-owned units inside Trump Parc East, a condo building on the south end of Central Park, went for an estimated 15% above the going rate. Add up all above-market selling, and it amounts to an estimated $6 million extra in Trump's pocket in his first three years as president. Or five times the government salary that Trump so famously donated over the same period.[56]

A constant cloud of suspicion hung over all the dealmaking, even transactions that would be fairly routine if the president weren't involved. In 2018, for example, Trump sold a plot of land in the Dominican Republic for $3.2 million,[57] ignoring the promise to do no new deals overseas while he served in office.[58] The president sold a Beverly Hills mansion for $13.5 million to a company connected to[59] Hary Tanoesoedibjo, the Indonesian tycoon, who has said he wants to follow the Trump playbook and become president of his own country.[60] Trump sold another 11 oceanside plots in Rancho Palos Verdes, California, at what seems to be fair market value,[61] for $23 million. In May 2018, the president sold a 4% stake in Spring Creek Towers, a federally subsidized housing project in Brooklyn, New York. The stake was small, but the amount of money was big—amounting to an estimated $33 million for the president.[62] Before Trump got the cash, however, Secretary of Housing and Urban Development Ben Carson had to sign off on the deal.[63] That put Carson in an uncomfortable spot. Could he be impartial when considering a proposal that affected his boss so personally? Even if Carson acted properly—and all indications are that he did—there were bound to be questions about whether

Trump had somehow benefited from being the boss of the man who approved his most lucrative deal while in office.[64]

DESPITE ITS REPUTATION, real estate is theoretically one of the most transparent industries in America. Buy jewelry or furniture and no one keeps any record of it. Buy a property, on the other hand, and local authorities document the purchase for posterity. That should make it easy to follow who is paying the president. And lots of the time, it is. Angela Chen, for instance, listed her name on property records showing her $15.9 million purchase from the president. But not everyone does that.

The most common way to disguise money in a real estate transaction is to funnel the funds through an LLC, or limited liability company. Set up an LLC, purchase the property through that LLC, and voilà—the name of the actual buyer disappears from the records. Usually the concern with LLCs is that they could allow dirty money to enter the banking system undetected. In transactions involving Trump, however, the concerns multiply, given that the recipient happens to be the president of the United States.

It's not easy to unwind such mysteries. On October 4, 2019, Trump received $2.4 million[65] in exchange for a 942-square-foot apartment on the corner of Sixth Avenue and 59th Street in New York City.[66] Property records name the buyer as Art Gardens LLC. The listed address for Art Gardens LLC is a three-story beige building in Cheyenne, Wyoming. Dig a little deeper and you'll find that the same address in Cheyenne is also home to a business called AAA Corporate Services, which specializes in setting up LLCs for other people. There is another clue, though. The second page of the deed lists a different address, one on 45th Street in New York.[67] Property records for that address reveal that its owner is another anonymous company, Smile

Caribbean LLC.[68] Documents filed with the New York department of state, however, show that the address for Smile Caribbean LLC is in Queens.[69] The building at that address used to be owned,[70] in part, by someone named Xiu Qong Li.

Getting closer. Xiu Qong Li's name also appears on a deed for a different apartment in the same building, which Trump sold for $2.9 million in March 2019. The buyer in that deal was technically called Koctagon LLC,[71] but if you trace the web far enough, Koctagon LLC also connects to the same Queens property in which Xiu Qong Li once held a stake.[72] And who is Xiu Qong Li? We don't know. Perhaps the buyer of the units, or maybe just someone affiliated with the buyer. No one seems eager to offer an explanation. Attempts to reach Xiu Qong Li proved unsuccessful. Neither the Trump Organization nor the White House was willing to clear up confusion about the sales. A lawyer who worked on one of the transactions said she was "not at liberty to disclose" the name of the buyer.[73] And letters to the apartments went unreturned. Thus, the mystery endures, and Trump walks away with $5.3 million[74] from who knows where.

None of this is particularly novel for Trump, but it is slightly more common now. Excluding a bulk sale to Hilton, Trump sold about 125 units inside his Las Vegas tower between January 1, 2013, and July 19, 2016, when he became the Republican nominee, according to a review of property records. Roughly one third of those condo-hotel units went to LLCs and other shell companies.[75] Other sellers in the building sold property to secretive entities at pretty much the same rate. After Trump won the nomination, others continued to sell about 36% of their units to shell companies, while Trump sold to those types of entities about 44% of the time. Once nominated, in other words, the sources of money flowing into Trump's empire got slightly more secretive than they had been before.

The sales that can be tracked are alarming on their own. But it's hard to look at the statistics concerning shell companies and say with any level of conviction that those sales are or aren't a way of funneling corrupt money into the Trump empire. Just as it was impossible in 1986, when *Forbes* examined the funds flowing into Trump Tower, to determine if any of it was drug money. The stakes are higher, with the recipient sitting in the Oval Office, but the problem is the same. Anonymity is, as it has always been, the point. No one knows, and, not knowing, there is very little anyone can do.

8

All in the Family

"NEPOTISM IS KIND OF A FACTOR OF LIFE"

The old Delmonico Hotel stands on the corner of New York City's 59th Street and Park Avenue, one of the most prestigious intersections in the United States. Donald Trump purchased the building, with its arched windows and brick facade, for a reported $115 million in 2002 and spent another $85 million or so converting it into luxury condominiums.[1] Retrofitted with Italian fixtures and marble finishes, he rebranded the place Trump Park Avenue. By the end of 2005 he had sold 91 units for $231 million, according to a review of property records—and still had another 31 units to spare.[2] The deal was Donald Trump at his best: recognizing an underperforming asset, dressing it up with some glamour, and selling it to a bunch of big-budgeted buyers.

There was one purchaser, however, who paid a relatively small sum of money. Just months after graduating from the University of Pennsylvania, Ivanka Trump reached a deal with her father for a 1,549-square-foot apartment.[3] The price: $1.5 million, or $968 per square foot.[4] The other buyers, by comparison, paid an average of $1,667 a square foot, meaning Ivanka got a discount of more than $1 million.[5] It's nice to be the daughter of the developer.

America's first daughter, who did not respond to a list of questions sent to both the Trump Organization and the White House, started her career outside of her father's real estate business. She joined another development firm called Forest City Ratner, working as a project manager for its retail division.[6] A year into that position, longing for more responsibility, she headed home, where her old man was waiting with an offer to become an executive at the Trump Organization. "Being 24 and 28, respectively, we're able to do things that we never would be able to do," Ivanka said in a 2006 interview with her brother Don Jr. "So we cut out years of sort of bureaucratic paper pushing."[7]

Inside Trump Tower, Ivanka also became a television star, joining her father onscreen for *The Apprentice* in 2006. Not long after, she began to develop her own brand. Her father represented successful, strong men. Ivanka, American heiress, wanted to stand for sophisticated working women. "I remember one of my earlier Christmas gifts was a Barbie, and I was devastated," she said on the set of Conan O'Brien's late-night talk show in 2007, "because my brothers had gotten Legos and Erector Sets. So to me, this was traumatic, and I wanted that. So I ended up taking my younger brother's Legos, bringing them into his room, to add insult to injury, locking him out, taking my mother's superglue—from the 1980s, there was plenty for her nails—and gluing the Legos together in a model of Trump Tower."[8]

It was a perfectly crafted tale, one stunningly similar to a story Donald Trump previously told about *his* brother. "Robert is two years younger than I am," Trump wrote in *The Art of the Deal,* "and we have always been very close, although he is much quieter and more easygoing than I am. One day we were in the playroom of our house, build-ing with blocks. I wanted to build a very tall building, but it turned out that I didn't have enough blocks. I asked Robert if I could borrow some of his, and he said, 'Okay, but you have to give them back when you're done.' I ended up using all of my blocks, and then all of his, and when I was done, I'd created a beautiful building. I liked it so much that I glued the whole thing together. And that was the end of Robert's blocks."[9]

Ivanka Trump is Donald Trump but 35 years younger, with an aristocratic air and a feminist twist. After joining the Trump Organi-zation, she technically worked for her older brother, Don Jr., but they operated more like equals.[10] And before long, their father began giving clues about whom he considered his heir or, in this case, heiress appar-ent. In 2007, when Ivanka was just 25, he added her to the board of Trump Entertainment Resorts—passing over her big brother. Ivanka earned $150,000 a year in director fees from the publicly traded com-pany, the same one her father had been bleeding cash from for years.[11] In 2009, days before the business filed for its second bankruptcy in five years, Donald and Ivanka both resigned from the board.[12]

To HER CREDIT, Ivanka Trump is the only one of the president's children who managed to monetize not just her last name, but also her first. In 2007, she partnered with fellow scion Moshe Lax, whose fam-ily traded in the diamond business, to launch an Ivanka Trump–branded jewelry line. Personally, the partnership proved to be fruitful. It was reportedly through Lax that Ivanka met her future husband, Jared Kushner.[13] But professionally, it turned into a mess. The state of New York ultimately claimed that Ivanka Trump Fine Jewelry failed to pay hundreds of thousands in taxes.[14] Lax also ended up getting sued by the Department of Justice for allegedly working with his family to conduct a number of schemes that helped shortchange the Internal Revenue Service of more than $60 million in taxes.[15] Lax denied the allegations and asked the court to dismiss the case.[16] As of May 2020, it remained active.[17]

Ivanka found better partners and expanded into other product lines, leaning on her father's connections. Marc Fisher Footwear, a Trump Tower tenant, added Ivanka Trump to its roster of brands. Fragrance giant Perfumania, which had previously created a Donald Trump–branded cologne, launched an Ivanka perfume.[18] And manufacturer G-III Apparel Group struck a deal to license the Ivanka Trump name for dresses, suits, sportswear, and jeans.[19]

The G-III partnership seemed to be the most lucrative. In exchange for using her name, the clothesmaker paid Ivanka an estimated 7% of all sales.[20] Her role made her closer to a celebrity endorser than a business tycoon, more Michael Jordan than Phil Knight. While G-III handled the nuts and bolts of the business, making sure products landed on shelves, Ivanka served as the face of the brand, promoting it on her oh-so-perfect social media accounts. "Getting all dolled up on the set of my photo shoot for my fall apparel & accessories campaign! #ivankatrump," she captioned one selfie.[21]

G-III CEO Morris Goldfarb could not have been more excited about the arrangement. "We believe we can help Ivanka build this into a mega brand," he told investors in a 2013 earnings call. "The retailer loves it. We believe the consumer is enthralled by Ivanka, who she is, how she acts, and how she dresses. And she will be front and center promoting this brand with us."[22]

G-III built a team for the rollout, and merchandise first hit stores in 2013. Macy's carried it in approximately 100 locations, Lord & Taylor had it in about 95, Bon-Ton put it in roughly two dozen, and Nordstrom slotted it in another 20 or so.[23]

In 2014, the first full year of production, sales started at an estimated $25 million.[24] The very next year, Donald Trump launched his presidential campaign and estimated revenues passed $50 million.[25] Much of that increase was a result of the mechanics of firing up a new brand, with smaller launches that develop into bigger sales. But some of it was undoubtedly due to Ivanka's boost in popularity, which only seemed to increase as her father's presidential run continued. Goldfarb nodded to the pickup in a December 2015 call with investors: "Ivanka Trump enjoyed stronger recognition."[26]

There's an old legend about Michael Jordan, which the basketball icon has denied but nonetheless offers an important business lesson.[27] In 1990, as the story goes, a North Carolina Democrat asked the superstar to back his candidacy. Jordan declined, explaining, "Republicans buy sneakers too." Ivanka Trump didn't have the option of steering entirely clear of politics, so she settled for leaving her own policy preferences a mystery. "Like many of my fellow millennials," she explained onstage at the Republican National Convention, wearing a pink Ivanka Trump dress that she would later promote on Twitter,[28] "I do not consider myself categorically Republican or Democrat. More than party affiliation, I vote based on what I believe is right for my family and for my country. Sometimes it's a tough choice. That is not the case this time." As the crowd began to cheer, her voice rose to match the noise. "As the proud daughter of your nominee, I am here to tell you that this is the moment, and Donald Trump is the person to make America great again." Cameras panned to well-dressed older women, standing and smiling. Elsewhere in the arena, a group of men began chanting "Trump! Trump! Trump!" Everyone loved Ivanka.[29]

Even the Clintons. "I have tremendous respect for Ivanka," said former first daughter Chelsea Clinton two months before the election.[30] Hillary agreed. "I respect his children," she told an estimated

66.5 million people watching the second-to-last presidential debate.[31] "His children are incredibly able and devoted, and I think that says a lot about Donald. I don't agree with nearly anything else he says or does, but I do respect that."[32]

IVANKA TRUMP APPARENTLY thought her father was going to lose the election. "His daughter called him and said, 'You're losing in a landslide, Pop,'" said Phil Ruffin, one of the president's closest friends, who was with him on election night.[33]

Days after he won, the president-elect welcomed *60 Minutes* correspondent Lesley Stahl into his Trump Tower penthouse—the one he claimed to never show anybody—for his first on-camera exclusive since the victory.[34] They set up cameras inside, with two rows of seats. Eric, Don Jr., and Tiffany, Trump's fourth child, sat in a row behind the president-elect, Melania, and Ivanka.*

"People think that you're going to be part of the administration, Ivanka," Stahl said.

"No," replied Ivanka. "I'm going to be a daughter. But I've said throughout the campaign that I'm very passionate about certain issues, and that I want to fight for them."

"But you won't be inside," Stahl asked.

---

* Before they sat down for the interview, Trump showed Stahl around his office—the massive room with a massive desk and massive windows, all overlooking Fifth Avenue and Central Park. From this perch, he launched into a tirade against the media.

"There were no cameras—there was nothing going on," Stahl later recalled. "I said, 'You know, that is getting tired. Why are you doing this? You're doing it over and over, and it's boring. And it's time to end that. You know, you've won the nomination. Why do you keep hammering this?'"

"You know why I do it?" Trump responded, according to Stahl. "I do it to discredit you all and demean you all so that when you write negative stories about me, no one will believe you."

"Wage equality, childcare—these are things that are very important for me," Ivanka responded. "I'm very passionate about education.
Really promoting more opportunities for women. So you know, there
are a lot of things that I feel deeply, strongly about. But not in a formal
administrative capacity."

Stahl changed topics. "Let me ask whether any of you think that
the campaign has hurt the Trump brand."

"I don't think it matters," Ivanka offered. "This is so much more
important. And more serious. And so that's the focus."[35]

But shortly after the close of the segment, which millions of people
watched from homes across the country,[36] Ivanka Trump's business
sent out a "style alert" to reporters. There was a photo of Ivanka, mid-
interview, with her left hand clasped over her right forearm, showing
off a golden bracelet. "Ivanka Trump wearing her favorite bangle from
the *Metropolis* Collection on '60 Minutes,'" read the text. A second
photo featured a close-up of the diamond-edged jewelry, which could
be yours, the alert made clear, for just $10,800.[37]

The backlash was immediate. "Ivanka Trump tries to cash in on
Donald's '60 Minutes' Interview," read the headline in the *New York
Post*.[38] "With Ivanka's Jewelry Ad, Trump Companies Begin to Seek
Profit off Election Result," proclaimed *The Washington Post*.[39] Donald
Trump may have known the presidency would mean a whole different
level of media scrutiny, but his children seemed unprepared. Their
entire lives, they had watched their father leverage fame for money—
and receive praise for doing so. Now, at the height of their own rele-
vancy, they were supposed to resist the temptation.

It wasn't a lesson they learned easily. Less than a week after the
60 Minutes interview, Donald Trump hosted Japanese prime minister
Shinzo Abe inside Trump Tower. Joining the meeting was Ivanka
Trump, who knew something about Japan. Less than two weeks earlier, she had applied for a trademark for her business in Japan.[40]

Which made sense, given that her business had recently reached an agreement[41] for a new deal with a Japanese clothing company named Sanei, whose largest shareholder happened to be a bank owned by the government of Japan.[42] On January 13, after *The New York Times* reported[43] the connection, Ivanka's business scuttled the deal.[44]

In December, Ivanka allowed the Eric Trump Foundation to auction off a coffee date with her as part of a fundraiser. By the middle of the month, the highest offers were north of $70,000, according to *The New York Times.* One bidder wanted to press the incoming first daughter about her father's plans for immigration, and another wanted to see what his plans were for Turkey, a country in which the bidder held investments. When the newspaper reached out to Eric, Ivanka's younger brother said he was still adjusting to the "new world" he was facing. His foundation eventually abandoned the auction.[45]

THE DAY AFTER Donald Trump's inauguration, roughly three million people across the country took to the streets for the Women's March, one of the largest demonstrations in American history.[46] Ivanka Trump, the women's advocate, was nowhere to be found. It's hard to demand power when you're already in power.

Since the moment Ivanka Trump founded her fashion business, her last name had been an asset. Now, in parallel with the troubles going on at her father's properties, it suddenly became a problem. Within weeks, Nordstrom announced that it was dropping Ivanka Trump apparel from its stores. "We've said all along we make buying decisions based on performance," the company explained in a statement it sent to reporters. "In this case, based on the brand's performance, we've decided not to buy it for this season."[47]

The president fumed. "My daughter Ivanka has been treated so unfairly by Nordstrom," he tweeted. "She is a great person—always pushing me to do the right thing! Terrible!"[48] His team joined in the fight. "They are using her, who has been a champion for women empowerment, women in the workplace, to get to him," adviser Kellyanne Conway said on Fox News. "Go buy Ivanka's stuff is what I would tell you. I hate shopping, and I'm going to go get some myself today."[49] Single-day sales shot up 219%, according to *The Washington Post*, which cited e-commerce tracker Lyst. Fanning outrage, however, is not a long-term business strategy. Within a week, the Ivanka Trump brand was back to its baseline.[50]

ON FEBRUARY 24, 2017, Eric Trump sat behind his desk inside Trump Tower, headquarters for the multibillion-dollar business he and his brother had just taken over, explaining how he got to where he was: "Nepotism is kind of a factor of life."[51]

That is certainly true in business, but it's not supposed to be the case in government. In 1967, six years after John F. Kennedy appointed his 35-year-old brother, Robert, to serve as attorney general, Congress passed an anti-nepotism law, banning public officials from appointing "any individual who is a relative." The statute specifically says the law applies to the president, and it names 27 different types of family members who count as relatives—including "daughter" and "son-in-law."[52]

Presidents in both parties have tried to bend the rules. Jimmy Carter considered handing his son an unpaid position in the White House before the Justice Department sent a letter saying he couldn't.[53] Bill Clinton gave his wife, Hillary, a leading role in the fight to reform healthcare. Opponents sued, and the U.S. Court of Appeals for the District of Columbia sided with the Clintons, noting that first ladies were allowed to help the president carry out official duties.[54]

Then came Trump. On January 9, 2017, the president-elect picked

Ivanka's husband, Jared Kushner, to be one of his top aides.[55] How did he justify it, given that the statute seems so clear? Well, on January 20, Trump's first day in office, the Justice Department issued a memo saying that another law, which gives the president broad powers to appoint officials inside the White House, overrode the anti-nepotism statute.[56]

"That's a bunch of baloney," says Richard Painter, George W. Bush's ethics lawyer. The Department of Justice can issue advice, through the Office of Legal Counsel, but that doesn't necessarily mean it is the law.[57] "They said all sorts of things to make the White House happy. We had torture memos we dealt with. You know, they've come up with all sorts of nonsense."[58]

Nonsense or not, the new memo freed Trump of the restrictions that had held back his predecessors. So what if Jimmy Carter couldn't have his son in the White House? On January 22, 2017, Jared Kushner was sworn in as a senior adviser to the president.

Ivanka Trump's role was less clear. She didn't have a title at the start of her father's presidency, but she sure seemed to be in the White House a lot, discussing issues that fit in with her personal brand. "A great discussion with two world leaders about the importance of women having a seat at the table!" Ivanka tweeted on February 13, 2017, captioning a photo of her sitting at the president's desk in the Oval Office, with her father standing to her right and Canadian prime minister Justin Trudeau to her left.[59]

The next month, reports surfaced that Ivanka's role was expanding. She was not an official employee, and she did not receive a salary, but she was getting an office in the West Wing, while beginning the process to obtain an official security clearance, which would allow her to review classified material.[60]

Richard Painter spoke with Jared and Ivanka's attorney. If Trump insisted on giving his family members White House jobs, despite the anti-nepotism statute, then they should at least be bound by the same rules as everyone else in the government, he reasoned. Ivanka should be an official employee, and she should disclose her financial holdings.

"I put a huge stink up," Painter says. "I made that clear. That's not going to fly. They were trying to say that we're going to volunteer. And Ivanka is going to sit there volunteering and have a volunteer position, so she shouldn't have to file a financial disclosure form or worry about financial conflicts. And I just said, 'No way. This is not junior league West Wing.'" As Painter saw it, Ivanka would not only put the country at risk by operating outside of the rules; she would put herself at risk. "I made it clear to their lawyer that they could end up in jail for that."[61]

Donald Trump could have resolved all of this by keeping his daughter out of policymaking, giving her a role more like the one she had described throughout the campaign—and even after the election. But Trump had worked alongside his daughter for 11 years, and he wasn't interested in stopping. So on March 29, 2017, he appointed her adviser to the president.[62] The White House became a family business.

THE DAY BEFORE the appointment, Ivanka Trump applied for 17 new trademarks with the Chinese government.[63] Following in her father's footsteps, she was planning to hold on to ownership of her business empire, which consisted largely of her name and deals she had signed to let other people use it. Hence the trademarks. The latest requests brought Ivanka's total number of outstanding applications to at least 41 at the time she took office, according to an analysis of documents accessible through a Chinese government database.[64]

As a private citizen, it made perfect sense that Ivanka was filing trademark requests. In China, there is known to be an entire cottage industry of trademark squatters who file for rights to names solely to ransom them down the line.[65] If Ivanka resisted filing for the trademarks, someone else could have swooped in and profited off her name. Some people had already tried, including one who submitted an application for "i vanka," complete with a logo of a long-haired businesswoman on the move.[66]

After the real Ivanka became a government official, the applications created additional headaches. In May 2018, the Chinese government approved seven Ivanka trademarks.[67] That same month, President Trump vowed to help a Chinese telecom giant, ZTE, that his administration had previously punished.[68] It seems unlikely that any American president, including Trump, would change policy based on whether his daughter got a trademark for an apparel business. But in taking a White House job and holding on to her assets, Ivanka left room to wonder. By April 2019 she had received 41 trademarks from China while in office.[69] Of all the trademarks she has received, the ones Ivanka applied for after her father became president got approved about 40% faster than those she requested before the Trumps moved to Washington.[70]

Similar questions arose around the world. After Ivanka met with the prime minister of Japan, his country approved three trademarks for her business, in less than one third of the time it had previously taken, according to an analysis of data from the World Intellectual Property Organization.[71] Canada registered three trademarks following Ivanka's sit-down with Trudeau. The Philippines, which named Trump business partner Jose Antonio special envoy to the United States just before Trump won the election, approved three more Ivanka trademarks.[72]

The presidency may have made business run smoother overseas, but Ivanka's brand was still facing an identity crisis at home. In April 2017, G-III announced Ivanka Trump's annual sales had ticked up $17.9 million,[73] which sounds great until you consider that it grew $29.4 million the previous year.[74] Revenues were supposed to be accelerating, not decelerating. But there's only so much that marketing muscle can do to shape the image of someone whose last name is on the front page of every newspaper day after day. The longer Ivanka stayed in office, the gloomier her financial picture looked. In the 12 months starting September 1, 2017, sales of Ivanka-branded merchandise dropped 48% from the previous year, according to research firm Rakuten Intelligence.[75]

In the middle of that period, G-III was rethinking its partnership. Ivanka's licensing agreement was set to expire on December 31, 2018, according to documents filed with the Securities and Exchange Commission.[76] Five months before it did, Ivanka announced that she was shuttering her business. The G-III deal, which provided Ivanka with an estimated $16 million over six years, died out with a whimper.[77] "The wind-down of it is negligible," the once exuberant Morris Goldfarb, CEO of G-III, told investors on an earnings call. "We won't miss a beat."[78]

IVANKA TRUMP SCORED a political victory months after joining the government, as the Trump administration was working with Congress on an overhaul to the federal tax code. Ivanka zeroed in on one particular provision, the child tax credit. At the time, the federal government gave taxpayers a $1,000 discount on their taxes for every child in their family. Partnering with allies in the Senate like Marco Rubio, Ivanka helped double that to $2,000, making good on her promise to fight for women and families in the White House.[79] "That's all she wanted," President Trump later recounted. "'Dad? Dad? We have to get that passed, Dad.' I said, 'Okay, Ivanka. Okay. Okay.'"[80]

Donald Trump was focused on other things, including a tweak that would have a bigger impact on his daughter's financial future than anything in her branding portfolio: he wanted to get rid of the estate tax, which he, like a lot of billionaires, detested.

In simplified terms, the estate tax worked like this: when someone died, the federal government counted up all their assets and took up to 40% of anything over $5.5 million (or $11 million for a couple), leaving the rest to the heirs.[81] To get around the law, super-rich people often opt to pass down their fortunes as early as possible. Billionaire Harold Hamm stuck almost all of the stock in his oil business in to an entity called "Harold Hamm Family LLC," which holds shares for his relatives while allowing Hamm to maintain control.[82] Rupert Murdoch did something similar with his shares of Fox, stuffing them into a family trust.[83] Before Mark Zuckerberg even had children, he started putting Facebook stock in a special type of trust that rich people often use to limit taxes for their heirs.[84]

Donald Trump took a different approach, keeping an estimated $3.1 billion of his family's $3.2 billion fortune for himself.[85]

It's a strategy that made no sense, especially since Trump did not have plans to hand his fortune to charity. "I'm of the old school," he once said. "I'd like to see my children take this great company that I've built—and it is a great company—and I'd like to see it go on for a long time."[86] By refusing to pass it down to his kids, however, he was putting that dream at risk. If the president, who took office at 70 years old, passed away, then his heirs would be stuck with an estimated $1.2 billion tax bill. And given that their father had only an estimated $130 million in cash, they would either have to sell some of the big properties they had inherited or else tie themselves down with debt in order to pay it.[87]

"All of planning, in one which way or another, requires divesting," says David Cannon, a New York City real estate trusts and estates attorney. "In the end, you got to give it up." And since Trump refused to give up his assets upon taking office, there's some consistency in him also refusing to hand over his holdings to protect his heirs from the estate tax.

One key difference between Trump and every other billionaire in America is that once he became president, he was actually in a position to change the law—and therefore transform his unorthodox approach into a sensible plan. So while Ivanka was working on the child tax credit, the president was working on saving her a fortune. He presented his plan to slash the tax as a way to shield small-time entrepreneurs.[88] Never mind that a couple could pass down $11 million to their kids tax-free, meaning truly small businesses were safe. "We are also going to protect millions of family businesses by ending the crushing, horrible, and unfair estate tax, also known as the death tax," Trump proclaimed in September 2017. "That means for those of you with small and family-owned businesses, your family won't have to sell the business in a fire sale just to pay a very, very high and unfair tax."[89]

Assuming Trump passed down his own family fortune evenly between his five children, eliminating the estate tax would have saved Don Jr., Ivanka, Eric, Tiffany, and Barron an estimated $250 million apiece. In other words, it would have been one of the most lucrative deals of Donald Trump's entire life. For most members of Congress, however, giving a massive tax break to President Trump and his fellow billionaires proved to be too much to stomach.

On December 22, 2017, the final version of the tax bill arrived in the Oval Office, with a modification—though not an elimination— of the estate tax. The new bill raised the amount millionaires could pass down tax-free, from $11 million per couple to $22 million.[90] The Trump kids would save just $4.6 million or so, rather than the $1.2 billion they could have protected if the estate tax had been completely wiped out. President Trump benefited from other changes in the tax code as well, though it's impossible to know exactly how much, since he famously refused to release his tax returns. Two pages of leaked filings from 2005 suggest changes besides the tweak to the estate tax could save Trump $11 million a year.[91] Sitting behind the Resolute

Desk, with sparkling cuff links, the president grabbed a black marker. "This is something I'm very proud of," he said. "Great for our country. Great for the American people."[92]

Good, but not as good as it could have been, for Ivanka Trump and her siblings. Not that their shot at a huge gift from Washington was entirely gone. In January 2019, Mitch McConnell and two other Republican senators introduced a new bill to repeal the estate tax.[93] If it ever makes it to Trump's desk, there's no question he will sign it. But even if it does not, Ivanka Trump should have plenty of money.

After all, she is married to Jared Kushner, heir to another rich real estate family. And unlike the Trumps, the Kushners have been careful about their estate planning, which helps explain how, according to financial documents obtained by *The New York Times*, Jared managed to build up a $324 million fortune by the time he was 35 years old.[94] In other words, he had more than six times as much money as Ivanka.[95]

9

Like Father, Like Son-in-Law

JARED KUSHNER'S WORLD OF CONFLICTS

A month and a half after signing the tax reform bill, Donald Trump sits inside the Oval Office, his back to a marble fireplace. A group of small-city officials and big-money investors are gathered before him, eager to share their thoughts on opportunity zones, a product of the new law that allows businesspeople to get huge tax breaks if they invest in beat-up neighborhoods.

"It's critically important," says billionaire Steve Case, who oversees $300 million of venture funds focused on middle America. Erin Stewart, mayor of New Britain, Connecticut, agrees: "This is an opportunity to transform a community like mine." The president notes that his daughter Ivanka has "been pushing this very hard" and asks her to speak last. "Creating the incentive to bring capital into communities that are currently being overlooked is just a tremendous opportunity," she says.[1]

A tremendous opportunity indeed. For struggling neighborhoods, who could use an extra hook to pull in money. For real estate investors, who are always looking for ways to minimize their tax bills.[2] And, coincidentally, for Ivanka's husband, Jared Kushner, whose portfolio was primed to profit off the new law.

Of the more-than 100 assets that Jared Kushner held after taking office, none were more valuable than his stake in a real estate startup he cofounded called Cadre.[3] The business functions like Amazon, except the only things for sale are commercial real estate investments, and the only shoppers allowed are rich people.[4] Just the kind of folks who might be drawn to a big tax break.

Before the Treasury Department even finished making rules for opportunity zones, in November 2018,[5] Cadre launched a product tailored to the new government giveaways, called Cadre Opportunity Zones.[6] The next year, Cadre was promoting its tax-friendly investments on Facebook: "Reduce your capital gains taxes with opportunity zones." It was also touting its early successes: "Cadre has received significant interest in the program and has opened several Opportunity Zone deals for investment."[7]

It's hard to blame Cadre for chasing a good opportunity. That's what companies do. What high-ranking government officials do, in most cases, is divest their assets. Jared Kushner went with a different approach. Although he got rid of a handful of high-profile properties, Kushner held on to an enormous portfolio, following in the footsteps of his father-in-law.[8] By doing so, he put both himself and Ivanka in a risky position. In order to guarantee that they were staying within the bounds of the law, the couple had to recuse themselves from White House business that would clearly affect either of their finances.[9] They did not, as Ivanka made apparent in the Oval Office gathering.

The effect: in January 2019, a government watchdog group named Citizens for Responsibility and Ethics in Washington asked the Department of Justice to open an investigation into Ivanka Trump's opportunity-zone efforts. "Government employees should never work on matters affecting their own finances, but Ivanka Trump appears to have done just that," said the group's executive director, Noah Bookbinder, in a statement. "Her actions are just the latest example of this administration's blatant and repeated disregard for ethics obligations."[10]

More than a year later, in February 2020, Kushner reportedly sold his stake in Cadre,[11] which by then was worth more than it had been when the real estate scion entered the White House.[12] Not wanting to leave money on the table, Kushner also secured a so-called certificate of divestiture from the Office of Government Ethics, allowing him to defer capital gains taxes on the sale, in accordance with federal rules meant to encourage officials to get rid of conflict-prone assets.[13] Kushner, in effect, managed to both hang on to the asset when he took office, then still get clearance to receive a tax break for ditching it three years later. Representatives for Jared Kushner and the Kushner Companies did not respond to multiple requests for comment.

Few players in Donald Trump's administration have attracted as much attention, or as much controversy, as Jared Kushner. The president's son-in-law got a rush of bad press for his stumbles with Cadre.[14] He got even more heat for his family's efforts to rehabilitate a troubled skyscraper, 666 Fifth Avenue. But those controversies are only part of the story. Jared Kushner's ethical issues go far deeper. Like his father-in-law, Kushner has continued to sell dozens of condos to opaque entities and collect millions in rent from undisclosed tenants.[15] More alarming: he has owed money to multiple banks with foreign government ties while serving in office.[16]

THE STORY OF Jared Kushner's rise is also the story of his father's downfall. Handsome and hardworking, Charles Kushner was the star of his family's New Jersey business dynasty, started by his own father Joseph Kushner, a Holocaust survivor.[17] Charles built up a portfolio of 25,000 apartments and turned into a political heavyweight. In 1997, he hosted President Bill Clinton in his office for a Democratic National Committee reception.[18] Five years later, he donated $1 million to the DNC.[19]

But Charles Kushner wasn't content merely pumping his own money into politics. Through various partnerships, Kushner diverted others' funds to politicians as well.[20] In 2003, one of Kushner's former employees sued him in a wrongful termination case, making allegations that Kushner was manipulating the books at his real estate firm and doling out political donations in other people's names.[21] The suit got dismissed, but officials inside the Federal Election Commission were soon closing in on Kushner. In June 2004, they reached a settlement that forced him to pay a $508,900 fine.[22]

Prosecutors at the Department of Justice also zeroed in on Kushner and found that he was using partnership money for things other than political donations—he used some to pay for private school and some to make charitable donations.[23] One of the people talking to the federal authorities during their investigation was Charles's own sister, Esther. Enraged that his sibling had turned against him, Charles plotted revenge. According to federal prosecutors, he paid $25,000 in cash to a couple of associates and instructed them to find a prostitute to seduce Esther's husband.[24]

When neither of the guys found a woman willing to carry out the plan, Charles took things into his own hands, finding someone in New York City, according to the prosecutors. He told her he would pay $7,000 to $10,000 if she slept with his brother-in-law. The woman went to New Jersey, where she approached her target in a diner parking lot, explained that her car had broken down, and asked for a ride back to her motel room. When they got to the motel, she told him he could come inside. He declined, but they exchanged phone numbers.

The next day, the woman was back in touch with Kushner's brother-in-law, and they met up, according to a criminal complaint detailing the allegations. One of Charles Kushner's henchmen installed a hidden camera in the motel room. After the woman successfully seduced Kushner's brother-in-law, the guy who set up the camera got the tape and delivered it to Charles at his office.[25]

While all of this was going on, the feds were digging deeper on Kushner's partnership scheme. On May 7, 2004, prosecutors sent letters to people Kushner knew, indicating that they were targets of the investigation. Two days later, Kushner instructed one of his associates to send the compromising video to his sister, Esther, specifically requesting that it arrive at her house before a family party.

Two months after that, federal prosecutors slammed Charles Kushner with criminal charges. He ultimately pleaded guilty to 16 counts of helping to prepare fraudulent and false tax returns, one count of lying to the FEC during its investigation, and one count of retaliating against a witness—for the plot aimed at his family members.[26] The prosecutor who signed the bottom of the agreement? Chris Christie, future governor of New Jersey, candidate for president, and adviser to Donald Trump.[27]

A JUDGE SENTENCED Charles Kushner to two years in prison, paving the way for his son Jared, just 23 years old when his father pleaded guilty, to take over the family business. The younger Kushner traveled to Alabama most weekends to visit his father,[28] until Charles got out of prison on August 25, 2006.[29] Within months, the Kushners were eyeing a 39-story tower in the heart of Manhattan, at 666 Fifth Avenue.

Buying the tower would send a signal—the Kushner family was back. They bid $1.8 billion, said to be the most anyone had ever paid for an office building in the United States.[30]

The financing came with complications. First, the banks did not want to hand a big pile of cash to Charles, a guy fresh out of federal prison. So Jared served as cosponsor of the loan, along with a partner of his dad's, George Gellert. Second, to justify the loan, the banks presumably needed to come up with an appraisal that valued the building at $1.8 billion or more. That didn't prove to be a problem, either— the appraisers pegged 666 Fifth Avenue at $2 billion.[31]

The numbers didn't make much sense. The Kushners were offering a record price, and the banks determined that they were actually *underpaying* by $200 million. So what if the Kushners would owe more in annual interest than the building was producing in yearly cash flow?[32] These were the go-go days before the Great Recession. Barclays, UBS, and others helped dole out $1.75 billion, put part of the loan into a package with a bunch of other debt, then sold it off in pieces to investors. In a document outlining the prospects of the property, the banks predicted its annual profits would soon soar 122% to $119 million a year.

Instead, the economy tanked, leaving the Kushner family stuck with a massive problem. More than 50% of the building's leases were set to expire by 2010.[33] Tenants fled, but the interest payments kept coming.[34]

No real estate investor wants to sell during a downturn, but sometimes there isn't much of a choice. In a series of deals, the Kushners offloaded much of the building they had just purchased.[35] When the smoke finally cleared, all they had left was a 50% share of the office space and half of the more than $1 billion loan that went with it.[36] One thing they never lost: confidence. They got in touch with Zaha Hadid, the legendary architect who designed the aquatic center for the

2012 Olympic Games in London, and she drew up a new plan for 666 Fifth Avenue, according to *The Wall Street Journal*. Hadid imagined a complete overhaul, which would include reducing the building to its steel frame and tacking on roughly 40 floors to make way for a retail space, an 11-story hotel, and luxury condominiums in the clouds.[37]

Big plans don't happen without big money. So the Kushners set off on a worldwide quest for cash, which eventually attracted major headlines. According to Bloomberg News, not many serious people took interest in the project at first. Why would they, given the Kushners' track record at the property? Once Donald Trump's political career began to take off, however, investors around the world had a look. A Qatari sheikh named Hamad bin Jassim Al-Thani contemplated putting $500 million from a private fund into the project in 2016. That deal never happened. Higher-ups managing a sovereign wealth fund from South Korea met with the Kushners. Bernard Arnault, the head of the LVMH retail empire and the richest man in France, fielded a pitch. An executive working for Saudi tycoon Fawaz Alhokair thought about investing through Alhokair's company, before ultimately concluding that the math didn't add up.[38]

While the search for suitors continued, Jared Kushner consolidated power inside Donald Trump's inner circle. Two days after the 2016 election, campaign chief Steve Bannon fired New Jersey governor Chris Christie, the man leading the Trump transition team. "The kid's been taking an ax to your head with the boss ever since I got here," Bannon told Christie, according to a book the governor published in 2019.[39] Kushner, and his business entanglements, stayed. On November 16, 2016, six days after Christie's departure, Jared Kushner walked into La Chine restaurant at the Waldorf Astoria hotel, where a table awaited him with $2,100 bottles of wine, according to *The New York Times*. At its head was Wu Xiaohui, chairman of Anbang Insurance Group, a financial giant known for its murky ownership structure. Anbang was considering investing in 666 Fifth Avenue. Wu raised a glass to Donald Trump, envisioning a bright economic future. But nothing ever seemed to come of it, and the Kushners remained searching for money as Jared moved to Washington.[40]

Kushner divested his stake in 666 Fifth Avenue and some other assets in 2017. But he did so in an unusual way, reportedly selling interests to a trust controlled by his family members.[41] Technically, that got the asset out of his portfolio. But was a scion of the Kushner empire really going to be uninterested in what happened to the family business he seemed poised to one day inherit? In August 2018, just six months before the Kushners' big loan came due,[42] a fund that counted Brookfield Property Partners among its investors swooped in and agreed to lease the building for 99 years, handing over $1.3 billion for the right to do so.[43] The largest outside shareholder of Brookfield Property Partners, with a noncontrolling 7% stake, was the Qatar Investment Authority.[44] "QIA played no role in Brookfield's investment decision," says Kerrie McHugh, a spokesperson for Brookfield.[45] Around the same time, however, the Qatar Investment Authority was also building out space inside President Trump's San Francisco skyscraper.[46]

AFTER THE FIFTH AVENUE project went sideways, the Kushners looked back to their home state of New Jersey. Right across the Hudson from Manhattan, in Jersey City, the family decided to construct a luxury residential tower. There would be a 24-hour doorman, sweeping views of Lower Manhattan,[47] a sauna, and on-site dry cleaning.[48] All of which made it odd that the Kushners partially financed the place with a government program called EB-5, designed to help impoverished areas.[49]

EB-5 was something of a distant, older cousin to the opportunity zone program. First enacted in 1990, the idea behind EB-5 was to boost the economy by allowing foreigners to invest in job-creating projects. In exchange for putting up $500,000 to support projects in downtrodden neighborhoods, the foreign investors could apply for green cards.[50] But the program didn't really work as expected. Instead of investing in poor parts of town, some developers used maps connecting wealthy neighborhoods, where they put their projects, to rough parts of town, which they avoided.[51] They then averaged the economic statistics of the whole area to qualify for the special incentives.[52]

It was gerrymandering, for profit rather than votes—and it was entirely legal. The Kushners got financing for the Jersey City tower after reportedly drawing their neighborhood in the shape of a fish-hook, with their project at one end and a poor neighborhood at the other.[53] They raised $50 million from 100 overseas investors.[54] Making it extra clear that this was not a rough part of town, the Kushner family reached a deal to brand the place with the Trump name.[55]

Emboldened, the Kushners also sought out another plot in Jersey City, this one in a middle-class neighborhood named Journal Square. In 2014, the Kushners paid $27 million for the land.[56] It sat in a prime location, almost directly on top of a train station that could shuttle commuters to Manhattan in 15 minutes. They laid out plans for twin skyscrapers,[57] which would soar over the neighborhood and, presumably, attract wealthy people who didn't want to pay the prices in Manhattan or Brooklyn but did want convenient access to New York City's Financial District.

Around the same time that the Kushners were scouring the globe for cash to rescue 666 Fifth Avenue, they were also apparently working with a Chinese company called the Qiaowai Group, as part of an attempt to secure EB-5 financing for the Journal Square project.[58] In May 2017, four months after Jared entered the White House, his sister

Nicole Meyer showed up at the Ritz-Carlton in Beijing. With more than 100 potential investors in the room, along with reporters from *The New York Times* and *The Washington Post,* Meyer emphasized how the project "means a lot to me and my entire family."[59] She explained how Jared used to run the family business but was now serving inside the Trump administration. And a slide flashed on the screen showing a photo of Jared's father-in-law, Donald Trump, identifying him as a "key decision maker" on the EB-5 program.[60]

The Kushner Companies later apologized for Meyer's remarks, saying she had not mentioned her brother as a way of attracting investors.[61] Regardless of her intent, the message that this was a Trump-connected property got through to those in the ballroom. "Even though this is the project of the son-in-law's family," one attendee told *The Washington Post,* "of course it is still affiliated."[62] Kushner's lawyer, when flooded with inquiries about the project, told reporters that Jared had already divested his interest.[63] In fact, Kushner held onto "contingent rights," which, according to a financial disclosure report filed with federal ethics officials, would give him "ownership interests" if certain targets were met.[64] On May 8, just after the lawyer issued a statement saying Kushner was out of the project, the president's son-in-law gave away the contingent interest to a trust held by his mother, a White House spokesperson told *The Washington Post.*[65]

Ethics experts shook their heads at all of this, but Charles Kushner, inside the family firm 12 years after he got out of prison, brushed aside any concerns. "You want to know what I think about ethics watchdogs?" he asked two reporters from *The Real Deal* in May 2018. "Do you really want to know what I think about those jerks?" Absolutely, one of the reporters responded. "I think they're a waste of time. They're guys who can't get a real job, ethics watchdog? Who gets a job—ethics watchdog? Give me a break."[66]

. . .

ON THE BANK of the East River in Williamsburg, Brooklyn, rests a
white warehouse, with sweeping views of Manhattan, that long ago
served as headquarters of wholesale grocer Austin, Nichols and Company. Today it is a luxury building, with a SoulCycle studio and an
Italian restaurant, topped with hundreds of residential condos. The
apartments run anywhere from several hundred thousand dollars to a
few million and come with 12-foot ceilings, oakwood floors, and hand-
painted tiles.[67] Residents enjoy greenery bursting along the pathways
outside and benches overlooking a small beach. It's an idyllic place.

Jared Kushner and his partners bought the old warehouse for a
reported $275 million in 2015.[68] As Donald Trump was revving up
his presidential campaign, Kushner's company was signing contracts
to sell off condos in the building.[69] By the day of the inauguration,
as Kushner was preparing to enter the White House, he already had
roughly 40 contracts for $48 million, according to a review of prop-
erty records.[70] But those deals had not yet closed, meaning the money
wasn't yet in Kushner's hands. His stake in the project is relatively
small, worth about $1 million, according to an analysis of Kushner's
financial disclosure reports.[71] That means he could have presumably
divested without much hassle. But he didn't.

Kushner put himself in an unusual situation. He was serving in the
White House while continuing to sell condos to undisclosed buyers—
just like his father-in-law. In the two-and-a-half years after he took office, Kushner and his partners sold more than 200 condos for nearly
$250 million, according to a review of property records.[72] Most of the
purchasers were surely run-of-the-mill house hunters, but some were not.
For instance, the first three buyers to sign contracts with Kushner's entity were companies called Gellert Kent One LLC, Gellert Kent Two

LLC, and Gellert Kent Three LLC, according to a review of local real estate records.[73] The documents list the "sole member" of those entities as George Gellert.[74] Four months after the Gellert companies closed on the properties, Donald Trump named George's son, Andrew, to be ambassador to Chile.[75]

Did the president appoint someone as an ambassador just because of a few condo purchases? No, the Kushner-Gellert ties run much deeper than that. Remember the Charles Kushner partner who served as co-sponsor on the 666 Fifth Avenue loan? That was George Gellert. Gellert also entered a new business venture, to purchase a New Jersey hotel, with the Kushner family after Trump appointed his son to be ambassador.[76] It seems clear that Andrew Gellert—a food executive who speaks "basic Spanish," according to a State Department write-up[77]—would not have been picked to serve as ambassador to Chile without his ties to the Kushners. Seven months after Trump tapped Gellert, the president withdrew the nomination.[78] Trump would not have been the first U.S. head of state to install a questionably qualified ambassador—his predecessors were also known for awarding such posts to political allies and old friends.[79] But he may be the first president to pick such an appointee based on his son-in-law's business connections.

The ethical problems with the Austin Nichols House, as the Brooklyn warehouse is now called, go deeper. Buyers might be able to curry favor with Kushner by picking up expensive condos, but the debtholders have the real leverage—literally. Their ties can also be kept quiet. Federal officials have to disclose loans made to them personally, but they do not have to say anything about debt their companies owe.[80] So, for instance, the $175 million mortgage that Kushner held with his partners does not show up on his federal financial disclosure reports.[81] Nor do the filings say anything about an August 2017 split of that loan, which left $50 million of it in the hands of a bank called Mega

International Commercial Bank, a wholly owned subsidiary of Mega Financial Holding Company.[82]

Mega Financial is 26% owned by government entities in Taiwan, and the majority of its board members come from Taiwan's ministry of finance.[83] Meanwhile, Taiwan is locked in a decades-long feud with neighboring China, in which the United States plays a peacekeeping role.[84] The loan documents, signed while Jared was in office, specifically name him as one of two guarantors of the debt.[85] That means that months after Trump took office, an overseas bank—partially owned by a government with a vested interest in U.S. foreign policy—held leverage over one of the president's top advisers and closest family members. And thanks to loophole-riddled disclosure laws, none of this has ever been previously reported.

NOT FAR FROM the Austin Nichols House, in a Brooklyn neighborhood called Dumbo, there is a four-building office complex in which Kushner retained a more valuable stake, which appears to be worth somewhere between $5 and $52 million, based on federal financial disclosures.[86] Though the precise value is difficult to ascertain, there is no question that the property is one of Jared's most valuable assets outside of Cadre. Packed with trendy tenants, the place serves as global headquarters for Etsy, which pays $12.4 million a year in annual rent.[87] Other occupants include WeWork ($8.7 million), a charter school ($3.8 million), a design studio ($1.6 million), and a brewery.[88] It's just the sort of up-and-coming scene where a real estate investor can make a fortune.[89]

Kushner and his partners bought the buildings, along with a fifth space nearby, for $240 million in 2013,[90] taking out $249 million in debt for the project from a French outfit called Natixis Real Estate Capital.[91] Natixis, in turn, passed that debt on to other banks. In April 2017, the partners filed documents revealing who else owned the debt besides Natixis. One of the lenders, with $27 million of the loan, happened to be Bank Hapoalim, an Israeli institution. That meant Kushner held financial ties to Israel even though he also served as one of President Trump's top officials working on a proposed peace plan for the country.[92]

The arrangement posed no legal hazards for Kushner,[93] but it did create an appearance issue. "We've got enough problems already where the United States is perceived as being biased in the Middle East toward one side," says Painter. "And then if you send a guy over there who's actually getting money from one side. I mean, you think how would the Israelis feel if we had somebody we sent over there to be a big negotiator who's getting a lot of money from some Palestinian bank."[94]

The issues did not end there. In 2018, the partners refinanced their four-building complex to make its debt load $480 million.[95] One of the lenders on that deal was Citigroup.[96] Around the same time Citigroup was helping with the loan, it was also lobbying in Washington on dozens of topics, including the North American Free Trade Agreement.[97] Jared Kushner, meanwhile, was working as one of Trump's top emissaries in the president's NAFTA negotiations.[98]

There was more. In February 2018, Ivanka Trump landed in South Korea to attend the closing ceremony of the Winter Olympics. When she wasn't watching the events, she stopped by the Blue House, South Korea's equivalent of the White House, to meet with President Moon Jae-in. They had dinner, and Ivanka briefed the head of state on new sanctions targeting North Korea, part of the American response to Pyongyang's continued nuclear aggression.[99] Such briefings are typically done by officials who hold security clearances. At the time, Ivanka was reportedly operating on only an interim security clearance.[100]

Later that year, Jared Kushner's lenders filed documents with the

Securities and Exchange Commission revealing yet another unusual business connection. The biggest holder of the Dumbo debt, with more than $220 million, had become a series of funds from a Seoul-based firm called Shinhan Financial Group.[101] Shinhan had previously gotten caught up in the dispute between North and South Korea, when it suffered a 2013 cyberattack that was rumored to come from Pyongyang.[102] Shinhan Financial Group's top 10 shareholders, according to an end-of-year report filed with the Securities and Exchange Commission, included the central banks of China (with a 1% stake)[103] and Norway (2%),[104] as well as the government of Singapore (3%). The largest shareholder, however, with a 9% stake, was a pension fund managed by the South Korean government—and ultimately under the purview of the South Korean president.[105]

In some ways, it was a similar arrangement as the one that allowed Taiwan to become a lender to Kushner and, if you assume shared marital finances, to his wife Ivanka. Flashy real estate often involves foreign money. It also tends to involve complex transactions, which can allow new lenders to get involved at any moment. In other words, it's a business perfectly calibrated to create stunning entanglements. Such as the one in South Korea, where Ivanka Trump found herself discussing matters of national security with a foreign leader who held leverage—albeit distant and indirect leverage—over her family's business.

10

Fill the Swamp

TRUMP'S TEAM

Amid all this intermingling of money and politics, it can be easy to forget that one of Donald Trump's key campaign promises was eliminating corruption in Washington. The slogan came about by accident. "It is time to drain the swamp in Washington, D.C.," Trump told a crowd in Green Bay, Wisconsin, on October 17, 2016, less than a month before the election. "This is why I am proposing a package of ethics reforms to make our government honest once again."[1] A smattering of people clapped.

Nine days later, however, standing behind a podium in Charlotte, North Carolina, Trump was railing against the "failed elites from Washington who have been wrong about virtually everything" when a supporter yelled out, "Drain the swamp!" Trump smiled. "You're right about the swamp—say it again," he instructed the person, prompting a chant to break out: "Drain the swamp! Drain the swamp! Drain the swamp!"[2]

About two weeks later, thousands of Trump supporters streamed into the New York Hilton Midtown hotel, on Sixth Avenue, around the corner from Trump Tower, to cheer on the man who promised to shake up Washington. A select few reportedly had access to an upstairs section, which included its own room off to the side for an even more exclusive crowd, the VIPs of VIPs.[3] People like billionaires Andy Beal, Harold Hamm, and David Koch.[4] Phil Ruffin recalls spending time with fellow Forbes 400 members Wilbur Ross, Richard LeFrak, and Carl Icahn. "You know, the usual group of guys," Ruffin explains.[5]

As the night rolled on, with Florida, North Carolina, Michigan, and Pennsylvania flashing red, the drinks flowed easily. There was plenty to celebrate. For the billionaires, a Trump presidency meant a friend in the White House. And a friend in the White House meant business opportunities. Icahn took advantage right away, leaving the party around 2 a.m. as financial markets plunged. "Carl left the party and started buying," Ross later said. "So he was smarter than I was. I stayed at the party. He went and bought and made a billion dollars."[6]

The opportunities didn't end that night. Trump soon started hearing from the tycoons about who to put in his cabinet. Forget draining the swamp—Trump decided to fill it up with friends, some of whom did not even have to take formal positions to wield influence. Consider Hamm, a fracking pioneer who had once reportedly co-chaired the reelection campaign for Oklahoma attorney general Scott Pruitt, a defender of the oil-and-gas industry.[7] Trump began considering Pruitt to run the Environmental Protection Agency. For a second opinion, the president-elect reached out to Icahn,[8] who owned a large stake in a refinery business that was suffering under federal environmental regulations.[9] Icahn spoke with Pruitt "four or five times" and came away impressed. "My hope is that Scott Pruitt is going to really be a breath of fresh air."[10] Pruitt got the nod to become administrator of the Environmental Protection Agency.

Icahn had other suggestions, too. Within days of the election, he sat down for dinner with Steven Mnuchin.[11] The two talked tax policy,[12] and Icahn determined that Mnuchin, a former Goldman Sachs partner worth an estimated $400 million,[13] would be a natural fit for Treasury secretary.[14] Trump made the appointment.

Icahn also got his own role, as "special advisor to the President on issues relating to regulatory reform."[15] Following the president's lead, Icahn did not divest his multibillion-dollar empire.[16] There was no question that Icahn had a personal interest in regulatory matters. ("I own refineries—obviously I have an agenda," he had said during the campaign.)[17] Other members of the administration do not share the president's and vice president's exemption from the federal conflict-of-interest law, which makes it a crime to take specific actions that will clearly affect personal holdings.[18] But the Trump team simply ignored all of that, issuing a press release implying that the regular rules did not apply. "Icahn will be advising the president in his individual capacity and will not be serving as a federal employee," the statement declared.[19]

Representatives for Icahn did not respond to a request for comment. But the suggestion seemed to be that, because Icahn wasn't taking a government paycheck, he did not have to comply with the conflict-of-interest statute. "That was ridiculous," says Richard Painter.[20] Especially since Icahn was, in fact, making money—just not from a government salary. From the night of Trump's election to the day after Icahn got his new job title, shares in his publicly traded investment firm jumped 33%, far outpacing the 6% increase in the overall stock market and boosting Icahn's personal fortune by an estimated $2 billion.[21]

IT WAS CLEAR from the start that Trump's own disregard for norms had inspired an ethics crisis across the government.[22] Predictable con-

sequences followed. Icahn's firm received a subpoena from federal investigators probing the investor's role in the Trump administration.[23]
In August 2017, Icahn stepped down, submitting an odd resignation
letter that seemed carefully drafted to counter claims that he had violated the conflict-of-interest law by saying he didn't actually do much.
"I had no duties whatsoever," Icahn wrote.[24]

Pruitt, a pauper compared with Icahn,[25] stumbled into his own
mess of ethics scandals. His agency spent $43,000 to install a phone
booth in Pruitt's office, a move the Government Accountability Office
later determined was against the law.[26] He reportedly got a deal to stay
for $50 a night in a property partially owned by the wife of a lobbyist
whose firm represented companies in the energy industry.[27] He also
talked to an aide about securing a mattress from the president's D.C.
hotel[28] and had her reach out to Chick-fil-A billionaire Dan Cathy to
inquire about "a potential business opportunity,"[29] later reported to be
having his wife become a Chick-fil-A franchisee.[30] Pruitt, who says he
did not tell an aide to ask about a franchise for his wife,[31] resigned in
July 2018.[32]

Trump appointed Tom Price to be secretary of Health and Human
Services.[33] Price ended up taking 21 trips on chartered, military, presidential, and commercial flights with costs totaling more than $1 mil-
lion. An inspector general concluded that Price's office failed to comply
with federal regulations.[34] Price, who says he wasn't responsible for
selecting flights, resigned as well.[35]

Interior secretary Ryan Zinke faced at least five investigations.
Some of those inquiries proved to be duds, but one of them reportedly
prompted the inspector general of the interior department to make a
referral to the Department of Justice.[36] Zinke, who could not be reached
for comment, also left the administration amid controversy.[37] Same with
Veterans Affairs chief David Shulkin.[38]

It's not as if misbehavior was inevitable. Secretary of State Rex Tillerson—who stepped down as CEO of ExxonMobil to enter the Trump administration, with an estimated $325 million fortune[39]—made a complete break from his former company, selling all of his shares and sacrificing millions of dollars to assume his new role with clean hands. "His ethics agreement serves as a sterling model for what we'd like to see with other nominees," said Walter Shaub, the top ethics official in the executive branch at the time.[40] Trump later got rid of Tillerson, who managed to leave Washington without ever getting caught up in a serious ethics scandal. "As I reflect upon the state of our American democracy," Tillerson said in a commencement address two months after his ouster, "I observe a growing crisis in ethics and integrity."[41]

Private equity tycoon Wilbur Ross also seemed to take conflicts of interest seriously at first. "I intend to be quite scrupulous about recusal and any topic where there is the slightest scintilla of doubt," he assured senators at his confirmation hearing in January 2017. The message seemed to sink in. "You have really made a very personal sacrifice," said Democratic senator Richard Blumenthal. "Your service has resulted in your divesting yourself of literally hundreds of millions of dollars in assets so that you could reach an agreement with the Office of Government Ethics. I don't want to embarrass you or presume, but obviously, of all the billions of dollars in holdings that you own now, you have divested more than 90%."[42]

Ross nodded along. His fellow cabinet appointees, including Tillerson, had endured bitter hearings. But not Ross. Republicans lauded his business experience, while Democrats touted his integrity. A month after the hearing, the Senate confirmed Ross easily, in a 72–27 vote.[43] At the time, however, no one on Capitol Hill knew the true story of Wilbur Ross. As later became apparent, he was the most ethically challenged cabinet secretary in an administration packed with them.

And unlike others who were dogged by scandal, and resigned in response, Ross remains in his powerful position.

IN 1990, ROSS found himself tangling with a young casino titan[44] named Donald Trump. The freewheeling days of the 1980s[45] had led to a slew of corporate bankruptcies; Ross, then at the investment bank Rothschild Inc., had built a reputation as one of the top restructuring advisers in the country.[46] Regardless of who he was representing, Ross's clients generally tended to come away with a fair share. "Wilbur, to me, was the master negotiator," says David Storper, Ross's former right-hand man, speaking on the record about his old boss for the first time. "Because he could end up picking somebody's pocket across the table, but they would also end up thanking him for it."[47]

The Trump Taj Mahal, in Atlantic City, was descending into bankruptcy,[48] which was bad news for Ross's client, an insurance company holding the casino's debt. On November 15, 1990, Ross talked with Carl Icahn, who also held about $155 million of the debt.[49]

Together, Ross and Icahn settled on a plan: the casino would enter into a prepackaged bankruptcy, and Trump would hold on to 50% of the equity. Ross and Icahn presumably could have knocked out the young mogul, but they instead kept him around, leaving Trump quite satisfied: "I think [Ross] is very talented, a fantastic negotiator."[50]

Ross collected hefty fees doing this kind of work, an estimated $6 million or more annually, but there was more money to be made. In 1997, while still working at Rothschild, he became a principal rather than a mere adviser, launching a $200 million private equity fund to invest in sick companies. Three years later, Ross bought out the fund and turned it into his own private equity shop—WL Ross & Co.[51] At 62 years old, an age at which most financiers are winding down, Ross was gearing up.[52] "He was just a workaholic," says Storper. "I mean, this is a guy that would call me up on a Thursday and be like, 'Why isn't the office open?' And I'm like, 'Because it's Thanksgiving.'"[53]

The hustle paid off. In 2001, Ross's firm began zeroing in on American steel companies. At first, WL Ross bet against the industry, shorting stocks so that he would make money if they fell. After they did, Ross began betting that he could profit off a resurgence. In Cleveland, he found a steel giant named the LTV Corporation that had recently declared bankruptcy. The company was struggling with a massive pension plan,[54] but Ross recognized that he could scoop up assets and leave the federal government stuck with pension liabilities.

To make sure the plan would work, Ross and his colleagues reached out to companies in the auto industry, who assured them that they would buy LTV products. Ross's team also met with unions, who agreed to loosen up labor restrictions with the understanding that WL Ross would bring back roughly half of the 7,500 jobs that had disappeared after the business went bankrupt.[55] And Ross met with officials inside the Commerce Department, concluding that George W. Bush's administration had to become more protectionist.[56]

In February 2002,[57] a bankruptcy judge approved WL Ross's plan to buy most of LTV's assets, for about $135 million, and to assume another $165 million or so in yearly environmental liabilities, while leaving the pension troubles behind. The next week, the Bush administration announced tariffs of up to 30% on steel imports. Ross looked like the smartest man on Wall Street. He combined LTV's assets with those of several other steel companies, including Bethlehem Steel in Pennsylvania and Acme Steel in Chicago. In 2003, Ross took the whole conglomerate, named International Steel Group, public.[58]

Securities filings listed Ross as the beneficial owner of 34% of the shares,[59] suggesting he was one of the wealthiest people in the country.

But most of the money in Ross's firm actually belonged to investors, rather than Ross personally. A *Forbes* reporter, apparently failing to distinguish between assets Ross managed and assets he owned, called the private equity tycoon to tell him that he was preparing to add Ross to the magazine's Forbes 400 ranking, with an estimated fortune of $1 billion.[60] It was far more than Ross was actually worth.

But Ross did not bother to correct him. "He said, 'Yep, fine, thank you,'" the reporter wrote in his notes.[61] Storper, who was in Ross's office at the time, remembers it similarly. "He said, 'Yeah, that's right,'" Storper says. "I never thought that he would actually be in the magazine."[62]

But there he was, not long after, with $1 billion listed next to his name. Wilbur Ross had snuck his way into the Forbes 400. "He's one of the easiest new guys I've put on [the Forbes 400] in a while," the reporter wrote in his notes. "Very low-key, said he didn't really want to be on, but at the same time wasn't going to fight success. He says he doesn't want to juice up his numbers at all."[63]

RIGHT AROUND THE time that the list came out,[64] Ross got married for the third time, to Hilary Geary, in a wedding fit for a billionaire. Roughly 40 people attended the ceremony in Southampton, the luxurious beach town 85 miles east of New York City. A Manhattan reception reportedly followed two days later, with 300 people celebrating inside the Rainbow Room, a restaurant on the 65th floor of 30 Rockefeller Plaza that once hosted the Astors, the Whitneys, and, naturally, the Rockefellers.[65]

Ross began to act like something of a Gilded Age industrialist. A man once known for wearing suspenders and mismatched socks,[66] he began dressing in stylish suits.[67] He collected million-dollar pieces of artwork.[68] He flew in private planes. And he threw his weight around in Republican politics. During the 2008 presidential election, Ross pushed his employees to donate money to Rudy Giuliani's campaign. "He was responsible for our bonuses," says someone who used to work with Ross, "so we were basically coerced."[69]

Ross also bought a new house in Palm Beach, Florida, shelling out $13.2 million.[70] One reason rich New Yorkers love Florida: there's no income tax in the Sunshine State,[71] meaning high-income New Yorkers can shield 9% of their annual paycheck from the government.

That meant real money to Ross, who sold his private equity firm in 2006 to Invesco for $100 million up front and the chance to earn another $275 million down the road.[72] When traveling, Ross was known for taking Invesco's private plane, leading to questions about who was picking up the tab for all of those flights.[73]

Ross could have avoided controversy by just flying commercial, of course, but that wasn't his style. "He'll take a chauffeured limousine for a block just to make sure he arrives in a chauffeured limousine,"[74] says Asher Edelman, a New York financier who served as inspiration for the character Gordon Gekko in the movie *Wall Street*.[75]

Ross's deceptions grew over the years. By the time *Forbes* called in 2007, he was likely worth $400 million or so.[76] But he kept up the myth, and the magazine put him down for $1.7 billion. In 2016, when Ross was probably up to about $600 million, he said he was at $3.7 billion.[77] The same reporter who made the mistake at *Forbes* ended up leaving the magazine and later worked on a competing list of rich people at *Bloomberg*, which also listed Ross with an inflated net worth.[78] Almost every other media outlet in the country fell in line, falsely touting Ross as a billionaire.

Outside of Ross's closest advisers, few people saw through the mirage. Investors poured money into Ross's funds, believing they were putting it in the hands of a billionaire with a magic touch.[79] Ross, in turn, charged management fees on the investors' money. He had figured out, in other words, how to spin fake billions into real millions.[80] David Wax, who served as the No. 3 person at Ross's firm, says, "Wilbur doesn't have an issue bending the truth."[81]

THERE WERE ALSO ill-gotten gains, according to investors, colleagues, and federal regulators. In 2005, right around the time that Ross started embracing the high life, Peter Lusk, a onetime vice chairman at WL Ross, sued for $20 million, alleging that Ross had deprived him of fees and interests he was promised. That case resulted in a settlement that insiders say cost about $10 million. When asked about the dispute in 2018, Ross replied, "The Lusk case ended with mutual confidentiality requirements."

A decade after Lusk sued, Ross was back in court, this time defending himself against Storper. In a $4 million suit, Ross's former right-hand man accused him of stealing his interests in private equity funds, then using phony documentation to try to cover it up. Lawyers for Ross conceded that their client had taken Storper's interest but said he was allowed to do so under partnership agreements. The parties settled in 2018 for an undisclosed sum.

A third former colleague, Joseph Mullin, sued WL Ross in 2017, saying he had not gotten $3.6 million he was owed.[82] "For no reason other than that they were in a position to do so, defendants looted Mr. Mullin's rightful carried interests and investment profits," the lawsuit said, "for the personal benefit of Wilbur L. Ross, Jr."[83] WL Ross denied the allegations, and a judge initially dismissed Mullin's suit on technical grounds.[84] But an appeals court overturned that decision in June 2019, leading to yet another settlement.[85]

Viewed individually, it's easy to write off any one of these cases as a run-of-the-mill Wall Street squabble. But take them together and a pattern emerges. Ross allegedly had a habit of grabbing assets from departed colleagues.[86]

They weren't the only alleged victims. Investors suffered, too. WL Ross promised its investors that it would pay back some fees it collected. But federal regulators concluded that the firm had not given back everything it should have. In 2016, the Securities and Exchange Commission accused Ross's firm of misleading and defrauding investors over an 11-year period.[87] WL Ross did not admit guilt, but it did agree to return $11.9 million to investors and hand over a $2.3 million fine.

In addition, WL Ross's parent company, Invesco, disclosed another $43 million in reimbursements and regulatory expenses associated with its private equity business in its 2015 annual report.[88] Four of Ross's former colleagues say those payments were also connected to WL Ross.[89]

The allegations were complicated. For example, the private equity firm was charging investors for money it had lost them, according to five former WL Ross employees and investors. If the firm made a bad deal, it was supposed to eventually calculate its management fees on the diminished value of the investment, rather than on the initial cost. But WL Ross allegedly continued to rack up fees based on the size of the original commitment. The firm was supposedly even charging fees for one investment that had dwindled down to virtually nothing.[90]

Ross was also allegedly taking fees he got from serving on the board of portfolio companies, according to former WL Ross employees.[91] Partnership agreements, however, required him to return some of that money to investors. It seemed typical of Ross's overall attitude. "He just acts so petty with some of this stuff," says Storper. "It's just a

game, you know. It's like, if you can keep something for free, why stick
your hand in the pocket? You just think you'll get away with it."[92]

EVENTUALLY IT DID START to catch up with Ross. By 2016, the SEC
was looking at allegations inside the firm, and Ross's former colleagues
were raising concerns about money that seemed to be disappearing
from their accounts. WL Ross funds were continuing to languish.[93]
Even *Forbes,* which had assigned a new reporter to estimate Ross's net
worth, was getting suspicious about why the private equity mogul was
willing to share values for his personal assets but not willing to back
up his numbers with hard evidence.[94] "I suggest we give another trim,"
the reporter wrote in her notes.

Fortunately for Ross, he had a way of alleviating these headaches.
Twenty-six years after helping out Trump in Atlantic City, he became
a big backer of Trump's presidential campaign, hosting a fundraiser in
the Hamptons and touting the candidate's trade proposals.[95] Trump,
in turn, offered him a spot in his cabinet. Moving to Washington
seemed a perfect way to leave behind a string of controversies and ce-
ment a legacy.

There was just one problem. By joining the government, Ross had
to file a public financial disclosure report, listing his assets and liabilities.[96] And lying to the government, unlike lying to *Forbes,* constituted
a federal crime.[97] So Ross told the truth, disclosing less than $700 mil-
lion in assets.[98]

In mid-2017, *Forbes*'s wealth editor assigned me to update Ross's net
worth estimate for the magazine's annual list of America's richest people. I reached out to Ross to ask about why his disclosure showed so
few assets when his assistant had told the magazine he had more than
$3 billion. On a Sunday afternoon in October, after a 16-hour flight
from Asia, Ross called.

He claimed the reason for the discrepancy was that he had moved most of his fortune into trusts for his family. "You're apparently not counting those, which are more than $2 billion," he said. "The way the Office of Government Ethics works, anything that is put into a trust of which you have no beneficial control—I mean have no beneficial interest—does not count in the assets that you have to disclose and divest of. So that's why the assets are somewhat small."[99]

Initially persuaded, I asked Ross when he had transferred those holdings. "Oh, a while back," he said. "Many months ago." When pressed, he got more specific. "Between the election and the nomination." Told that he might be removed from the Forbes 400, given that the assets were apparently held by his family members, Ross feigned indifference. "I don't care if I'm on the list or not. That frankly doesn't matter. But what I don't want is for people to suddenly think I've lost a lot of money when it's not true."

When the story came out, quoting the commerce secretary's statements about a transfer of billions of dollars of assets to his family members shortly before taking office,[100] other outlets picked up on it,[101] and the Commerce Department realized it had a problem. A department spokesperson issued a statement directly contradicting Ross's previous statement, insisting that there had been no multibillion-dollar transfer during that period and saying there must have been a misunderstanding.[102]

There was no misunderstanding, as an audio recording of the conversation shows. It seems clear that Ross was simply doing what he had done for years: lying about his assets in a way that was difficult to detect. Before finishing this book, I sent Ross a detailed list of questions outlining the allegations against him. "It is not Mr. Ross' responsibility to correct false statements," replied an attorney working with the commerce secretary, declining to directly respond to the questions. In light of those comments, however, I reviewed all of my sources once again, including those that supported information I had previously published.

The truth is that after speaking with 21 of Ross's former colleagues and associates, a clear story emerges, which only starts with Ross's net worth deceptions.[103] "There's no way you could make that money," says Storper. "You would be by far, like, the home run king. It wouldn't be hitting 763 home runs. It would be hitting a million home runs."[104] Why wasn't Ross content with the amount of money he had?[105] Wax, the former No. 3 at WL Ross, offers one explanation: "You're talking about somebody who is as egotistical as they come."[106]

ROSS'S YEARNING FOR importance quickly became apparent in Washington. One of the first stories about him, published 16 days before the Senate confirmed him as commerce secretary, had nothing to do with governance. "A Palm Beach Power Hostess Prepares for Trump's Washington," read the headline in *The New York Times*. The story focused on Ross's wife, Hilary, quoting her stepdaughter and close friends, who painted her as something of a bipartisan Jackie Kennedy.

"If any one couple can help socially lubricate the new Washington social scene," the novelist Jay McInerney told the *Times,* "it will be Hilary and Wilbur. They've always mixed with Republicans and Democrats, like myself, at their dinner table, and we could use some of that spirit more than ever at this fraught moment."[107]

The Rosses certainly did seem to socialize a lot, including with some of their old associates in the business world.[108] On May 18, 2017, Ross had lunch in the basement of the White House[109] with Bill Furman, the CEO of a publicly traded railcar manufacturer called the Greenbrier Companies.[110] At the time, Ross also owned a stake in the company.[111] He was putting himself in danger of violating the criminal conflict-of-interest law, which generally bars public officials from taking actions that will clearly benefit their own holdings.[112]

A spokesman for the Commerce Department dismissed those

concerns: "There was a purely social lunch with Mr. Furman at which Secretary Ross paid the bill," he said in a statement. "No items specific to Greenbrier have been before the secretary during his tenure at Commerce."[113] But that was not entirely true. Twelve days after his discussion with Ross, Furman wrote a letter to the Commerce Department, weighing in on a review of steel imports that the commerce secretary was considering.[114]

In March 2017, Ross had a meeting with the CEO of Chevron, while his wife apparently still held more than $250,000 of stock in the energy company.[115] From a legal standpoint, there is no difference if a conflict-producing asset is held by an official or the spouse of an official.[116] Ross's calendars show that the agenda for that meeting included discussing oil and gas developments, tax reform, and trade issues—the sorts of topics that could trigger a criminal conflict-of-interest violation.

About a week after that, Ross had a different meeting, this time with the CEO of Boeing,[117] a company in which Ross's wife apparently held nearly $3 million of stock.[118] The inspector general of the Commerce Department seems to be investigating all of this. Policies prohibit confirming or denying the existence of any ongoing investigation, but when asked about fallout from the Chevron and Boeing meetings, a Commerce official named Robert Johnston hinted at a probe anyway: "The matter is under review."[119]

On October 25, 2017, Ross sold his interests in another problematic investment, Navigator Holdings, a shipping company.[120] One of Navigator's largest customers happened to be a Russian petrochemicals giant whose top owners included two of Vladimir Putin's cronies.[121] On October 26, *The New York Times* reached out to Ross about his connection to Navigator.[122]

Five days later, Ross opened a short position in the shipping firm,[123] setting himself up to benefit if the article—still days from publication—caused the company's shares to decline. The story came out on November 5, and, while shares did not drop immediately, they did trickle downward over the next week and a half, when Ross closed out his short position, apparently with a small profit.[124] Insider trading experts expressed skepticism about whether Ross's actions were actually illegal,[125] but they generally seemed to agree that they were, as Columbia professor John Coffee Jr. put it, "sleazy as hell."[126]

The day after Ross shorted Navigator, he filed a new document with the federal government declaring that he had divested everything he promised he would. Above his signature sat an ominous warning: "Any intentionally false or misleading statement or response provided in this certification is a violation of law punishable by a fine or imprisonment, or both."[127]

Ross's filing was, in fact, false. He said he had gotten rid of everything, but he still owned more than $10 million worth of stock in Invesco,[128] over $250,000 of stock in Greenbrier,[129] at least $50,000 in Air Lease Corporation,[130] and more than $1,000 in BankUnited.[131]

Ross defended himself by saying he simply didn't realize what he owned. It was an unusual explanation, given that he had made hundreds of millions of dollars by focusing on his assets.[132] But it also seemed to be the only explanation that left Ross with some legal wiggle room. Federal law prohibits *intentionally* making false statements, but unintentionally doing so is not a crime.[133]

Nor is holding on to conflict-ridden assets that government ethics officials do not fully understand—and therefore do not require officials to divest. One of the interests that Ross kept was a stake in Diamond S Shipping, an international transporter in which he had invested during his time at WL Ross.[134] His filings disclosed the stake, but they did not mention that one of the main investors in the company was a Chinese sovereign wealth fund.[135] That meant the secretary of commerce had decided to remain in business with China while serving the United States.[136]

The conflicts got even messier. Ross delegated many of his tasks to a deputy, Wendy Teramoto, who had worked with him at WL Ross, where she remained an employee even after taking a role inside the Commerce Department.[137] According to Teramoto's own financial disclosure report, she served on the board of directors for Diamond S Shipping, the company largely owned by a Chinese sovereign wealth fund, until July 2017[138]—meaning she apparently had close business ties to China at the same time that she worked a trade deal on behalf of the United States. A lawyer for the company, when asked about the arrangement, replied with three words, "Resigned March 2017," suggesting that Teramoto's filing was false.[139] Teramoto did not respond to a request for comment. Regardless of when exactly she left the board, there's no question she played a major role in the China negotiations. "Really a lot of the work was done by Wendy Teramoto, my chief of staff," Ross said in a television interview trumpeting the agreement.[140]

The deal seemed relatively friendly toward China, in contrast to President Trump's hard-line rhetoric.[141] Which made sense, of course, given the business ties of the people negotiating it. It's unlikely that President Trump knew about Ross's overlapping interests, but he did sense that something was not right. "I can't believe you made this deal," he fumed to Ross, according to Bob Woodward's book *Fear*. "Why didn't you tell anybody? You didn't tell me about this. You just went off and did it on your own.[142]

"I thought you were a killer," Trump added. "When you were on Wall Street, you made some of these deals. But you're past your prime. You're not a good negotiator anymore. I don't know what it is, but you've lost it. I don't trust you. I don't want you doing any more negotiations."[143]

THE PRESIDENT MAY HAVE been angry, but he let Ross keep his position, leaving the commerce secretary to work on other things like overseeing the U.S. Census. It wasn't a flashy job, but it was an important one. The census, a once-every-decade count of all the people living in the United States, determines how much money the federal government sends to each part of the country, for things like healthcare programs, schools, housing, food stamps, financial aid, highways, and so on.[144] Add everything up and the census affects over $900 billion a year[145]—more money than the entire annual budgets of all but seven countries in the world. The census also decides which parts of the United States have the loudest voices in Washington. Census figures determine how many congresspeople[146] come from every area and how many electoral college votes come from every state.[147] Put simply, the census is the foundation for understanding who gets power and money.

Shortly after Trump became president, his administration started batting around the idea of adding a question on the census asking respondents whether they were citizens or not. It seemed like a simple question, but Democrats feared it would scare immigrants—documented and undocumented—into not responding to the census, which could push funding and representation more toward Republican-leaning parts of the country. As secretary of commerce, Wilbur Ross had authority over whether to add the question or not.[148] Experts did not think it was a good idea. Six former Census Bureau directors wrote to Ross, expressing concerns about adding the new question. The chief scientist inside the Census Bureau explained that the question would have "an adverse impact on self-response and, as a result, on the accuracy and quality of the 2020 Census."

Lots of people, especially in immigrant communities, would not answer the question, internal Census Bureau data, based on responses from a similar government survey, suggested. In cases where people did respond to a citizenship question, more than 20% of noncitizens lied, claiming they were in fact citizens. Asking for citizenship status was actually an unreliable way of figuring out who was a citizen. A better way to get an accurate count of citizens, according to the Census Bureau's chief scientist, was not to ask a question but instead to pull records from other parts of the government, like the Social Security Administration, U.S. Citizenship and Immigration Services,[149] and the Internal Revenue Service.

On March 26, 2018, Wilbur Ross tossed that aside and decided to add the question anyway.[150] He said it was necessary in order to properly enforce the Voting Rights Act. "Even if there is some impact on responses," Ross said, "the value of more complete and accurate data derived from surveying the entire population outweighs such concerns."[151] Never mind that his staff had determined that asking the question could in fact result in data that was *less* accurate.

Lawsuits and congressional inquiries followed.[152, 153] Ross had testified to Congress that "the Department of Justice, as you know, initiated the request for inclusion of the citizenship question,"[154] even though records showed that Ross was working to add a citizenship question long before the Department of Justice made its request. In another hearing, a member of Congress had asked Ross whether anyone from the White House had discussed the matter with Ross. He replied, "I'm not aware of any such," without mentioning that chief strategist Steve Bannon had reached out to Ross in relation to a possible citizenship question.[155] It is illegal to lie to Congress.[156]

When subpoenaed by Congress for additional documentation,[157] Ross and Attorney General William Barr, who replaced Jeff Sessions in February 2019,[158] refused to hand over documents.[159] The House voted to place both cabinet officials in contempt of Congress. Not surprisingly, the Justice Department declined to prosecute them.[160]

Three federal judges ruled against the Trump administration's decision to add the question, finding that its Voting Rights Act explanation was merely a pretext.[161] The case eventually landed in the Supreme Court, where America's top justices ruled that the administration could theoretically add a citizenship question, but not under the "contrived" circumstances it was presenting.[162] Dishonesty, in other words, thwarted the Trump administration's plans to add a citizenship question to the census.

Ross's former colleagues took it all in. They had seen Ross manipulate numbers for years, but this was different from tricking a magazine. Ross now seemed to be lying in regard to the numbers that underpin American democracy. "I almost wish I could just like sit him down and talk to him and say, 'What the fuck have you done?'" says Storper. "'How do you wear an American flag pin? I mean, you're a hypocrite.'"[163]

11

2020 Money

CAMPAIGN CASH AND
CORONAVIRUS COSTS

At some point on Inauguration Day 2017—between the stop at the White House, the parade down Pennsylvania Avenue, and the speech in front of the Capitol—Donald Trump found time to officially declare, with the Federal Election Commission, that he was running for reelection in 2020.[1] George W. Bush and Barack Obama had waited more than two years after taking office to file their reelection papers.[2] But Trump had a different plan.

During the 2016 election, he spent $66 million of his own money running for president,[3] funding most of the effort by himself[4] until he secured the Republican nomination and got reinforcements.[5] After he won the election, his friend Tom Barrack had helped fill a new pot with $107 million from people pitching in to fund the inaugural festivities.[6] Some of that money reportedly ended up at the Trump International Hotel, which was nice for the president.[7] But that dried up after the inauguration was over. Trump needed a new pile of cash.

His 2020 campaign, beginning January 20, 2017, provided it. By kicking off the campaign on the first day of his presidency, Donald Trump ensured that he could continue charging for things like rent, legal expenses, food, lodging, and so on. And since he was no longer donating his own money, that meant that by Trump's third anniversary in office, he had shifted $2 million from his supporters to his business.[8]

Some of those payments were hard to reconcile. Take the money flowing into Trump Tower Commercial LLC, the entity through which[9] the president owns his famous Fifth Avenue tower in New York City.[10] From 2017 to 2019, Trump Tower collected $1.3 million from the campaign, more than any other company in the Trump empire.[11] In addition, the Republican National Committee, working in concert with the Trump campaign, sent another $225,000 to Trump Tower Commercial LLC.[12] Federal filings list the purpose of those payments as "rent,"[13] but when asked, the Trump campaign would not say how much space it was renting.

The campaign leased additional square footage a handful of blocks from Trump Tower in another Trump building, yielding more money to the president.[14] It's even harder to make sense of those payments, which flowed through a company named Trump Plaza LLC and totaled $84,000 from 2017 to 2019.[15] Trump Plaza LLC controls a property on Third Avenue and 61st Street in Manhattan, with retail space, eight townhomes,[16] and 128 parking spaces.[17] But it's not clear what the Trump campaign was renting. There was no sign of the campaign in the retail portion, and a third party appeared to sublease the garage space, leaving just the apartments as possible campaign locations.

Since neither the Trump campaign nor the Trump Organization would explain the reason for the payments, I decided to stake out the side-by-side apartment buildings on 61st Street for 14 hours in November 2018. During that time, I saw seven people walk in or out of the properties. Of the six who were willing to talk, none could explain what the campaign could possibly be renting.[18] Neither could a man working behind the desk on the property. "I've been here since the beginning," he said. "If there was any kind of office rented out for campaigning or whatever, I would know about it."[19] A staffer on the 2016 campaign, who did not want to speak on the record, offered one possible explanation, saying people had sometimes used an apartment at Trump Plaza as a landing pad.[20] Of course, a hotel—even a Trump hotel—could have presumably served the same purpose. But that would not have necessarily ensured an average of $3,850[21] per month for the president.

Yet another Trump company, named Trump Restaurants LLC, also rented space to the campaign. That entity appears to be connected to a handful of eateries in the basement of Trump Tower. I took the escalator downstairs and the only thing that appeared to be run by the campaign was a small T-shirt stand, wedged in between the Trump Grill and Trump's Ice Cream Parlor. The campaign paid Trump Restaurants LLC an average of $3,000[22] per month in rent for what appears to be roughly 60 square feet; that is, about $600 per square foot annually.[23] To put that in perspective, Gucci, which rents a Fifth Avenue store upstairs, pays an estimated $460[24] per square foot every year. "That's robbery,"[25] said one New York City real estate expert, looking at the T-shirt stand from inside the Trump Tower atrium. Two others said the payments could be justified, given that smaller spaces tend to charge more money per square foot.[26]

Additional funds went to Trump National Doral, Mar-a-Lago, the D.C. hotel, and so on. One different Trump company collected $259,000 in legal and IT consulting expenses from 2017 to 2019. In January 2019, a business set up to lease Trump's private jet, named Tag Air

Inc.,[27] accepted a $2,750[28] payment from the campaign. It's not clear what flight expense that payment covered. Trump tends to get around in a nicer jet these days: Air Force One.

None of this self-dealing should come as a surprise. Donald Trump, after all, learned the ways of life at the foot of Fred Trump, a man whose business model relied on funneling money through related entities to benefit himself. Donald Trump had been siphoning funds in similar fashion for years. Just ask the old shareholders of Trump Hotels & Casino Resorts. Or the donors to the Eric Trump Foundation. Or the people looking after the Secret Service budget. Or Donald Trump himself, who was talking to the press about running for president 17 years before he took office. "It's very possible," he said at the time, "that I could be the first presidential candidate to run and make money on it."[29]

BUSINESS, HOWEVER, IS unpredictable. Just because you're skimming money from one pot doesn't mean you're getting richer overall. Trump's decision to keep his assets while serving as president was a gamble that paid off miserably. In the first year he sat in the White House, his net worth decreased by an estimated $400 million.[30] That had as much to do with markets as with politics. Even the president is not immune to declining Manhattan real estate values.[31]

From 2018 to the start of 2020, the president's net worth remained steady at $3.1 billion.[32] During those years, assets closely aligned with Trump's name—like Trump Tower and Trump National Doral—suffered.[33] Those not branded "Trump" did better, like 1290 Avenue of the Americas, in New York City, and 555 California Street, in San Francisco. Taken together, it all evened out, leaving the president with the same net worth for two years, even as the stock market surged.[34]

Then came the coronavirus. The Trump administration didn't

think much of it at first, as it was taking hold in China. "I think it will help to accelerate the return of jobs to North America," commerce secretary Wilbur Ross predicted on January 30.[35] The next month, the number of cases in the United States creeped up to two dozen.[36] Trump stayed optimistic. "It's going to disappear," the president said. "One day—it's like a miracle—it will disappear."[37] Wishful thinking, both for the country and for Trump's businesses, especially his hotels and golf clubs, which need people to leave the house in order to make money.

By mid-March, it was clear that the virus was not, in fact, going to disappear. Markets dove 34% as the effects rippled through the economy. Trump's own fortune plunged by an estimated $1 billion from March 1 to March 18.[38] Golf industry insiders worried about how everything would play out as the summer months approached. "If we could open up in a week or two and put all this behind us, this would be a bad memory come August," said Matthew Galvin, CEO of Morningstar Golf and Hospitality. "But if this persists through April and May and into June, then all bets are off."[39]

Hoping to stem the carnage, Congress passed a $2 trillion[40] relief package on March 27, 2020, the largest in U.S. history. A key part of that plan was a $349 billion loan proposal called the Paycheck Protection Program. The idea was simple: The federal government would offer businesses loans, and if those businesses kept their employees around for eight weeks, the loans would be forgiven.[41] Hotel companies were among the biggest beneficiaries, which should have been good news for Trump.

Instead, his reputation for self-dealing finally caught up with him. Fearing that taxpayer money would end up in the president's pocket,[42] legislators inserted a provision into the bill preventing the Trump Organization—and all other businesses owned by officials in high office—from taking the bailout loans.[43] "It's a shame," says Merrick

Dresnin, who used to serve as director of human resources for the Trump hotel in Washington, D.C. "To a certain extent, I'm glad I'm not there because it would be rough not to have that opportunity because it is going to save some companies. But yeah, I'm not sure what's going to happen with them."[44]

What happened was mass layoffs, which had already started before Congress passed the bill and only increased afterward. They hit Trump's hotels, clubs, and golf courses in California, Illinois, New York, Florida, Hawaii, Nevada, Virginia, and Washington, D.C. In all, the Trump Organization fired or furloughed more than 2,400 workers.[45]

Frankie Ortiz, a chef at Trump National Doral, was one of them. "We were busy all the way through the first week of March, when everything hit hard here in south Florida," he says. "Everybody started canceling events and canceling weddings and everything else. I mean, by March 18, which was the day I was laid off, we had no more events. I mean, events way up until August were canceled."[46]

Before long, Trump National Doral—the president's most important golf property, which generates $76 million[47] of annual revenue—shut down with the rest of the country.

On June 10, Eric Trump shared some good news with his 3.7 million Twitter followers: "We are incredibly excited to be reopening all hospitality at Trump Doral, Miami on June 18th!" He noted that "the courses are impeccable" and included a couple of links where Trump fans could make reservations.[48] President Trump amplified the advertisement, retweeting it to more than 80 million followers while pointing out, "The Trump family didn't ask the federal government for money to carry this and many other very expensive to carry properties!"[49]

The presidential promotion, however, didn't seem to help much.

Trump National Doral only booked 38 of its 643 rooms on the day of the reopening, according to two front desk agents. I made one of those 38 reservations.

"Welcome to Trump National," a masked employee said at the front desk. The resort had installed new safety features, like circular signs on the floor telling guests to stand several feet apart while waiting to check in. There wasn't much of a wait, though, given the lack of customers. Most of the people on site seemed to be staff.

At the pool, music blared over the speakers—"I Don't Care" by Ed Sheeran and Justin Bieber—but there were no guests there to enjoy the party. The golf pro shop was similarly quiet. "There's nobody here," said an employee walking nearby. Afternoon rains had cleared players off the course, so the resort had apparently decided to call it an early day. I walked all 18 holes of the famous Blue Monster course, which was, as Eric Trump had promised, in impeccable condition. But the only people enjoying it were non-golfers—a couple of joggers ran on the sixth hole, some little kids played in the sand traps on the 11th, and a pair of fishermen cast their lines near the 15th.

In the restaurant near the lobby, I found a handful of people. A group of older guys sat together without masks, drinking martinis and opining on sports and politics. One of them told a bartender that the concerns over the coronavirus were the media's fault. "They're trying to beat your boy," he said. "They're trying to take Donald down. That's what it's all about." Seconds later, he seemed to allow the possibility that COVID-19 was a real threat, just not one he was too worried about: "If I get it, I get it."

Amidst all of this, the virus continued to spread across the country. More than 3,000 Floridians tested positive for coronavirus on June 18, 2020, the day of the reopening. It was a state record—though not for long. Two weeks later, Florida was registering 10,000 new cases per day, making it the most infectious state in the nation.[50]

·　·　·

DESPITE THE TROUBLES, President Trump projected confidence. "You know, I'm very under-levered and everything, so that's good," he told a reporter who asked about the impact the virus was having on his businesses.[51] But Trump wasn't necessarily under-leveraged, at least not at his two most important hospitality properties, Doral and the Washington, D.C., hotel.

The Trump Organization took on $125 million[52] in debt at Doral, an amount that it could seemingly service in good times—but only barely.[53] In 2017, the Trump Organization generated earnings of just $4.3 million at the resort.[54] The next year, business improved, yielding $9.7 million of profits (measured as earnings before interest, taxes, depreciation, and amortization).[55] Annual debt service on the property could hit $3 to $3.5 million in 2020.[56] Given the state of affairs midway through the summer, it seemed unlikely it would make that much by year-end.

The situation appeared to be even worse at the president's hotel in Washington, D.C. The Trump Organization had a $170 million[57] mortgage against that property. Even with interest rates down, a loan of that size could require $4 to $5 million in annual interest payments. That property seemed to be struggling to produce enough profit to cover its interest expenses in boom times.[58] Amidst the coronavirus crisis, it's probably a safe bet that the place is losing money.

When borrowers can't pay what they owe, they are left with a handful of options. They can (a) negotiate with lenders, (b) refinance their loans, (c) inject cash from other holdings, or (d) declare bankruptcy. The most appealing solution, from a borrower's perspective, is to negotiate with lenders. No surprise, then, that the Trump Organization reportedly took steps in that direction in late March, reaching out to Deutsche Bank, which holds the loans on both the D.C. hotel and the Miami golf resort.[59]

That put Deutsche Bank in an awkward position. If it gave Trump a break on his loans, it would be doing a financial favor to the president of the United States, whose administration happened to be simultaneously pursuing an investigation of the bank. If Deutsche Bank refused to work with Trump and instead left him in a vulnerable position, then it could risk retaliation by the president. It was a nightmarish conflict of interest, involving hundreds of millions of dollars and a president in crisis.

And it wasn't just Trump's hotels that were in trouble. The virus had also pushed more people to shop online rather than in brick-and-mortar spaces, like the 125,000 square feet that Trump owns near Fifth Avenue.[60] The value of office space took a hit, too, with investors wondering how America's great work-from-home experiment would affect long-term leases with corporate tenants.

Trump, of course, did not have to be invested in this portfolio of assets. In fact, if he had just liquidated his $3.5 billion fortune at the time he took office, and then reinvested it in a broad-based, conflict-free mutual fund modeling the S&P 500, he would have avoided four years of financial controversies. He might have had to pay a big capital gains tax at the start—since Trump is exempt from the primary conflict-of-interest statute, there is some debate about whether he would have qualified for the tax-dodging benefit meant to ease the pain of divesting for other officials.[61]

But even if he paid the maximum possible federal and state capital gains tax, there would have still been no issues with the emoluments clause. No decline in his golf business. No concerns about tenants causing conflicts. No worries about who bought his condos. No bad example followed by Ivanka, Jared, or members of his cabinet.

And, with all that money invested in the broader market rather than in his assortment of properties, President Trump would have been an estimated $415 million richer.[63]

MISSED OPPORTUNITY

After Donald Trump won the 2016 election, he faced a choice about what to do with his business. One option was to sell everything and assume the presidency free of conflicts of interest. Instead, Trump chose to hang on to his assets—and all the trouble that came with them. Setting aside the political ramifications, it was a terrible business decision. If Trump had just sold everything at the start, paid the maximum possible federal and state capital gains taxes, then reinvested in the S&P 500, he would have been an estimated $415 million richer by March 2020.

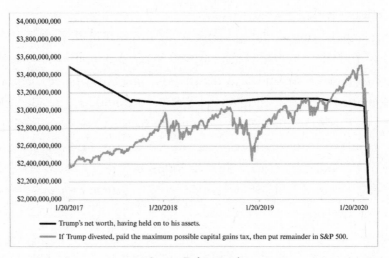

Source: *Forbes* research

APPENDIX

WHO PAYS THE PRESIDENT RENT?

TENANT	EST. ANNUAL RENT	PROPERTY
Gucci	$22 million	Trump Tower
Equitable Holdings	$13 million	1290 Ave. of the Americas
Nike	$13 million	6 East 57th
Neuberger Berman	$9.6 million	1290 Ave. of the Americas
Bank of America	$6.5 million	555 California
Cushman & Wakefield	$4.8 million	1290 Ave. of the Americas
Walgreens Boots Alliance	$3.8 million	40 Wall, 1290 Ave. of the Americas
Venable	$3.7 million	1290 Ave. of the Americas
Morgan Stanley	$3.1 million	555 California
Dodge & Cox	$2.9 million	555 California
Kirkland & Ellis	$2.9 million	555 California
UBS	$2.8 million	555 California
Green Ivy Schools	$2.6 million	40 Wall
Bryan Cave Leighton Paisner	$2.5 million	1290 Ave. of the Americas
Hachette Book Group	$2.5 million	1290 Ave. of the Americas
JPMorgan Chase & Co.	$2.5 million	1290 Ave. of the Americas
Linklaters	$2.4 million	1290 Ave. of the Americas
State Street Bank and Trust Company	$2.4 million	1290 Ave. of the Americas

TENANT	EST. ANNUAL RENT	PROPERTY
Enterprise Parking	$2.3 million	Trump Plaza, Trump Int'l Hotel & Tower (NYC), Trump World Tower, Trump Parc
Columbia University	$2.1 million	1290 Ave. of the Americas
Country-Wide Insurance Company	$2.1 million	40 Wall
Goldman Sachs	$2 million	555 California
New York Sports Clubs	$2 million	Trump Park Avenue
Regus	$1.9 million	555 California
Industrial & Commercial Bank of China	$1.9 million	Trump Tower
Fenwick & West	$1.9 million	555 California
Hadassah	$1.6 million	40 Wall
Thornton Tomasetti	$1.6 million	40 Wall
Jean-Georges	$1.6 million	Trump Int'l Hotel & Tower (NYC)
Work Better	$1.5 million	40 Wall
Jones Day	$1.5 million	555 California
McKinsey & Company	$1.5 million	555 California
Marc Fisher Footwear	$1.4 million	Trump Tower
Companies tied to Tommy Hilfiger	$1.4 million	Trump Tower
Atane	$1.3 million	40 Wall
Foresters Financial	$1.3 million	40 Wall
Harry Fox Agency	$1.3 million	40 Wall
Ripple	$1.2 million	555 California
IBISWorld	$1.2 million	40 Wall
KKR	$1.2 million	555 California
Sidley	$1.2 million	555 California
LendingHome	$1.1 million	555 California
Rahr Enterprises	$1 million	Trump Tower
TB Alliance	$900,000	40 Wall
The Quad Preparatory School	$900,000	40 Wall
Microsoft	$900,000	555 California
Abbott Capital	$700,000	1290 Ave. of the Americas

TENANT	EST. ANNUAL RENT	PROPERTY
HQ Capital	$700,000	1290 Ave. of the Americas
Supercell	$700,000	555 California
Wells Fargo	$700,000	555 California
Nuts Factory	$700,000	Trump Plaza
Blue Shield of California	$600,000	555 California
Consilio	$600,000	40 Wall
Girl Scouts of Greater New York	$600,000	40 Wall
Magna	$600,000	40 Wall
TIAA	$600,000	555 California
Cenegenics	$600,000	40 Wall
Santander Bank	$500,000	1290 Ave. of the Americas
TD Bank	$500,000	1290 Ave. of the Americas
Jaffe & Velazquez	$500,000	40 Wall
LERA Consulting Structural Engineers	$500,000	40 Wall
Newman Myers Kreines Harris	$500,000	40 Wall
Foran Glennon Palandech Ponzi & Rudloff	$500,000	40 Wall
Foley and Lardner	$500,000	555 California
Pret A Manger	$500,000	Trump Parc East
Upper East Café	$500,000	Trump Plaza
Donald J. Trump For President	$500,000	Trump Tower
AllianceBernstein	$500,000	555 California
ICF	$450,000	40 Wall
NFP	$450,000	40 Wall
Garrison Investment Group	$400,000	1290 Ave. of the Americas
Access Intelligence	$400,000	40 Wall
Derive Technologies	$400,000	40 Wall
Rita Gray Center	$400,000	40 Wall
Norton Rose Fulbright	$400,000	555 California
GNC	$400,000	Trump Plaza

TENANT	EST. ANNUAL RENT	PROPERTY
UN Plaza Grill	$400,000	Trump World Tower
Legacy Business School	$400,000	Trump Tower
Tubi	$350,000	555 California
Accounting & Compliance Int'l	$350,000	40 Wall
Aegis Capital Corp	$350,000	40 Wall
Bay Crest Partners	$350,000	40 Wall
Camacho Mauro Mulholland	$350,000	40 Wall
Cammack Retirement Group	$350,000	40 Wall
Harris St. Laurent	$350,000	40 Wall
Hidrock Properties	$350,000	40 Wall
ID PR	$350,000	40 Wall
Katz & Rychik	$350,000	40 Wall
PFM	$350,000	40 Wall
Rosenblatt Securities	$350,000	40 Wall
Telstra	$350,000	40 Wall
The Heffner Agency	$350,000	40 Wall
Zaremba Brown	$350,000	40 Wall
Galeries Bartoux	$350,000	Trump Parc East
Casa Barilla	$300,000	1290 Ave. of the Americas
KNT-CT Holdings Co., Ltd.	$300,000	1290 Ave. of the Americas
Halperin Battaglia Benzija	$300,000	40 Wall
Bay Club	$300,000	555 California
Mephisto	$300,000	Trump Plaza
NCheng	$300,000	40 Wall
United Advisors	$300,000	40 Wall
HMI Capital	$300,000	555 California
EY	$300,000	555 California
Boyce Technologies	$250,000	40 Wall
Neapolitan Express	$250,000	40 Wall
Centerview Partners	$250,000	555 California
Servcorp	$250,000	555 California
DirectView	$225,000	40 Wall

TENANT	EST. ANNUAL RENT	PROPERTY
The World Bar	$225,000	Trump World Tower
Jajan & Associates	$200,000	40 Wall
Covala Group	$200,000	40 Wall
Paulson Investment Company	$200,000	40 Wall
Symbelle Beauty Spa	$200,000	Trump Plaza
Dalbir Singh & Associates	$175,000	40 Wall
Elite Brands	$175,000	40 Wall
Livermore Trading Group	$175,000	40 Wall
Solomon Blum Heymann	$175,000	40 Wall
PCCP	$175,000	555 California
Sushi Nakazawa	$150,000	D.C. hotel
Dos Toros Taqueria	$150,000	1290 Ave. of the Americas
J's Cleaners	$150,000	Trump Plaza
Staple Street Capital	$150,000	1290 Ave. of the Americas
JH Darbie & Co.	$150,000	40 Wall
Piper Sandler Companies	$150,000	555 California
Global Kitchen	$125,000	1290 Ave. of the Americas
Grandfield & Dodd	$125,000	40 Wall
Hinch Newman	$125,000	40 Wall
LaRocca Hornik Rosen & Greenberg	$125,000	40 Wall
Meridian Equity Partners	$125,000	40 Wall
Metroloft Management	$125,000	40 Wall
Prime Executions	$125,000	40 Wall
Prodigy Network	$125,000	40 Wall
Qatar Investment Authority	$125,000	555 California
Anthony Cristiano	$125,000	Trump Int'l Hotel & Tower Chicago
Roberto Bezjon Salon	$125,000	Trump Parc East
Teresa's Brick Oven Pizza and Café	$100,000	1290 Ave. of the Americas
Collaborative Construction Management	$100,000	40 Wall
Mercury Media	$100,000	40 Wall

TENANT	EST. ANNUAL RENT	PROPERTY
Daiwa Capital Markets	$100,000	555 California
Sumitomo Mitsui Banking Corp	$100,000	555 California
World Zionist Organization	$100,000	40 Wall
Earl of Sandwich	$75,000	1290 Ave. of the Americas
Authentic8	$75,000	555 California
The Vault Restaurant	$50,000	555 California
The Tsang Law Firm	$25,000	40 Wall
Wellness on Wall	$25,000	40 Wall
World Currency Exchange	$25,000	Trump Tower
A Shine and Co.	$5,000	555 California
Poke Bar	$5,000	555 California
The Trump Organization	$0	Trump Tower
Just Salad		1290 Ave. of the Americas
Coastal Management		40 Wall
Verizon Communications		40 Wall
Fox Corporation		Trump Int'l Hotel & Tower (NYC)
Hopsteiner		Trump Tower
NBC		D.C. hotel
CNN		D.C. hotel
Brioni		D.C. hotel

Annual rent we can account for: $177 million

TOTAL COMMERCIAL RENT: $191 million

*Note: Estimates for 1290 Avenue of the Americas, 555 California and the
D.C. hotel—buildings in which Donald Trump does not own 100%
of the equity—represent the rent attributable to the president.

ACKNOWLEDGMENTS

Books usually have only one name on the cover, which doesn't make much sense if you understand the process of writing one. It took a crowd of people to put together *White House, Inc.*, and without each of them, this book would not exist.

I didn't know it at the time, but the process started in late 2016, just after Donald Trump's election. America had chosen its first billionaire president, and *Forbes*, which prides itself on billionaire coverage, needed someone to focus on Trump's businesses. Randall Lane, the editor of the magazine, called me into his office and asked if I would be interested in the assignment. I'll be forever grateful to him for giving me the opportunity to chase the story of a lifetime.

Randall and a few other people also suggested that I write a book, which was something I had never seriously considered. Thanks to *Forbes-Life* editor Michael Solomon, my agent, David McCormick, author Michael Lewis, and Penguin Random House editor Merry Sun. Without your gentle encouragement, I would have never had the confidence to give this a shot.

I always knew I was lucky to work at *Forbes*, but the magazine's support throughout this process—even when it dragged on longer than I had anticipated—confirmed how fortunate I am. It's a special place with hard working people. Among them: Rich Behar, Steve Bertoni, Abe Brown, Deniz Çam, Kerry Dolan, Matt Drange, Noah Kirsch, Luisa Kroll, Matt Schifrin, Katya Soldak, Chase Peterson-Withorn, Michela Tindera, and Jen Wang, who all worked on stories referenced in this book. It's an honor to call them colleagues.

It is also an honor to compete against some of the best reporters in the business, including many who wrote other stories I've cited. Thanks for your groundbreaking work, David Barstow, Andrea Bernstein, Russ Buettner, Susanne Craig, Zach Everson, David Fahrenthold, David Kocieniewski, Derek Kravitz, Eric Lipton, Ilya Marritz, Martyn McLaughlin, Caleb Melby, Jonathan O'Connell, Joshua Partlow, Al Shaw, and Heather Vogell. I know I'm missing plenty of others—please forgive me. Thanks as well to the reporters who chronicled Trump long before he got into politics, including Wayne Barrett, Gwenda Blair, David Cay Johnston, and Tim O'Brien.

The unsung heroes of journalism are fact-checkers. I was lucky enough to have a team of all-stars reviewing this book. Thank you to Daniela Sirtori-Cortina, Anastassia Gliadkovskaya, and especially Natalie Robehmed, who spent months combing through every word. No one deserves more credit than you.

Writing a book can be scary, but I knew I was in good hands with the team at Penguin Random House. My editor, Merry Sun, deserves a second thank you. She made this book better in ways big (encouraging me to rethink the entire premise) and small (helping format endnotes). Thank you to copy editor Will Palmer for cleaning up the mess, to Jane Cavolina for whipping the endnotes into shape, to Amanda Lang and Regina Andreoni for helping make sure it got into readers' hands, to lawyer Linda Friedner for keeping me out of trouble, and to the members of the managing and production editorial team—Jessica Regione, Megan Gerrity, and Nicole Celli—for patiently guiding us through the process.

Writing a book can also be lonely. Thanks to my friends, who assured me that they would still hang out with me after I disappeared for a year.

(I hope it's true!) Thanks to my family, who cheered me up by talking about Ohio State football, Camp Kawanhee, and lots of other things that have nothing to do with Donald Trump. Thanks Dad, Mom, Will, Rees, and Ken for also agreeing to review the book and offer suggestions.

Most important, thanks to my wife, Kate. We made the decision to take on this project together, and I don't think either of us really knew what we were getting into. But even when it meant working late into the night, even when it meant missing weddings, even when it meant not getting home to see our families, you remained supportive. Nothing about this was easy, but you made it easier. Thank you for constantly reminding me, without ever explicitly telling me, that there are more important things than investigating Trump's business. For example, your work treating coronavirus patients in the hospital. And yes, I'll be doing the dishes for the next 10 years.

NOTES

PROLOGUE

1. Vornado Realty Trust, Form 10-K, Securities and Exchange Commission, February 18, 2020, 7, www.sec.gov/ix?doc=/Archives/edgar/data/899689/000089968920000007/vno -12312019x10k.htm.

2. San Francisco Assessor-Recorder, 555 California Owner LLP, HWA 555 Owners LLC, March 5, 2005; Donald Trump, OGE Form 278e, U.S. Office of Government Ethics, 5 C.F.R. part 2634 (hereafter "Donald Trump, OGE Form 278e"), May 15, 2019, 82, 51; Trump International Hotel Liquor License Filings with Trust Info, ProPublica, January 26, 2017, 7, www.documentcloud.org/documents/3442581-Trump-International-Hotel -Liquor-License-Filings#document/p7; Vornado Realty Trust, Supplemental Operating and Financial Data, for the quarter ended September 30, 2019, 37, https://extapps2.oge .gov/201/Presiden.nsf/PAS+Index/12DAC79CC95F849085258142002703CA/$FILE /Trump,%20Donald%20J.%20%20final278.pdf.

3. Dan Alexander, "Trump's Net Worth Drops $1 Billion as Coronavirus Infects the President's Business," *Forbes,* April 2, 2020, www.forbes.com/donald-trump/#1e4e73d42899.

4. Vornado Green Book, 15.

5. Analysis of Vornado Realty Trust, Supplemental Operating and Financial Data, for the quarter and year ended December 31, 2019, 50.

6. San Francisco Assessor-Recorder, Notice of Non-Responsibility, HWA 555 Owners LLC, Qatar Investment Authority Advisor (USA) Inc., August 30, 2018; Qatar Investment Authority Advisory, April 12, 2020, www.qiaadvisory.com.

7. Donald Trump, OGE Form 278e, 82.

8. Trump International Hotel Liquor License Filings, 7.

9. *CIA World Factbook,* s.v. "Qatar, Geography," https://www.cia.gov/library/publications /the-world-factbook/geos/print_qa.html.

10. Congressional Research Service, "Qatar: Governance, Security, and U.S. Policy," December 4, 2018, 2, 10, crsreports.congress.gov/product/pdf/R/R44533/42.

11. Independent Statistics and Analysis, U.S. Energy Information Administration, Natural Gas.

12. *CIA World Factbook,* s.v. "Country Comparison: GDP per Capita," https://www.index mundi.com/g/r.aspx?v=67&t=100.

13. *CIA World Factbook,* s.v. "Qatar, Government" https://www.cia.gov/library/publications /the-world-factbook/geos/qa.html; "Qatar: Governance, Security, and U.S. Policy," 6.

14. "Qatar: Governance, Security, and U.S. Policy," 9–10; *CIA World Factbook,* s.v. "Qatar, Transnational Issues," www.cia.gov/library/publications/the-world-factbook/geos/qa.html.

15. "Qatar: Governance, Security, and U.S. Policy," 17–18.

16. U.S. Department of State, "Integrated Country Strategy: Qatar," www.state.gov/wp -content/uploads/2019/01/ICS-Qatar_UNCLASS_508.pdf; White House, "Remarks by President Trump in Christmas Video Teleconference with Members of the Military," December 27, 2018, www.whitehouse.gov/briefings-statements/remarks-president-trump -christmas-video-teleconference-members-military/.

17. U.S. Department of State, "U.S. Relations with Saudi Arabia," Bilateral Relations Fact Sheet, Bureau of Near Eastern Affairs, November 26, 2019, www.state.gov/u-s-relations -with-saudi-arabia/.

18. U.S. Department of State, "U.S. Relations with United Arab Emirates," Bilateral Relations Fact Sheet, Bureau of Near Eastern Affairs, November 4, 2019, www.state.gov/u-s -relations-with-united-arab-emirates/.

19. "Qatar: Governance, Security, and U.S. Policy," 11.

20. White House, "A Look Back at the U.S.-Saudi Friendship," May 20, 2017, www.white house.gov/articles/look-back-u-s-saudi-friendship/.

21. U.S. Department of Justice, Supplemental Statement Pursuant to the Foreign Agents Registration Act of 1938, as amended, MSLGROUP Americas, Inc. d/b/a Qorvis MSL-GROUP, 43, 44, efile.fara.gov/docs/5483-Supplemental-Statement-20170531-25.pdf.

22. "Qatar: Governance, Security, and U.S. Policy," 11.

23. "Qatar: Governance, Security, and U.S. Policy," 11–12.

24. Donald Trump, Twitter, June 6, 2017, twitter.com/realDonaldTrump/status/872062159 789985792.

25. "Remarks by President Trump and Amir Tamim Bin Hamad Al Thani of the State of Qatar Before Bilateral Meeting," White House, April, 10, 2018, www.whitehouse.gov /briefings-statements/remarks-president-trump-amir-tamim-bin-hamad-al-thani-state -qatar-bilateral-meeting/.

26. Clerk of the United States House of Representatives, Lobbying Disclosure Act of 1995 (Section 5), Mercury, April 18, 2018, https://soprweb.senate.gov/index.cfm?event=getFilingDet ails&filingID=8DB08FC0-72E6-48ED-83E9-CCAA76D02AD0&filingTypeID=51; Clerk of the United States House of Representatives, Lobbying Disclosure Act of 1995 (Section 5), Choharis Law Group, PLLC, May 31, 2018, https://soprweb.senate.gov /index.cfm?event=getFilingDetails&filingID=01CF7DCA-8AF6-4FDB-93F8 -DFD1C9A6F11C&filingTypeID=51; Clerk of the United States House of Representatives, Lobbying Disclosure Act of 1995 (Section 5), Mercury, July 19, 2018, https://soprweb.sen ate.gov/index.cfm?event=getFilingDetails&filingID=7ACFF985-1B4A-426A-9CD9 -B6ACBB384414&filingTypeID=60; Clerk of the United States House of Representatives, Lobbying Disclosure Act of 1995 (Section 5), Mercury, October 16, 2018, https:// soprweb.senate.gov/index.cfm?event=getFilingDetails&filingID=2FC4BD54 -C7E1-418A-A7FF-E7084D46584E&filingTypeID=69; Clerk of the United States House of Representatives, Lobbying Disclosure Act of 1995 (Section 5), Choharis Law Group, PLLC, March 6, 2019.

27. White House, "Joint Statement from the President of the United States Donald J. Trump and His Highness Sheikh Tamim Bin Hamad Al-Thani, Amir of the State of Qatar," July 9, 2019, www.whitehouse.gov/briefings-statements/joint-statement-president-united-states -donald-j-trump-highness-sheikh-tamim-bin-hamad-al-thani-amir-state-qatar/.

28. Source, text message to author, November 5, 2019.

29. San Francisco Assessor-Recorder, Notice of Non-Responsibility, 1–3.

30. Text messages from source to author.

31. Qatar Investment Authority Advisory (USA) Inc., https://www.qiaadvisory.com.

32. Spokesperson for the White House, email to author, May 15, 2020.

33. Harry Cameron, email to author, May 15, 2020; Wendi Kopsick, email to author, May 14, 2020.

34. U.S. Constitution, art. I, § 9, National Archives, www.archives.gov/founding-docs/constitution-transcript.

35. "Donald Trump FULL news conference," CBC News, January 11, 2017, www.youtube.com/watch?v=L-I_M9sKXFs.

36. San Francisco Assessor-Recorder, Notice of Non-Responsibility, 1.

37. "Qatar: Governance, Security, and U.S. Policy," 4.

38. "Remarks by President Trump and Amir Tamim Bin Hamad Al Thani."

39. "Remarks by President Trump at a Dinner Hosted by the Secretary of the Treasury in Honor of the Amir of the State of Qatar," July 8, 2019, www.whitehouse.gov/briefings-statements/remarks-president-trump-dinner-hosted-secretary-treasury-honor-amir-state-qatar/.

40. U.S. Department of the Treasury, "Treasury Cash Room," www.treasury.gov/about/history/Pages/cash-room.aspx.

41. "Remarks by President Trump at a Dinner Hosted by the Secretary of the Treasury in Honor of the Amir of the State of Qatar."

42. White House Press Office, email to author, July 8, 2019; subject: WH in-town pool report #13.

43. Analysis of White House Press Office email to author.

44. "Joint Statement from the President of the United States Donald J. Trump and His Highness Sheikh Tamim Bin Hamad Al-Thani, Amir of the State of Qatar."

45. "#1135 Bruce Flatt," Forbes, as of May 2, 2020, www.forbes.com/profile/bruce-flatt/#20005b2c5ddf.

46. White House Press Office email; Donald Trump, Twitter, July 9, 2019, twitter.com/realDonaldTrump/status/1148679238431793152.

47. NYC Department of Finance, Office of the City Register, TST/TMW, 666 Fifth, LP, ℅ Tishman Speyer Properties LP, 666 Fifth Associates LLC, ℅ The Kushner Companies, January 11, 2007, 9, a836-acris.nyc.gov/DS/DocumentSearch/DocumentImageView?doc_id=2007011101722001; analysis of U.S. Office of Government Ethics; 5 C.F.R. part 2634, Form Approved: OMB No. (3209-0001) (March 2014) Executive Branch Personnel Public Financial Disclosure Report (OGE Form 278e), Kushner, Jared, July 20, 2017, 56, 69, 80; Prospectus Supplement, GE Commercial Mortgage Corporation, Securities and Exchange Commission, April 26, 2007, B-3, www.sec.gov/Archives/edgar/data/1215087/000119312507103115/d424b5.htm; Q2 2019 Interim Report, Brookfield Property Partners, LP, 52: https://bpy.brookfield.com/-/media/Files/B/Brookfield-BPY-IR-V2/quarterly-reports/2019/bpy-2q19-interim-report-with-cover.pdf.

48. Brookfield Property Partners, Form 20-F, Securities and Exchange Commission, 118, www.sec.gov/Archives/edgar/data/1545772/000154577220000007/bpy201920-f.htm.

49. White House Press Office email, 3.

50. White House Press Office email, 2–3.

51. Analysis of Qatar Investment Authority, "Our Governance," www.qia.qa/About/Our Governance.aspx.

52. "Remarks by President Trump at a Dinner Hosted by the Secretary of the Treasury in Honor of the Amir of the State of Qatar."

53. Donald Trump, OGE Form 278e.

54. Donald Trump, OGE Form 278e.

55. "#1001 Donald Trump," *Forbes,* as of May 2, 2020, www.forbes.com/profile/donald
-trump/#ec9fbed47bdb.

CHAPTER ONE: ART OF THE SELF-DEAL

1. CNN/ORC International Poll, September 20, 2015, 2, i2.cdn.turner.com/cnn/2015/im
ages/09/20/rel10a.pdf.

2. Randall Lane, "Inside the Epic Fantasy That's Driven Donald Trump for 33 Years,"
Forbes, September 29, 2015, www.forbes.com/sites/randalllane/2015/09/29/inside-the-epic
-fantasy-thats-driven-donald-trump-for-33-years/#145e4f012037.

3. Donald Trump and Allen Weisselberg, interviewed by Randall Lane, Chase Peterson-
Withorn, and Kerry Dolan, September 21, 2015.

4. Steve Forbes's profile on Forbes.com, www.forbes.com/sites/steveforbes/#7e5bde7ae726.

5. Federal Election Commission, campaign finance data, analysis of campaign finance contributions to Donald J. Trump for President, January 1–September 21, 2015, www.fec
.gov/data/receipts/?data_type=processed&committee_id=C00580100&two_year_trans
action_period=2016&min_date=01%2F01%2F2015&max_date=09%2F21%2F2015.

6. Crown Building Deed, April 17, 2015, Grantor: Lexington Building Co. LLC, Grantee:
730 Fifth Retail, LLC, NYC Department of Finance, document ID 2015042300534001,
a836-acris.nyc.gov/DS/DocumentSearch/DocumentImageView?doc_id=2015042
300534001.

7. Analysis of SHVO, "730 Fifth Avenue, New York, NY," www.shvo.com/aman-new-york/;
Gilbane Building Company, "Crown Building at 730 Fifth Avenue for OKO Group,"
www.gilbaneco.com/project/crown-building-at-730-fifth-avenue-for-oko-group/; Prospectus Supplement, Wells Fargo Commercial Mortgage Trust 2012-LC5, Securities and Exchange Commission, July 20, 2012, www.sec.gov/Archives/edgar/data/850779/000153
949712000571/prospectus-supplement.htm.

8. Wells Fargo Bank, N.A., "Distribution Date Statement," June 17, 2016, U.S. Securities and
Exchange Commission, www.sec.gov/Archives/edgar/data/1556601/000105640416005001
/wcm12lc5_ex991-201606.htm.

9. The Trump Organization, "40 Wall Street," www.trump.com/commercial-real-estate
-portfolio/40-wall-street.

10. Prospectus Supplement, Wells Fargo Commercial Mortgage Trust 2015-LC22, Securities
and Exchange Commission, August 3, 2015, www.sec.gov/Archives/edgar/data/850779
/000153949715001541/n537_pros-x14.htm.

11. Wells Fargo Bank, N.A., "Distribution Date Statement," June 17, 2016.

12. Wells Fargo Bank, N.A., "Distribution Date Statement," September 30, 2016, www
.sec.gov/Archives/edgar/data/1651164/000105640416006331/wcm15l22_ex991
-201610.htm.

13. Donald Trump and Tony Schwartz, *Trump: The Art of the Deal* (New York: Random
House, 1987).

14. Howard Rudnitsky, "No Mr. Nice Guy," *Forbes,* September 13, 1993.

15. Trump Hotels & Casino Resorts Inc., Form 10-Ks, Securities and Exchange Commission,
March 27, 1996, 88, www.sec.gov/Archives/edgar/data/943320/0000950130-96-000986
.txt; March 29, 2002, www.sec.gov/Archives/edgar/data/943320/000095013002002301
/d10k405.txt.

16. Lane, "Inside the Epic Fantasy."

17. *Forbes* archives.

18. Monte Burke, "As Ivanka Trump Enters Her Prime She Has Never Been More Important
to the Family Business," *Forbes,* March 25, 2013, www.forbes.com/sites/monteburke

/2013/03/25/as-ivanka-trump-enters-her-prime-she-has-never-been-more-important
-to-the-family-business/#40f230af6f9e.

19. Miami-Dade Property Appraiser, June 11, 2012, purchase price of $104,843,300. Trump
himself cites a purchase price of $150 million: Trump and Weisselberg interview.

20. Mortgage, Assignment of leases and rents, fixture filing and security agreement, Trump
Endeavor 12 LLC, Deutsche Bank Trust Company Americas, August 7, 2015; Mortgage,
Assignment of leases and rents, fixture filing, and security agreement, Trump Endeavor
12 LLC, Deutsche Bank Trust Company Americas, June 11, 2012.

21. Trump and Weisselberg interview.

22. Dan Alexander, "Trump's Net Worth Drops $1 Billion as Coronavirus Infects the Presi-
dent's Business," *Forbes,* April 2, 2020, www.forbes.com/donald-trump/#1e4e73d42899.

23. Trump and Weisselberg interview.

24. Lane, "Inside the Epic Fantasy."

25. Jennifer Fernandez, "Donald Trump's 1985 Apartment Looks Exactly How You'd Imagine It," *Architectural Digest,* July 27, 2016, www.architecturaldigest.com/story/donald
-trump-1985-apartment-looks-exactly-how-youd-imagine-it.

26. Jess Cagle and Charlotte Triggs, "At Home with Donald Trump and His Family," September
30, 2015, *People,* people.com/celebrity/at-home-with-donald-trump-and-his-family/.

27. Donald Trump, interviewed by Scott Pelley, "Trump Gets Down to Business on *60
Minutes,*" September 27, 2015, www.cbsnews.com/news/donald-trump-60-minutes-scott
-pelley/.

28. Erin Carlyle, Chase Peterson-Withorn, and Jennifer Wang, "Trump by the Numbers,"
Forbes, October 19, 2015.

29. Chase Peterson-Withorn, "Donald Trump Has Been Lying About the Size of His Penthouse," *Forbes,* May 3, 2017, www.forbes.com/sites/chasewithorn/2017/05/03/donald
-trump-has-been-lying-about-the-size-of-his-penthouse/#19adabe31ef8.

30. Carlyle, Peterson-Withorn, and Wang, "Trump by the Numbers."

31. Thomas M. Wells, "Donald Trump Hired Me as an Attorney, Please Don't Support Him
for President," *Huffington Post,* August 2, 2016, www.huffpost.com/entry/donald-trump
-hired-me-as-an-attorneyplease-dont_b_579e52dee4b00e7e269fb30f.

32. Michael D'Antonio, "Trump's Parents Are Still Watching Him," February, 23, 2019, CNN,
www.cnn.com/2019/01/23/opinions/fred-mary-trump-presidential-influence-dantonio
/index.html.

33. Gwenda Blair, *The Trumps: Three Generations of Builders and a President* (New York:
Simon & Schuster, 2015), chap. 7, 117, 120–21.

34. "Franklin D. Roosevelt," White House, www.whitehouse.gov/about-the-white-house
/presidents/franklin-d-roosevelt/.

35. "The Federal Housing Administration (FHA)," U.S. Department of Housing and Urban
Development, www.hud.gov/program_offices/housing/fhahistory.

36. Preceding two paragraphs: Blair, *The Trumps,* 146–190.

37. "Homes and Community Renewal," New York State, Housing Finance Agency, hcr
.ny.gov/housing-finance-agency; Blair, *The Trumps,* 205.

38. Blair, *The Trumps,* 213–14.

39. *Housing Act of 1954: Hearings on H.R. 7839, Day 1, Before the Select Comm. on Banking
and Currency,* 83rd Cong. (1954) (testimony of Fred Trump), www.washingtonpost
.com/wp-stat/graphics/politics/trump-archive/docs/fred-trump-cong-testimony-1954
-housing-act.pdf.

40. Blair, *The Trumps,* 214–15.

41. *FHA Investigation: Hearings on S. Res. 229, Before the Senate Committee on Banking and
Currency,* 83rd Cong. (1954) (testimony of Fred Trump), 402–4, https://www.washing

tonpost.com/wp-stat/graphics/politics/trump-archive/docs/fha-investigation
-1954-part-1.pdf; "'Trump Revealed': The Reporting Archive," *Washington Post,* August
30, 2016, www.washingtonpost.com/graphics/politics/trump-revealed-book-reporting
-archive/?itid=sf; State of New Jersey Department of Law and Public Safety, Division of
Gaming Enforcement, Report to the Casino Control Commission, Trump Plaza Corporation, October 16, 1981, 35 (hereafter "Trump Plaza Casino Commission report").

42. FHA *Investigation: Hearings on S. Res. 229*, executive session, June 18, 1954, 405-406;
"'Trump Revealed,'" *Washington Post.*

43. FHA *Investigation: Hearings on S. Res. 229*, 406; "'Trump Revealed': The Reporting Archive," *Washington Post.*

44. Trump Plaza Casino Commission report, 35.

45. Trump and Schwartz, *Art of the Deal*, 72, 73, 75.

46. The White House, "Donald J. Trump," https://www.whitehouse.gov/people/donald-j
-trump/.

47. Trump Plaza Casino Commission report, 37, 36, 40, 41, 44, 85, 43, 141, 31.

48. Trump Plaza Casino Commission report, 85; Morris Kaplan, "Major Landlord Accused of
Antiblack Bias in City," *New York Times*, October 16, 1973, www.nytimes.com/times
-insider/2015/07/30/1973-meet-donald-trump/.

49. Federal Bureau of Investigation, "Trump Management Company," Part 1, 10, 37, vault
.fbi.gov/trump-management-company.

50. Trump and Schwartz, *Art of the Deal*, 99.

51. United States Senate, "Have You No Sense of Decency?," senate.gov/artandhistory/his
tory/minute/Have_you_no_sense_of_decency.htm; Hearings before the Permanent Subcommittee on Investigations of Committee On Governmental Affairs, United States Senate, April 1988, 108, 229, 230, 251, ncjrs.gov/pdffiles1/Digitization/125163NCJRS.pdf;
Jonathan Mahler and Matt Flegenheimer, "What Donald Trump Learned from Joseph
McCarthy's Right-Hand Man," *New York Times*, June 20, 2016, www.nytimes.com
/2016/06/21/us/politics/donald-trump-roy-cohn.html.

52. Trump and Schwartz, *Art of the Deal*, 99.

53. "Realty Outfit Loses Suit for 100-Million," *New York Times*, January 26, 1974, www
.nytimes.com/1974/01/26/archives/realty-outfit-loses-suit-for-100million.html.

54. This and preceding paragraph: Trump and Schwartz, *Art of the Deal*, 99, 136, 121, 122.

55. Trump Plaza Casino Commission report, 31.

56. Trump and Schwartz, *Art of the Deal*, 131.

57. "Three Lawmakers Are Critical of Commodore Tax Relief," *New York Times,* April 26, 1976,
https://www.nytimes.com/1976/04/26/archives/3-lawmakers-are-critical-of-commodore-tax
-relief.html.

58. Trump and Schwartz, *Art of the Deal*, 133.

59. Blair, *The Trumps*, 289.

60. Judy Klemesrud, "Donald Trump, Real Estate Promoter, Builds Image as He Buys Buildings," *New York Times,* November 1, 1976, www.nytimes.com/1976/11/01/archives/donald
-trump-real-estate-promoter-builds-image-as-he-buys-buildings.html.

61. Sean Kilachand, "The Forbes 400 Hall of Fame: 36 Members of Our Debut Issue Still in
Ranks," September 20, 2012, www.forbes.com/sites/seankilachand/2012/09/20/the-forbes
-400-hall-of-fame-36-members-of-our-debut-issue-still-in-ranks/#60a0dd984113.

62. Jonathan Greenberg, "Trump Lied to Me About His Wealth to Get onto the Forbes 400.
Here Are the Tapes," April 20, 2018, www.washingtonpost.com/outlook/trump-lied-to
-me-about-his-wealth-to-get-onto-the-forbes-400-here-are-the-tapes/2018/04/20/ac762b08
-4287-11e8-8569-26fda6b404c7_story.html.

63. Trump Plaza Casino Commission report, 63.

64. Greenberg, "Trump Lied to Me About His Wealth."

65. Dan Alexander, "Donald Trump Gained More Money Under Obama than Any Other Presidency," March 7, 2018, www.forbes.com/sites/danalexander/2018/03/07/donald-trump -gained-more-money-under-barack-obamas-tenure-than-any-other-presidency/#46470e 0726db.

66. Analysis of Trump Plaza Casino Commission report.

67. Trump Plaza Casino Commission report, 23–73.

68. Greenberg, "Trump Lied to Me About His Wealth."

69. Audio of phone conversation between Jonathan Greenberg and "John Barron" (Donald Trump), May 17, 1984. *Washington Post,* April 19, 2018, www.washingtonpost.com/video /national/audio-from-may-17-1984-phone-conversation/2018/04/20/bab5f61e-4429-11e8 -b2dc-b0a403e4720a_video.html.

70. "Fred Charles Trump, Donald John Trump," *Forbes,* October 1, 1984; "Donald John Trump," *Forbes,* October 28, 1985.

71. Greenberg, "Trump Lied to Me About His Wealth."

72. Michael D'Antonio, *The Truth About Trump* (St. Martin's Publishing Group), 133.

73. Trump Plaza Casino Commission report, 56, 32.

74. Eamonn Fingleton, "Golden Boy," *Forbes,* February 28, 1983.

75. Harold Seneker, Dolores Lataniotis, Graham Button, and Vicki Contavespi, "Donald John Trump," in "The Forbes 400," *Forbes,* October 23, 1989.

76. Dan Alexander and Chase Peterson-Withorn, "How Trump Is Trying and Failing to Get Rich Off His Presidency," *Forbes,* October 12, 2018, www.forbes.com/sites/danalexander /2018/10/02/how-trump-is-tryingand-failingto-get-rich-off-his-presidency /#6e787a2e3b1a.

77. "Donald John Trump," *Forbes.*

78. Barbara Res, interviewed by author, September 14, 2018.

79. John, Merwin, "Who's Getting Clipped," *Forbes,* November 5, 1984.

80. Greg Burks, "Even the Model Costs $50,000," *Forbes,* October 23, 1989. Another *Forbes* article reported that the yacht was 289 feet; Katherine, Weisman, "A Superyacht of One's Own," *Forbes,* October 22, 1990.

81. Frank Lynn, "Big Donors to Top City Officials Named," *New York Times,* December 23, 1986.

82. Property Record for Mar-a-Lago, December 5, 1985, Palm Beach County, Florida.

83. Graham Button, "43rd Annual Report on American Industry," *Forbes,* January 7, 1991.

84. Allan Sloan, "You Can't Win Them All," *Forbes,* December 26, 1988.

85. Blair, *The Trumps,* 148.

86. Richard L. Stern and John Connolly, "Manhattan's Favorite Guessing Game—How Rich Is Donald Trump?," *Forbes,* May 14, 1990.

87. Dan Alexander, "Vintage Trump Ads Say a Lot About the President," *Forbes,* September 28, 2017, www.forbes.com/sites/danalexander/2017/09/19/trump-vintage-old-ads-advertisement -forbes-president-donald.

88. State of New Jersey Casino Control Commission, hearing on the petition of Trump Plaza Associates, Trump's Castle Associates, Trump Taj Mahal Associates, and Trump Management Corporation, August 16, 1990, 16, 36, 42, 47, 57.

89. David Barstow, Suzanne Craig, and Russ Buettner, "Trump Engaged in Suspect Tax Schemes as He Reaped Riches from His Father," *New York Times,* October, 2, 2018, https://www.nytimes.com/interactive/2018/10/02/us/politics/donald-trump-tax-schemes -fred-trump.html.

90. State of New Jersey Department of Law and Public Safety, Division of Gaming Enforcement, Complainant vs. Trump's Castle Associate, Limited Partnership, d/b/a, Trump Casino Resort by the Bay, April 3, 1991, 4, www.washingtonpost.com/wp-stat/graphics/politics/trump-archive/docs/stipulation-castle-fred-trump.pdf.

91. State of New Jersey Casino Control Commission, Public Meeting 91-20, June 26, 1991, 21.

92. Barstow, Craig, and Buettner, "Trump Engaged in Suspect Tax Schemes."

93. Laura Jereski and Jason Zweig, "Step Right Up, Folks," *Forbes,* March 4, 1991.

94. Matthew Schifrin and Jason Zweig, "Dr. Feelgood," *Forbes,* March 4, 1991.

95. Trump Hotels & Casino Resorts, Form 10-K, 1995, 38, sec.gov/archives/edgar/data/943320/0000950130-96-000986.txt.

96. "Watch Donald Trump's 1995 DJT IPO And Eventual Bankruptcy," CNBC, November 30, 2018, https://www.youtube.com/watch?v=1rsXb6p_jdA.

97. Trump Hotels & Casino Resorts, Form 10-K, 1995, 43.

98. Trump Hotels & Casino Resorts, Form 10-K, 1995, 43.

99. Trump Hotels & Casino Resorts, Form S-1, Feb. 2, 1996, 5-6, sec.gov/archives/edgar/data/943320/0000950130-96-000349.txt.

100. Trump Hotels & Casino Resorts Inc., Form 10-K, Securities and Exchange Commission, March 28, 1997, 1, F-9, www.sec.gov/Archives/edgar/data/943320/0000940180-97-000299.txt.

101. Analysis of Trump Hotels & Casino Resorts Inc., Form 10-K, Securities and Exchange Commission, March 28, 1997, 69, F-9.

102. Trump Hotels & Casino Resorts Inc., Form 8-K, Securities and Exchange Commission, June 26, 1996, 3, www.sec.gov/Archives/edgar/data/943320/0000940180-97-000299.txt.

103. Riva Atlas, "Greedy, Greedy," *Forbes,* August 26, 1996.

104. Trump Hotels & Casino Resorts Inc., Form 10-K, Securities and Exchange Commission, March 28, 1997, 15.

105. Trump Hotels & Casino Resorts Inc., Form 10-K, Securities and Exchange Commission, March 27, 1996, 101, www.sec.gov/Archives/edgar/data/943320/0000950130-96-000986.txt; Trump Hotels & Casino Resorts Inc., Form 10-K, Securities and Exchange Commission, March 28, 1997, 12, 16, 72.

106. Atlas, "Greedy, Greedy."

107. Trump Hotels & Casino Resorts Inc., Form 10-K, Securities and Exchange Commission, March 31, 1998, F-4, www.sec.gov/Archives/edgar/data/943320/0001047469-98-012801.txt.

108. Trump Hotels & Casino Resorts Holdings LP, Form 10-K, Securities and Exchange Commission, March 28, 1997, 64.

109. Trump Hotels & Casino Resorts Inc., Form 10-K, Securities and Exchange Commission, March 28, 1997, F-28.

110. Analysis of documents: Trump Hotels & Casino Resorts Inc., Form 10-Ks, Securities and Exchange Commission, March 28, 1997, 64; March 30, 2000, 59; March 19, 2003, 55; March 31, 2005, 58.

111. Analysis of documents: Trump Hotels & Casino Resorts Inc., Form 10-Ks, Securities and Exchange Commission, March 31, 1998, 66; March 30, 2000, 59, www.sec.gov/Archives/edgar/data/943322/000095013000001801/0000950130-00-001801.txt; March 31, 2001, 56, www.sec.gov/Archives/edgar/data/943322/000095013001500465/d10k405.txt; March 29, 2002, 59–60, www.sec.gov/Archives/edgar/data/943322/000095013002002305/d10k405.txt; March 19, 2003, 55-56, www.sec.gov/Archives/edgar/data/943322/000095013003002754/d10k.htm; March 30, 2004, F-23, www.sec.gov/Archives/edgar/data/943320/000119312504053673/d10k.htm; March 31, 2005, F-30, www.sec.gov/Archives/edgar/data/943320/000119312505067289/d10k.htm.

112. Analysis of annual reports.
113. Trump Hotels & Casino Resorts Inc., Form 10-K, Securities and Exchange Commission, March 31, 1999, 49, www.sec.gov/Archives/edgar/data/943322/0000950110-99-000449.txt.
114. Trump Hotels & Casino Resorts Inc., Form 10-K, Securities and Exchange Commission, March 27, 1996, 99, 46, 93.
115. Trump Hotels & Casino Resorts Inc., Form 10-K, Securities and Exchange Commission, March 30, 2000, 1, 8, 63, 52.
116. Analysis of Trump Hotels & Casino Resorts Inc., Form 10-Ks.
117. Trump Hotels & Casino Resorts Inc., Form 10-K, Securities and Exchange Commission, March 31, 2005, 2.
118. Trump Hotels & Casino Resorts Holdings, Form 10-Ks, Securities and Exchange Commission, March 28, 1997, 56; March 27, 1996, 88.
119. Trump Hotels & Casino Resorts Holdings, Form 10-K, Securities and Exchange Commission, March 28, 1997, 58, 71, 56.
120. Trump Hotels & Casino Resorts Inc., Form 10-K, Securities and Exchange Commission, March 29, 2002, 35; "Donald Trump," in "The Forbes 400," *Forbes,* October 14, 1996; "Forbes 400 Richest in America," *Forbes,* September 2001.
121. Trump Hotels & Casino Resorts Inc., Form 10-K, Securities and Exchange Commission, March 29, 2002, 35, 57.
122. Police Athletic League, "Programs," www.palnyc.org/programs-overview.
123. Police Athletic League, Inc., Form 990, Department of the Treasury, Internal Revenue Service, 2001, 28.
124. The Donald J. Trump Foundation, Form 990, U.S. Department of the Treasury, Internal Revenue Service, 2001, 19.
125. Analysis of the Donald J. Trump Foundation, Form 990s, 2001–2016.
126. David A. Fahrenthold, "Trump Boasts About His Philanthropy but His Giving Falls Short of His Words," *Washington Post,* October 29, 2016, www.washingtonpost.com/politics/trump-boasts-of-his-philanthropy-but-his-giving-falls-short-of-his-words/2016/10/29/b3c03106-9ac7-11e6-a0ed-ab0774c1eaa5_story.html.
127. David A. Fahrenthold, "Trump Pays IRS a Penalty for His Foundation Violating Rules with Gift to Aid Florida Attorney General," *Washington Post,* September 1, 2016, www.washingtonpost.com/news/post-politics/wp/2016/09/01/trump-pays-irs-a-penalty-for-his-foundation-violating-rules-with-gift-to-florida-attorney-general/.
128. Dan Alexander, "How Donald Trump Shifted Kids-Cancer Charity Money Into His Business," *Forbes,* June 6, 2017, forbes.com/sites/danalexander/2017/06/06/how-donald-trump-shifted-kids-cancer-money-into-his-business; Fahrenthold, "Trump Boasts About His Philanthropy."
129. Analysis of Donald J. Trump Foundation, Form 990s.
130. Barstow, Craig, and Buettner, "Trump Engaged in Suspect Tax Schemes."
131. Analysis of S&P 500; Barstow, Craig, and Buettner, "Trump Engaged in Suspect Tax Schemes."
132. Alexander, "Trump's Net Worth Drops $1 Billion."
133. Timothy L. O'Brien, "What's He Really Worth?," *New York Times,* October 23, 2005, www.nytimes.com/2005/10/23/business/yourmoney/whats-he-really-worth.html.
134. Dan Alexander and Chase Peterson-Withorn, "Trump's Secret Windfall: The Crown Jewels of His Fortune Are 2 Skyscrapers He Didn't Want—And Doesn't Control," *Forbes,* March 7, 2019, www.forbes.com/sites/danalexander/2019/03/07/trumps-secret-windfall-the-crown-jewels-of-his-fortune-are-2-skyscrapers-he-didnt-wantand-doesnt-control/#213f1f9122e5; Alexander, "Trump's Net Worth Drops $1 Billion."

135. "Donald Trump Presidential Campaign Announcement," June 16, 2015, www.c-span.org
     /video/?326473-1/donald-trump-presidential-campaign-announcement.

CHAPTER TWO: MOSCOW MONEY

1. Stephen Battaglio, "14 Million Viewers for Republican Presidential Debate a Record for
   CNBC," October 29, 2015, www.latimes.com/entertainment/envelope/cotown/la-et-ct
   -ratings-debate-cnbc-20151029-story.html.
2. Third Republican Primary Debate, October 28, 2015, www.youtube.com/watch?v=wp
   COloV3DZk&feature=youtu.be&t=2452.
3. Letter of Intent, I.C. Expert Investment Company, Trump Acquisition, LLC, *BuzzFeed,*
   October 28, 2015, 162, www.documentcloud.org/documents/5719169-Trump-Moscow
   .html#document/p163.
4. Anna Shepeleva, telephone interview with author, March 26, 2019.
5. Letter of Intent, I.C. Expert Investment Company.
6. Donald Trump and Tony Schwartz, *Trump: The Art of the Deal* (New York: Random
   House, 1987), 27.
7. Deposition of Donald Trump, Superior Court of New Jersey, Law Division, Camden
   County, Donald J. Trump v. Timothy L. O'Brien, Time Warner Book Group Inc. and
   Warner Books Inc., December 19, 2007.
8. Dan Alexander and Richard Behar, "The Truth Behind Trump Tower Moscow: How
   The President Risked Everything for a (Relatively) Tiny Deal," *Forbes,* May 23, 2019,
   www.forbes.com/sites/danalexander/2019/05/23/the-truth-behind-trump-moscow-how
   -the-president-risked-everything-for-a-relatively-tiny-deal/#6b7e8610bc32.
9. Robert S. Mueller, *Report on the Investigation into Russian Interference in the 2016 Presidential Election,* March 2019, 119, www.justice.gov/storage/report.pdf (hereafter "Mueller
   report").
10. Tom Hamburger, Rosalind S. Helderman, and Michael Birnbaum, "Inside Trump's Fi-
    nancial Ties to Russia and His Unusual Flattery of Vladimir Putin," *Washington Post,*
    June 17, 2016, www.washingtonpost.com/politics/inside-trumps-financial-ties-to-russia
    -and-his-unusual-flattery-of-vladimir-putin/2016/06/17/dbdcaac8-31a6-11e6-8ff7
    -7b6c1998b7a0_story.html.
11. Alexander and Behar, "The Truth Behind Trump Tower Moscow."
12. Donald Trump, Twitter, November 11, 2013, twitter.com/realDonaldTrump/status/3999
    39505924628480.
13. Mueller report.
14. Alexander and Behar, "The Truth Behind Trump Tower Moscow."
15. Analysis of Knight Frank research, Moscow Residential Real Estate Market, 2; Letter of
    Intent, I.C. Expert Investment Company, 6.
16. Yulia Parado, email to author, May 21, 2019.
17. Emin Agalarov, email to author, May 16, 2019.
18. Mueller report.
19. Emin Agalarov email.
20. Alan Cullison, "Ukrainians Flock to See Yanukovych's Mansion," *Wall Street Journal,*
    www.wsj.com/articles/ukrainians-flock-to-see-yanukovychs-mansion-1393107191.
21. United States District Court for the District of Columbia, United States v. Paul Manafort
    Jr., Criminal No. 17-201-1 (ABJ)(S-5), Violations: 18 U.S.C. § 371, 1–23.
22. Agence France-Presse, "Vladimir Putin describes secret meeting when Russia decided
    to seize Crimea," March 9, 2015, theguardian.com/world/2015/mar/09/vladimir-putin

-describes-secret-meeting-when-russia-decided-to-seize-crimea; "Putin Says Plan to Take Crimea Hatched Before Referendum," Reuters, March 9, 2015, www.reuters.com/article /us-ukraine-crisis-putin-crimea/putin-says-plan-to-take-crimea-hatched-before -referendum-idUSKBN0M51DG20150309.

23. Charge d'Affaires Harry R. Kamian, "Russia's Continued Illegal Occupation of Crimea," March 1, 2018, ru.embassy.gov/russias-continued-illlegal-occupation-crimea/; Alison Smale and Steven Erlanger, "Ukraine Mobilizes Reserve Troops, Threatens War," *New York Times,* March 1, 2014, www.nytimes.com/2014/03/02/world/europe/ukraine .html.

24. Congressional Research Service, "Ukraine: Background, Conflict with Russia, and U.S. Policy," April 29, 2020, fas.org/sgp/crs/row/R45008.pdf.

25. "Joint Statement on Crimea by President of the European Council Herman Van Rompuy and President of the European Commission José Manuel Barroso," March 16, 2014, www .consilium.europa.eu/uedocs/cms_Data/docs/pressdata/en/ec/141566.pdf.

26. "EU Meeting on Ukraine: David Cameron's Speech," March 6, 2014, www.gov.uk/gov ernment/speeches/eu-meeting-on-ukraine-david-camerons-speech.

27. "Remarks to the Press by Vice President Joe Biden with Prime Minister Donald Tusk of Poland," March 18, 2014, obamawhitehouse.archives.gov/the-press-office/2014/03/18 /remarks-press-vice-president-joe-biden-prime-minister-donald-tusk-poland.

28. "President Obama Announces New Ukraine-Related Sanctions," March 17, 2014, obama whitehouse.archives.gov/blog/2014/03/17/president-obama-announces-new-ukraine -related-sanctions.

29. "Treasury Sanctions Russian Officials, Members of the Russian Leadership's Inner Cir-cle, and an Entity for Involvement in the Situation in Ukraine," U.S. Department of the Treasury, March 20, 2014, www.treasury.gov/press-center/press-releases/Pages/jl23331 .aspx.

30. Phyllis Berman and Lea Goldman, "Cracked De Beers," *Forbes,* September 15, 2003.

31. Katya Soldak, "Crimean Punishment," *Forbes,* April 14, 2014.

32. Analysis of residential real estate data from Federal Statistic Services, 2019.

33. Emin Agalarov, email to author, May 16, 2019.

34. Analysis of New York City property records.

35. "Conversation with Donald Trump," C-SPAN, December 15, 2014, www.c-span.org /video/?323309-1/conversation-donald-trump.

36. Mueller report, 12.

37. United States District Court for the District of Columbia, United States of America v. Internet Research Agency LLC, Criminal No. (18 U.S.C. §§ 2, 371, 1349, 1028A), Feb-ruary 16, 2018, 13 (hereafter "USA v. Internet Research Agency").

38. Mueller report, 33.

39. *USA v. Internet Research Agency,* 17.

40. *USA v. Internet Research Agency,* 5.

41. Mueller report, 34, 26.

42. Mueller report, 42, 41, 42.

43. Alexander and Behar, "The Truth Behind Trump Tower Moscow."

44. Dan Alexander, "Exclusive Investigation: Inside the Wild Plan to Create a Fake Trump Tower," *Forbes,* August 1, 2017, www.forbes.com/sites/danalexander/2017/08/01/exclu sive-investigation-inside-the-wild-plan-to-create-a-fake-trump-tower/#7712c6ba547d.

45. Mueller report, 78.

46. Giorgi Rtskhiladze, email to author, January 31, 2017; Giorgi Rtskhiladze, interviewed by author, May 15, 2019.

47. Mueller report, 78.

48. Giorgi Rtskhiladze, interviewed by author, May 15, 2019.

49. Mueller report, 78.

50. Alexander and Behar, "The Truth Behind Trump Tower Moscow."

51. United States District Court, Eastern District of New York, United States of America Against Felix Sater, Cr. No. 98-1101, 7, 10, 11.

52. Alexander and Behar, "The Truth Behind Trump Tower Moscow."

53. *Hearing with Michael Cohen, Former Attorney to President Donald Trump, Before the House Committee on Oversight and Reform,* 116th Cong., First Session, February 27, 2019, Serial No. 116–03, 108, docs.house.gov/meetings/GO/GO00/20190227/108969/HHRG -116-GO00-20190227-SD003.pdf.

54. Felix Sater, telephone interview with author, April 24, 2019.

55. Phil Ruffin, telephone interview with author, February 8, 2017.

56. Donald Trump and Allen Weisselberg, interviewed by Randall Lane, Chase Peterson-Withorn, and Kerry Dolan, September 21, 2015,

57. Letter of Intent, I.C. Expert Investment Company, 37, 44–45.

58. Analysis of Knight Frank research, Moscow Residential Real Estate Market, 44–45.

59. Analysis of Letter of Intent, I.C. Expert Investment Company, 196; Felix Sater, telephone interview with author, April 24, 2019.

60. "User Clip: Michael Cohen testifies before House Oversight Cmte," C-SPAN, March 2, 2019, https://www.c-span.org/video/?c4783868/user-clip-michael-cohen-testifies-house -oversight-cmte.

61. Felix Sater, telephone interview with author, April 24, 2019.

62. Emails between Felix Sater and Michael Cohen, *BuzzFeed,* October 28, 2015, 67, www .documentcloud.org/documents/5719169-Trump-Moscow.html#document/p67.

63. Public Library of U.S. Diplomacy, Cable, "Bio Note: Yuri Molchanov, St. Petersburg Vice Governor for Property and Land Issues, Investments, Strategic Projects and for Liaison with Such Organizations," February 5, 2007, https://wikileaks.org/plusd/cables/07MOSCO W468_a.html.

64. "#556 Andrei Molchanov," *Forbes,* March 10, 2010, www.forbes.com/lists/2010/10/bil lionaires-2010_Andrei-Molchanov_5ZJC.html.

65. LSR Group, Corporate Governance, Board of Directors, Andrey Mochanov, www.lsr group.ru/en/about-us/corporate-governance/board-of-directors/andrey-molchanov.

66. Vladimir Putin biography, Kremlin, putin.kremlin.ru/bio/page-3.

67. LSR Group Annual Report 2008, 16, 17, 61.

68. "#1867 Andrei Molchanov," *Forbes,* March, 6, 2018, www.forbes.com/profile/andrei -molchanov/#28edb66938b6.

69. Emails between Felix Sater and Michael Cohen, 69.

70. "Ukraine-Related Sanctions," U.S. Department of the Treasury, September 12, 2014, www.treasury.gov/resource-center/sanctions/ofac-enforcement/pages/20140912.aspx.

71. Felix Sater, telephone interview with author, May 15, 2019.

72. Molly Woodward, email to author and Richard Behar, May 23, 2019.

73. Alexander and Behar, "The Truth Behind Trump Tower Moscow."

74. Felix Sater, telephone interview with author, April 24, 2019.

75. Andrey Rozov to Michael Cohen, *BuzzFeed,* October 28, 2015, 18, www.document cloud.org/documents/5719169-Trump-Moscow.html#document/p18.

76. Alexander and Behar, "The Truth Behind Trump Tower Moscow."

77. "Treasury Sanctions Russian Officials."

78. Alexander and Behar, "The Truth Behind Trump Tower Moscow."

79. From "November 3, 2015" to here is from: Emails between Felix Sater and Michael Cohen, 202.

80. Michael Cohen hearing, House Oversight Committee, 109.

81. Felix Sater, telephone interview with author, May 15, 2019.

82. Michael Cohen hearing, House Oversight Committee.

83. Text messages between Felix Sater and Michael Cohen, 223.

84. This and preceding three paragraphs: Text messages between Felix Sater and Michael Cohen, 230–35.

85. Bank of Russia, "On Measures to Enhance Financial Stability of JSC GenBank," press release, August 10, 2017.

86. "Treasury Sanctions Russian Officials."

87. This and preceding five paragraphs: Text messages between Felix Sater and Michael Cohen, 237–41.

88. This and preceding two paragraphs: Mueller report, 81–83, 348.

89. This and preceding six paragraphs: Text messages between Felix Sater and Michael Cohen, 242–67.

90. Felix Sater, telephone interview with author, May 15, 2019.

91. Mueller report, 86.

92. Alexander and Behar, "The Truth Behind Trump Tower Moscow."

93. This and preceding paragraph: Mueller report, 121, 118.

94. "Watch Live: Former Trump Lawyer Michael Cohen Testifies Before the House Oversight Committee," February, 27, 2019, www.youtube.com/watch?v=_lmOUXYLHzw&t=1h17m13s.

95. This and preceding three paragraphs: Mueller report, 118–26.

96. "Republican Primary Debate," YouTube, March 10, 2016, www.youtube.com/watch?v=h2nj-zCV-XM&feature=youtu.be&t=5196.

97. Ali Vitali, "Donald Trump: There's No Proof Putin Killed Journalists," NBC News, www.nbcnews.com/politics/2016-election/donald-trump-says-there-s-no-proof-putin-killed-journalists-n483451.

98. "Presidential Candidate Donald Trump Rally in Madison, Alabama," C-SPAN, February 28, 2016, www.c-span.org/video/?405393-1/donald-trump-campaign-rally-huntsville-alabama&transcriptQuery=putin&start=1774.

99. Mueller report, 133–35.

100. Ellen Nakashima, "Russian Government Hackers Penetrated DNC, Stole Opposition Research on Trump," *Washington Post,* June 14, 2016, www.washingtonpost.com/world/national-security/russian-government-hackers-penetrated-dnc-stole-opposition-research-on-trump/2016/06/14/cf006cb4-316e-11e6-8ff7-7b6c1998b7a0_story.html; David E. Sanger, and Nick Corasaniti, "D.N.C. Says Russian Hackers Penetrated Its Files, Including Dossier on Donald Trump," *New York Times,* June 14, 2016, www.nytimes.com/2016/06/15/us/politics/russian-hackers-dnc-trump.html.

101. WikiLeaks, wikileaks.org/dnc-emails/.

102. Wikileaks, "Re: Debbie . . . please approve . . . team thinks this is the right approach . . .'High Road'," May 21, 2016, wikileaks.com/dnc-emails/emailid/7883; Wikileaks, "Re: Sanders: If I'm elected, DNC leader would be out," May 21, 2016, wikileaks.com/dnc-emails/emailid/9999.

103. DNC, "Statement From DNC Chair On Presiding Convention and Concluding Tenure," July 24, 2016, static.politico.com/f4/45/f8fb7eb6449da7c79f1bb3a64303/untitled.pdf.

104. "Donald Trump News Conference," C-SPAN, July 27, 2016, www.c-span.org/video/?413263-1/donald-trump-urges-russia-find-hillary-clinton-emails-criticizes-record-tpp.

105. Mueller report, 57.
106. "Watch: Donald Trump Recorded Having Extremely Lewd Conversation About Women in 2005," *Washington Post,* October 7, 2016, www.washingtonpost.com/video/national /watch-donald-trump-recorded-having-extremely-lewd-conversation-about-women -in-2005/2016/10/07/3bf16d1e-8caf-11e6-8cdc-4fbb1973b506_video.html.
107. Jane Mayer, "The Danger of President Pence," *New Yorker,* October 16, 2017, www .newyorker.com/magazine/2017/10/23/the-danger-of-president-pence.
108. This and preceding two paragraphs: Mueller report, 15, 56, 239–40, 78; Wikileaks, "HRC Paid Speeches," January 25, 2016, wikileaks.org/podesta-emails/emailid/927; Wikileaks, "Re: From time to time I get the questions in advance," March 12, 2016, wikileaks.org/podesta-emails/emailid/57027; CNN, "Full Rush Transcript Hillary Clinton Part//CNN TV One Democratic Presidential Town Hall, March 13, 2016, cnnpressroom.blogs.cnn.com/2016/03/13/full-rush-transcript-hillary-clinton-partcnn -tv-one-democratic-presidential-town-hall/; Donna Brazile, "Donna Brazile: Russian DNC Narrative Played Out Exactly As They Hoped," *TIME,* March 17, 2017, time. com/4705515/donna-brazile-russia-emails-clinton/; Text messages from Giorgi Rtskh-iladze to Michael Cohen obtained by author.
109. Preceding two paragraphs: Mueller report, 157, 153.
110. "Statement by the President on Actions in Response to Russian Malicious Cyber Activity and Harassment," December 29, 2016, obamawhitehouse.archives.gov/the-press-office /2016/12/29/statement-president-actions-response-russian-malicious-cyber-activity.
111. Mueller report, 177.
112. United States District Court for the District of Columbia, United States of America v. Michael T. Flynn, Violation: 18 U.S.C. § 1001 (False Statements), December 1, 2017, 3, www.justice.gov/file/1015126/download.
113. Mueller report, 179.
114. *United States of America v. Michael T. Flynn*, 3.
115. Mueller report, 180.
116. Donald J. Trump, Twitter, December 30, 2016, twitter.com/realdonaldtrump/status /814919370711461890.
117. David Ignatius, "Why Did Obama Dawdle on Russia's Hacking?," *Washington Post,* January 12, 2017, www.washingtonpost.com/opinions/why-did-obama-dawdle-on-russias-hacking /2017/01/12/75f878a0-d90c-11e6-9a36-1d296534b31e_story.html.
118. This and previous paragraph: Mueller report, 214–50.
119. United States v. Michael T. Flynn, 2017, Doc. No. 3, United States District Court, District of Columbia; United States v. Michael T. Flynn, 2017, Doc. No. 1, United States District Court, District of Columbia; United States v. Michael T. Flynn, 2017, Doc. No. 4, United States District Court, District of Columbia.
120. United States v. Michael T. Flynn, 2017, Doc. 151, United States District Court, District of Columbia.
121. Dan Alexander, "Why the Next Big Trump Project Could Be a Las Vegas Casino," *Forbes,* March 20, 2017, www.forbes.com/sites/danalexander/2017/03/20/conflict-conflicts -of-interest-emoluments-clause-trump-ruffin-phil-russia-treasury-profits-hotel-las-vegas -casino/#7ab7e92c79b1.
122. Phil Ruffin, interviewed by author, February 15, 2017.
123. "Russian Election Interference," C-SPAN, March 20, 2017, www.c-span.org/video/?425087 -1/fbi-director-investigating-links-trump-campaign-russia.
124. "FBI Oversight," C-SPAN, May 3, 2017, www.c-span.org/video/?427708-1/fbi-director -defends-decision-reveal-clinton-email-probe-election.
125. Mueller report, 276–77.

126. "James Comey's Interview with ABC News Chief Anchor George Stephanopoulos," ABC News, April 16, 2018, abcnews.go.com/Site/transcript-james-comeys-interview-abc-news -chief-anchor/story?id=54488723.

127. Mueller report, 283.

128. This and preceding two paragraphs: Mueller report, 290.

CHAPTER THREE: THE TAKEOVER

1. "Watch Live: Donald Trump Holds His First Press Conference as President-Elect," CBS News, YouTube, January 11, 2017, www.youtube.com/watch?v=0l4bQYZcaQk.

2. Ken Bensinger, Miriam Elder, and Mark Schoofs, "These Reports Allege Trump Has Deep Ties to Russia," *BuzzFeed*, January 10, 2017, www.buzzfeednews.com/article/ken bensinger/these-reports-allege-trump-has-deep-ties-to-russia.

3. "Watch Live: Donald Trump Holds His First Press Conference as President-Elect."

4. "Russia/U.S. Presidential Election: Further Details of Trump Lawyer Cohen's Secret Liaison with the Kremlin," *BuzzFeed*, 18, www.documentcloud.org/documents/3259984 -Trump-Intelligence-Allegations.html.

5. Robert S. Mueller, *Report on the Investigation into Russian Interference in the 2016 Presidential Election*, March 2019, 139, www.justice.gov/storage/report.pdf.

6. "U.S. Presidential Election: Republican Candidate Donald Trump's Activities in Russia and Compromising Relationship with the Kremlin," *BuzzFeed*, 2, www.documentcloud .org/documents/3259984-Trump-Intelligence-Allegations.html.

7. "Watch Live: Donald Trump Holds His First Press Conference as President-Elect."

8. Donald Trump, Twitter, November 30, 2016, twitter.com/realDonaldTrump/status/803 926488579973120, twitter.com/realDonaldTrump/status/803927774784344064, twitter .com/realDonaldTrump/status/803930240661811200, twitter.com/realDonaldTrump/sta tus/803931490514075648.

9. Donald Trump, OGE Form 278e, U.S. Office of Government Ethics, 5 C.F.R. part 2634 (hereafter "Donald Trump, OGE Form 278e"), May 15, 2019, 41; Deutsche Bank Annual Report 2019, 16, www.db.com/ir/en/download/Deutsche_Bank_Annual_Report_2019 .pdf; Investors Bancorp Inc., Form 10-K, Securities and Exchange Commission, December 31, 20191-2, https://www.sec.gov/ix?doc=/Archives/edgar/data/1594012/000159401 220000013/isbc-12312019x10k.htm.

10. Analysis of USAspending.gov and property records.

11. Analysis of Prospectus Supplement, Wells Fargo Commercial Mortgage Trust 2012-LC5, Securities and Exchange Commission, July 20, 2012, A 3-33, www.sec.gov/Archives /edgar/data/850779/000153949712000571/prospectus-supplement.htm; Industrial and Commercial Bank of China Limited, Annual Report 2018, 77, v.icbc.com.cn/userfiles /Resources/ICBCLTD/download/2019/2018AnnualReport20190425.pdf; analysis of property records, Bank of India Annual Report 2018–2019, 63.

12. "GSA and Trump Organization Reach Deal on Old Post Office Lease, U.S. General Services Administration," June 5, 2013, www.gsa.gov/about-us/newsroom/news-releases /gsa-and-trump-organization-reach-deal-on-old-post-office-lease; Leased Facility Inventory Report, U.S. Postal Service, January 25, 2018; Freddie Mac Structured Pass-Through Certificates (SPCs), Series K-SCT, February 25, 2010, 79; Donald Trump, OGE Form 278e, May 15, 2018, 22.

13. Government-Wide Ethics Laws Conflicts of Interest, 18 U.S.C. § 208, www.govinfo.gov /content/pkg/USCODE-2012-title18/pdf/USCODE-2012-title18-partI-chap11-sec208.pdf.

14. National Park Service, "Jimmy Carter," 2, nps.gov/jica/planyourvisit/upload/peanut-bro chure-2018-508.pdf.

15. Edward T. Pound, "Reagan's worth put at $4 million," *The New York Times*, February 23, 1981, nytimes.com/1981/02/23/us/reagan-s-worth-put-at-4-million.html; Stephen Labaton, "Most of the Clintons' Wealth Held by Mrs. Clinton, Disclosure Form Shows," *The New York Times*, May 18, 1994, nytimes.com/1994/05/18/us/most-of-clintons-wealth-held-by-mrs-clinton-disclosure-form-shows.html; Public Papers of the Presidents of the United States: George H. W. Bush, "Statement by Press Secretary Fitzwater on the President's Federal Income Tax Return," April, 15, 1991, govinfo.gov/content/pkg/ppp-1991-book1/html/ppp-1991-book1-doc-pg371-2.htm; "Press Briefing by Ari Fleischer," August 22, 2001, georgewbush-whitehouse.archives.gov/news/briefings/text/20010822.html.

16. Barack Obama, OGE Form 278e, U.S. Office of Government Ethics, 5 C.F.R. part 2634, May 4. 2014, 3.

17. U.S. Constitution, art. I, § 9, cl. 8, Senate.gov, www.senate.gov/civics/constitution_item/constitution.htm#a1_sec9.

18. In the United States District Court for the Southern District of New York, Citizens for Responsibility and Ethics in Washington, Plaintiff, v. Donald J. Trump, in his official capacity as President of the United States of America, Defendant, January 23, 2017.

19. President-Elect Donald Trump news conference, C-SPAN, January 11, 2017, www.c-span.org/video/?421482-1/president-elect-donald-trump-election-year-hacking-i-russia.

20. "Watch Live: Donald Trump Holds His First Press Conference as President-Elect."

21. Walter Shaub, interviewed by author, May 15, 2020.

22. Walter Shaub, "OGE Director Walter Shaub Asks Trump to Do More to Resolve Conflicts of Interest," YouTube, January 11, 2017, www.youtube.com/watch?v=R58fJ7Eetbg.

23. "Watch Live: Donald Trump Holds First Press Conference as President-Elect."

24. Alexander Hamilton, *Federalist* no. 75, www.congress.gov/resources/display/content/The+Federalist+Papers#TheFederalistPapers-75.

25. Zephyr Teachout, *Corruption in America* (Cambridge, MA: Harvard University Press, 2014), 1.

26. Articles of Confederation, from "A Century of Lawmaking for a New Nation: U.S. Congressional Documents and Debates, 1774–1875, Statutes at Large," memory.loc.gov/cgi-bin/ampage?collId=llsl&fileName=001/llsl001.db&recNum=127.

27. Teachout, *Corruption in America*, 26.

28. U.S. Constitution, art. I, § 9, National Archives, https://www.archives.gov/founding-docs/constitution-transcript#toc-section-9.

29. Teachout, *Corruption in America*, 28–29; William Short to Thomas Jefferson, May 2, 1791, National Archives, Founders Online, https://founders.archives.gov/documents/Jefferson/01-20-02-0103#TSJN-01-20-0139-fn-0001.

30. "Thomas Jefferson: A Revolutionary World," Library of Congress, www.loc.gov/exhibits/jefferson/jeffworld.html.

31. "From Thomas Jefferson to John Adams, September 4, 1823," National Archives, Founders Online, https://founders.archives.gov/documents/Jefferson/98-01-02-3737.

32. Daniel Feller, "Andrew Jackson: Domestic Affairs," University of Virginia Miller Center, millercenter.org/president/jackson/domestic-affairs.

33. *Encyclopedia Britannica*, s.v. "Spoils System," www.britannica.com/topic/spoils-system.

34. R. Albion Taylor, *Federal Employment under the Merit System* (Washington, D.C.: United States Civil Service Commission, 1940), 80–81.

35. K. D. Ackerman, *Dark Horse: The Surprise Election and Political Murder of James A. Garfield* (New York: Carroll & Graf Publishers, 2003), 376, http://archives.org/details/darkhorseupris00acke/page/376/mode/2up.

36. Jay Bellamy, "A Stalwart of Stalwarts," *Prologue Magazine* 48, no. 3 (Fall 2016), www.archives.gov/publications/prologue/2016/fall/guiteau.

37. Ackerman, *Dark Horse*, 376; Jay Bellamy, "A Stalwart of Stalwarts," *Prologue Magazine* 48, no. 3 (Fall 2016), www.archives.gov/publications/prologue/2016/fall/guiteau.

38. "Chester A. Arthur," White House, http://www.whitehouse.gov/about-the-white-house /presidents/chester-a-arthur/.

39. Richard White, *The Republic for Which It Stands: The United States During Reconstruction and the Gilded Age, 1865–1896* (New York: Oxford University Press, 2017), 467.

40. William T. Horner, *Ohio's Kingmaker: Mark Hanna, Man and Myth* (Athens: Ohio University Press, 2010), 186–87.

41. Quentin R. Skrabec, *Henry Clay Frick: The Life of the Perfect Capitalist* (Jefferson, NC: McFarland & Co., 2010), 159.

42. Lewis L. Gould, "William McKinley: Campaigns and Elections," University of Virginia Miller Center, millercenter.org/president/mckinley/campaigns-and-elections.

43. Jacob S. Hacker and Paul Pierson, *Winner-Take-All Politics: How Washington Made the Rich Richer and Turned Its Back on the Middle Class* (New York: Simon & Schuster, 2010), 171.

44. The American Presidency Project, Statistics, Data Archive Elections, 1986, www.presi dency.ucsb.edu/statistics/elections/1896.

45. "How the Fight Was Won," *New York Times,* November 11, 1896, timesmachine.ny times.com/timesmachine/1896/11/11/108261619.html.

46. "Timeline," Theodore Roosevelt Papers, Library of Congress, www.loc.gov/collections /theodore-roosevelt-papers/articles-and-essays/timeline/.

47. Nathan Miller *Theodore Roosevelt: A Life* (New York: William Morrow, 1992), 334–41.

48. Randall E. Adkins, *The Evolution of Political Parties, Campaigns, and Elections: Landmark Documents*, 1787–2007, (Washington, D.C.: CQ Press, 2008), 157–59.

49. "Appendix 4: The Federal Election Campaign Laws: A Short History," Federal Election Commission, transition.fec.gov/info/appfour.htm; P. Laider and M. Turek, *Basic Documents in Federal Campaign Finance Law* (Krakow, Poland: Jagiellonian University Press, 2015), 15–17.

50. "Papers Relating to the Foreign Relations of the United States, with the Annual Message of the President Transmitted to Congress, December 7, 1903," Office of the Historian, Foreign Service Institute, United States Department of State, http://history.state.gov/his toricaldocuments/frus1903/message-of-the-president.

51. Teachout, *Corruption in America*, 189.

52. Federal Election Commission, "Mission and History," www.fec.gov/about/mission-and -history/.

53. "Select Committee on Presidential Campaign Activities (The Watergate Committee)," A History of Notable Senate Investigations, United States Senate, https://www.senate.gov /artandhistory/history/common/investigations/Watergate.htm.

54. Memorandum for Richard T. Burgess, Office of the President, Re: Conflict of Interest Problems Arising out of the President's Nomination of Nelson A. Rockefeller to Be Vice President Under the Twenty-Fifth Amendment to the Constitution, fas.org/irp/agency /doj/olc/082874.pdf.

55. "Confirmation of Nelson A. Rockefeller as Vice President of the United States," December 17, 1974, Committee on the Judiciary, House of Representatives, United States, 24, https://ir.lawnet.fordham.edu/cgi/viewcontent.cgi?article=1013&context=twentyfifth _amendment_watergate_era; Jake Miller, "Conflicts of Interest: Donald Trump 2017 vs. Nelson Rockefeller 1974," *Face the Nation*, CBS, January 13, 2017, https://www.cbsnews .com/news/conflicts-of-interest-donald-trump-2017-vs-nelson-rockefeller-1974/.

56. "Nomination of Nelson A. Rockefeller of New York to Be Vice President of the United States: Hearings Before the Committee on Rules and Administration," United States Senate, Ninety-third Congress, Second Session, 1974, 19.

57. "Nomination of Nelson A. Rockefeller of New York to be Vice President of the United States," 48–57.

58. Linda Charlton, "Goldwater Now Undecided on Rockefeller Nomination," *New York Times,* October 25, 2019, www.nytimes.com/1974/10/25/archives/goldwater-now-undecided-on -rockefeller-nomination-goldwater-in.html.

59. "Nomination of Nelson A. Rockefeller," 58, 478, 510.

60. Mayer, *Dark Money,* 235.

61. This and preceding three paragraphs: Jane Mayer, *Dark Money: The Hidden History of the Billionaires Behind the Rise of the Radical Right* (New York: Anchor, 2016), 146, 231, 288–91, 234–37; Betsy DeVos, "Hard-Earned American Dollars That Big Brother Has Yet to Find a Way to Control," *Roll Call,* September 6, 1997; Ann Southworth, "Lawyers and the Conservative Counterrevolution," Law & Social Inquiry, *Journal of the American Bar Foundation* 43, no. 4 (Fall 2018): 1698–1728.

62. Citizens United v. Federal Election Commission, 558 US 310 (2010), November 14, 2008, www.oyez.org/cases/2008/08-205.

63. Supreme Court of the United States, Syllabus, Citizens United v. Federal Election Commission Appeal from the United States District Court for the District of Columbia No. 08–205, argued March 24, 2009, reargued September 9, 2009, decided January 21, 2010, transition.fec.gov/law/litigation/cu_sc08_opinion.pdf.

64. David D. Kirkpatrick, "A Quest to End Spending Rules for Campaigns," *New York Times,* January 25, 2010, www.nytimes.com/2010/01/25/us/politics/25bopp.html.

65. Mayer, *Dark Money,* 228.

66. "PAC Table 1," Federal Election Commission, https://transition.fec.gov/press/summaries /2012/tables/pac/PAC1_2012_24m.pdf.

67. Analysis of data from Center for Responsive Politics.

68. Bloomberg, Michael R., Candidate for President, ID: P00014530, Democratic Party, Financial Summary, Federal Election Commission, www.fec.gov/data/candidate/P00014530 /?cycle=2020&election_full=true.

69. Steyer, Tom, Candidate for President, ID: P00012716, Democratic Party, Financial Summary, Federal Election Commission, www.fec.gov/data/candidate/P00012716/.

70. "Part 2 of the CNN/NYT Democratic Presidential Debate," CNN, October 16, 2019, www.cnn.com/videos/politics/2019/10/16/part-2-cnn-nyt-democratic-presidential -debate-ohio-october-15-2019.cnn.

71. Analysis of data from Center for Responsive Politics; Steyer, Tom, Candidate for President, ID: P00012716, Democratic Party, Financial Summary.

72. Steven Bertoni, "Billionaire Sheldon Adelson Says He Might Give $100M to Newt Gingrich or Other Republican," February 21, 2012, www.forbes.com/sites/stevenbertoni /2012/02/21/billionaire-sheldon-adelson-says-he-might-give-100m-to-newt-gingrich -or-other-republican/#7349436e4400.

73. Analysis of data from Center for Responsive Politics.

74. "Donald Trump Presidential Campaign Announcement Full Speech (C-SPAN)," You-Tube, June 16, 2015, www.youtube.com/watch?v=apjNfkysjbM.

75. "Donald J. Trump, Inaugural Address," YouTube, January 20, 2017, www.youtube.com /watch?v=4GNWldTc8VU&feature=youtu.be.

76. Mattathias Schwartz and Lee Fang, "Spot the Billionaires Given Special Seats on Donald Trump's Inaugural Platform," *The Intercept,* January 21, 2017, theintercept.com/2017 /01/21/identify-trump-donors/.

77. Dan Alexander, Chase Peterson-Withorn, and Michaela Tindera, "The Definitive Net Worth of Donald Trump's Cabinet," July 25, 2019, www.forbes.com/sites/michelatin dera/2019/07/25/the-definitive-net-worth-of-donald-trumps-cabinet/#62df1cb76a15.

78. Alexander, Peterson-Withorn, and Tindera, "The Definitive Net Worth."

79. Richard L. Stern and John Connolly, "Manhattan's Favorite Guessing Game—How Rich Is Donald Trump?," *Forbes,* May 14, 1990; deed between RMB Partners Ltd. and Plaza Operating Partners Ltd., July 21, 1988.

80. Reports of Donations Accepted for Inaugural Committee, 58th Presidential Inauguration Committee, April 18, 2017, docquery.fec.gov/pdf/286/201704180300150286/2017041 80300150286.pdf#navpanes=0.

81. Richard Painter, telephone interview with author, August 2, 2019.

82. A representative for Joseph Craft did not respond to a request for comment. "Chairman Risch Opening Statement at Nomination Hearing for the Honorable Kelly Craft to Be the U.S. Ambassador to the United Nations," United States Senate, June 19, 2019, http:// www.foreign.senate.gov/press/chair/release/chairman-risch-opening-statement-at-nomi nation-hearing-for-the-honorable-kelly-craft-to-be-the-us-ambassador-to-the-united-na tions.

83. This and preceding paragraph: Reports of Donations Accepted for Inaugural Committee, 58th Presidential Inauguration Committee, 63, 41, 102.

84. Donald Trump, "Memorandum on Construction of the Dakota Access Pipeline," January 24, 2017, www.presidency.ucsb.edu/documents/memorandum-construction-the-dakota -access-pipeline.

85. Analysis of Energy Transfer Equity LP, Form 10-Ks, Securities and Exchange Commission, 2016 and 2017; analysis of stock price.

86. Reports of Donations Accepted for Inaugural Committee, 58th Presidential Inauguration Committee, 81, 153, 356.

87. Analysis of SEC documents; analysis of stock price. "I support Trump for the ideology he represents and not for personal reasons," Peterffy explained in an email, when asked about his donation. "I thought it was important that he start in the job with a great momentum." Representatives for Ricketts and Schwab did not answer questions about their donations. Kalen Holliday, email to author, May 11, 2020.

88. Dan Alexander, "Trump Nominee Ricketts and Family See Fortune Jump $700M Since Election," *Forbes,* January 18, 2017, www.forbes.com/sites/danalexander/2017/01/18/trump -nominee-ricketts-and-family-see-fortune-jump-700m-since-election/#5c667bd92286.

89. Analysis of Form 4, Statement of Changes in Beneficial Ownership, Securities and Exchange Commission, Schwab, Charles R., www.sec.gov/Archives/edgar/data/316709/000 122520816043577/xslF345X03/doc4.xml, www.sec.gov/Archives/edgar/data/316709/00 0122520816041427/xslF345X03/doc4.xml; analysis of stock price, Charles Schwab Corporation.

90. Rebecca Ballhaus, "Todd Ricketts, Co-Owner of the Chicago Cubs, Ends Bid for Commerce Post," *Wall Street Journal,* April 20, 2017, www.wsj.com/articles/todd-ricketts -co-owner-of-the-chicago-cubs-ends-bid-for-commerce-post-1492638729.

91. Representatives for Barrack did not answer a set of questions sent before the publication of this book. 58th Presidential Inaugural Committee, "Return of Organization Exempt from Income Tax," Internal Revenue Service, 2016, apps.irs.gov/pub/epostcard/cor/8144 63688_201710_990O_2917941215256354.pdf.

92. "Pre-Inauguration Dinner Arrivals, Part 1," C-SPAN, January 17, 2017, www.c-span.org /video/?422081-1/guests-arrive-invitation-dinner-president-elect-donald-trump.

93. Chairman's Global Dinner invitation list, ProPublica, February 5, 2019, www.document cloud.org/documents/5727935-Chairman-s-Global-Dinner-invitation-list.html.

94. "Architectural overview," Andrew W. Mellon Auditorium, mellonauditorium.com/history.

95. This and preceding paragraph: Dan Alexander, "In Trump They Trust: Inside the Global Web of Partners Cashing In on the President," *Forbes,* March 20, 2017, www.forbes.com

/sites/danalexander/2017/03/20/in-trump-they-trust-inside-the-global-web-of-partners
-cashing-in-on-the-president/#6f6ef0db7605.

96. Phil Ruffin, telephone interview with author, February 15, 2017.

97. "Financial Performance of Trump D.C. Hotel for February 2017," *Washington Post*, August 11, 2017, apps.washingtonpost.com/g/documents/business/february-performance/2525/?tid=lk_inline_manual_19.

98. Maggie Haberman, Sharon LaFraniere, and Ben Protess, "At Trump's Inauguration, $10,000 for Makeup and Lots of Room Service," January 14, 2019, *New York Times*, https://www.nytimes.com/2019/01/14/us/politics/trump-inauguration-spending.html.

99. Haberman, LaFraniere, and Protess, "At Trump's Inauguration, $10,000."

100. Ilya Marritz and Justin Elliott, "Trump's Inauguration Paid Trump's Company—With Ivanka in the Middle," ProPublica and WNYC, December 14, 2018, www.propublica.org/article/trump-inc-podcast-trumps-inauguration-paid-trumps-company-with-ivanka-in-the-middle.

101. This and preceding four paragraphs: Eric Trump, interviewed by author, February 24, 2017.

102. Dan Alexander, "Why the Next Big Trump Project Could Be a Las Vegas Casino," *Forbes*, March 20, 2017, www.forbes.com/sites/danalexander/2017/03/20/conflict-conflicts-of-interest-emoluments-clause-trump-ruffin-phil-russia-treasury-profits-hotel-las-vegas-casino/#6c50b74e79b1.

103. Phil Ruffin interview.

104. Eric Trump, interviewed by author, February 24, 2017.

105. Donald Trump, OGE Form 278e, May 15, 2018, 3, 40.

106. Grant Bargain and Sale Deed, Trump Ruffin Tower I, LLC, Yu Zhang, Clark County Recorder, October 4, 2018, gisgate.co.clark.nv.us/assessor/webimages/default.asp?appID=1&txtdocNum=20181004:02723.

107. Los Angeles County Registrar-Recorder/County Clerk, May 31, 2019, 908 North Canon LLC.

108. Abram Brown, "Wine, Murder and Cigars: My Evening at Home with the Trump-Loving Indonesian Billionaire Who Just Bought the President's Beverly Hills Mansion," *Forbes*, June 14, 2019, www.forbes.com/sites/abrambrown/2019/06/14/wine-murder-and-cigars-my-evening-at-home-with-the-trump-loving-indonesian-billionaire-who-just-bought-the-presidents-beverly-hills-mansion/#3a05674a79e4.

CHAPTER FOUR: PRESIDENTIAL PALACE

1. Jennifer Steinhauer, "Trump Kicks Away Obama Traditions Even at the Dinner Table," *New York Times*, December 14, 2018, www.nytimes.com/2018/12/14/us/politics/trump-food-restaurants.html; Jessica Sidman, "Why It Doesn't Matter That Trump Never Dines Out in D.C.," *Washingtonian*, March 19, 2019, www.washingtonian.com/2019/03/19/why-it-doesnt-matter-that-trump-never-dines-out-in-dc/.

2. Author's audio recording, December 8, 2019. Subsequent seven paragraphs are from this recording.

3. U.S. Department of Justice, email to author, December 10, 2019.

4. Jonathan O'Connell and David Fahrenthold, "Barr Books Trump's Hotel for $30,000 Holiday Party," *Washington Post*, August, 27, 2019, www.washingtonpost.com/business/2019/08/27/cheers-barr-books-trumps-hotel-holiday-party/.

5. U.S. Department of Justice, email to author, December 10, 2019.

6. Richard L. Stern and John Connolly, "Manhattan's Favorite Guessing Game: How Rich Is Donald?," *Forbes,* May 14, 1990, www.forbes.com/sites/danalexander/2019/05/08 /why-we-took-trump-off-the-forbes-400-during-his-decade-of-tax-losses/#3c51e8c33d91. Also see document labeled "Trump Plaza deed"; p. 4 has the date, https://a836-acris.nyc .gov/DS/DocumentSearch/DocumentImageView?doc_id=FT_1510000259351, July 21, 1988.

7. Dan Alexander, "Vintage Trump Ads Say a Lot About the President," *Forbes,* September 19, 2017, www.forbes.com/sites/danalexander/2017/09/19/trump-vintage-old-ads-advertise ment-forbes-president-donald/#5f8e32835100.

8. Reuters, "Trump's Plaza Hotel Bankruptcy Plan Approved," *New York Times,* December 12, 1992, www.nytimes.com/1992/12/12/business/company-news-trump-s-plaza-hotel-bank ruptcy-plan-approved.html.

9. Chase Peterson-Withorn and Abram Brown, "Three Decades of Trump," *Forbes,* October 19, 2015.

10. Allan Sloan, "You Can't Win Them All," *Forbes,* December 26, 1988.

11. Peterson-Withorn and Brown, "Three Decades of Trump."

12. Riva Atlas, "More Trumpery," *Forbes,* August 16, 1993.

13. Riva Atlas, "Dollars for Donald," *Forbes,* September 14, 1992.

14. Trump Hotels & Casino Resorts, Inc., Form 10-K, March 31, 1993, 1–2, www.sec.gov /Archives/edgar/data/943320/0000950110-99-000452.txt.

15. Trump Hotels & Casino Resorts, Inc., Form 10-K, March 31, 2005, 2, www.sec.gov /Archives/edgar/data/943320/000119312505067289/d10k.htm.

16. Trump Entertainment Resorts, Inc., Trump Entertainment Resorts Holdings, L.P., Trump Entertainment Resorts Funding, Inc., Form 10-K/A, March 14, 2006, F-13, www.sec.gov /Archives/edgar/data/943320/000119312506119514/d10ka.htm.

17. Trump Entertainment Resorts, Inc., Trump Entertainment Resorts Holdings, L.P., Trump Entertainment Resorts Funding, Inc., Form 10-K/A, March 12, 2009, ii, www .sec.gov/Archives/edgar/data/943320/000119312509055503/d10k.htm.

18. Charlie Reiss, telephone interview with author, 2018.

19. Dan Alexander, "Why the Next Big Trump Project Could Be a Las Vegas Casino," *Forbes,* March 20, 2017, www.forbes.com/sites/danalexander/2017/03/20/conflict-conflicts -of-interest-emoluments-clause-trump-ruffin-phil-russia-treasury-profits-hotel-las-vegas -casino/#24290a1f79b1.

20. Charlie Reiss interview.

21. Daniela Sirtori, "How Trump's Plan to Have His Name on a Brazil Beachfront Tower Went Bust," *Forbes,* March 7, 2017, www.forbes.com/sites/danielasirtori/2017/03/20/bra zil-beachfront-bomb/#6c2bebc04418; Chloe Sorvino, "For Trump, St. Vincent and the Grenadines Became the Isle of Disappointment," *Forbes,* March 20, 2017, www.forbes .com/sites/chloesorvino/2017/03/20/trump-golf-course-development-st-vincent-and-the -grenadines-isle-of-disappointment/#1ded319e2f8f; Chloe Sorvino, "Inside the Bankruptcy of the Puerto Rican Golf Course Trump Managed," *Forbes,* March 20, 2017, www.forbes.com/sites/chloesorvino/2017/03/20/puerto-rico-trump-bankruptcy-golf -course/#7d1df8174bfe; Dan Alexander, "Exclusive Investigation: Inside the Wild Plan to Create a Fake Trump Tower," *Forbes,* August, 1, 2017, www.forbes.com/sites/danalexan der/2017/08/01/exclusive-investigation-inside-the-wild-plan-to-create-a-fake-trump -tower/#69a0b8da547d.

22. Noah Kirsch, "Inside the Chaos at Trump's Panama City Ocean Club," *Forbes,* March 20, 2017, www.forbes.com/sites/noahkirsch/2017/03/20/inside-the-chaos-at-trumps-panama -city-ocean-club/#6b0d72041bdc.

23. Donald Trump, OGE Form 278e, U.S. Office of Government Ethics, 5 C.F.R. part 2634 (hereafter "Donald Trump, OGE Form 278e"), May 15, 2019, 8, 14, 13.

24. "Part 2: Donald Trump Jr. Testifies in Zakarian Lawsuit," *Washington Post,* September 30, 2016, www.washingtonpost.com/video/politics/part-2-donald-trump-jr-testifies-in-zakarian -lawsuit/2016/09/30/f5e797dc-873e-11e6-b57d-dd49277af02f_video.html.

25. Donald Trump, OGE Form 278e, May 15, 10; "Donald Trump Deposition, Part 1," *New York Daily News,* YouTube, September 30, 2016, www.youtube.com/watch?v=3dqE9Ns -RJM.

26. "Donald Trump Jr. Deposition, Part 1," *New York Daily News,* YouTube," https://www .youtube.com/watch?v=jbDeBY-1drU.

27. "Old Post Office, Washington, D.C.," U.S. General Services Administration, www.gsa .gov/historic-buildings/old-post-office-washington-dc.

28. "Old Post Office Building Redevelopment Environmental Assessment," U.S. General Services Administration in Cooperation with the National Capital Planning Commission, December 2012, 13, www.gsa.gov/cdnstatic/OPO_EA_Public_Draft_508.pdf.

29. "Old Post Office, Washington, D.C."

30. Landlord and Tenant: The Trump Administration's Oversight of the Trump International Hotel Lease, Statement of Mr. Dan Mathews, Commissioner, Public Buildings Service, U.S. General Services Administration, September 25, 2019, www.gsa.gov/about -us/newsroom/congressional-testimony/landlord-and-tenant-the-trump-administrations -oversight-of-the-trump-international-hotel-lease.

31. "Old Post Office Building Redevelopment Environmental Assessment," 15.

32. "Waldorf Astoria Hotels & Resorts Reveals Proposal to Redevelop the Old Post Office Building into a New and Exciting Destination on Pennsylvania Ave," Hilton, November 7, 2011, newsroom.hilton.com/corporate/news/waldorf-astoria-hotels-resorts-reveals -proposal-to-redevelop-the-old-post-office-building-into-a-new-and-exciting -destination-on-pennsylvania-ave.

33. "Old Post Office Building Redevelopment Environmental Assessment," 15.

34. "GSA and Trump Organization Reach Deal on Old Post Office Lease," U.S. General Services Administration, June 5, 2013, www.gsa.gov/about-us/newsroom/news-releases /gsa-and-trump-organization-reach-deal-on-old-post-office-lease.

35. Trump International Hotel Ribbon Cutting Ceremony.

36. "Donald Trump Jr. Deposition, Part 1."

37. Kevin Terry to Donald J. Trump Jr., 72; "Part 2: Donald Trump Jr. Testifies in Zakarian Lawsuit."

38. Chase Peterson-Withorn, "Here's How Much Don Jr., Eric and Ivanka Trump Are Worth," *Forbes,* November 8, 2019, https://www.forbes.com/sites/chasewithorn/2019/11 /08/heres-how-much-don-jr-eric-and-ivanka-trump-are-worth/#36a15b7f75ed; Ivanka Trump, OGE Form 278e, May 14, 2019, s3.amazonaws.com/storage.citizensforethics .org/wp-content/uploads/2019/06/14143951/TRUMP-IVANKA_Annual-Report-2019 Pending-WH-Action-1.pdf.

39. Donald Trump, OGE Form 278e, May 15, 2019, 76; Trump International Hotel Liquor License Filings with Trust Info, ProPublica, January 26, 2017, www.documentcloud.org /documents/3442581-Trump-International-Hotel-Liquor-License-Filings#document/p7; Kevin Terry to Donald J. Trump Jr., 72.

40. "Donald Trump Deposition, Part 1."

41. "Donald Trump Presidential Campaign Announcement," C-SPAN, October 26, 2016, www.c-span.org/video/?326473-1/donald-trump-presidential-campaign-announcement.

42. "Donald Trump Deposition, Part 1."

43. Statement from the Entertainment Division of Univision Communications Inc., Univision PR Team, June 25, 2015, corporate.univision.com/press/2015/06/25/statement-from-the-entertainment-division-of-univision-communications-inc-on-june-25-2015/.

44. "Donald Trump Deposition," Part 1.

45. "Part 2: Donald Trump Jr. Testifies in Zakarian Lawsuit."

46. "Donald Trump Jr. Deposition, Part 1."

47. Merrick Dresnin, interviewed by author, May 13, 2020.

48. Merrick Dresnin, telephone interview with author, January 5, 2020.

49. Beatrice Dumitrache, telephone interview with author, January 11, 2020.

50. Trump International Hotel Ribbon Cutting Ceremony.

51. Telephone interview with author, January 7, 2020.

52. Preceding four paragraphs: "Evaluation of GSA's Management and Administration of the Old Post Office Building Lease," January 16, 2019, 2–10, 45, 24, https://www.gsaig.gov/content/evaluation-gsas-management-and-administration-old-post-office-building-lease.

53. Citizens for Responsibility and Ethics in Washington, Restaurant Opportunities Centers United, Inc., Jill Phaneuf, and Eric Goode v. Donald J. Trump, in his official capacity as President of the United States of America, Docket No. 18-474, United States Court of Appeals for the Second Circuit, s3.amazonaws.com/storage.citizensforethics.org/wp-content/uploads/2017/01/03160142/2019-09-13-111-Opinion-1.pdf.

54. Richard Blumenthal, et al., Appellees, v. Donald J. Trump, in His Official Capacity as President of the United States of America, Appellant, Appeal from the United States District Court for the District of Columbia (No. 1:17-cv-01154) No. 19-5237, www.cadc.uscourts.gov/internet/opinions.nsf/2EFD382E65E33B3C852585070055D091/$file/19-5237-1827549.pdf.

55. "Emoluments Lawsuit," Office of the Attorney General for the District of Columbia, Maryland and D.C., oag.dc.gov/about-oag/emoluments-lawsuit.

56. "Emoluments Lawsuit," Office of the Attorney General for the District of Columbia, Maryland and D.C., http://oag.dc.gov/about-oag-emoluments-lawsuit.

57. "Conflicts of Interest and the President," Morgan Lewis Trump Trust, White Paper, ProPublica, 6, www.documentcloud.org/documents/3400512-Morgan-Lewis-Trump-Trust-White-Paper.html.

58. Elijah E. Cummings to George Sorial, regarding Trump Organization payment to Treasury, March 12, 2018, 1, oversight.house.gov/sites/democrats.oversight.house.gov/files/2018-03-12.EEC%20to%20Sorial-Trump%20Organization%20re%20Trump%20Org.%20Payment%20to%20Treasury.pdf.

59. "Donation of Profits from Foreign Government Patronage, Trump Organization," 5–6, oversight.house.gov/sites/democrats.oversight.house.gov/files/documents/Trump%20Org%20Pamphlet%20on%20Foreign%20Profits.pdf.

60. "Trump Organization to Robert Menendez," fax, April 6, 2018, 9, www.foreign.senate.gov/imo/media/doc/Trump%20Org%20response%20to%20RM%20re%20Hotel%20Foreign%20Profits.pdf.

61. Bernard Condon, "Trump Org Donates Nearly $200k to Cover Foreign Profits," AP, February 25, 2019, apnews.com/a4349ac80a7048bdb61f017fffd9623f; Jonathan O'Connell, "Trump Organization Reports Small Bump in Foreign Government Profits in 2018," *Washington Post,* www.washingtonpost.com/business/economy/trump-organization-reports-small-bump-in-foreign-government-profits-in-2018/2019/02/24/b49f3b6c-3872-11e9-a2cd-307b06d0257b_story.html.

62. Donald Trump, OGE Form 278e, May 15, 2019, 10, and May 15, 2018, 20.

63. Author's audio recording, December 8, 2019; Beatrice Dumitrache, telephone interview with author; Merrick Dresnin, interviewed by author, May 13, 2019.

64. Author's audio recording, December 8, 2019.

65. Beatrice Dumitrache, telephone interview with author.

66. Beatrice Dumitrache, telephone interview with author; Michel Rivera, telephone interview with author, December 5, 2019.

67. Author's audio recording, December 8, 2019.

68. Beatrice Dumitrache, telephone interview with author; author's audio recording, December 8, 2019.

69. Author's audio recording, December 8, 2019.

70. Tom Sietsema, "Trump's First D.C. Dinner as President: An Overcooked, $54 Steak. With Ketchup," *Washington Post,* February 27, 2017, www.washingtonpost.com/lifestyle /food/trumps-first-dc-dinner-as-president-an-overcooked-54-steak-with-ketchup /2017/02/27/c98895b4-fd19-11e6-8f41-ea6ed597e4ca_story.html.

71. Telephone interview with author, January 7, 2020.

72. Michel Rivera, telephone interview with author.

73. Liz Johnstone, "Tracking President Trump's Visits to Trump Properties," NBC News, December 29, 2017, updated October 22, 2019, www.nbcnews.com/politics/donald-trump /how-much-time-trump-spending-trump-properties-n753366.

74. Julie Bykowicz, "Trump Hotel May Be Political Capital of the Nation's Capital," AP News, March 5, 2017, apnews.com/cc2e2c2b6b4d4417afff3aa5f768be10.

75. Michel Rivera, telephone interview with author; Beatrice Dumitrache, telephone interview; author's audio recording, December 8, 2019.

76. Beatrice Dumitrache, telephone interview with author.

77. Kevin McCarthy (@RepKevinMcCarthy), "Family dinner," Facebook, photo of Kevin McCarthy, Jim Jordan, Mark Meadows, et al., February 12, 2020, www.facebook.com /RepKevinMcCarthy/photos/a.10150114697283176/10157079091968176.

78. Katrina Pierson (@katrinapierson), Instagram photo, July 4, 2019, www.instagram.com /p/BzgH3yrAPvG/; Tyler Gadsden Ziolkowski, Facebook, photo of Kellyanne Conway, June 14, 2019, www.facebook.com/photo.php?fbid=164961211207375.

79. Said Bilani (@saidbilani), Instagram photo of Jeanine Pirro, September 26, 2019, www .instagram.com/p/B23-j5ehyxA/; Andre Soriano (@officialandresoriano), Instagram photo of Laura Ingraham, February 2, 2020, www.instagram.com/p/B8EMNSng2RF/.

80. *1100 Pennsylvania*, 1100pennsylvania.substack.com.

81. Author's screenshot, "Zach Everson counts as of 2-17-2020," 1100 Pennsylvania.

82. House Oversight Committee, press releases, November 30, 2016 2020, oversight.house .gov/investigations/trump-hotel-in-washington-dc?page=2.

83. FEC Form 1, "Jim Jordan for Congress," October 10, 2019, 2, docquery.fec.gov/pdf/416 /201910109163791416/201910109163791416.pdf.

84. FEC data, "Jim Jordan for Congress," May 16, 2018–June 20, 2019, www.fec.gov/data/dis bursements/?data_type=processed&committee_id=C00416594&recipient_name=blt +prime&recipient_name=trump&two_year_transaction_period=2020&two_year_trans action_period=2018&min_date=01%2F01%2F2017&max_date=12%2F31%2F2020.

85. FEC data, "Meadows for Congress," October 2, 2017–December 18, 2019, www.fec.gov /data/disbursements/?data_type=processed&committee_id=C00503094&recipient _name=blt+prime&recipient_name=trump&two_year_transaction_period=2018&two _year_transaction_period=2020&min_date=01%2F01%2F2017&max_date=12 %2F31%2F2020.

86. FEC Form 1, "Meadows for Congress," April 15, 2019, 2, docquery.fec.gov/pdf/527 /201904159146355527/201904159146355527.pdf.

87. "Michael R. Pence," White House, www.whitehouse.gov/people/mike-pence/.

88. FEC data, "Greg Pence for Congress," November 27, 2017–March 14, 2019, www.fec.gov /data/disbursements/?data_type=processed&committee_id=C00658401&recipient _name=blt+prime&recipient_name=trump&two_year_transaction_period=2018&two _year_transaction_period=2020&min_date=01%2F01%2F2017&max_date=12 %2F31%2F2020.

89. FEC Form 1, "Greg Pence for Congress," 2, docquery.fec.gov/pdf/836/20181022913058 9836/201810229130589836.pdf.

90. FEC data, Republican National Committee, www.fec.gov/data/disbursements/?data_type =processed&committee_id=C00003418&recipient_name=blt+prime&recipient_name =trump&two_year_transaction_period=2020&two_year_transaction_period=2018 &min_date=01%2F01%2F2017&max_date=12%2F31%2F2020.

91. FEC data, 2017–2019, www.fec.gov/data/disbursements/?data_type=processed&recipient _name=benjamin+bar&recipient_name=blt+prime&recipient_name=old+post+office &recipient_name=opo&recipient_name=trump&two_year_transaction_period=2016 &two_year_transaction_period=2018&two_year_transaction_period=2020&min_date =01%2F01%2F2017&max_date=12%2F31%2F2020.

92. Merriam-Webster, s.v. "The Origins of 'Lobbyist,'" www.merriam-webster.com/words-at -play/the-origins-of-lobbyist.

93. Peggy Kern, "A Big Business and Growing: Online Extra for the Influence Business," National Conference of State Legislatures, January 2009, www.ncsl.org/research/ethics /lobbying-a-big-business-and-growing.aspx; Philip A. Wallach, "America's Lobbying Addiction," Brookings Institution, April 13, 2015, www.brookings.edu/blog/fixgov/2015 /04/13/americas-lobbying-addiction/.

94. Zach Everson, 1100pennsylvania.substack.com; "Trump First Tuesdays," Facebook Group, www.facebook.com/trumpfirsttuesdays/.

95. Jonathan O'Connell, "From Trump Hotel Lobby to White House, Malaysian Prime Minister Gets VIP Treatment," *Washington Post,* September 12, 2017, www.washington post.com/politics/from-trump-hotel-lobby-to-white-house-malaysian-prime-minister -gets-vip-treatment/2017/09/12/1b296f54-97d1-11e7-87fc-c3f7ee4035c9_story.html.

96. Melanie Schmitz, "Exclusive: Kuwaiti Embassy Will Host Its 2018 Independence Day Party at Trump's Hotel," ThinkProgress, January 26, 2018, thinkprogress.org/kuwaiti -embassy-trump-hotel-2018-0c03ad3c8145/; Telephone interview with author, January 7, 2020; Supplemental Statement Pursuant to the Foreign Agents Registration Act of 1938, General Delegation of the PLO, May 9, 2018, 16, efile.fara.gov/docs/5244-Supplemental -Statement-20180509-31.pdf.

97. Jose Manuel del Gallego Romualdez, "Our Special 120th Independence Day DC Celebration," *Philippine Star,* April 22, 2018, www.philstar.com/opinion/2018/04/22/1808198 /our-special-120th-independence-day-dc-celebration; Telephone interview with author, January 7, 2020.

98. Beatrice Dumitrache, telephone interview with author, January 11, 2020.

99. Eleanora Movsisian (@eleanoramovs), Instagram photo of Anatoly Antonov, January 2, 2018 www.instagram.com/p/Bdc71BYHQGz/.

100. *Interview of Kurt Volker, Before the House Permanent Select Committee on Intelligence, Committee on Oversight and Reform, and Committee on Foreign Affairs,* 116th Cong., October 3, 2019, 42, 308, docs.house.gov/meetings/IG/IG00/CPRT-116-IG00-D007.pdf.

101. Supplemental Statement Pursuant to the Foreign Agents Registration Act of 1938, General Delegation of the PLO, May 9, 2018, 43–44: efile.fara.gov/docs/5244-Supplemental -Statement-20180509-31.pdf.

102. Author's screenshot, "Zach Everson counts as of 2-17-2020," February 17, 2020.

103. Beatrice Dumitrache, telephone interview with author.

104. Ethics in Government Act of 1978, section 101(d), subsection (f), 5, 2, 1, www.govinfo .gov/content/pkg/USCODE-2010-title5/pdf/USCODE-2010-title5-app-ethicsing.pdf.

105. U.S. Office of Government Ethics, Public Financial Disclosure Guide, Stock, www.oge .gov/Web/278eGuide.nsf/2f96d42716636dbf85257f490052263c/59a975c885aebd0685 257f45006ee3a6?OpenDocument; Bond (municipal), www.oge.gov/Web/278eGuide.nsf /2f96d42716636dbf85257f490052263c/5591e83a6a795d9985257f450065ed76?Open Document; Bond (corporate), www.oge.gov/Web/278eGuide.nsf/2f96d42716636dbf85 257f490052263c/9bb3604a7aa3035d85257f450065c91e?OpenDocument.

106. U.S. Office of Government Ethics, Public Financial Disclosure Guide, Real Estate Holding Company (including REITs), www.oge.gov/Web/278eGuide.nsf/Content/6+-+Other+ Assets+&+Income+Document-Real+Estate+Holding+Company+(including+REITs).

107. Donald Trump, OGE Form 278e, May 15, 2019, 20, 10.

108. John Haltiwanger, "Trump Made $40.8 Million Last Year from a Hotel That Critics Say He's Using to Illegally Profit from the Presidency," *Business Insider,* May 16, 2019, www .businessinsider.com/trump-made-millions-last-year-from-his-hotel-near-the-white -house-2019-5.

109. Steve Reilly and Nick Penzenstadler, "Trump's Company Earned $40M from Washington Hotel in 2017, Disclosure Shows," *USA Today,* May 16, 2018, www.usatoday.com /story/news/2018/05/16/trumps-dc-hotel-earns-his-company-40-m-during-first-year -office/616833002/.

110. Craig Karmin and Julie Bykowicz, "Trump Organization Exploring Sale of Marquee Washington Hotel," *Wall Street Journal,* October 25, 2019, www.wsj.com/articles/trump -organization-exploring-sale-of-marquee-washington-hotel-11572019874; David A. Fahr -enthold and Jonathan O'Connell, "In New Financial Disclosure, Trump Reports Apparent Payment Through His Personal Attorney to Adult-Film Star," *Washington Post,* May 16, 2018, www.washingtonpost.com/politics/in-new-financial-disclosure-trump-reports -apparent-payment-through-his-personal-attorney-to-adult-film-star/2018/05/16 /cf6171f2-592c-11e8-b656-a5f8c2a9295d_story.html; Eric Lipton and Annie Karni, "Checking In at Trump Hotels, for Kinship (and Maybe Some Sway)," *New York Times,* September 7, 2019, www.nytimes.com/2019/09/07/us/politics/trump-hotel.html.

111. Dan Alexander, "10 Things We Learned from Trump's Financial Disclosure Report," *Forbes,* May 17, 2018, www.forbes.com/sites/danalexander/2018/05/17/10-things-we-learned -from-trumps-financial-disclosure-report/#f4466e915766.

112. U.S. Office of Government Ethics, Public Financial Disclosure Guide, Real Estate Holding Company (including REITs).

113. Ivanka Trump, OGE Form 278e, U.S. Office of Government Ethics, 5 C.F.R. part 2634, 3.

114. "GSA Outleases and the Trump Old Post Office Hotel: Statement of the Honorable Emily W. Murphy, Administrator, U.S. General Services Administration, Before the House Transportation and Infrastructure Subcommittee on Economic Development, Public Buildings and Emergency Management," January 28, 2020, www.gsa.gov/about-us /newsroom/congressional-testimony/gsa-outleases-and-the-trump-old-post-office-hotel.

115. Jonathan O'Connell, "The General Services Administration Removed Trump Hotel Data from Its Website. You Can Read It Here," *Washington Post,* August 11, 2017, www .washingtonpost.com/news/business/wp/2017/08/11/government-removes-trump-hotel -data-from-website-says-it-was-posted-accidentally/.

116. "April performance"; O'Connell, "The General Services Administration," 2; Trump Old Post Office LLC, Monthly Statement Certificate, assets.documentcloud.org/documents /3923499/April-performance.pdf.

117. "Trends in the Hotel Industry USA Edition 2019," CBRE, 32.

118. Dan Wasiolek, telephone interview with author, January 10, 2020.

119. Kara Scannell and Gloria Borger, "Exclusive: Trump DC Hotel Sales Pitch Boasts of Millions to Be Made from Foreign Governments," CNN, November 14, 2019, www.cnn.com/2019/11/14/politics/exclusive-trump-hotel-investor-pitch/index.html.

120. Donald Trump, OGE Form 278e, part 2634, May 15, 2018, 20, and May 15, 2019, 10.

121. Brian Friedman, telephone interview with author, January 8, 2020.

122. Leasehold Deed of Trust, Assignment of Leases and Rents, Fixture Filing and Security Agreement, Trump Old Post Office LLC and Deutsche Bank Trust Company Americas, Washington, D.C., Recorder of Deeds, Doc No. 2014073616, August 12, 2014.

123. Donald Trump, OGE Form 278e, May 15, 2019, 41.

124. Effective Federal Funds Rate (FEDFUNDS), fred.stlouisfed.org/series/FEDFUNDS.

125. Donald Trump, OGE Form 278e, May 15, 2019, 41.

126. Brian Friedman, telephone interview with author, January 8, 2020.

127. Karmin and Bykowicz, "Trump Organization Exploring Sale"; Eric Lipton and Maggie Haberman, "Trumps Put Their Washington Hotel on the Market," *New York Times,* October 25, 2019, www.nytimes.com/2019/10/25/us/politics/trump-hotel-washington.html; Dan Berman and Christie Johnson, "Trump Organization Explores Selling DC Hotel," CNN, October 25, 2019, www.cnn.com/2019/10/25/politics/trump-washington-dc-hotel/index.html.

128. Brian Friedman, interviewed by author, January 10, 2020.

129. Author's audio recording, December 8, 2019.

130. Brian Friedman interview, January 10, 2020.

131. Brian Friedman interview, January 10, 2020. A concierge at the Four Seasons clarified that there is just one Warhol in that hotel. It is a print of *Indian Head Nickel.*

132. Brian Friedman interview, January 10, 2020.

133. Karmin and Bykowicz, "Trump Organization Exploring Sale."

134. Michael Bellisario, telephone interview with author, January 10, 2020.

135. Bill Moyer, telephone interview with author, January 7, 2020.

136. Dan Wasiolek, telephone interview with author, January 10, 2020.

137. Telephone interview with author, January 7, 2020; Bill Moyer, telephone interview with author; Dan Wasiolek, telephone interview with author; Michael Bellisario, telephone interview with author; Joel Paige, telephone interview with author, March 9, 2020; Kevin Brown, telephone interview with author, March 9, 2020; Bjorn Hanson, telephone interview with author, March 9, 2020.

138. Brian Friedman interview.

139. Michael Bellisario, telephone interview with author; Bill Moyer, telephone interview with author.

140. Bill Moyer, telephone interview with author.

141. Michael Bellisario, telephone interview with author.

CHAPTER FIVE: BAD LIE

1. "Briefing by Secretary Tillerson, Secretary Mnuchin, and Secretary Ross on President Trump's Meetings with President Xi of China," April 7, 2017, www.whitehouse.gov/briefings-statements/briefing-secretary-tillerson-secretary-mnuchin-secretary-ross-president-trumps-meetings-president-xi-china/; "President Trump at Mar-a-Lago Dinner Table with Chinese President Xi Jinping (FNN)," Fox 10 Phoenix, YouTube, April 6, 2017, www.youtube.com/watch?v=wMVwnzJTrx4.

2. International Monetary Fund, "GDP, current prices, Billions of U.S. dollars," www.imf
    .org/external/datamapper/NGDPD@WEO/OEMDC/ADVEC/WEOWORLD.
3. "President Trump at Mar-a-Lago Dinner Table."
4. "Fox Business: Maria Bartiromo Interviews Donald Trump—April 12, 2017," Factbase
    Videos, YouTube, www.youtube.com/watch?v=L_NkAv1HLjA.
5. "Statement by President Trump on Syria (C-SPAN)," YouTube, April 13, 2017, www
    .whitehouse.gov/briefings-statements/statement-president-trump-syria/.
6. "Lunch Program, Part 1: A Conversation with Wilbur L. Ross, Jr., Secretary, U.S. Dept.
    of Commerce," Milken Institute, YouTube, June 26, 2017, www.youtube.com/watch?v=
    5ipA_FP8zSg.
7. Donald J. Trump, Twitter, January 18, 2017, twitter.com/realdonaldtrump/status/821772
    494864580614; Donald J. Trump, Twitter, February 11, 2017, twitter.com/realdonald
    trump/status/830558065715998726; Donald J. Trump, Twitter, November 22, 2017,
    twitter.com/realdonaldtrump/status/933301876975718401.
8. Chase Peterson-Withorn, "Donald Trump Has Gained More than $100 Million on Mar-
    a-Lago," *Forbes,* April 23, 2018, www.forbes.com/sites/chasewithorn/2018/04/23/donald
    -trump-has-gained-more-than-100-million-on-mar-a-lago/#1a30b0915adc.
9. Donald Trump, OGE Form 278e, U.S. Office of Government Ethics, 5 C.F.R. part 2634
    (hereafter "Donald Trump, OGE Form 278e"), July 15, 2015, 16; May 16, 2016, 16; June
    14, 2017, 16.
10. "Donald Trump Deposition, Part 1," *New York Daily News,* YouTube, September 30,
    2016, www.youtube.com/watch?v=3dqE9Ns-RJM.
11. Robert Frank, "Mar-a-Lago Membership Fee Doubles to $200,000," CNBC, Janu-
    ary 25, 2017, www.cnbc.com/2017/01/25/mar-a-lago-membership-fee-doubles-to-200000
    .html.
12. The press office for the U.S. State Department did not respond to requests for comment.
    Christine Stapleton, "Trump Picks Another Mar-a-Lago Member for Ambassador," *Palm
    Beach Daily News*, November 14, 2018, www.palmbeachdailynews.com/news/20181114
    /trump-picks-another-mar-a-lago-member-for-ambassador.
13. "#468 Isaac Perlmutter," *Forbes,* www.forbes.com/profile/isaac-perlmutter/#d377d26cafbf.
14. Representatives for Isaac Perlmutter did not respond to requests for comment. Isaac Arn-
    sdorf, "The Shadow Rulers of the VA," ProPublica, August 7, 2018, www.propublica.org
    /article/ike-perlmutter-bruce-moskowitz-marc-sherman-shadow-rulers-of-the-va.
15. Dan Alexander, "How Trump Is Trying—And Failing—To Get Rich Off His Presi-
    dency," *Forbes,* October 2, 2018, www.forbes.com/sites/danalexander/2018/10/02/how
    -trump-is-tryingand-failingto-get-rich-off-his-presidency/#3a04c83e3b1a.
16. Spokesperson for the Trump Organization, email to author, March 12, 2020.
17. Walter Shaub, "Mar-a-Lago Isn't the 'Winter White House.' It's Just an Embarrassing
    Cash Grab," *Washington Post,* May 7, 2018, www.washingtonpost.com/news/postevery
    thing/wp/2018/05/07/mar-a-lago-isnt-the-winter-white-house-its-just-an-embarrassing
    -cash-grab/.
18. Donald Trump, OGE Form 278e, May 15, 2019, 5.
19. Analysis of Donald Trump, OGE Form 278e, May 15, 2019, 5–11.
20. Vornado Realty Trust, Supplemental Operating and Financial Data, for the quarter and
    year ended December 31, 2018, 43, 48; analysis of 40 Wall Street CREFC Servicer Report,
    October 18; analysis of Trump Tower CREFC Servicer Report, October 18, 2019; analysis
    of Trump Plaza CREFC Servicer Report, October 11; analysis of Trump International
    Hotel & Tower CREFC Servicer Report, October 18; Jonathan O'Connell, Twitter, No-
    vember 15, 2019, https://twitter.com/OConnellPostbiz/status/1195364225939648515;

NYC Department of Finance, Notice of Property Value, January 15, 2017, a836-mspuvw
-dofptsz.nyc.gov/PTSCM/StatementSearch?bbl=1012920069&stmtDate=20170115&stmt
Type=NPV; Nathan Strauss (Tiffany), email to author, August 22, 2018; Charlie Brooks
(Nike), email to author, October 3, 2017; Kimberly Benza (Trump Organization), email to
author, September 12, 2019; analysis of property records; NYC Department of Finance,
Notices of Property Value, January 15, 2020, a836-edms.nyc.gov/dctm-rest/repositories
/dofedmspts/StatementSearch?bbl=1010117001&stmtDate=20200115&stmtType=NPV;
a836-edms.nyc.gov/dctm-rest/repositories/dofedmspts/StatementSearch?bbl=
1013401001&stmtDate=20200115&stmtType=NPV; a836-edms.nyc.gov/dctm-rest/reposi
tories/dofedmspts/StatementSearch?bbl=1013401002&stmtDate=20200115&stmtType=
NPV; a836-edms.nyc.gov/dctm-rest/repositories/dofedmspts/StatementSearch?bbl=101011
4001&stmtDate=20200115&stmtType=NPV; Chicago CBD, Office Q3 2019, Cushman
& Wakefield, 1; Anthony Cristiano Chicago, "Our Story," anthonycristiano.com/story
.html.

21. Analysis of Donald Trump, OGE Form 278e, May 15, 2019, 5–11; Ivanka Trump, OGE
Form 278e, U.S. Office of Government Ethics, May 14, 2019, 4.

22. Alexander, "How Trump Is Trying—And Failing."

23. "In Conversation with: Donald Trump," Golf.com, YouTube, May 15, 2014, www.you
tube.com/watch?v=z5rpTuRgL0E&t=321s.

24. "Samuel L. Jackson Finds Out He's in a Feud with Donald Trump," *Late Night with Seth
Meyers*, YouTube, January 5, 2016, www.youtube.com/watch?v=Tu2xnbaI3Ds.

25. "Anthony Anderson: Donald Trump Cheats at Golf," *Late Night with Seth Meyers*, You-
Tube, February 17, 2016, www.youtube.com/watch?v=KAR9QkES6wQ.

26. "About Trump International West Palm Beach," a letter from Jim Fazio, www.trumpinter
nationalpalmbeaches.com/about.

27. Donald Trump, OGE Form 278e, May 15, 2019, 8.

28. Analysis of Trump's 2019 financial disclosure report, interviews with seven golf industry
experts, Society of Golf Appraiser's report, ClubCorp 2016 annual report, Donald Trump,
OGE Form 278e, U.S. Office of Government Ethics 5 C.F.R. art 2634, 05/15/2019, Society of Golf Appraiser, 2019 Survey, http://www.golfappraisers.org/Portals/0/Survey/SGA
_2019_Survey_.pdf, Securities and Exchanges Commission, Form 10-K, ClubCorp Holdings Inc, for the fiscal year ended December 27, 2016 https://www.sec.gov/Archives/edgar
/data/1577095/000157709517000061/0001577095-17-000061-index.htm.

29. Ashley Hoffman, "15 Surprising Facts About Trump's Bedminster Golf Club in New
Jersey," *Time*, May 15, 2017, time.com/4765663/bedminster-golf-club-trump-visit-facts/.

30. "Experience Trump National Bedminster," www.trumpnationalbedminster.com/welcome.

31. Jonathan O'Connell and David A. Fahrenthold, "Trump Visits His For-Profit Golf
Course During California Trip," *Washington Post*, April 5, 2019, www.washingtonpost
.com/politics/trumps-california-visit-comes-as-decisions-loom-for-his-seaside-golf
-course-there/2019/04/05/cf957f88-57b9-11e9-8ef3-fbd41a2ce4d5_story.html; Victoria Kim,
"From the Archives: Trump Sues City for $100 million," *Los Angeles Times*, December 20,
2008, www.latimes.com/politics/la-pol-ca-donald-trump-sued-rancho-palos-verdes-golf
-course-story.html; Troy McMullen, "Trump Tees Off," *Wall Street Journal*, February 4,
2005, www.wsj.com/articles/SB110748670379645928.

32. Monmouth County Document Summary Sheet, Coastal Title Agency Inc., Shadow Isle
Golf Club LLC, Trump National Golf Club Colts Neck LLC, September 10, 2008, 3.

33. Anonymous source close to Trump's golf business, telephone interview with author, October 19, 2017.

34. Donald Trump, OGE Form 278e, May 15, 2019, 9.

35. Analysis of Trump's 2019 financial disclosure report, interviews with seven golf industry experts, Society of Golf Appraiser's report, ClubCorp 2016 annual report, Donald Trump, OGE Form 278e, U.S. Office of Government Ethics 5 C.F.R. art 2634, 05/15/2019, Society of Golf Appraiser, 2019 Survey, http://www.golfappraisers.org/Portals/0/Survey/SGA_2019_Survey_.pdf Securities and Exchanges Commission, Form 10-K, ClubCorp Holdings Inc, for the fiscal year ended December 27, 2016 https://www.sec.gov/Archives/edgar/data/1577095/000157709517000061/0001577095-17-000061-index.htm.

36. Florida Traffic Crash Report, HSMV Crash Report Number 77685828, November 27, 2009.

37. "Tiger Woods' Full Apology Speech," CNN, YouTube, February 19, 2010, www.youtube.com/watch?v=Xs8nseNP4s0.

38. Palm Beach County Sheriff's Office, Toxicology Report, Eldrick T. Woods, June 1, 2017.

39. Analysis of Rancho Palos Verdes government data.

40. Loudon County, Virginia, Trump National Golf Club, Washington, D.C., Appeal Application, Case # 26251, 13.

41. Palm Beach County, Trump National Golf Club Jupiter, Petition/Review Form, Petition/Review #: P16-2647, January 12, 2017, 20.

42. Iredell County Assessor's Office, Appeal Summary, Point Lake & Golf Club Inc., TNGC Charlotte LLC.

43. Ken Alkins, "How Donald Trump Is Rebuilding a Mooresville Golf Club Fit for a . . . Trump," *Charlotte Business Journal,* April 5, 2013.

44. Analysis of Trump's 2019 financial disclosure report, interviews with seven golf industry experts, Society of Golf Appraisers' report, and ClubCorp 2016 annual report. Donald Trump, OGE Form 278e, U.S. Office of Government Ethics, 5 C.F.R. part 2634, May 15. 2019; Society of Golf Appraisers, "The Investor's Tour Salient Indicators," 2019 survey, http://www.golfappraisers.org/Portals/0/Survey/SGA_2019_Survey_.pdf; Securities and Exchange Commission, Form 10-K, ClubCorp Holdings Inc., for the fiscal year ended December 27, 2016, https://www.sec.gov/Archives/edgar/data/1577095/000157709517000061/0001577095-17-000061-index.htm.

45. Anonymous source close to Trump's golf business, telephone interview with author, November 19, 2017.

46. "Our Properties," Trump Golf, www.trumpgolf.com/Our-Courses; Donald Trump, OGE Form 278e, May 15, 2019, 4–11, 17.

47. Former golf club employee, interview with author, May 29, 2020.

48. This and preceding six paragraphs: George Schwab, telephone interview with author, January 8, 2020.

49. Former golf club employee, interviewed by author, May 29, 2020.

50. David A Fahrenthold and Joshua Partlow, "How Two Housekeepers Took On the President—and Revealed That His Company Employed Undocumented Immigrants," *Washington Post,* December 4, 2019, www.washingtonpost.com/politics/how-two-undocumented-housekeepers-took-on-the-president--and-revealed-trumps-long-term-reliance-on-illegal-immigrants/2019/12/04/3dff5b5c-0a15-11ea-bd9d-c628fd48b3a0_story.html; Miriam Jordan, "Making President Trump's Bed: A Housekeeper Without Papers," *New York Times,* December 6, 2018, www.nytimes.com/2018/12/06/us/trump-bedminster-golf-undocumented-workers.html.

51. George Schwab, telephone interview with author.

52. Matthew Galvin, telephone interview with author, March 10, 2020.

53. Analysis of Loudon County Property Records; Donald Trump, OGE Form 278e, May 15, 2019, 10, 78, 46; Trump International Hotel Liquor License Filings with Trust Info,

ProPublica, January 26, 2017, 7, www.documentcloud.org/documents/3442581-Trump
-International-Hotel-Liquor-License-Filings#document/p7.

54. George Schwab, telephone interview with author.

55. "Trump Says He Is 'Very Much of a Germaphobe,'" *Washington Post,* January 12, 2017,
www.washingtonpost.com/videopolitics/trump-says-he-is-very-much-of-a-germaphobe
/2017/01/12/1e4af06c-d8b0-11e6-a0e6-d502d6751bc8_video.html; Daniel Lippman, "The
Purell Presidency: Trump Aides Learn the President's Real Red Line," *Politico,* July 7,
2019, www.politico.com/story/2019/07/07/donald-trump-germaphobe-1399258; "Trump's
History of Germaphobia," *Washington Post,* YouTube, June 17, 2019, www.youtube.com
/watch?v=KLpDxsokZD4.

56. George Schwab, telephone interview with author.

57. Former golf club employee interview.

58. "President Trump Shares Story About His Brother's Alcohol Addiction During Opioid
Speech," NBC News, October 26, 2017, www.youtube.com/watch?v=Q9yJSjdp_go.

59. George Schwab, telephone interview with author.

60. Ian Gillule, telephone interview with author, 2017.

61. Analysis of property records, Miami-Dade Property Appraiser.

62. "Trump National Doral Fact Sheet," www.trumphotels.com/press-release/trump-national
-doral-fact-sheet/183.

63. Preceding eight paragraphs: Donald Trump and Allen Weisselberg, interviewed by Randall Lane, Chase Peterson-Withorn, and Kerry Dolan, September 21, 2015.

64. "Trump International Golf Links Scotland," Trump Organization, YouTube, August 23,
2012, www.youtube.com/watch?v=LkbPo8_Qd5Y.

65. "Trump Expands Golf & Hospitality Portfolio with Purchase of Highly Acclaimed
Doonbeg Golf Club, Ireland," press release, February 11, 2014, web.archive.org/web
/20140702005458/http://www.trump.com/_files/pdf/Doonbeg.pdf.

66. TIGL Ireland Enterprises Limited, Abridged Financial Statements, for the period ended
December 31, 2014, 7, 33, 4, 10.

67. Trump and Weisselberg interview.

68. Analysis of Trump International Golf Club Scotland Limited, Abbreviated Accounts,
Annual Reports 2006–2018 Companies House.

69. Analysis of TIGL Ireland Enterprises Limited, Abridged Financial Statements, Annual
Reports 2014–2018.

70. TIGL Ireland Enterprises Limited, Abridged Financial Statements, 4; the Trump Organization, "The Trump Story," https://www.trump.com/timeline.

71. "V. Trump Endeavor 2017," Miami-Dade County Value Adjustment Board, video, December 13, 2017.

72. Donald Trump, OGE Form 278e, May 15, 2018, 6, and May 15, 2019, 65, 46; Trump
International Hotel Liquor License Filings, 7.

73. Value Adjustment Board Report, Trump Endeavor 12 LLC, November 14, 2017, 5.

74. Preceding five paragraphs: "V. Trump Endeavor 2017" video.

75. "World Golf Championships–Mexico Championship Debuts in 2017," PGA Tour, June 1,
2016, www.pgatour.com/tournaments/wgc-mexico-championship/en/news/2016/06/01
/world-golf-championships-mexico-championship-debuts-in-2017.html.

76. Bob Harig, "PGA Tour Moves Tournament from Trump Doral to Mexico City," ESPN,
June 1, 2016, www.espn.com/golf/story/_/id/15876975/pga-tour-move-event-miami-trump
-doral-resort-mexico-city-2017.

77. "V. Trump Endeavor 2017" video.

78. Joel Paige, telephone interview with author, March 9, 2020.

79. "V. Trump Endeavor 2017" video.
80. Value Adjustment Board Report, Trump Endeavor 12 LLC, November 14, 2017, 237.
81. This and preceding paragraph: Alexander, "How Trump Is Trying—And Failing."
82. Value Adjustment Board Report, Trump Endeavor 12 LLC, November 14, 2017, 225–27.
83. Donald Trump, OGE Form 278e, May 15, 2019, 7.
84. Matias Magarinos, telephone interview with author, January 8, 2020.
85. Analysis of annual reports from Companies House.
86. SLC Turnberry Limited, Annual Report and Financial Statements, for the year ended December 31, 2017, Companies House, 5–12.
87. Analysis of annual reports for SLC Turnberry Limited, Companies House, 2014–2018.
88. Analysis of TIGL Ireland Enterprises Limited, Abridged Financial Statements, for the period ended December 31, 2016, 4.
89. Analysis of TIGL Ireland Enterprises Limited, Abridged Financial Statements, Annual Reports 2014–2018.
90. Trump International Golf Club Scotland Limited, Directors' Reports and financial statements for the years ended December 31, 2012, 9; December 31, 2013, 9; December 31, 2014, 8; December 31, 2015, 9; December 31, 2016, 9; December 31, 2017, 12; December 31, 2018, 12; Companies House. All figures measured in British pounds sterling.
91. Trump International Golf Club Scotland Limited, Directors' Report and financial statements for the year ended December 31, 2016, Companies House, 9.
92. Trump International Golf Club Scotland Limited, Directors' Report and financial statements for the year ended December 31, 2017, Companies House, 12, 4.
93. Trump International Golf Club Scotland Limited, Directors' Reports and financial statements for the years ended December 31, 2015, 18; December 31, 2017, 21; December 31, 2018, 21; Companies House.
94. Analysis of Trump International Golf Club Scotland Limited, Directors' Reports and financial statements for the years ended December 31, 2012; December 31, 2013; December 31, 2014; December 31, 2015; December 31, 2016; December 31, 2017; December 31, 2018; Companies House.
95. "Trump Submits £150 Million Investment Plans," Trump Estate, July 19, 2018, www.thetrumpestate.com/2018/07/19/media-release-trump-submits-150-million-investment-plans/.
96. "Conflicts of Interest and the President," Morgan Lewis, White Paper, January 11, 2017, 3, www.documentcloud.org/documents/3400512-Morgan-Lewis-Trump-Trust-White-Paper.html.
97. Trump International Golf Club Scotland Limited, Directors' Report and financial statements for the year ended December 31, 2018, Companies House, 5.
98. Analysis of Trump International Golf Club Scotland Limited, Directors' Reports and financial statements for the years ended December 31, 2017; December 31, 2018; IGL Ireland Enterprises Limited, Abridged Financial Statements for the periods ended December 31, 2017; December 31, 2018; SLC Turnberry Limited, Annual Reports and Financial Statements for the years ended December 31, 2017; December 31, 2018, Companies House; Value Adjustment Board Report, Trump Endeavor 12 LLC, November 14, 2017, 236–37.
99. Anonymous source close to Trump's golf business, telephone interviews with author, October 19, 2017, and May 13, 2020.
100. Liz Johnstone, "Tracking President Trump's Visits to Trump Properties," NBC News, December 20, 2017, screenshot as of March 2, 2020, https://www.nbcnews.com/politics/donald-trump/how-much-time-trump-spending-trump-properties-n753366.
101. Doug Rutherford, telephone interview with author, January 7, 2020.

102. Brad Heath, Fredreka Schouten, Steve Reilly, Nick Penzenstadler, and Aamer Madhani, "Trump Gets Millions from Golf Members. CEOs and Lobbyists Get Access to President," *USA Today*, September 6, 2017, www.usatoday.com/story/news/2017/09/06/trump-gets-millions-golf-members-ceos-and-lobbyists-get-access-president/632505001/.

103. Analysis of Disbursements, Omar Navarro for Congress, Federal Election Commission, www.fec.gov/data/disbursements/?data_type=processed&committee_id=C00592048&recipient_name=trump+national&two_year_transaction_period=2020&two_year_transaction_period=2018&min_date=01%2F01%2F2017&max_date=12%2F31%2F2020.

104. "Election Results for the U.S. Senate and U.S. House of Representatives, Federal Elections 2018," 53, www.fec.gov/resources/cms-content/documents/federalelections2018.pdf.

105. FEC Form 1, "Kipnis for Congress," March 2, 2018, docquery.fec.gov/pdf/209/201808039119352209/201808039119352209.pdf.

106. Analysis of Disbursements, Kipnis for Congress, Federal Election Commission, www.fec.gov/data/disbursements/?data_type=processed&committee_id=C00684324&recipient_name=trump+national&two_year_transaction_period=2018&two_year_transaction_period=2020&min_date=01%2F01%2F2017&max_date=12%2F31%2F2020.

107. MacArthur Victory, PAC—Nonqualified ID: C0064692, Federal Election Commission, www.fec.gov/data/committee/C00646927/?tab=about-committee; FEC Form 1, "MacArthur Victory," June 2, 2017, docquery.fec.gov/pdf/478/201706029055300478/201706029055300478.pdf; FEC Form 1, "Tom MacArthur for Congress," May 9, 2016, docquery.fec.gov/pdf/868/201810309133556868/201810309133556868.pdf; "Disbursements, MacArthur Victory," Federal Election Commission, www.fec.gov/data/disbursements/?data_type=processed&committee_id=C00646927&recipient_name=trump+national&two_year_transaction_period=2020&two_year_transaction_period=2018&min_date=01%2F01%2F2017&max_date=12%2F31%2F2020.

108. Analysis of Disbursements, Republican National Committee, Federal Election Commission www.fec.gov/data/disbursements/?data_type=processed&committee_id=C00003418&recipient_name=doral&recipient_name=mar-a-lago&two_year_transaction_period=2018&two_year_transaction_period=2020&min_date=01%2F01%2F2017&max_date=12%2F31%2F2020.

109. FEC Form 1, "Statement of Organization, Trump Victory," January 15, 2020, docquery.fec.gov/pdf/323/202001159167186323/202001159167186323.pdf.

110. Disbursements, Trump Victory, Federal Election Commission, www.fec.gov/data/disbursements/?data_type=processed&committee_id=C00618389&recipient_name=doral&recipient_name=mar-a-lago&two_year_transaction_period=2020&two_year_transaction_period=2018&min_date=01%2F01%2F2017&max_date=12%2F31%2F2020.

111. Analysis of disbursements data for Trump Golf properties, Federal Election Commission, www.fec.gov/data/disbursements/?data_type=processed&recipient_name=doonbeg&recipient_name=doral&recipient_name=ferry+point&recipient_name=mar+a+lago&recipient_name=pine+hill&recipient_name=trump+international&recipient_name=trump+national&recipient_name=trump+national+golf&recipient_name=turnberry&two_year_transaction_period=2020&two_year_transaction_period=2018&min_date=01%2F01%2F2017&max_date=12%2F31%2F2020.

112. Derek Kravitz, Derek Willis, Paul Cronan, Mark Schifferli, and Charlie Smart, "Paying the President," ProPublica, June 27, 2018, projects.propublica.org/paying-the-president/.

113. Alexandra Alper, "Democrats Slam Pence for Staying at Trump Hotel in Ireland," Reuters, September 3, 2019, www.reuters.com/article/us-ireland-usa-pence-trump/democrats-slam-pence-for-staying-at-trump-hotel-in-ireland-idUSKCN1VO11X; Nicholas Wu, "Aide Defends Mike Pence for Staying at Trump Hotel in Ireland on President's Suggestion,"

USA Today, September 3, 2019, www.usatoday.com/story/news/politics/2019/09/03/pences -decision-stay-doonbeg-ireland-trump-hotel-criticized/2195539001/.

114. "Remarks by President Trump at the Announcement of State Opioid Response Grants," White House, September 4, 2019, www.whitehouse.gov/briefings-statements/remarks -president-trump-announcement-state-opioid-response-grants/.

115. "Secret Service Payments to Trump Properties (Jan–June 2017)," November 21, 2019, Property of the People, propertyofthepeople.org/document-detail/?doc-id=6556375-Secret -Service-Payments-to-Trump-Properties-Jan.

116. When asked about the payments, a Secret Service spokesperson responded, "For operations security reasons, the Secret Service cannot discuss specifically nor in general terms the means and methods we utilize to carry out our protective responsibilities." United States Secret Service, email to author, May 14, 2020.

117. Analysis of Secret Service Payments to Trump Properties (Jan–June 2017), November 21, 2019, Property of the People, propertyofthepeople.org/document-detail/?doc-id=6556375 -Secret-Service-Payments-to-Trump-Properties-Jan.

118. Virginia Canter, telephone interview with author, May 13, 2020.

119. Analysis of *Trump National Golf Club LLC v. Ossining Town,* Westchester Supreme Court Index Number 67432/2015, October 1, 2019, 2; analysis of Donald Trump, OGE Form 278e, May 15, 2019, 9.

120. Documents obtained through a public records request from the City of Rancho Palos Verdes, 2015–2019.

121. Palm Beach County, Trump National Golf Club Jupiter, Petition/Review Form, Petition/ Review #: P16-2647, January 12, 2017, 73; analysis of Donald Trump, OGE Form 278e, May 15, 2019, 5.

122. Donald Trump, OGE Form 278e, May 15, 2019, 7; "License Agreement Between Trump Ferry Point LLC and City of New York Department of Parks & Recreation," February 21, 2012.

123. Analysis of Trump Golf Links at Ferry Point Quarterly gross receipts and golf course activities, 2015–2018.

124. "Press Briefing by Acting Chief of Staff Mick Mulvaney," White House, October 17, 2019, www.whitehouse.gov/briefings-statements/press-briefing-acting-chief-staff-mick-mulvaney/.

125. "President Trump Participates in a Bilateral Meeting with the Chancellor of Germany," White House, YouTube, August 26, 2019, www.youtube.com/watch?v=Q2gxAoxc0IM& t=990s.

126. Analysis of Value Adjustment Board Report, Trump Endeavor 12 LLC, November 14, 2017, 214–15.

127. "Press Briefing by Acting Chief of Staff Mick Mulvaney."

128. U.S. Constitution, art. II, § 1, para. 7, National Archives, www.archives.gov/founding -docs/constitution-transcript#toc-section-1–2.

129. "Press Briefing by Acting Chief of Staff Mick Mulvaney."

130. "Mick Mulvaney Walks Back Quid Pro Quo Comments," Fox News, YouTube, October 20, 2019, www.youtube.com/watch?v=I4Zjtcml7lU.

131. Donald J. Trump, Twitter, October 19, 2019, twitter.com/realDonaldTrump/status/1185 726930764611589, twitter.com/realDonaldTrump/status/1185726931611852802, twitter .com/realdonaldtrump/status/1185735579327193093.

132. Chris Christie, interviewed on *This Week,* ABC, October 20, 2019, https://abcnews.go .com/Politics/week-transcript-10-20-19-secretary-state-mike/story?id=66394461.

133. "Mick Mulvaney Walks Back Quid Pro Quo Comments."

CHAPTER SIX: ALL THE PRESIDENT'S TENANTS

1. U.S. Constitution, art. I, § 9, https://www.archives.gov/founding-docs/constitution -transcript.
2. Dan Alexander and Matt Drange, "Trump's Biggest Potential Conflict of Interest Is Hiding In Plain Sight," *Forbes,* February 13, 2018, https://www.forbes.com/sites/danalexander /2018/02/13/trump-conflicts-of-interest-tenants-donald-business-organization-real-estate -assets-pay/#70381bb848f9; Bloomberg News, "China's Biggest Bank to Reduce Its Space at Trump Tower," January 9, 2019, https://www.bloomberg.com/news/articles/2019-01-09 /china-s-biggest-bank-said-to-reduce-space-at-nyc-s-trump-tower.
3. Industrial and Commercial Bank of China, New York Branch, http://www.icbkus.com /icbc/%E6%B5%B7%E5%A4%96%E5%88%86%E8%A1%8C/%E7%BA%BD%E7 %BA%A6%E7%BD%91%E7%AB%99/en/.
4. Industrial and Commercial Bank of China Limited, Annual Report 2018, 77, http:// v.icbc.com.cn/userfiles/Resources/ICBCLTD/download/2019/2018AnnualReport 20190425.
5. Prospectus Supplement, Wells Fargo Commercial Mortgage Trust 2012-LC5, Securities and Exchange Commission, July 20, 2012, A-3-33, https://www.sec.gov/Archives/edgar /data/850779/000153949712000571/prospectus-supplement.htm; Donald Trump, OGE Form 278e, U.S. Office of Government Ethics, 5 C.F.R. part 2634 (hereafter "Donald Trump, OGE Form 278e"), May 15, 2019, 79, 59, 60; Trump International Hotel Liquor License Filings with Trust Info, ProPublica, January 26, 2017, 7, https://www.document cloud.org/documents/3442581-Trump-International-Hotel-Liquor-License-Filings #document/p7.
6. Prospectus Supplement, Wells Fargo, July 20, 2012.
7. "Remarks by President Trump and Prime Minister Johnson of the United Kingdom in Working Breakfast, Biarritz, France," White House, August 25, 2019, https://www.white house.gov/briefings-statements/remarks-president-trump-prime-minister-johnson-united -kingdom-working-breakfast-biarritz-france/.
8. Donald Trump and Allen Weisselberg, interviewed by Randall Lane, Chase Peterson-Withorn, and Kerry Dolan, September 21, 2015.
9. Analysis of Wells Fargo Commercial Mortgage Trust 2012-LC5, Commercial Mortgage Pass-Through Certificates Series 2012-LC5, Form 10-D, SEC, March 17, 2016, https:// www.sec.gov/Archives/edgar/data/1556601/000105640416004079/wcm12lc5_ex991 -201603.htm.
10. "Eric Trump: How to Manage Under Pressure," Yahoo Finance, YouTube, October 10, 2019, https://youtu.be/BCR3mo4hYdo?t=873.
11. SL Green Realty Corp, Third Quarter 2018, September 30, 2018, 6, https://www.sec.gov /Archives/edgar/data/1040971/000104097118000022/a18q3supplemental.htm.
12. "China's Biggest Bank to Reduce Its Space at Trump Tower," Bloomberg News, January 9, 2019, https://www.bloomberg.com/news/articles/2019-01-09/china-s-biggest-bank-said -to-reduce-space-at-nyc-s-trump-tower.
13. "Eric Trump: How to Manage Under Pressure."
14. The Trump Organization, Twitter, December 18, 2018, https://twitter.com/Trump/status /1075083401827368962.
15. Prospectus Supplement, Wells Fargo, July 20, 2012.
16. Jonathan O'Connell, "Trump Organization Reports Small Bump in Foreign Government Profits in 2018," *Washington Post,* February 24, 2019, https://www.washingtonpost.com /business/economy/trump-organization-reports-small-bump-in-foreign-government -profits-in-2018/2019/02/24/b49f3b6c-3872-11e9-a2cd-307b06d0257b_story.html.

17. Eric Trump's Facebook page, https://www.facebook.com/EricTrump/posts/3549736508 431729.

18. Prospectus Supplement, Wells Fargo, July 20, 2012.

19. Analysis of Trump Tower CREFC Servicer Report, October 18, 2019.

20. Research conducted by the author for *Forbes*.

21. Alexander and Drange, "Trump's Biggest Potential Conflict of Interest."

22. "Conflicts of Interest and the President," Morgan Lewis, White Paper, January 11, 2017, ProPublica, 1–2, www.documentcloud.org/documents/3400512-Morgan-Lewis-Trump -Trust-White-Paper.html.

23. Alan Garten, email to author, January 25, 2018.

24. Research conducted by the author for *Forbes*.

25. Alan Garten email to author.

26. San Francisco Assessor-Recorder, 555 California Owner LP and HWA 555 Owners LLC, March 6, 2006; analysis of Donald Trump, OGE Form 278e, May 15, 2019, 51, 52, 59, 79, 82; Trump International Hotel Liquor License Filings, 7; New York City Department of Finance Office of the City Register, Deed, Jamestown 1290, L.P., HWA 1290 III LLC, HWA 1290 IV LLC and HWA 1290 V LLC, May 3, 2006, https://a836-acris.nyc.gov /DS/DocumentSearch/DocumentImageView?doc_id=2006042900019002.

27. Analysis of Vornado Realty Trust, Supplemental Operating and Financial Data, for the Quarter and Year ended December 31, 2019, 45, 50.

28. Analysis of Trump Tower CREFC Servicer Report, October 18, 2019; analysis of Vornado Realty Trust, Supplemental Operating and Financial Data, for the Quarter and Year ended December 31, 2019, 45, 50; Alexander and Drange, "Trump's Biggest Potential Conflict of Interest"; analysis of 40 Wall Street CREFC Servicer Report, October 18, 2019; NYC Department of Finance Notice of Property Value Tax Year 2020–21, JAB (Acquisition) Ltd., January 15, 2020, 2; analysis of Trump International Hotel and Tower CREFC Servicer Report, October 18, 2019; Trump Plaza CREFC Servicer Report, October 11, 2019; NYC Department of Finance Notice of Property Value Tax Year 2020–21, 845, United Nations Plaza Comm1, the Donald J. Trump Revocable Trust, January 15, 2020, https://a836-edms.nyc.gov/dctm-rest/repositories/dofedmspts/StatementSearch?bbl =1013401001&stmtDate=20200115&stmtType=NPV; Chicago CBD, Office Q3 2019, Cushman & Wakefield, 1; Anthony Cristiano Chicago, "Our Story," https://anthonycri stiano.com/story.html; Jonathan O'Connell, Twitter, November 15, 2019, https://twitter .com/OConnellPostbiz/status/1195364225939648515.

29. A spokesperson for the White House referred inquiries to the Trump Organization. The Trump Organization did not respond to inquiries from the author. White House spokesperson, email to author, May 15, 2020.

30. Alexander and Drange, "Trump's Biggest Potential Conflict of Interest."

31. Wendi Kopsick, email to author, May 14, 2020.

32. Dan Alexander, "Trump's Secret Windfall: The Crown Jewels of His Fortune Are 2 Skyscrapers He Didn't Want—And Doesn't Control," *Forbes,* March 7, 2019, https://www .forbes.com/sites/danalexander/2019/03/07/trumps-secret-windfall-the-crown -jewels-of-his-fortune-are-2-skyscrapers-he-didnt-wantand-doesnt-control/#16a6c0fe22e5.

33. The 35 tenants are:

    Starbucks: Starbucks Store Locator, 555 California St., San Francisco, CA, https:// www.starbucks.com/store-locator?map=37.787509,-122.346548,5z&place=555 %20California%20St,%20San%20Francisco,%20CA,%20USA. Clerk of the United States House of Representatives, LD-2 Disclosure Form, Starbucks Corporation, July 13, 2018, https://disclosurespreview.house.gov/ld/ldxmlrelease/2017/3A/30096 4395.xml.

TD Bank: 1290 Ave. of the Americas, https://www.tdbank.com/net/absearch/Loca
tionDetails.aspx?branchID=43336. Clerk of the United States House of Representatives, LD-2 Disclosure Form, TD Ameritrade Holding Company, July 19, 2019,
https://disclosurespreview.house.gov/ld/ldxmlrelease/2017/3A/300964395.xml.

Walgreens Boots Alliance: Walgreens—Store #14485, 40 Wall St., New York, NY
10005, https://www.walgreens.com/locator/duane+reade-40+wall+st-new+york-ny
-10005/id=14485. Clerk of the United States House of Representatives, LD-2 Dis
closure Form, Walgreen Co., July 19, 2017, https://disclosurespreview.house.gov
/ld/ldxmlrelease/2017/Q2/300889383.xml.

JPMorgan Chase: Chase Radio City, 51 W. 51st St., New York, NY 10019, https://locator
.chase.com/ny/new-york/51-w-51st-st. Clerk of the United States House of Representatives, LD-2 Disclosure Form, JPMorgan Chase Holdings LLC, January 21, 2020,
https://disclosurespreview.house.gov/ld/ldxmlrelease/2019/Q4/301127627.xml.

Santander: Santander Bank, Branch 1290 Ave. of the Americas, New York, NY 10019.
https://locations.santanderbank.com/ny/new-york/1290-avenue-of-the-americas
.html. Clerk of the United States House of Representatives, LD-2 Disclosure Form,
Santander Holdings USA, Inc., January 21, 2020, https://disclosurespreview.house
.gov/ld/ldxmlrelease/2019/Q4/301125142.xml.

Columbia University: ColumbiaDoctors Midtown, 51 West 51st St., New York, NY
10019, https://www.columbiadoctors.org/columbiadoctors-midtown. Clerk of the
United States House of Representatives, LD-2 Disclosure Form, The Trustees of
Columbia University in the City of New York, October 21, 2019, https://disclosure
spreview.house.gov/ld/ldxmlrelease/2019/Q3/301073411.xml.

Equitable Holdings: Form 10-K, Equitable Holdings Inc., Securities and Exchange
Commission, 1290 Ave. of the Americas, https://www.sec.gov/Archives/edgar/data
/1333986/000133398620000015/eqh201910-k.htm. Clerk of the United States House
of Representatives, LD-2 Disclosure Form, AXA Equitable Life Insurance Company, April 19, 2018, https://disclosurespreview.house.gov/ld/ldxmlrelease/2018/Q1
/300949322.xml.

State Street: State Street Office Locations, New York, International Fund Services
(N.A), LLC., State Street Bank and Trust Company, National Association, 1290
Ave. of the Americas, 10th Floor, https://www.statestreet.com/about/office-locations
.html. Clerk of the United States House of Representatives, LD-2 Disclosure Form,
State Street Bank and Trust Co., April 17, 2018, https://disclosurespreview.house
.gov/ld/ldxmlrelease/2018/Q1/300946501.xml.

Venable: Venable LLP, New York—1290 Ave. of the Americas, https://www.venable
.com/offices/new-york-ny-1290. Clerk of the United States House of Representatives LD-2 Disclosure Form, Venable LLP on behalf of Overstock.com, Inc.,
April 20, 2018, https://disclosurespreview.house.gov/ld/ldxmlrelease/2018/Q1
/300955312.xml.

Neuberger Berman: Neuberger Berman, Office Locations, Firm Headquarters, New
York, 1290 Ave. of the Americas, https://www.nb.com/en/global/office-locations.
Clerk of the United States House of Representatives, LD-2 Disclosure Form, Neuberger Berman Group, LLC, April 18, 2018, https://disclosurespreview.house.gov
/ld/ldxmlrelease/2018/Q1/300948238.xml.

Bryan Cave: Bryan Cave Leighton Paisner, Locations, 1290 Ave. of the Americas,
https://www.bclplaw.com/en-US/offices/index.html. Clerk of the United States
House of Representatives, LD-2 Disclosure Form, Bryan Cave Leighton Paisner
LLP, January 18, 2020, https://disclosurespreview.house.gov/ld/ldxmlrelease/2019
/Q4/301121323.xml.

Nike: Charlie Brooks (Nike), email to author, October 3, 2017. Clerk of the United States House of Representatives, LD-2 Disclosure Form, Nike, Inc., October 11, 2017.

Hadassah, Women's Zionist Organization for America: Hadassah, Mailing Address, 40 Wall St., https://www.hadassah.org/about/index.html. Clerk of the United States House of Representatives, LD-2 Disclosure Form, Hadassah, The Women's Zionist Organization Of America, Inc., December 23, 2019, https://disclosurespreview .house.gov/ld/ldxmlrelease/2019/Q4/301102668.xml.

Girl Scouts of Greater New York: Girl Scouts of Greater New York, 40 Wall St., Suite 708, New York, NY 10005, https://www.girlscoutsnyc.org/en/about-girl-scouts/who -we-are/Termsandconditions.html. Clerk of the United States House of Representatives, LD-2 Disclosure Form, Girl Scouts of the U.S.A., April 17, 2017, https://dis closurespreview.house.gov/ld/ldxmlrelease/2017/Q1/300866531.xml.

Verizon: XO Communications, 40 Wall St., 16th Floor, New York, NY 10005, https:// www.xo.com/contact-us/sales/sales-office-locations/new-york. Clerk of the United States House of Representatives, LD-2 Disclosure Form, Verizon Communications Inc. and various subsidiaries, https://disclosurespreview.house.gov/ld/ldxmlrelease /2019/Q2/301045883.xml.

TB Alliance: TB Alliance Contact New York: 40 Wall St., 24th floor, New York, NY 10005, https://www.tballiance.org/contact. Clerk of the United States House of Representatives, LD-2 Disclosure Form, Global Alliance for TB Drug Development (TB Alliance), January 15, 2020, https://disclosurespreview.house.gov/ld/ldxmlre lease/2019/Q4/301106262.xml.

Capital One: Capital One, 502 Park Ave., New York, NY 10022, https://locations.capi talone.com/location/branch_46062. Clerk of the United States House of Representatives, LD-2 Disclosure Form, Capital One Financial Corporation, January 21, 2020, https://disclosurespreview.house.gov/ld/ldxmlrelease/2019/Q4/301126733.xml.

Fox: Federal Communications Commission, Antenna Lease, TV Intercity Relay License— WCQ510—Fox Television Stations, LLC, Trump International Hotel & Tower, https://wireless2.fcc.gov/UlsApp/UlsSearch/licensePathsSum.jsp?licKey=972519. Clerk of the United States House of Representatives, LD-2 Disclosure Form, 21st Century Fox, January 22, 2018, https://disclosurespreview.house.gov/ld/ldxmlrelease /2017/Q4/300934008.xml.

GNC: GNC at Trump Plaza https://www.gnc.com/store-details?StoreID=2564. Clerk of the United States House of Representatives, LD-2 Disclosure Form, General Nutrition Center, January 17, 2020 https://disclosurespreview.house.gov/ld/ldxmlre lease/2019/Q4/301110446.xml.

Bank of America: Bank of America locations, San Francisco Main Financial Center & ATM, 315 Montgomery St., San Francisco, CA 94104, US, https://locators.banko famerica.com/ca/sanfrancisco/financial-centers-san-francisco-16793.html. Clerk of the United States House of Representatives, LD-2 Disclosure Form, Bank of America Corporation, April 17, 2020, https://disclosurespreview.house.gov/ld/ldxmlre lease/2020/Q1/301169480.xml. Clerk of the United States House of Representatives, LD-2 Disclosure Form, TRGroup (also doing business as ACT—Alliance for Competitive Taxation), July 20, 2018, https://disclosurespreview.house.gov/ld/ldx mlrelease/2018/Q2/300974132.xml. Clerk of the United States House of Representatives, LD-1 Disclosure Form, TRGroup, Inc., April 12, 2013, https://disclosure spreview.house.gov/ld/ldxmlrelease/2013/RR/300567882.xml.

Jones Day: Jones Day, San Francisco, Address, 555 California St., 26th Floor Tenant at 555 California St., https://www.jonesday.com/en/locations/united-states/san-francisco?tab

=overview-b562c134-cdfe-4884-b2c1-c5a82b916e06. Clerk of the United States House of Representatives, LD-2 Disclosure Form, Jones Day, January 21, 2020, https://disclosurespreview.house.gov/ld/ldxmlrelease/2019/Q4/301124734.xml.

Microsoft: Vornado Realty Trust, Office, San Francisco, 555 California St., Tenant Profile, Microsoft, https://www.vno.com/office/property/555-california-street/3311899/landing. Clerk of the United States House of Representatives, LD-2 Disclosure Form, Microsoft, July 17, 2017, https://disclosurespreview.house.gov/ld/ldxmlrelease/2017/Q2/300885784.xml.

Morgan Stanley: Morgan Stanley, San Francisco Complex Office, 555 California St., https://advisor.morganstanley.com/san-francisco-complex. Clerk of the United States House of Representatives, LD-2 Disclosure Form, Morgan Stanley & Co. LLC, January 21, 2020, https://disclosurespreview.house.gov/ld/ldxmlrelease/2019/Q4/301127679.xml.

Foley and Lardner: Foley & Lardner LLP, San Francisco, 555 California St., https://www.foley.com/en/offices/san-francisco. Clerk of the United States House of Representatives, LD-2 Disclosure Form, Foley & Lardner LLP, April 20, 2018, https://disclosurespreview.house.gov/ld/ldxmlrelease/2018/Q1/300953010.xml.

Sidley: Sidley, San Francisco, Locations, 555 California St., https://www.sidley.com/en/locations/offices/san-francisco. Clerk of the United States House of Representatives, LD-2 Disclosure Form, Sidley Austin LLP, January 17, 2020, https://disclosurespreview.house.gov/ld/ldxmlrelease/2019/Q4/301109093.xml.

Wells Fargo: Wells Fargo Advisors, San Francisco, CA, Branch, 555 California St., https://home.wellsfargoadvisors.com/001_PCA7. Clerk of the United States House of Representatives, LD-2 Disclosure Form, Wells Fargo & Company, January 21, 2020, https://disclosurespreview.house.gov/ld/ldxmlrelease/2019/Q4/301128953.xml.

TIAA: Symphony Asset Management Office, 555 California St., https://www.nuveen.com/en-us/people/investment-specialists/symphony-asset-management. Clerk of the United States House of Representatives, LD-2 Disclosure Form, TIAA, January 17, 2018, https://disclosurespreview.house.gov/ld/ldxmlrelease/2017/Q4/300925614.xml.

UBS: UBS Locations, UBS Financial Services Inc. 555 California St., San Francisco CA 94104, https://www.ubs.com/locations/united-states/san-francisco/555-california-street/ubs-financial-services-inc-846.html. Clerk of the United States House of Representatives, LD-2 Disclosure Form, UBS Americas Inc., January 6, 2020, https://disclosurespreview.house.gov/ld/ldxmlrelease/2019/Q4/301103411.xml.

Authentic8: Authentic8, Office Locations, San Francisco, 555 California St., Suite 3360, San Francisco, CA 94104, https://www.authentic8.com/contact-us/. Clerk of the United States House of Representatives, LD-2 Disclosure Form, Authentic8, Inc., January 21, 2019.

Goldman Sachs: Goldman Sachs, Office Locations, 555 California St., 45th Floor, San Francisco, CA 94104, https://www.goldmansachs.com/our-firm/locations.html. Clerk of the United States House of Representatives, LD-2 Disclosure Form, The Goldman Sachs Group, Inc., January 21, 2020, https://disclosurespreview.house.gov/ld/ldxmlrelease/2019/Q4/301125366.xml.

EY: EY-Parthenon, Locations, 555 California St., https://www.linkedin.com/company/ey-parthenon. Clerk of the United States House of Representatives, LD-2 Disclosure Form, Ernst & Young LLP (Washington Council Ernst & Young), July 19, 2017, https://disclosurespreview.house.gov/ld/ldxmlrelease/2017/Q2/300889383.xml.

McKinsey: McKinsey Locations, 555 California St., https://www.mckinsey.com/locations. Clerk of the United States House of Representatives, LD-2 Disclosure Form,

McKinsey & Company, January 21, 2020, https://disclosurespreview.house.gov/ld /ldxmlrelease/2019/Q4/301124836.xml.

KKR: KKR Locations, 555 California St., https://www.kkr.com/our-firm/locations. Lobbied the Executive Office of the President, according to this filing. Clerk of the United States House of Representatives, LD-2 Disclosure Form, Kohlberg Kravis Roberts & Company, January 19, 2018, https://disclosurespreview.house.gov/ld /ldxmlrelease/2017/Q4/300929718.xml.

Ripple Labs: Ripple Careers, 315 Montgomery St., https://ripple.com/company/careers/. Clerk of the United States House of Representatives, LD-2 Disclosure Form, Ripple Labs, Inc., April 20, 2020 https://disclosurespreview.house.gov/ld/ldxmlrelease/2020 /Q1/301175934.xml.

Blue Shield of California: Vornado Realty Trust, Supplemental Operating and Financial Data, for the Quarter and Year Ended December 31, 2019, 50. Clerk of the United States House of Representatives, LD-2 Disclosure Form, Blue Shield of California, January 17, 2020, https://disclosurespreview.house.gov/ld/ldxmlrelease /2019/Q4/301110772.xml,https://news.blueshieldca.com/2018/03/22/blue-shield -foundation-new-sf-headquarters.

34. Analysis of lobbying reports listed above.
35. The 30 tenants are:

Columbia University: ColumbiaDoctors Midtown, 51 West 51st St., New York, NY 10019, https://www.columbiadoctors.org/columbiadoctors-midtown. USASpend ing.gov, recipient profile, Trustees of Columbia University in the City of New York, https:// www.usaspending.gov/#/recipient/104cf824-0647-4d9a-199a-89fe 3de4bf9e-P/latest. USASpending.gov, recipient profile, Trustees of Columbia University in the City of New York, The, https://www.usaspending.gov/#/recipient /03aa78e7-78f5-7779-fc3e-8890eeec17ce-P/latest. USASpending.gov, recipient profile, Teachers College, Columbia University, https://www.usaspending.gov/#/recipi ent/ba4aadbf-3e8e-0e42-231c-1fa9b6c4f67a-P/latest.

Verizon: XO Communications, 40 Wall St., 16th Floor, New York, NY 10005, https:// www.xo.com/contact-us/sales/sales-office-locations/new-york. USASpending.gov, recipient profile, Verizon Communications Inc., https://www.usaspending.gov/#/re cipient/7c0b8b81-6424-176c-cf87-b06062671a1b-P/latest.

ICF: ICF Company Locations, 40 Wall St., https://www.icf.com/company/locations. USASpending.gov, recipient profile, ICF International, Inc., https://www.usaspend ing.gov/#/recipient/992f0d92-dfad-d76d-675d-b35f3e49616c-P/latest.

Microsoft: Vornado Realty Trust, Office, San Francisco, 555 California St., Tenant Profile, Microsoft https://www.vno.com/office/property/555-california-street/3311899 /landing. USASpending.gov, recipient profile, Microsoft Corporation, https://www .usaspending.gov/#/recipient/13f1c931-edc1-d2bc-07a6-c809332ae02a-P/latest.

EY: EY-Parthenon, Locations, 555 California Street, https://www.linkedin.com/com pany/ey-parthenon. USASpending.gov, recipient profile, Ernst & Young LLP, https:// www.usaspending.gov/#/recipient/1ff8dfe9-cd9d-4a69-7e85-0c991 96102bd-P/latest.

McKinsey: McKinsey Locations, 555 California St., https://www.mckinsey.coom/loca tions. USASpending.gov, recipient profile, McKinsey & Company, Inc., https:// www.usaspending.gov/#/recipient/8507105f-01f7-1eff-2e79-72eb0ca1c157-P/latest.

Wells Fargo: Wells Fargo Advisors, San Francisco, CA Branch, 555 California St., https://home.wellsfargoadvisors.com/001_PCA7. USASpending.gov, recipient profile, Wells Fargo & Company, https://www.usaspending.gov/#/recipient/741dda66 -0b1e-50fb-13de-36849bc84de2-P/latest.

TD Bank: TD Bank Location, 1290 Ave. of the Americas, https://www.tdbank.com
/net/absearch/LocationDetails.aspx?branchID=43336. USASpending.gov, recipient
profile, Toronto-Dominion Bank, The, https://www.usaspending.gov/#/recipient
/624ea65e-82e8-40af-8292-0ed547b92317-P/latest.

State Street: State Street Office Locations, New York, International Fund Services (N.A),
LLC., State Street Bank and Trust Company, National Association, 1290 Ave. of
the Americas, 10th Floor, https://www.statestreet.com/about/office-locations.html.
USASpending.gov, recipient profile, State Street Corporation, https://www.usaspend
ing.gov/#/recipient/fc579aa9-04f0-5671-eca3-ac40cece3e17-P/latest.

Cushman & Wakefield: Cushman & Wakefield, New York, 1290 Ave. of the Americas,
https://www.cushmanwakefield.com/en/offices/offices-search#q=new%20york.
USASpending.gov, recipient profile, Cushman & Wakefield of Washington D.C.
Inc., https://www.usaspending.gov/#/recipient/04f337d9-6e18-1137-e2b3-ebcf260
017bb-P/latest.

Walgreens Boots Alliance: Walgreens—Store #14485, 40 Wall St., New York, NY 10005,
https://www.walgreens.com/locator/duane+reade-40+wall+st-new+york-ny-10005/id
=14485. USASpending.gov, recipient profile, Walgreen Co., https://www.usaspend
ing.gov/#/recipient/b4ada01a-e703-73a5-5f27-bfbc66a17055-C/latest.

Thornton Tomasetti: Thornton Thomasetti, Locations, New York, Wall St., 40 Wall St.,
https://www.thorntontomasetti.com/location/new-york-wall-street. USASpending.gov,
recipient profile, Thornton Tomasetti, Inc., https://www.usaspending.gov/#/recipi
ent/4126336f-d844-0f26-76dd-68a0d6da0db1-P/latest.

Neuberger Berman: Neuberger Berman, Office Locations, Firm Headquarters, New
York, 1290 Ave. of the Americas, https://www.nb.com/en/global/office-locations
.USASpending.gov, recipient profile, Neuberger Berman Group LLC, https://www
.usaspending.gov/#/recipient/5170f055-5598-da10-4122-7d9601e03f55-P/latest
.USASpending.gov, recipient profile, Neuberger Berman Investment Advisers LLC,
https://www.usaspending.gov/#/recipient/09203f48-2618-a89b-3256
-085ede1dc339-P/latest.

Bank of America: Bank of America locations, San Francisco Main Financial Center &
ATM, 315 Montgomery St., San Francisco, CA 94104, https://locators.banko
famerica.com/ca/sanfrancisco/financial-centers-san-francisco-16793.html. USASpend
ing.gov, recipient profile, Bank of America Corporation, https://www.usaspend
ing.gov/#/recipient/89397a6a-2e67-286e-b3db-2b4a7ce50ee1-P/latest.

JPMorgan: Chase Radio City 51 W. 51st St., New York, NY 10019, https://locator
.chase.com/ny/new-york/51-w-51st-st. USASpending.gov, recipient profile, JPMor
gan Chase & Co., https://www.usaspending.gov/#/recipient/1c544118-2827-1d28
-4c03-61ae95ffcece-P/latest.

Hadassah, Women's Zionist Organization for America: Hadassah, Mailing Address,
40 Wall St., https://www.hadassah.org/about/index.html. USASpending.gov, re
cipient profile, Hadassah, The Women's Zionist Organization of America, Inc,
https://www.usaspending.gov/#/recipient/1722729e-e45a-90d8-da20-10b9b9
1e9cc6-P/latest.

Goldman Sachs: Goldman Sachs, Office Locations, 555 California Street, 45th Floor,
San Francisco, CA 94104, https://www.goldmansachs.com/our-firm/locations.html.
USASpending.gov, recipient profile, The Goldman Sachs Group Inc., https://www
.usaspending.gov/#/recipient/ea005464-deb1-d923-d064-0e7a4fac12ef-P/latest.

Equitable Holdings: Form 10-K, Equitable Holdings Inc., Securities and Exchange
Commission, 1290 Ave. of the Americas, https://www.sec.gov/Archives/edgar/data/
1333986/000133398620000015/eqh201910-k.htm. USASpending.gov, recipient pro-

file, AXA, https://www.usaspending.gov/#/recipient/27861b3d-d862-329b-8b97-44e
41dec453e-P/latest.

Ibisworld: Ibisworld, Contact Us, United States HQ, New York, T40 Wall St., 15th
Floor, New York, NY 10005, USA, https://www.ibisworld.com/contact-us/. USAS
pending.gov, recipient profile, Ibisworld, Inc., https://www.usaspending.gov/#/re
cipient/75bb2a11-c8a0-c939-0d92-b65194237b23-P/latest.

LERA Consulting: LERA Offices, New York City Headquarters, 40 Wall St., Floor 23,
https://www.lera.com/blank. USASpending.gov, recipient profile, Lera Consulting
Structural Engineers, RLLP, https://www.usaspending.gov/#/recipient/885986a9-b8ad
-d8e4-6f31-9bf929d33b0b-P/latest.

Norton Rose Fulbright: Norton Rose Fulbright, Location, San Francisco, Norton Rose
Fulbright US LLP, 555 California St., https://www.nortonrosefulbright.com/en-us
/locations/san-francisco. USASpending.gov, recipient profile, Norton Rose Fulbright US LLP https://www.usaspending.gov/#/recipient/85a4bc16-6452-e008-ca51
-56288f5c874b-P/latest.

Access Intelligence: Access Intelligence, Contact, Locations, 40 Wall St., 50th Floor,
https://www.accessintel.com/contact/. USASpending.gov, recipient profile, Access
Intelligence LLC, https://www.usaspending.gov/#/recipient/dbc9a66f-149c-18b3-dd79
-f710b97a9bd6-P/latest.

GNC: GNC at Trump Plaza, https://www.gnc.com/store-details?StoreID=2564. US
ASpending.gov, recipient profile, GNC Holdings INC., https://www.usaspending
.gov/#/recipient/daf8398f-6b58-9631-da8a-eb5dc53bdd89-P/latest.

Authentic8: Authentic8, Office Locations, San Francisco, 555 California St., Suite
3360, San Francisco, CA 94104, https://www.authentic8.com/contact-us/. USAS
pending.gov, recipient profile, Authentic8, Inc., https://www.usaspending.gov/#/re
cipient/20047998-03d6-dc13-3748-3503d4ef255a-P/latest.

Telstra: Telstra, Enterprise, Our Global Offices, New York, NY Office, 40 Wall St.,
https://www.telstra.com.au/business-enterprise/about-enterprise/our-global-offices.
USASpending.gov, recipient profile, Telstra Corporation Limited, https://www.us
aspending.gov/#/recipient/269ae5af-1a6a-9c8e-c7e0-797b7b511227-P/latest.

Nike: Charlie Brooks (Nike), email to author, October 3, 2017. USASpending.gov, recipient profile, Nike, https://www.usaspending.gov/#/recipient/50488510-e78b-4827
-b28c-4bebedba80e6-P/latest.

Morgan Stanley: Morgan Stanley, San Francisco Complex Office, 555 California St.,
https://advisor.morganstanley.com/san-francisco-complex. USASpending.gov, recipient profile, Morgan Stanley, https://www.usaspending.gov/#/recipient/133f6029-d54c
-0d69-fdec-fe79706b0af3-P/latest.

Regus: Regus, 315 Montgomery St., https://www.regus.com/offices/united-states/cali
fornia/san-francisco/office-space/california-san-francisco-315-montgomery. USASpen
ding.gov, recipient profile, Regus Management Group LLC, https://www.usaspend
ing.gov/#/recipient/cda94608-919f-b8d5-ca8c-0d9c6336dcc7-P/latest.

Girl Scouts of Greater New York: Girl Scouts of Greater New York, 40 Wall St., Suite
708, New York, NY 10005, https://www.girlscoutsnyc.org/en/about-girl-scouts/who
-we-are/Termsandconditions.html. USASpending.gov, recipient profile, Girl Scouts
of the United States of America, https://www.usaspending.gov/#/recipient/4b7890
65-1425-9651-7c1d-aed11965db69-P/latest.

New York Sports Club: Address, 502 Park Ave., Tenant, https://www.newyorksports
clubs.com/clubs/59th-park. USASpending.gov, recipient profile, Town Sports International Holdings, Inc., https://www.usaspending.gov/#/recipient/fb0cb458-36e2
-5ed7-4c8d-34a9a2c6215b-P/latest.

36. Analysis of contracts from 2018 to 2019.

37. The 17 tenants are:

Walgreens Boots Alliance: Walgreens—Store #14485, 40 Wall St., New York, NY 10005, https://www.walgreens.com/locator/duane+reade-40+wall+st-new+york-ny-10005/id= 14485. Walgreens Boots Alliance, Inc., Form 10-K, Securities and Exchange Commission, for the fiscal year ended August 31, 2018, 84–85, https://www.sec.gov/Archives/edgar/data/1618921/000162828018012472/wba-2018831x10k.htm.

JPMorgan: Chase Radio City 51 W. 51st St., New York, NY 10019, https://locator.chase.com/ny/new-york/51-w-51st-st. JPMorgan Chase & Co., Form 10-K, Securities and Exchange Commission, for the fiscal year ended December 31, 2017, 269, https://www.sec.gov/Archives/edgar/data/19617/000000196171800057/corp10k2017.htm.

Santander Bank: Santander Bank, Branch 1290 Ave. of the AmericasNew York, NY 10019, https://locations.santanderbank.com/ny/new-york/1290-avenue-of-the-americas.html. Banco Santander, Form 20-F, Securities and Exchange Commission, for the fiscal year ended December 31, 2018, 98, https://www.sec.gov/Archives/edgar/data/891478/000155837019002417/san-20181231x20f.htm.

Garrison Investment Group: Garrison Investment Group, 1290 Ave. of the Americas, https://www.garrisoninv.com. "SEC Charges New York Investment Advisers with Entering into Prohibited Transactions, Other Violations, Administrative Proceeding," File No. 3-19452, September 13, 2019, https://www.sec.gov/enforce/ia-5345-s.

State Street: State Street Office Locations, New York, International Fund Services (N.A), LLC, State Street Bank and Trust Company, National Association, 1290 Ave. of the Americas, 10th Floor, https://www.statestreet.com/about/office-locations.html. State Street Corporation, Form 10-K, Securities and Exchange Commission, for the fiscal year ended December 31, 2018, 33, https://www.sec.gov/Archives/edgar/data/93751/000000937511900336/stt-20181231_10k.htm.

Atane: HAKS, Corporate HQ, 40 Wall St., http://www.haks.net/Preview/Locations.php. Investigations, U.S. Department of Transportation, and the District Attorney's Office of New York, "FHWA Suspends 21 New York and New Jersey Individuals and Companies," May 1, 2019, https://www.oig.dot.gov/library-item/37243.

Verizon: XO Communications 40 Wall St., 16th Floor, New York, NY 10005, https://www.xo.com/contact-us/sales/sales-office-locations/new-york. "FCC Settles E-Rate Investigation with Verizon," FCC, 32 FCC Rcd 7723 (9), October 17, 2017, https://www.fcc.gov/document/fcc-settles-e-rate-investigation-verizon.

JH Darbie & Co.: JH Darbie & Co. Corporate Headquarters, 40 Wall St., http://jhdarbie.com/sv/contact. "SEC Charges Broker-Dealer, CEO with Net Capital Rule Violations," Administrative Proceeding, File No. 3-18409, March 27, 2018, https://www.sec.gov/enforce/34-82951-s.

Magna Group: Contact Us, 40 Wall St., https://www.mag.na/contact/. "SEC Files Charges in Elaborate Microcap Stock Fraud," February 15, 2019, https://www.sec.gov/news/press-release/2019-13.

SS&C Technologies: SS&C Technologies, Offices, 40 Wall St., Wayback Machine, https://web.archive.org/web/20190604125233/https:/www.ssctech.com/about-us/offices. SS&C Technologies Holdings Inc., Form 10-K, Securities and Exchange Commission, for the fiscal year ended December 31, 2018, 85, https://www.sec.gov/Archives/edgar/data/1402436/000156459019005753/ssnc-10k_20181231.htm.

Capital One: Capital One, 502 Park Ave., New York, NY 10022, https://locations.capitalone.com/location/branch_46062. Capital One Financial Corporation, Form 10-K,

Securities and Exchange Commission, for the fiscal year ended December 31, 2018, 209, https://www.sec.gov/ix?doc=/Archives/edgar/data/927628/000092762819000093 /cof-12312018x10k.htm.

Bank of America: Bank of America locations, San Francisco Main Financial Center and ATM 315 Montgomery St., San Francisco, CA 94104, US, https://locators.banko famerica.com/ca/sanfrancisco/financial-centers-san-francisco-16793.html. "U.S. At- torney's Office Announces $2.5 Million Settlement with Bank of America for Trading Ahead and Obstructing the CME's Investigation," U.S. Department of Justice, U.S. Attorney's Office, Western District of North Carolina, September 22, 2017, https:// www.justice.gov/usao-wdnc/pr/us-attorneys-office-announces-25-million -settlement-bank-america-trading-ahead-and.

Microsoft: Vornado Realty Trust, Office, San Francisco, 555 California St., Tenant Profile, Microsoft, https://www.vno.com/office/property/555-california-street/331 1899/landing. "Hungary Subsidiary of Microsoft Corporation Agrees to Pay $8.7 Million in Criminal Penalties to Resolve Foreign Bribery Case," U.S. Department of Justice, Office of Public Affairs, July 22, 2019, https://www.justice.gov/opa/pr /hungary-subsidiary-microsoft-corporation-agrees-pay-87-million-criminal -penalties-resolve.

Morgan Stanley: Morgan Stanley, San Francisco Complex Office, 555 California St., https://advisor.morganstanley.com/san-francisco-complex. "SEC Charges Morgan Stanley in Connection with Failure to Detect or Prevent Misappropriation of Client Funds," June 29, 2018, https://www.sec.gov/news/press-release/2018-124.

Wells Fargo: Wells Fargo Advisors, San Francisco, CA Branch, 555 California St., https://home.wellsfargoadvisors.com/001_PCA7. Wells Fargo 2018 Annual Report, 216, https://www08.wellsfargomedia.com/assets/pdf/about/investor-relations/annual -reports/2018-annual-report.pdf.

UBS: UBS Locations, UBS Financial Services Inc. 555 California St., San Francisco CA 94104, https://www.ubs.com/locations/united-states/san-francisco/555-california-street /ubs-financial-services-inc-846.html. UBS Group AG, Form 20-F, Securities and Exchange Commission, for the fiscal year ended December 31, 2017, 381.

Goldman Sachs: Goldman Sachs, Office Locations, 555 California St., 45th Floor, San Francisco, CA 94104, https://www.goldmansachs.com/our-firm/locations.html. "CFTC Orders Goldman Sachs to Pay $1 Million for Recordkeeping Violations," November 26, 2019, https://www.cftc.gov/PressRoom/PressReleases/8086-19.

38. See Magna Group, above.
39. See Capital One, above.
40. See Microsoft, above.
41. Abu Dhabi Tourism and Culture, January 27, 2017, Wayback Machine, https://web.ar chive.org/web/20170127204046/https://tcaabudhabi.ae/en/who.we.are/our.offices.aspx
42. U.S. Department of Justice, Supplemental Statement Pursuant to the Foreign Agents Reg- istration Act of 1938, as amended, https://efile.fara.gov/docs/6134-Supplemental-State ment-20161004-8.pdf.
43. Abu Dhabi Tourism and Culture, January 27, 2017.
44. Abu Dhabi Tourism and Culture, Wayback Machine, May 2, 2017, https://web.archive .org/web/20170502022859/https://tcaabudhabi.ae/en/who.we.are/our.offices.aspx
45. Bank of India website, author's screenshot, October 31, 2019.
46. Research conducted by author for *Forbes*.
47. Vornado Green Book, October 23, 2019, 15, http://fliphtml5.com/twmd/aygt/basic.
48. Bank of India Annual Report 2018–2019, 63, https://www.bankofindia.co.in/pdf/AN NUAL_REPORT_20192.pdf.

49. "Vornado Realty Trust Supplemental Operating and Financial Data for the Quarter Ended September 30, 2019," 48, Vornado Green Book, 15.

50. Photograph taken at 555 California Street by author, December 2019.

51. Text messages to author, November 2019; San Francisco Assessor-Recorder, Notice of Non-Responsibility, HWA 555 Owners LLC, Qatar Investment Authority Advisor (USA) Inc., August 30, 2018.

52. "President-Elect Donald Trump News Conference," C-SPAN, January 11, 2017, https://www.c-span.org/video/?421482-1/president-elect-donald-trump-election-year-hacking-i-russia.

53. Richard Painter, interviewed by author, July 27, 2017.

54. HQ Capital Private Equity LLC, 1290 Ave. of the Americas, Floor 10, https://hqcapital.com/en/company/offices/.

55. HQ Capital, "History," https://hqcapital.com/en/company/history/.

56. Chris Newlands, "Quandts Family Office Expands Client Base," *Financial Times,* October 22, 2015, https://www.ft.com/content/572803f0-6d06-11e5-8171-ba1968cf791a.

57. Edward Giltenan, "Quandt Family Buy a BMW," *Forbes,* October 5, 1987.

58. "Stefan Quandt," *Forbes,* https://www.forbes.com/profile/stefan-quandt/#10b35e371e49.

59. "The Protocol Amending the Tax Convention with Spain," Senate Consideration of Treaty Document 113-4, https://disclosurespreview.house.gov/ld/ldxmlrelease/2019/Q4/301125142.xml.

60. Vornado Realty Trust, Q2 2012 Earnings Call, August 7, 2012; Vornado Green Book, 67.

61. Analysis of Vornado Green Book, 65, 8; Equitable Holdings spokesperson, telephone interview with author, May 15, 2020.

62. AXA Equitable Holdings, Inc., Form 10-K, Securities and Exchange Commission, December 31, 2018, 97, https://www.sec.gov/Archives/edgar/data/1333986/000133398619000010/eqhs-1and10xk.htm.

63. "Remarks by President Trump Before Air Force One Departure," August 18, 2019, White House, https://www.whitehouse.gov/briefings-statements/remarks-president-trump-air-force-one-departure-12/.

64. Clerk of the United States House of Representatives, Lobbying Disclosure Act of 1995 (Section 5), Jones Day, https://disclosurespreview.house.gov/ld/ldxmlrelease/2019/Q4/301124734.xml.

65. Analysis of Vornado Green Book, 13; analysis of Vornado Realty Trust, Supplemental Operating and Financial Data, for the Quarter and Year ended December 31, 2019, 50.

66. Venable Offices, New York—1290 Ave. of the Americans, https://www.venable.com/offices.

67. Analysis of Vornado Green Book, 67, 65.

68. Clerk of the United States House of Representatives, Lobbying Disclosure Act of 1995 (Section 5), Venable LLP, January 21, 2020, https://disclosurespreview.house.gov/ld/ldxmlrelease/2019/Q4/301124704.xml; July 22, 2019, https://disclosurespreview.house.gov/ld/ldxmlrelease/2019/Q2/301054637.xml; April 18, 2019, https://disclosurespreview.house.gov/ld/ldxmlrelease/2019/Q1/301028707.xml; October 21, 2019, https://disclosurespreview.house.gov/ld/ldxmlrelease/2019/Q3/301073765.xml.

69. Sberbank, "Shareholder Structure," https://www.sberbank.com/investor-relations/share-profile/shareholder-structure.

70. Clerk of the United States House of Representatives, Lobbying Disclosure Act of 1995 (Section 5), Venable LLP, January 21, 2020; Defending Elections from Threats by Establishing Redlines Act of 2019, S. 1060, § 201, § 101, 116th Cong. (2019), First Session, April 8, 2019, https://www.congress.gov/bill/116th-congress/senate-bill/1060/text?q=%7B%22search%22%3A%5B%22as%22%5D%7D&r=87&s=1#toc-idA56783BD8F5140

649B72C1AA9AE7BCA9; Defending American Security from Kremlin Aggression Act of 2019, S. 482, § 501, 116th Cong. (2019), First Session, February 13, 2019, http://www .congress.gov/bill/116th-congress-senate-bill/482/text?q=%7B%22search%22%3A%5B %22Defending+American+Security+from+Kremlin+Aggression+Act+of+2019%22%5D %7D&r=1.

71. Brendan McCormick, email to author, May 14, 2020.

72. "Remarks by President Trump in Listening Session with the Retail Industry Leaders Association and Member Company CEOs," White House, February 15, 2017, https://www .whitehouse.gov/briefings-statements/remarks-president-trump-listening-session-retail -industry-leaders-association-member-company-ceos/.

73. "Stefano Pessina," *Forbes,* https://www.forbes.com/profile/stefano-pessina/#3295ed2868dc.

74. Prospectus Supplement, Wells Fargo Commercial Mortgage Trust 2015-LC22, Securities and Exchange Commission, August 3, 2015, A-3-6, https://www.sec.gov/Archives/edgar /data/850779/000153949715001541/n537_pros-x14.htm; Walgreen Boots Alliance, Form 10-K, Securities and Exchange Commission, for the fiscal year ended August 31, 2019, 1, https://www.sec.gov/Archives/edgar/data/1618921/000161892119000069/wba -2019831x10k.htm.

75. Richard C. Morais, "Psst . . . Wanna Buy Some Augmentin?" *Forbes,* April 12, 2004.

76. "The Club's New Members," *Forbes,* March 15, 2004.

77. "Stefano Pessina," *Forbes.*

78. Mark Scott, "Walgreen to Take Stake in Alliance Boots for $6.7 Billion," *New York Times,* June 19, 2012, https://dealbook.nytimes.com/2012/06/19/walgreens-to-take-45 -stake-in-alliance-boots-for-6-7-billion/.

79. Walgreens Boots Alliance, Schedule 14 A, Securities and Exchange Commission, 42, https://www.sec.gov/Archives/edgar/data/1618921/000120677419003835/wba3593081 -def14a.htm.

80. "Statement of Acting Chairman Maureen K. Ohlhausen Regarding the Walgreens/Rite Aid Transaction," September 19, 2017, https://www.ftc.gov/system/files/documents/pub lic_statements/1255033/1710181_walgreens_rite_aid_statement_of_acting_chairman _ohlhausen.pdf.

81. "White House Listening Session on the Retail Industry," C-SPAN, February 15, 2017, https:// www.c-span.org/video/?424083-1/president-trump-holds-listening-session-retail-industry.

82. Clerk of the United States House of Representatives, LD-2 Disclosure Forms, Clerk of the United States House of Representatives, Lobbying Disclosure Act of 1995 (Section 5), Walgreen Co., April 20, 2017, https://disclosurespreview.house.gov/ld/ldxmlrelease/2017 /Q1/300874995.xml; July 20, 2017, https://disclosurespreview.house.gov/ld/ldxmlrelease /2017/Q2/300891899.xml; October 11, 2017, https://disclosurespreview.house.gov/ld/ldxm lrelease/2017/Q3/300902629.xml; January 10, 2018, https://disclosurespreview.house.gov /ld/ldxmlrelease/2017/Q4/300922546.xml.

83. "White House Listening Session on the Retail Industry," C-SPAN.

84. "Walgreens Boots Alliance Secures Regulatory Clearance for Purchase of Stores and Related Assets from Rite Aid, "Walgreens Boots Alliance, September 19, 2017, https://www .walgreensbootsalliance.com/news-media/press-releases/2017/walgreens-boots-alliance -secures-regulatory-clearance-purchase.

85. Analysis of FTC commissioner biographies, https://www.ftc.gov/about-ftc/commission ers, https://www.ftc.gov/about-ftc/biographies/former-commissioners.

86. "Statement of Commissioner Terrell McSweeny Regarding the Walgreens/Rite Aid Transaction," Federal Trade Commission, https://www.ftc.gov/system/files/documents/public _statements/1255043/1710181_walgreens_rite_aid_statement_of_commissioner_mc sweeny.pdf.

87. "Statement of Acting Chairman Maureen K. Ohlhausen Regarding the Walgreens/Rite Aid Transaction."

88. "President Donald J. Trump Announces Tenth Wave of Judicial Nominees," White House January 23, 2018, https://www.whitehouse.gov/presidential-actions/president-donald-j-trump-announces-tenth-wave-judicial-nominees/.

89. Phil Caruso, Walgreens Media Relations, email to author, January 26, 2018.

90. Maureen Ohlhausen, email to author, May 11, 2020.

91. "Remarks by President Trump Before Marine One Departure," White House, January 21, 2017, https://www.whitehouse.gov/briefings-statements/remarks-president-trump-marine-one-departure-3/; Donald Trump, Twitter, July 24, 2018, https://twitter.com/realdonaldtrump/status/1021917767467982854.

92. Analysis of Vornado Green Book, 67.

93. "Remarks by President Trump in Strategy and Policy Forum," February 3, 2017, https://www.whitehouse.gov/briefings-statements/remarks-president-trump-strategy-policy-forum/.

94. "Remarks by the President at the AARP," Obama White House Archives, February 23, 2015, https://obamawhitehouse.archives.gov/the-press-office/2015/02/23/remarks-president-aarp.

95. Morgan Stanley, San Francisco Complex Office, 555 California St., https://advisor.morganstanley.com/san-francisco-complex.

96. Clerk of the United States House of Representatives, LD-2 Disclosure Form, Morgan Stanley, April 19, 2017, https://disclosurespreview.house.gov/ld/ldxmlrelease/2017/Q1/300868933.xml.

97. "Economic Report of the President, February 2018, "White House, 84, https://www.whitehouse.gov/wp-content/uploads/2018/02/ERP_2018_Final-FINAL.pdf.

98. "Economic Report of the President, February 2020," White House, 135, https://www.whitehouse.gov/wp-content/uploads/2020/02/2020-Economic-Report-of-the-President-WHCEA.pdf.

99. "Regulation Best Interest, A Small Entity Compliance Guide," Securities and Exchange Commission, https://www.sec.gov/info/smallbus/secg/regulation-best-interest#Introduction.

100. Clerk of the United States House of Representatives, LD-2 Disclosure Form, JPMorgan Chase Holdings LLC, January 22, 2019, https://disclosurespreview.house.gov/ld/ldxmlrelease/2018/Q4/301016536.xml.

101. Alexander and Drange, "Trump's Biggest Potential Conflict of Interest."

102. Clerk of the United States House of Representatives, LD-2 Disclosure Form, The Trustees of Columbia University in the City of New York, July 22, 2019, https://disclosurespreview.house.gov/ld/ldxmlrelease/2019/Q2/301054999.xml.

103. Analysis of VNDO 2012-6AVE Commercial Mortgage Pass-Through Certificates, Morningstar, https://ratingagency.morningstar.com/PublicDocDisplay.aspx?i=NFoOdtw2Vyo%3D&m=i0Pyc%2Bx7qZZ4%2BsXnymazBA%3D%3D&s=LviRtUKXqs8kml5dHt7FTeE2SZmY0Fvqd4iX49Mk%2F9UapyiFTEO6TA%3D%3D.

104. Clerk of the United States House of Representatives, LD-2 Disclosure Form, Nike, Inc., January 16, 2020, https://disclosurespreview.house.gov/ld/ldxmlrelease/2019/Q4/301106721.xml.

105. Dan Alexander and Matt Drange, "Landlord in Chief," *Forbes,* February 13, 2018, https://www.forbes.com/trump-tenants/#30aeed91d320.

106. Clerk of the United States House of Representatives, LD-2 Disclosure Form, Ripple Labs, Inc., April 18, 2019, https://disclosurespreview.house.gov/ld/ldxmlrelease/2019/Q1/301029911.xml.

107. Analysis of Vornado financial statement, April 2, 2018, https://www.sec.gov/Archives/edgar/data/899689/000110465918022863/a18-9693_1ex99d1.htm; analysis of Vornado Green Book.

108. Girl Scouts of Greater New York, 40 Wall St., Suite 708 New York, NY 10005, https://www.girlscoutsnyc.org/en/about-girl-scouts/who-we-are/Termsandconditions.html.

109. Michael Lopes, email to author, May 13, 2020.

110. Clerk of the United States House of Representatives, LD-2 Disclosure Form, Girl Scouts of the U.S.A., April 17, 2017, https://disclosurespreview.house.gov/ld/ldxmlrelease/2017/Q1/300866531.xml.

111. "President Donald J. Trump Proclaims June 2017 as Great Outdoors Month," May 31, 2017, https://www.whitehouse.gov/presidential-actions/president-donald-j-trump-proclaims-june-2017-great-outdoors-month/.

112. U.S. Government Accountability Office, "Decision, Matter of Oracle America Inc.," November 14, 2018, 2, https://www.gao.gov/assets/700/695586.pdf.

113. U.S. Government Accountability Office, Oracle America Inc.

114. Analysis of Vornado Q3 2019 Financial Supplement, 48, 13, 48, and additional documents.

115. U.S. Government Accountability Office, "Decision in the matter of IBM-U.S., Federal File B-407073.3, B-407073.4, B-407073.5, B-407073.6," June 6, 2013, https://www.gao.gov/assets/660/655241.pdf.

116. Congressional Research Service, the Department of Defense's JEDI Cloud Program, August 2, 2019, https://crsreports.congress.gov/product/pdf/R/R45847.

117. Marco Rubio, Twitter, August 1, 2019, https://twitter.com/marcorubio/status/1157047946405240832.

118. Guy Snodgrass, *Holding the Line* (New York: Sentinel, 2019), 309.

119. U.S. Department of Defense, "Report on the Joint Enterprise Defense Infrastructure (JEDI) Cloud Procurement," April 13, 2020, 102, https://media.defense.gov/2020/Apr/15/2002281438/-1/-1/1/REPORT%20ON%20THE%20JOINT%20ENTERPRISE%20DEFENSE%20INFRASTRUCTURE%20(JEDI)%20CLOUD%20PROCUREMENT%20DODIG-2020-079.PDF.

120. James Mattis, Secretary of Defense, Letter of Resignation, December 20, 2018, https://media.defense.gov/2018/Dec/20/2002075156/-1/-1/1/letter-from-secretary-james-n-mattis.pdf.

121. "Remarks by President Trump and Prime Minister Rutte of the Netherlands Before Bilateral Meeting," White House, July 18, 2019, https://www.whitehouse.gov/briefings-statements/remarks-president-trump-prime-minister-rutte-netherlands-bilateral-meeting/.

122. "Secretary of Defense Esper Media Engagement En Route to Sydney, Australia," U.S. Department of Defense, August 2, 2019, https://www.defense.gov/Newsroom/Transcripts/Transcript/Article/1925072/secretary-of-defense-esper-media-engagement-en-route-to-sydney-australia/.

123. "Statement from Chief Pentagon Spokesperson Jonathan Rath Hoffman on DOD Cloud Update," U.S. Department of Defense, October 22, 2019, https://www.defense.gov/Newsroom/Releases/Release/Article/1995650/statement-from-chief-pentagon-spokesperson-jonathan-rath-hoffman-on-dod-cloud-u/.

124. "Contracts for October 25, 2019, "U.S. Department of Defense, https://www.defense.gov/Newsroom/Contracts/Contract/Article/1999639/.

125. Richard Painter, interviewed by author, May 11, 2020; Don Fox, interviewed by author, May 12, 2020; Virginia Canter, interviewed by author, May 13, 2020; Walter Shaub, interviewed by author, May 15, 2020; Marilyn Glynn, interviewed by author, May 16, 2020.

126. "Armed Services," C-SPAN, October 29, 2019" U.S. Department of Defense, https://www.c-span.org/video/?465480-1/armed-services.

127. U.S. Department of Defense, "Report on the Joint Enterprise Defense Infrastructure (JEDI) Cloud Procurement," 8, 9.

128. Elissa Brown, email to author, May 11, 2020.

129. Analysis of Prospectus Supplement, Wells Fargo Commercial Mortgage Trust 2012-LC5, Securities and Exchange Commission, July 20, 2012, A-3-33, https://www.sec.gov/Ar chives/edgar/data/850779/000153949712000571/prospectus-supplement.htm; analysis of Nike lease, 7, November 30, 1995, New York City Department of Finance, Office of the City Register, https://a836-acris.nyc.gov/DS/DocumentSearch/DocumentImageView?doc _id=FT_1180004945118.

130. Dan Alexander and Matt Drange, "Poorer President," *Forbes,* November 14, 2017.

131. Analysis of USASpending.gov, recipient profile, Microsoft Corporation, https://www.us aspending.gov/#/recipient/13f1c931-edc1-d2bc-07a6-c809332ae02a-P/latest.

132. A spokesperson for Columbia declined to comment on the record. Analysis of USASpend ing.gov, recipient profile, Trustees of Columbia University in the City of New York, https:// www.usaspending.gov/#/recipient/01daf754-a68e-fbe9-8f28 -0246869c54ac-P/latest; Trustees of Columbia University in the City of New York, The, https://www.usaspending.gov/#/recipient/03aa78e7-78f5-7779-fc3e-8890eeec17ce-P/lat est; Teachers College, Columbia University, https://www.usaspending.gov/#/recipient /ba4aadbf-3e8e-0e42-231c-1fa9b6c4f67a-P/latest.

133. Representatives for ICF did not respond to multiple requests for comment. USASpend ing.gov, recipient profile, ICF International, Inc., https://www.usaspending.gov/#/recipient /992f0d92-dfad-d76d-675d-b35f3e49616c-P/latest.

134. A spokesperson for McKinsey declined to comment on the record. Steven Roth, "Chair-man's Letter," 12, Securities and Exchange Commission, https://www.sec.gov/Archives /edgar/data/899689/000089183617000044/ex_99-1.htm.

135. USASpending.gov, recipient profile, McKinsey & Company, Inc., https://www.usa spending.gov/#/recipient/8507105f-01f7-1eff-2e79-72eb0ca1c157-P/latest.

136. USASpending.gov, recipient profile, Wells Fargo & Company, https://www.usaspending .gov/#/recipient/741dda66-0b1e-50fb-13de-36849bc84de2-P/latest.

137. "Consumer Financial Protection Bureau Fines Wells Fargo $100 Million for Widespread Illegal Practice of Secretly Opening Unauthorized Accounts," CFPB, September 8, 2016, 5, https://www.consumerfinance.gov/about-us/newsroom/consumer-financial-protection -bureau-fines-wells-fargo-100-million-widespread-illegal-practice-secretly-opening -unauthorized-accounts/, https://www08.wellsfargomedia.com/assets/pdf/about/investor -relations/annual-reports/2016-annual-report.pdf.

138. A spokesperson for Wells Fargo declined to comment. USASpending.gov, recipient pro-file, Wells Fargo & Company, https://www.usaspending.gov/#/recipient/741dda66-0b1e -50fb-13de-36849bc84de2-P/latest.

139. Analysis of federal contracting data from usaspending.gov.

140. Analysis of tenant payments.

141. Walgreens Boots Alliance. HAKS. Verizon. JH Darbie & Co. Magna Group. SS&C Technologies.

142. Prospectus Supplement, Wells Fargo Commercial Mortgage Trust 2015-LC22, Securities and Exchange Commission, August 3, 2015, A-3-6, https://www.sec.gov/Archives/edgar /data/850779/000153949715001541/n537_pros-x14.htm.

143. "Twenty-One Individuals and Companies Indicted in New York Corruption and Fraud Scheme," Office of Inspector General, U.S. Department of Transportation, April 18, 2018, https://www.oig.dot.gov/library-item/36482.

144. "New York City Construction Management Company Principals Plead Guilty and Agree to Forfeit $3 Million," Office of Inspector General, U.S. Department of Transportation, May 13, 2019, https://www.oig.dot.gov/library-item/37254.

145. Quaiser Hashmi, telephone interview with author, May 20, 2020.

146. Capital One Financial Corporation, Form 10-K, Securities and Exchange Commission, for the year ended December 31, 2018, 209, https://www.sec.gov/ix?doc=/Archives/edgar/data/927628/000092762819000093/cof-12312018x10k.htm.

147. "SEC Charges UBS Financial Services Inc. with Anti-Money Laundering Violations," U.S. Securities and Exchange Commission, November 17, 2018, https://www.sec.gov/enforce/34-84828-s.

148. "Bill Cumbelich," CBRE, https://www.cbre.com/people-and-offices/bill-cumbelich; Vornado Green Book, 15; analysis of Vornado Realty Trust, Supplemental Operating and Financial Data, for the Quarter and Year ended December 31, 2019, 48.

149. "SEC Charges Barclays with FCPA Violations Related to Its Hiring Practices," Securities and Exchange Commission, Administrative Proceeding, File No. 3-19537, September 27, 2019, https://www.sec.gov/enforce/34-87132-s.

150. U.S. Department of Defense, "Report on the Joint Enterprise Defense Infrastructure (JEDI) Cloud Procurement," 34; U.S. Department of Defense, contracts for October 25, 2019, https://www.defense.gov/Newsroom/Contracts/Contract/Article/1999639/.

151. "SEC Charges Microsoft Corporation with FCPA Violations," Securities and Exchange Commission, July 22, 2019, https://www.sec.gov/enforce/34-86421-s-0.

152. Spokesperson for Fox Television Stations, telephone interview with author, January 26, 2018; Prospectus Supplement, Wells Fargo Commercial Mortgage Trust 2016-LC24, Securities and Exchange Commission, September 15, 2016, A-1-1, A-1-15, https://www.sec.gov/Archives/edgar/data/850779/000153949716003632/n725_x15.htm.

153. Spokesperson for CNN, email to author, April 21, 2020; Jonathan O'Connell, Twitter, November 15, 2019, https://twitter.com/OConnellPostbiz/status/1195364225939648515; DC.gov Office of Tax and Revenue, Property detail, https://www.taxpayerservicecenter.com/RP_Detail.jsp?ssl=PI0003230079.

CHAPTER SEVEN: CASHING IN

1. Coral Davenport, "Rick Perry, Ex-Governor of Texas, Is Trump's Pick as Energy Secretary," *New York Times*, December 13, 2016, nytimes.com/2016/1/13/us/politics/rick-perry-energy-secretary-trump.html.

2. Margaret Brennan, "Rex Tillerson Opens Up in Rare, Wide-Ranging Interview," CBS News, February 18, 2018, https://www.cbsnews.com/news/rex-tillerson-secretary-of-state-60-minutes-interview/.

3. "Wilbur Ross Arrival at Trump Tower," C-SPAN, December 15, 2016, https://www.c-span.org/video/?420221-105/wilbur-ross-arrival-trump-tower.

4. "Paul Ryan at Trump Tower," C-SPAN, December 9, 2016, https://www.c-span.org/video/?419850-2/house-speaker-speaks-reporters-trump-tower.

5. "Senate Majority Leader Mitch McConnell at Trump Tower," C-SPAN, January 9, 2017, https://www.c-span.org/video/?421399-2/senate-majority-leader-mitch-mcconnell-trump-tower.

6. "Technology Summit at Trump Tower," C-SPAN, December 14, 2016, https://www.c-span.org/video/?420133-1/president-elect-donald-trump-holds-technology-summit.

7. Chase Peterson-Withorn, "Woman with Chinese Government Connections Bought Jared and Ivanka's Penthouse," *Forbes,* January 17, 2019, https://www.forbes.com/sites/chasewithorn/2019/01/17/woman-with-chinese-government-connections-bought-jared-and-ivankas-penthouse/#4ba3078b22d9.

8. NYC Department of Finance, Office of the City Register, Trump Park Avenue LLC, Xiao Yan Chen, February 21, 2017, 10, https://a836-acris.nyc.gov/DS/DocumentSearch

/DocumentImageView?doc_id=2017022300040002; Donald Trump, OGE Form 278e, U.S. Office of Government Ethics, 5 C.F.R. part 2634 (hereafter "Donald Trump, OGE Form 278e"), May 15, 2019, 77, 64; Trump International Hotel Liquor License Filings with Trust Info, ProPublica, January 26, 2017, 7, https://www.documentcloud .org/documents/3442581-Trump-International-Hotel-Liquor-License-Filings #document/p7.

9. Also known as Xiao Yan Chen.

10. "Access," Global Alliance Associates, LLC, https://gaa.lucita.org/about_overview_access .shtml.

11. NYC Department of Finance, Office of the City Register, Trump Park Avenue LLC, Xiao Yan Chen.

12. Analysis of property records.

13. Analysis of property records.

14. "Donald J. Trump Files Personal Financial Disclosure Statement with Federal Election Commission," Wayback Machine, July 15, 2015, https://web.archive.org/we/201508240 10812/https://www.donaldjtrump.com/press-releases/donald-j.-trump-files-personal -financial-disclosure-statement-with-federal.

15. Analysis of Wells Fargo Commercial Mortgage Trust 2012-LC5, Commercial Mortgage Pass-Through Certificates Series 2012-LC5, Form 10-D, Securities and Exchange Commission, March 17, 2016, 13, A-1-2, https://www.sec.gov/Archives/edgar/data/1556601 /000105640416004079/wcm12lc5_ex991-201603.htm.

16. Donald Trump, OGE Form 278e, May 15, 2019, and July 15, 2015.

17. 40 Wall Street: Analysis of more than 100 SEC filings related to COMM 2015-CCRE24 Mortgage Trust, Wells Fargo Commercial Mortgage Trust 2015-LC22, and COMM 2015-LC23 Mortgage Trust, https://www.sec.gov/cgi-bin/browse-edgar?company =lc22&match=contains&CIK=&filenum=&State=&Country=&SIC=&owner=ex clude&Find=Find+Companies&action=getcompany,   https://www.sec.gov/cgi-bin /browse-edgar?company=lc23&match=contains&CIK=&filenum=&State=& Country=&SIC=&owner=exclude&Find=Find+Companies&action=getcompany, https://www.sec.gov/cgi-bin/browse-edgar?company=ccre24&match=contains &CIK=&filenum=&State=&Country=&SIC=&owner=exclude&Find=Find +Companies&action=getcompany.

Trump Plaza: Analysis of dozens of SEC filings for COMM 2014-CCRE19 Mortgage Trust, https://www.sec.gov/cgi-bin/browse-edgar?company=COMM+2014-CCRE19 +Mortgage+Trust&match=&CIK=&filenum=&State=&Country=&SIC=&owner =exclude&Find=Find+Companies&action=getcompany.

Trump International Hotel & Tower (NYC): Analysis of dozens of SEC filings for Wells Fargo Commercial Mortgage Trust 2016-LC24, https://www.sec.gov/cgi-bin/browse -edgar?company=Wells+Fargo+Commercial+Mortgage+Trust+2016-LC24 &match=contains&CIK=&filenum=&State=&Country=&SIC=&owner=exclude &Find=Find+Companies&action=getcompany.

555 California Street: Analysis of a dozen supplements to quarterly reports filed by Vornado Realty Trust, https://investors.vno.com/quarterly-earnings-calendar/quarterly -earnings/default.aspx#.

Trump Park Avenue: Analysis of property record: https://a836-acris.nyc.gov/DS/Docu mentSearch/DocumentImageView?doc_id=2010072801017012; Donald Trump, OGE Form 278e, May 15, 2019; Patrick Birney, assistant vice president of financial operations at the Trump Organization, email to author, February 14, 2019; 6 E. 57th St., "Analysis of information from Bloomberg terminal on Fifty-Seventh Street Associates LLC."

Trump Tower: Prospectus Supplement, Wells Fargo Commercial Mortgage Trust 2012-LC5, Securities and Exchange Commission, July 20, 2012, A-3-33, https://www.sec.gov/Archives/edgar/data/850779/000153949712000571/prospectus-supplement.htm.

Doral: Analysis of financial disclosure, interest rate benchmarks, and property records; Donald Trump, OGE Form 278e, May 15, 2019; 1-Month London Interbank Offered Rate (LIBOR), based on U.S. Dollar (USD1MTD156N), https://fred.stlouisfed.org/series/USD1MTD156N; 3-Month London Interbank Offered Rate (LIBOR), based on U.S. Dollar (USD3MTD156N), https://fred.stlouisfed.org/series/USD3MTD156N; 6-Month London Interbank Offered Rate (LIBOR), based on U.S. Dollar (USD6MTD156N), https://fred.stlouisfed.org/series/USD6MTD156N; 12-Month London Interbank Offered Rate (LIBOR), based on U.S. Dollar (USD12MD156N), https://fred.stlouisfed.org/series/USD12MD156N; Bank Prime Loan Rate (DPRIME), https://fred.stlouisfed.org/series/DPRIME; Mortgage, Assignment of Leases and Rents, Fixture Filing and Security Agreement, Trump Endeavor 12 LLC, Deutsche Bank Trust Company Americas, August 7, 2015, and June 11, 2012.

D.C. Hotel: Analysis of financial disclosure, interest rate benchmarks and property records; Donald Trump, OGE Form 278e, May 15, 2019; 1-Month London Interbank Offered Rate (LIBOR), based on U.S. Dollar (USD1MTD156N), https://fred.stlouisfed.org/series/USD1MTD156N; 3-Month London Interbank Offered Rate (LIBOR), based on U.S. Dollar (USD3MTD156N), https://fred.stlouisfed.org/series/USD3MTD156N; 6-Month London Interbank Offered Rate (LIBOR), based on U.S. Dollar (USD6MTD156N), https://fred.stlouisfed.org/series/USD6MTD156N; 12-Month London Interbank Offered Rate (LIBOR), based on U.S. Dollar (USD12MD156N), https://fred.stlouisfed.org/series/USD12MD156N; Bank Prime Loan Rate (DPRIME), https://fred.stlouisfed.org/series/DPRIME; Leasehold Deed of Trust, Assignment of Leases and Rents, Fixture Filing and Security Agreement, Trump Old Post Office LLC and Deutsche Bank Trust Company Americas, Washington, D.C., Recorder of Deeds, Doc No. 2014073616, August 12, 2014.

Trump International Hotel & Tower Chicago: Analysis of financial disclosure, interest rate benchmarks, Patrick Birney email, and *New York Times* story; Donald Trump, OGE Form 278e, May 15, 2019; 1-Month London Interbank Offered Rate (LIBOR), based on U.S. Dollar (USD1MTD156N), https://fred.stlouisfed.org/series/USD1MTD156N; 3-Month London Interbank Offered Rate (LIBOR), based on U.S. Dollar (USD3MTD156N), https://fred.stlouisfed.org/series/USD3MTD156N; 6-Month London Interbank Offered Rate (LIBOR), based on U.S. Dollar (USD6MTD156N), https://fred.stlouisfed.org/series/USD6MTD156N; 12-Month London Interbank Offered Rate (LIBOR), based on U.S. Dollar (USD12MD156N), https://fred.stlouisfed.org/series/USD12MD156N; Bank Prime Loan Rate (DPRIME), https://fred.stlouisfed.org/series/DPRIME; Patrick Birney email; Ford Fessenden and Iaryna Mykhyalyshyn, "What Donald Trump Owns and Owes," *New York Times,* August 20, 2016, https://www.nytimes.com/interactive/2016/08/20/us/elections/donald-trump-owns-and-owes-debt-properties.html.

1290 Avenue of the Americas: Vornado Realty Trust, Supplemental Operating and Financial Data, for the quarter and year ended December 31, 2019; analysis of financial disclosure report, property records, and Patrick Birney email; Donald Trump, OGE Form 278e, May 15, 2019; Loudon County Property Record, Trump Natl Golf Club Wash DC LLC, PARID: 005401940000, May 1, 2009, Monmouth County Document Summary Sheet, Coastal Title Agency, Transaction ID

Number: 1157169, September 10, 2008, Monmouth County Document Summary Sheet, Coastal Title Agency, Transaction ID Number: 1157169, September 10, 2008; Patrick Birney email.

Seven Springs: Analysis of property records, interview and financial disclosure report; Donald Trump, OGE Form 278e, May 15, 2019; Westchester County Recording and Endorsement Page, Seven Springs LLC, Control No. 401960076, June 22, 2000; Westchester County Recording and Endorsement Page, Seven Springs LLC, Control No. 401960090, June 22, 2000; Telephone interview with author, September 29, 2017.

Spring Creek Towers: Analysis of financial disclosure report, interview, and debt circular; Donald Trump, OGE Form 278e, May 15, 2019; Telephone interview with author, 2018.; Freddie Mac Structured Pass-Through Certificates (SPCs), Series K-SCT, December 31, 2007.

124 Woodbridge Road: Analysis of interest rates, disclosure report, and property records; 6-Month London Interbank Offered Rate (LIBOR), based on U.S. Dollar (USD6MTD156N), https://fred.stlouisfed.org/series/USD6MTD156N; Donald Trump, OGE Form 278e, May 15, 2018; Palm Beach County, Florida, Mortgage, 124 Woodbridge Rd., Account No. 1764760, December 28, 1993; Palm Beach County, Florida, Satisfaction of Mortgage, 124 Woodbridge Rd., Account No. 1764760, December 28, 1993.

1094 South Ocean: Analysis of interest rates, disclosure report, and property records; Donald Trump, OGE Form 278e, May 15, 2018; 6-Month London Interbank Offered Rate (LIBOR), based on U.S. Dollar (USD6MTD156N), https://fred.stlouis fed.org/series/USD6MTD156N; Palm Beach County, Florida, Mortgage, 1094 S. Ocean Blvd., February 3, 1994; Palm Beach County, Florida, Satisfaction of Mortgage, 1094 S. Ocean Blvd., Loan # 7071764752, June 15, 2017.

1125 S Ocean: Analysis of property record and financial disclosure report; Palm Beach County, Florida, Mortgage, 1125 S. Ocean Blvd., Loan No. 1700158, May 17, 2018; Donald Trump, OGE Form 278e, May 15, 2019.

Trump International Hotel Las Vegas: Analysis of property records, financial disclosure report, and email from spokesperson for the Trump Organization; Clark County property recorder, Trump Ruffin Tower I LLC, Instrument No. 201807260001873; Donald Trump, OGE Form 278e, May 15, 2019; email from Trump Organization to author, September 12, 2019.

18. Analysis of documents from note 17.

19. Analysis of documents from note 17.

20. Analysis of Donald Trump, OGE Form 278e, May 15, 2019, 41; Russ Choma, "Donald Trump Has Never Explained a Mysterious $50 Million Loan. Is It Evidence of Tax Fraud?," September 2019, *Mother Jones*, https://www.motherjones.com/politics/2019/09 /donald-trump-has-never-explained-a-mysterious-50-million-chicago-unit-acquisition -loan-is-it-evidence-of-tax-fraud/.

21. Scott Amey, telephone interview with author, May 15, 2020; Virginia Canter telephone interview; Don Fox, telephone interview with author, May 12, 2020; Richard Painter interview.

22. Donald Trump, Twitter, April 19, 2019, https://twitter.com/realDonaldTrump/status /1163472273388576768.

23. Donald Trump, Twitter, August 19, 2019, https://twitter.com/realDonaldTrump/status /1164914609180033026.

24. Donald Trump, Twitter, September 6, 2019, https://twitter.com/realdonaldtrump/status /1169948967947395072.

25. Donald Trump, Twitter, September 11, 2019, https://twitter.com/realDonaldTrump/status/1171735692428419072.
26. Research conducted by the author for *Forbes*.
27. Dan Alexander, "Vintage Trump Ads Say a Lot About the President," *Forbes*, September 19, 2017, www.forbes.com/sites/danalexander/2017/09/19/trump-vintage-old-ads-advertisement-forbes-president-donald.
28. Eamonn Fingleton, "Golden Boy," *Forbes*, February 28, 1983; Donald Trump and Allen Weisselberg, interviewed by Randall Lane, Chase Peterson-Withorn, and Kerry Dolan, September 21, 2015.
29. Fingleton, "Golden Boy."
30. Allan Dodds Frank, "See No Evil," *Forbes*, October 6, 1986.
31. U.S. Department of the Treasury, "National Money Laundering Risk Assessment," 38, http://home.treasury.gov/system/files/1362018NMLRA_12-18.pdf; Office of the Comptroller of the Currency, Bank Secrecy Act (BSA & Related Regulations), https://www.occ.treas.gov/topics/supervision-and-examination/bsa/bsa-related-regulations/index-bsa-and-related-regulations.html.
32. "The Trump Story," Trump Organization, https://www.trump.com/timeline.
33. Supreme Court of the State of New York, County of New York, *Deutsche Bank Trust Company Americas Against Donald J. Trump*, Index No. 603483/08 8, https://iapps.courts.state.ny.us/fbem/DocumentDisplayServlet?documentId=QFCiQXhOS1rG_PLUS_19nbsqurQ==.
34. Email to author, March 2018.
35. Analysis of property records, Cook County Recorder of Deeds.
36. Phil Ruffin, telephone interview with author, February 8, 2017.
37. Phil Ruffin, telephone interview.
38. Analysis of property records, NYC Department of Finance.
39. Analysis of property records, City of Rancho Palos Verdes.
40. Analysis of various property records.
41. Analysis of property records in New York, California, Florida, Virginia, Nevada, and Illinois; author interviews with Mario Molinari (February 28, 2020), Jonathan Schaede (March 5, 2020), Arun Jagtiani (March 4, 2020), Dana Koch (March 9, 2020), Jack McCabe (March 10, 2020), background source (March 4, 2020), Mark Boyland (February 27, 2020), Jim Renwick (March 8, 2020), Brian Milton (March 3, 2020); email from Isaac Klein (March 10, 2020); data from Gail Lissner (March 3, 2020) and Truman Fleming (February 26, 2020).
42. Matea Gold, "Trump's 'Huuuuuge' Caribbean Estate Is on the Market for $28 Million, Prompting Questions," *Washington Post*, May 17, 2017, https://www.washingtonpost.com/politics/trumps-huuuuuge-caribbean-estate-is-on-the-market-for-28-million-prompting-questions/2017/05/17/cf3f99c0-372b-11e7-b373-418f6849a004_story.html.
43. Mario Molinari, Jonathan Schaede, and Arun Jagtiani interviews.
44. Sotheby's International Realty, "Chateau des Palmiers," sothebysrealty.com/eng/sales/detail/180-I-83146-qz6f4w/chateau-des-palmiers-terres-basses-mi-97150.
45. Mario Molinari interview.
46. New York State Board of Elections President and Vice-President Election Returns, November 8, 2016, 28, https://www.elections.ny.gov/NYSBOE/elections/2016/General/2016President.pdf.
47. Analysis of property records, Trump Park Avenue, and property listings: 502 Park Ave., 12E, New York, NY 10022, Trump International Realty; 502 Park Ave., 8H, New York, NY 10022, Trump International Realty; Trump International Realty Luxury Listing Book, 6, https://issuu.com/trumpinternationalrealty100/docs/listing_brochure_winter_2016

_revise?e=22923278/42751226; 502 Park Ave., PH21, Trump International Realty, Way-back Machine, https://web.archive.org/web/20181121211835/https://www.trumpinterna tionalrealty.com/listings/new-york.

48. Analysis of property records, Trump Park Avenue.

49. "The Elliman Report: 2010—2019 Manhattan Decade," Co-op and condo sales prepared by Miller Samuel Real Estate Appraisers," Douglas Elliman, 2020, 10, http://www.elli man.com/resources/siteresources/commonresources/static%20pages/images/corporate -resources/q4_2019/manhattan%2010yr%202019.pdf.

50. Analysis of property records, Trump Tower.

51. Christine Miller Martin, email to author, March 5, 2020.

52. Dan Alexander, "Why the Next Big Trump Project Could Be a Las Vegas Casino," *Forbes,* March 20, 2017, https://www.forbes.com/sites/danalexander/2017/03/20/conflict -conflicts-of-interest-emoluments-clause-trump-ruffin-phil-russia-treasury-profits-hotel -las-vegas-casino/#3490710f79b1.

53. Silver State Election Night Results 2016, Clark County, https://www.nvsos.gov/silverstat e2016gen/county-results/clark.shtml.

54. Silver State Election Night Results 2016, U.S. President, https://www.nvsos.gov/silver state2016gen/.

55. Silver State Election Night Results 2016, Washoe County, https://www.nvsos.gov/silver state2016gen/county-results/washoe.shtml.

56. Preceding three paragraphs: Analysis of property records; data sent to author by Truman Fleming of Vegas Paradise Homes.

57. Donald Trump, OGE Form 278e, May 15, 2019, 40, 3.

58. "President-Elect Donald Trump News Conference," C-SPAN, January 11, 2017, https:// www.c-span.org/video/?421482-1/president-elect-donald-trump-election-year-hacking -i-russia.

59. Los Angeles County Registrar-Recorder/County Clerk, 809 North Canon LLC, Hillcrest Asia Limited, May 31, 2019, 3; Recorder's Office, Los Angeles County, 225 Canon LLC, July 10, 2013, MNC Tower 28th Floor, https://premier.ctic.com/services/document.ashx ?qs=dG9rZW49YlI4UEpaTjhNJTJmRXNiZHMyS2Jqc0h5dHFoU3BCbUtvUkx BT3JwUzVaMzg4alhxWDYzcSUyZjBZaTFiJTJmVXlzTmJxWkklMmZ1JTJiVzZtRHlY SUpIZEpqZ1NrR1NVeGZIcjE0YTI5T3hrczE1REx6TmFjJTNkJmZpcHM 9MDYwMzcmdHBkb2M9Q0FMT1NBJTNhMjAxMyswMTAxMDI0NiZyZWNvc mRpbmc9MDclMmYxMCUyZjIwMTMmYXBuPSZhaWQ9NzImdj0xLjEmcD1hJm RvY3VtZW50PTEzLTEwMTAyNDYmZmlkPTImZng9Mg%3D%3D; MNC Land, http://tinyurl.com/y73z26k8.

60. Abram Brown, "Meet the Donald Trump of Indonesia: Another Billionaire Who Wants to Be President," *Forbes,* March 20, 2017, https://www.forbes.com/sites/abrambrown /2017/03/20/donald-trump-hary-tanoesoedibjo-indonesia/#5e73ac2b50b1.

61. Documents obtained through a public records request from the City of Rancho Palos Verdes.

62. NYC Department of Finance, Office of the City Register, Starrett City Inc., BSC Hous-ing Company, Inc., May 4, 2018, 33, https://a836-acris.nyc.gov/DS/DocumentSearch /DocumentImageView?doc_id=2018050400965001; Donald Trump, OGE Form 278e, May 15, 2019, 40.

63. NYC Department of Finance, Office of the City Register, Starrett City Inc., BSC Hous-ing Company, Inc., May 4, 2018, 5, https://a836-acris.nyc.gov/DS/DocumentSearch /DocumentImageView?doc_id=2018050400965004.

64. Dan Alexander and Chase Peterson-Withorn, "Donald Trump's Sons Have Sold More than $100 Million of His Real Estate Since He Took Office," *Forbes,* October 2, 2019,

https://www.forbes.com/sites/danalexander/2019/10/02/donald-trump-has-sold-more-than-100-million-of-real-estate-since-taking-office/#3c4b4b091090.

65. NYC Department of Finance, Office of the City Register, Trump CPS LLC., Art Gardens LLC, October 21, 2019, 10, https://a836-acris.nyc.gov/DS/DocumentSearch/DocumentImageView?doc_id=2019100900802001.

66. NYC Department of Finance, Notice of Property Value, Tax Year 2020–21, 3, https://a836-edms.nyc.gov/dctm-rest/repositories/dofedmspts/StatementSearch?bbl=1010117002&stmtDate=20200115&stmtType=NPV.

67. NYC Department of Finance, Office of the City Register, Trump CPS LLC, Art Gardens LLC; AAA Corporate Services, "What We Offer," https://aaacorpservices.com/what-we-offer/.

68. NYC Department of Finance, Office of the City Register, Document ID 2013010900761001d, https://a836-acris.nyc.gov/DS/DocumentSearch/DocumentImageView?doc_id=2013010900761001; NYC Department of Finance, Notice of Property Value, Tax Year 2020–21, https://a836-edms.nyc.gov/dctm-rest/repositories/dofedmspts/StatemenSearch?bbl=1012601143&stmtDate=20200115&stmtType=NPV.

69. Analysis of New York Secretary of State documents.

70. NYC Department of Finance, Office of the City Register, Ruibiao Su, Mark Man Zhang, 1–2, https://a836-acris.nyc.gov/DS/DocumentSearch/DocumentImageView?doc_id=2018031401007003.

71. NYC Department of Finance, Office of the City Register, Trump CPS LLC, Koctagon LLC, March 12, 2019, 2, 11, https://a836-acris.nyc.gov/DS/DocumentSearch/DocumentImageView?doc_id=2019031200759001.

72. NYC Department of Finance, Office of the City Register, Koctagon LLC, Trump Parc East Condominium board of managers, 3, https://a836-acris.nyc.gov/DS/DocumentSearch/DocumentImageView?doc_id=2019031200759002. Koctagon LLC lists its address as 70 West 45th St., #39C—the same one we saw earlier, owned by Smile Caribbean LLC, which in turn is registered at a property formerly owned by Xiu Qong Li.

73. Karen Masuko, telephone interview with author, May 13, 2020.

74. NYC Department of Finance, Office of the City Register, Trump CPS LLC, Koctagon LLC, March 12, 2019, https://a836-acris.nyc.gov/DS/DocumentSearch/DocumentImageView?doc_id=2019031200759001; NYC Department of Finance, Office of the City Register, Koctagon LLC, Trump Parc East Condominium board of managers, https://a836-acris.nyc.gov/DS/DocumentSearch/DocumentImageView?doc_id=2019031200759002.

75. Analysis of property records.

CHAPTER EIGHT: ALL IN THE FAMILY

1. David W. Dunlap, "Residential Real Estate; Dowager Going Condo in Un-Trumplike Way," *New York Times*, August 16, 2002, https://www.nytimes.com/2002/08/16/nyregion/residential-real-estate-dowager-going-condo-in-un-trumplike-way.html; Peter Grant, "Trump to Buy New York Hotel In Deal Valued at $115 Million," *Wall Street Journal*, November 30, 2001, https://www.wsj.com/articles/SB1007068496576738440.

2. Analysis of New York City Property Records.

3. Deed, November 18, 2003. Grantor: Trump Park Avenue LLC, document ID: 2003111700539001, https://a836-acris.nyc.gov/DS/DocumentSearch/DocumentImageView?doc_id=2003111700539001.

4. Deed, October 6, 2004. Grantor: Trump Park Avenue LLC. Grantee: Ivanka Trump. Document ID: 2004090300223001, https://a836-acris.nyc.gov/DS/DocumentSearch/DocumentImageView?doc_id=2004090300223001.

5. Analysis of New York City real estate records.

6. Analysis of Schedule 14A, Trump Entertainment Resorts, Securities and Exchange Commission, 6, https://www.sec.gov/Archives/edgar/data/943320/000119312508062814/ddef14a.htm.

7. "The Donald Interviews the Kids," *Forbes,* YouTube October 30, 2006, https://www.youtube.com/watch?v=Vc0k1CMl6_o.

8. "Ivanka Trump on 'Late Night with Conan O'Brien'-3/16/07," YouTube, June 9, 2016, https://www.youtube.com/watch?v=wEzEhjhB2Ic.

9. Donald Trump and Tony Schwartz, *The Art of the Deal* (New York: Random House, 1987), 73, https://archive.org/stream/TrumpDonaldTheArtOfTheDeal/Trump+Donald+-+The+Art+Of+The+Deal_djvu.txt.

10. Stephane Fitch, "The Real Apprentices," *Forbes,* October 9, 2006, https://www.forbes.com/free_forbes/2006/1009/056.html.

11. Analysis of Schedule 14A, Trump Entertainment Resorts, Securities and Exchange Commission, 12.

12. Trump Entertainment Resorts, Analysis of Amended and Restated Services Agreement, July 16, 2010, Securities and Exchange Commission, https://www.sec.gov/Archives/edgar/data/943320/000119312510161799/dex103.htm.

13. Ben Schreckinger, "The Trouble with Ivanka's Business Partner," *Politico,* August 27, 2017, https://www.politico.com/magazine/story/2017/08/27/ivanka-trump-business-partner-215544.

14. Analysis of New York State Department of State, State Tax Warrant Notice System, Ivanka Trump Fine Jewelry, https://appext20.dos.ny.gov/stwarrants_public/stw_warrants?p_name=IVANKA+TRUMP+FINE+JEWELRY&p_lapsed=0.

15. Amended Complaint: *United States of America v. Moshe Lax et al.*, June 6, 2019, Doc. No. 106, United States District Court for the Eastern District of New York, 1:18-cv-04061-ILG-PK.

16. Answer: *United States of America v. Moshe Lax et al.*, August 5, 2019, Doc. No. 129, United States District Court for the Eastern District of New York, 1:18-cv-04061-ILG-PK.

17. Docket: *United States of America v. Lax et Al.*, U.S. District Court Eastern District of New York (Brooklyn), 1:18-cv-04061-ILG-PK.

18. "Ivanka Trump Launches Her First Fragrance," Business Wire, February 13, 2013, https://www.businesswire.com/news/home/20130213005078/en/Ivanka-Trump-Launches-Fragrance.

19. "G-III Apparel Group, Ltd. Signs License for Ivanka Trump Brand," Business Wire, December 10, 2010, https://www.businesswire.com/news/home/20121210005152/en/G-III-Apparel-Group-Ltd.-Signs-License-Ivanka.

20. Chase Peterson-Withorn, "Here's How Much Don Jr., Eric and Ivanka Trump Are Worth," *Forbes,* November 8, 2019, https://www.forbes.com/sites/chasewithorn/2019/11/08/heres-how-much-don-jr-eric-and-ivanka-trump-are-worth/#53be84f675ed.

21. Ivanka Trump, Twitter.com, May 10, 2013, https://twitter.com/ivankatrump/status/332929344215318528.

22. G-III Apparel Group, Q2 2014 Earnings Call, September 4, 2013, 8:30 a.m. ET.

23. G-III Apparel Group, Q3 2014 Earnings Call, December 4, 2013.

24. G-III Apparel Group, Q4 2013 Earnings Call, April 2, 2013.

25. G-III Apparel Group, Q3 2015 Earnings Call, December 3, 2014; G-III Apparel Group annual report for the fiscal year ended January 31, 2016, 39, Securities and Exchange Commission, https://www.sec.gov/Archives/edgar/data/821002/000157104916013440/t1600804-10k.htm.

26. G-III Apparel Group, Q3 2016 Earnings Call, December 2, 2015.

27. Laura Wagner, "'Republicans Buy Sneakers, Too,'" *Slate,* July 28, 2016, https://slate.com /culture/2016/07/did-michael-jordan-really-say-republicans-buy-sneakers-too.html.

28. Ivanka Trump, Twitter, July 22, 2016, https://twitter.com/IvankaTrump/status/75649214 6484580352.

29. "Ivanka Trump Introduces Donald Trump at the Republican National Convention," C-SPAN, July 21, 2016, https://www.c-span.org/video/?c4612799/ivanka-trump-introduces -donald-trump-republican-national-convention.

30. "Chelsea Clinton Vows to Remain Friends with Ivanka Trump," *Politico,* September 9, 2016, https://www.politico.com/story/2016/09/chelsea-clinton-ivanka-trump-friends-227950.

31. "Second Presidential Debate of 2016 Draws 66.5 Million Viewers," Nielsen, October 10, 2016, https://www.nielsen.com/us/en/insights/article/2016/second-presidential-debate-of -2016-draws-66-5-million-viewers/.

32. "Presidential Candidates Debate," C-SPAN, October 9, 2016, https://www.c-span.org /video/?414227-1/presidential-nominees-debate-washington-university&start=5449.

33. Phil Ruffin, interviewed by author, February 15, 2017.

34. "The 45th President," *60 Minutes,* CBS, November 13, 2016, https://www.cbsnews.com /news/60-minutes-donald-trump-family-melania-ivanka-lesley-stahl/.

35. "The 45th President," *60 Minutes.*

36. Dominic Patten, "Donald Trump's '60 Minutes' Sit-Down Delivers Season High; Lags Behind Obama 2008 Interview & Sean Penn on El Chapo—Update," *Deadline,* November 15, 2016, https://deadline.com/2016/11/donald-trump-60-minutes-interview-ratings -rise-seahawks-patriots-sunday-night-football-rises-nbc-nfl-cbs-1201853888/.

37. Katie Rosman, Twitter, November 14, 2016, https://twitter.com/katierosman/status/798 345538236272641; Eric Lipton, Twitter, November 14, 2016, https://twitter.com/Eric LiptonNYT/status/798386072594083841.

38. Kate Sheehy and Daniel Halper, "Ivanka Trump Tries to Cash In on Donald's '60 Minutes' Interview," *New York Post,* November 15, 2016, https://nypost.com/2016/11/15 /ivanka-trump-uses-60-minutes-interview-to-hawk-10k-bracelet/.

39. Drew Harwell, "With Ivanka's Jewelry Ad, Trump Companies Begin to Seek Profit off Election Result," *Washington Post,* November 15, 2016, https://www.washingtonpost .com/news/wonk/wp/2016/11/15/with-ivankas-jewelry-ad-trump-companies-begin -to-seek-to-profit-off-the-election/.

40. Analysis of trademarks filed on Wipo.

41. "Abigail Klem, IT Operations LLC, to the Honorable John Conyers, Jr.," May 17, 2017, https://judiciary.house.gov/sites/democrats.judiciary.house.gov/files/documents/it%20 operations%20response%20letter.

42. "Company Info," Sanei International, https://www.sanei.net/company/; Corporate Governance, TSI Holdings Co. Ltd, https://www2.tse.or.jp/disc/36080/140120160613421939 .pdf; "Moody's Affirms Development Bank of Japan's A1 Ratings," Moody's Investors Service, https://www.moodys.com/research/Moodys-affirms-Development-Bank-of-Japans-A1 -ratings-outlook-stable--PR_398363.

43. Matt Flegenheimer, Rachel Abrams, Barry Meier, and Hiroko Tabuchi, "Business Since Birth: Trump's Children and the Tangle That Awaits," New York Times, December 4, 2016, https://www.nytimes.com/2016/12/04/us/politics/trump-family-ivanka-donald-jr.html.

44. "Abigail Klem, IT Operations LLC, to the Honorable John Conyers, Jr."

45. Eric Lipton and Maggie Haberman, "Available to the Highest Bidder: Coffee with Ivanka Trump," *New York Times,* December 15, 2016, https://www.nytimes.com/2016/12/15 /us/politics/ivanka-trump-charity-auction.html.

46. Women's March Annual Report for the Year Ending December 31, 2017, 5, https://static1
.squarespace.com/static/5c3feb79fcf7fdce5a3c790b/t/5c422af80e2e725f8f0ea8f8
/1547840252450/2017%2BWM%2BAnnual%2BReport_LoRes.pdf.

47. Anne D'Innocenzio, "Nordstrom to Drop Ivanka Trump's Clothing, Accessories Line,"
AP News, February 3, 2017, https://apnews.com/19ae5b3f6808496f804b16111dcccd7c
/nordstrom-drop-ivanka-trumps-clothing-accessories-line.

48. Donald Trump, Twitter, February 8, 2017, https://twitter.com/realdonaldtrump/status
/829356871848951809.

49. "Kellyanne Conway on Ivanka Trump's Fashion Line: 'Go Buy It Today!,'" Fox News,
February 9, 2017, https://insider.foxnews.com/2017/02/09/kellyanne-conway-ivanka-trump
-retailers-go-buy-her-stuff.

50. Kristine Phillips, "'Go Buy Ivanka's Stuff,' Kellyanne Conway Said. Then the First
Daughter's Fashion Sales Exploded," *Washington Post,* March 10, 2017, https://www
.washingtonpost.com/news/business/wp/2017/03/10/go-buy-ivankas-stuff-kellyanne
-conway-said-then-the-first-daughters-fashion-sales-exploded/.

51. Eric Trump, interviewed by author, February 24, 2017.

52. Government-Wide Ethics Laws Conflicts of Interest, 5 U.S.C. § 3110, https://www.gov
info.gov/content/pkg/USCODE-2010-title5/pdf/USCODE-2010-title5-partIII-sub
partB-chap31-subchapI-sec3110.pdf.

53. Richard Painter, interviewed by author, August 2, 2019.

54. Association of American Physicians and Surgeons, Inc., et al., Appellees, v. Hillary Rod-
ham Clinton, et al., Appellants, 1993, United States Court of Appeals, District of Columbia Circuit, https://law.resource.org/pub/us/case/reporter/F2/997/997.F2d.898.93-5092.93
-5086.html.

55. "President-Elect Donald J. Trump Names Jared Kushner Senior Advisor to the President,"
press release, January 9, 2017, https://www.presidency.ucsb.edu/documents/press-release
-president-elect-donald-j-trump-names-jared-kushner-senior-advisor-the.

56. "Application of the Anti-Nepotism Statute to a Presidential Appointment in the White
House Office," January 20, 2017, https://www.justice.gov/olc/file/971166/download.

57. Marilyn Glynn, telephone interview with author, May 16, 2020; Walter Shaub, telephone
interview with author, May 15, 2020; Virginia Canter, telephone interview with author,
May 13, 2020; Don Fox, telephone interview with author, May 12, 2020.

58. Richard Painter, interview.

59. Ivanka Trump, Twitter, February 13, 2017, https://twitter.com/ivankatrump/status/831
270847671316483.

60. Annie Karni, "Ivanka Trump Set to Get West Wing Office as Role Expands," *Politico,*
March 20, 2017, https://www.politico.com/story/2017/03/ivanka-trump-white-house
-236273; Barney Henderson, "Ivanka Trump Given West Wing Office and Security Clearance in Expanded White House Role," *The Telegraph,* March 20, 2017, https://www
.telegraph.co.uk/news/2017/03/20/ivanka-trump-given-west-wing-office-security
-clearance-expanded/; Rachel Abrams, "Despite a Trust, Ivanka Trump Still Wields
Power over Her Brand," *New York Times,* March 20, 2017, https://www.nytimes.com/2017
/03/20/business/despite-trust-ivanka-trump-still-wields-power-over-her-brand.html; Betsy
Klein, "Ivanka Trump's Growing West Wing Role Raises Questions," CNN, March 22,
2017, https://edition.cnn.com/2017/03/22/politics/ivanka-trump-west-wing-white-house
/index.html; John Santucci and Adam Kelsey, "Ivanka Trump to Receive White House
Office, Security Clearance," ABC News, March 20, 2017, https://abcnews.go.com/Politics
/ivanka-trump-receive-white-house-office-security-clearance/story?id=46263737.

61. Richard Painter interview.

62. Ivanka Trump, OGE Form 278e, U.S. Office of Government Ethics, July 21, 2017, 5 C.F.R. part 2634, 3.
63. Analysis of trademarks included in Chinese government database, http://wsjs.saic.gov.cn/.
64. Analysis of trademarks included in Chinese government database.
65. Sophie Brown, "Brand Wars: Battling China's Trademark 'Squatters,'" CNN, July 18, 2014, http://edition.cnn.com/2014/07/17/world/asia/china-trademarks-squatters-penfolds /index.html; "China Grapples with Trademark Infringement—of Its Own Brands," *The Economist*, October 4, 2018, https://www.economist.com/business/2018/10/04/china -grapples-with-trademark-infringement-of-its-own-brands.
66. Trademark application, i vanka, Chinese government database, http://wsjs.saic.gov.cn/.
67. Analysis of Ivanka Trump trademarks included in Chinese government database, http:// wsjs.saic.gov.cn/.
68. Donald Trump, Twitter, May 13, 2018, https://twitter.com/realDonaldTrump/status /995680316458262533.
69. Analysis of Ivanka Trump trademarks included in Chinese government database.
70. Analysis of Ivanka Trump trademarks. included in Chinese government database.
71. Analysis of Ivanka Trump Trademarks filed with World Intellectual Property Organization.
72. Analysis of Ivanka Trump trademarks filed with Wipo; Dan Alexander, "In Trump They Trust: Inside The Global Web of Partners Cashing In on the President," *Forbes*, March 20, 2017, https://www.forbes.com/sites/danalexander/2017/03/20/in-trump-they-trust-inside -the-global-web-of-partners-cashing-in-on-the-president/#3ccf21757605.
73. Analysis of G-III Apparel Group, Ltd., Form 10-K, Securities and Exchange Commission, for the fiscal year ended January 31, 2018, 51, https://www.sec.gov/Archives/edgar /data/821002/000114420418018565/tv489439-10k.htm.
74. Analysis of G-III Apparel Group, Ltd., Form 10-K, Securities and Exchange Commission, for the fiscal year ended January 31, 2017, 45, https://www.sec.gov/Archives/edgar /data/821002/000157104917003132/t1700141-10k.htm.
75. Research provided to the author by Rakuten Intelligence.
76. Analysis of G-III Apparel Group, Ltd., Form 10-K, Securities and Exchange Commission, for the fiscal year ended January 31, 2017, 45.
77. Analysis of G-III earnings calls and annual reports; Peterson-Withorn, "Here's How Much Don Jr., Eric and Ivanka Trump Are Worth."
78. G-III Apparel Group, Q2 2019 Earnings Call, September 6, 2018.
79. "Get Ready for Taxes: Here's How the New Tax Law Revised Family Tax Credits," IRS, November 7, 2018, https://www.irs.gov/newsroom/get-ready-for-taxes-heres-how-the-new -tax-law-revised-family-tax-credits.
80. "Remarks by President Trump at the American Farm Bureau Federation's 100th Annual Convention, New Orleans, Louisiana," White House, January 15, 2019, https://www .whitehouse.gov/briefings-statements/remarks-president-trump-american-farm-bureau -federations-100th-annual-convention-new-orleans-louisiana/.
81. Instructions for Form 706 (Rev. August 2017) for decedents dying after December 31, 2016, United States Estate (and Generation-Skipping Transfer) Tax Return, U.S. Department of the Treasury, Internal Revenue Service, https://www.irs.gov/pub/irs-prior/i706 --2017.pdf; U.S. Department of the Treasury, Internal Revenue Service, 26 CFR 601.602: Tax Forms and Instructions, https://www.irs.gov/pub/irs-drop/rp-16-55.pdf.
82. Continental Resources, Inc., Schedule 14 A, Proxy Statement, 11, https://www.sec .gov/Archives/edgar/data/732834/000119312520094812/d795514ddef14a.htm #tx795514_33.

83. Fox Corporation, Schedule 14 A, Proxy Statement, 50, https://www.sec.gov/Archives /edgar/data/1754301/000119312519252169/d802602ddef14a.htm.

84. Facebook, Inc., Schedule 14A, Proxy Statement, 96, https://www.sec.gov/Archives/edgar /data/1326801/000132680115000019/facebook2015proxystatement.htm.

85. Matt Drange and Dan Alexander, "Poorer President," *Forbes*, November 14, 2017; Chase Peterson-Withorn, "Donald Trump's Financial Carelessness Could Cost His Kids $1.3 Billion in Taxes," *Forbes*, August 8, 2019, https://www.forbes.com/sites/chasewithorn /2019/08/09/donald-trumps-financial-carelessness-could-cost-his-kids-13-billion-in -taxes/#11ebfd4465db.

86. *Meet the Press,* NBC, January 10, 2016, https://archive.org/details/KNTV_20160110 _160300_Meet_the_Press/start/1053/end/1113.

87. Alexander and Drange, "Poorer President."

88. "President Defends Puerto Rico Hurricane Response Touts Tax Cuts Plan," C-SPAN, September 29, 2017, https://archive.org/details/CSPAN_20170930_014000_President _Defends_Puerto_Rico_Hurricane_Response_Touts_Tax_Cuts_Plan/start/1416/end /1476?q=%22estate+tax%22.

89. "President Trump Pitches Tax Cuts in National Association of Manufacturers . . . ," C-SPAN, September 29, 2017, https://archive.org/details/CSPAN_20170929_154000 _President_Trump_Pitches_Tax_Cuts_in_National_Association_of_Manufacturers . . . /start/1158/end/1218?q=%22fire+sale+just+to+pay%22.

90. "How the Trump Tax Plan Will Affect You," U.S. Congressman Peter DeFazio, https:// defazio.house.gov/how-the-trump-tax-plan-will-affect-you; "IRS Issues Guidance on Transition Tax on Foreign Earnings," IRS, December 29, 2017, https://www.irs.gov /newsroom/irs-issues-guidance-on-transition-tax-on-foreign-earnings; guidance under Section 965, Notice 2018-07, https://www.irs.gov/pub/irs-drop/n-18-07.pdf.

91. "Donald Trump's Tax Documents from 2005," *New York Times,* March 14, 2017, https:// www.nytimes.com/interactive/2017/03/14/us/politics/document-Donald-Trump-2005 -Tax.html; Dan Alexander, "President Trump Could Save $11 Million a Year from New Tax Bill," *Forbes,* December 18, 2017, https://www.forbes.com/sites/danalexander/2017 /12/18/president-trump-could-save-11-million-a-year-from-new-tax-bill/#60de939f2337.

92. "Trump Signs Tax Bill," Fox Business, YouTube, December 22, 2017, https://www.you tube.com/watch?v=dAxREsm8Ws8.

93. "Thune Leads Colleagues in Reintroducing Legislation to Permanently Repeal the Death Tax," Senator John Thune, January 28, 2019, https://www.thune.senate.gov/public /index.cfm/2019/1/thune-leads-colleagues-in-reintroducing-legislation-to-permanently -repeal-the-death-tax.

94. Jesse Drucker and Emily Flitter, "How Jared Kushner Avoided Paying Taxes," *New York Times*, October 13, 2018, https://www.nytimes.com/2018/10/13/business/kushner-paying -taxes.html.

95. Peterson-Withorn, "Here's How Much Don Jr., Eric and Ivanka Trump Are Worth."

CHAPTER NINE: LIKE FATHER, LIKE SON-IN-LAW

1. "President Trump Remarks on Domestic Violence," C-SPAN, February 14, 2018, https:// www.c-span.org/video/?441190-1/president-trump-opposes-domestic-violence &start=252.

2. Steve Bertoni, "An Unlikely Group of Billionaires and Politicians Has Created the Most Unbelievable Tax Break Ever," *Forbes,* July 18, 2018, https://www.forbes.com/sites/for

besdigitalcovers/2018/07/17/an-unlikely-group-of-billionaires-and-politicians-has
-created-the-most-unbelievable-tax-break-ever/.

3. Jared Kushner, OGE Form 278e, U.S. Office of Government Ethics, 5 C.F.R. part 2634,
Annual Report 2019 for Calendar Year 2018 (hereafter "Jared Kushner, OGE Form
278e"), May 15, 2019, 9, https://s3.amazonaws.com/storage.citizensforethics.org/wp-content
/uploads/2019/06/14143054/KUSHNER-JARED_Annual-Report-2019Pending-WH
-Action.pdf.

4. Cadre, "Our Company," http://cadre.com/our-team/.

5. Cadre, Twitter, November 29, 2018, https://twitter.com/CadreRE/status/10681973899
68777216.

6. Cadre, Opportunity Zones, https://cadre.com/investing-with-us/opportunity-zones/.

7. Cadre, "Join the Cadre Opportunity Zones Program," screenshot captured October 15,
2019.

8. Jared Kushner, OGE Form 278e, May 15, 2019.

9. Scott Amey, telephone interview with author, May 15, 2020; Virginia Canter, telephone
interview with author, May 13, 2020; Don Fox, telephone interview with author, May 12,
2020; Richard Painter, telephone interview with author, May 11, 2020.

10. "CREW Files Conflict of Interest Complaint Against Ivanka Trump," Citizens for Responsibility and Ethics in Washington, January 4, 2019, https://www.citizensforethics
.org/press-release/crew-files-conflict-of-interest-complaint-against-ivanka-trump/.

11. Jennifer Jacobs and Caleb Melby, "Jared Kushner Divests from Startup Cadre over Future
Conflict Concerns," Bloomberg, February 28, 2020, https://www.bloomberg.com/news
/articles/2020-02-28/kushner-divests-from-startup-firm-cadre-over-conflict-concerns
?sref=CG50Q9x0.

12. Jared Kushner, OGE Form 278e, U.S. Office of Government Ethics, 5 C.F.R. part 2634,
July 20, 2017, 38; Jared Kushner, OGE Form 278e, U.S. Office of Government Ethics, 5
C.F.R. part 2634, July 31, 2019, 19.

13. Jared Kushner, Certificate of Divestiture, U.S. Office of Government Ethics, Certificate
No. OGE-2020-023, February 26, 2020.

14. Anne Applebaum, "Want to Secretly, Legally Send Money to Jared Kushner? Here's How
to Do It," *Washington Post*, June 13, 2019; Jon Swaine, "Company Part-Owned by Jared
Kushner Got $90m from Unknown Offshore Investors since 2017," *Guardian*, June 10,
2019, http://www.theguardian.com/us-news/2019/jun/10/jared-kushner-real-estate-cadre
-goldman-sachs; Stephen Braun, "AP: Ivanka, Kushner Could Profit from Tax Break They
Pushed," AP News, https://apnews.com/a2f9b8bba398423ab84689805c0a72bc.

15. Analysis of New York City property records.

16. Shinhan Financial Group Co., Form 20-F, Securities and Exchange Commission, Annual
Report Pursuant to Section 13 or 15(d) of the Securities Exchange Act of 1934 for the
fiscal year ended December 31, 2018, April 30, 2019, 250, https://www.sec.gov/Archives
/edgar/data/1263043/000119312519127582/d669014d20f.htm; Free Writing Prospectus
Structural and Collateral Term Sheet Benchmark 2018-B8, November 29, 2018, 6; NYC
Department of Finance, Second Amended and Restated Mortgage, Document ID
2017090800269001, August 25, 2017, 53, 73, https://a836-acris.nyc.gov/DS/Document
Search/DocumentImageView?doc_id=2017090800269001; Mega International Commercial Bank, "Annual Report 2018," 41, https://www.megabank.com.tw/en-us/-/media
/mega/files/bank/about/annul-report/2018/mega_annual_report_2018.pdf?la=zh-tw
&hash=8FDF6EB95067AF32E151BBAD29FA317B.

17. Rae Kushner, oral history interview, United States Holocaust Memorial Museum, https://
collections.ushmm.org/search/catalog/irn504520.

18. "Remarks at a Democratic National Committee Reception in Florham Park, New Jersey," Public Papers of the Presidents of the United States: William J. Clinton, govinfo.gov/content/pkg/ppp-1997-book2/html/ppp-1997-book2-doc-pg1319.htm.

19. Steven Bertoni, "Exclusive Interview: How Jared Kushner Won Trump the White House," *Forbes*, November 22, 2016, http://www.forbes.com/sites/stevenbertoni/2016/11/22/exclusive-interview-how-jared-kushner-won-trump-the-white-house.

20. "Real Estate Developer to Pay $508,900 Civil Penalty to Federal Election Commission," Federal Election Commission, June 30, 2004, https://www.fec.gov/updates/real-estate-developer-to-pay-508900-civil-penalty-to-federal-election-commission.

21. United States District Court for the District of New Jersey Civil Action No. 03-504, Robert Yontef, Plaintiff, v. Westminster Manager LLC, D/B/A Kushner Companies, Charles Kushner and Richard Stadtmaue, Defendants, February 4, 2003.

22. Federal Election Commission, "Real Estate Developer to Pay $508,900 Civil Penalty to Federal Election Commission."

23. United States District Court, District of New Jersey, United States of America v. Charles Kushner, Crim. No. 04-580, August 18, 2004.

24. United States District Court, District of New Jersey, United States of America v. Charles Kushner, Magistrate No. 04-6120, July 12, 2004; United States District Court, District of New Jersey, United States of America v. Charles Kushner, Crim. No. 04-580, August 18, 2004.

25. This and preceding paragraph: United States District Court, District of New Jersey, United States of America v. Charles Kushner, Magistrate No. 04-6120, July 12, 2004.

26. This and preceding paragraph: United States District Court, District of New Jersey, United States of America v. Charles Kushner, Crim. No. 04-580, August 18, 2004.

27. "Political Contributor, Developer Charles Kushner Pleads Guilty to Tax Fraud, Witness Retaliation and Making False Statements to the Federal Election Commission," U.S. Department of Justice, August 18, 2004, http://www.justice.gov/archive/tax/usaopress/2004/txdv04kush0818_r.htm; United States District Court, District of New Jersey, United States of America v. Charles Kushner, Crim. No. 04-580, August 18, 2004.

28. Bertoni, "Exclusive Interview: How Jared Kushner."

29. Federal Bureau of Prisons, Charles Kushner, https://www.bop.gov/inmateloc/.

30. Charles V. Bagli, "A Big Deal, Even in Manhattan: A Tower Goes for $1.8 Billion," *New York Times*, December 7, 2006, http://kushner.com/wp-content/uploads/2016/08/NYTimesABigDeal.pdf.

31. Prospectus Supplement, GE Commercial Mortgage Corporation, Securities and Exchange Commission, April 26, 2007, Series 2007-C1 Trust, B-3, https://www.sec.gov/Archives/edgar/data/1215087/000119312507103115/d424b5.htm.

32. Analysis of SEC documents.

33. This and preceding three paragraphs: Analysis of Prospectus Supplement, GE Commercial Mortgage Corporation, Securities and Exchange Commission, April 26, 2007, Series 2007-C1 Trust, B-5, S-87, https://www.sec.gov/Archives/edgar/data/1215087/000119312507103115/d424b5.htm.

34. Prospectus Supplement, GE Commercial Mortgage Corporation, Securities and Exchange Commission, April 26, 2007, Series 2007-C1 Trust, B-5; Vornado Realty Trust, Q3 2012 Earnings Call, November 2, 2012; Orrick, Harington & Sutcliffe, "Learn About Our Locations and the Markets We Serve," http://www.orrick.com/en/locations; Newmark Knight Frank, "Norton Rose Fulbright Takes 107,215 SF at 1301 Avenue of the Americas," May 6, 2015, http://www.ngkf.com/home/media-center/press-releases.aspx?d=6956#sthash.4HrEYsF9.vQVFBDje.dpbs.

35. Bertoni, "Exclusive Interview: How Jared Kushner."
36. Vornado Realty Trust, Form 10-K, Securities and Exchange Commission, Annual Report Pursuant to Section 13 or 15(d) of the Securities Exchange Act of 1934 for the Fiscal Year Ended December 31, 2012, 152, https://www.sec.gov/Archives/edgar/data/899689/0000 89968913000004/vno2012form10k420pm.htm.
37. Peter Grant, "Jared Kushner's White House Role Complicates Skyscraper Deal," *Wall Street Journal,* March 21, 2017, https://www.wsj.com/articles/jared-kushners-white-house-role-complicates-skyscraper-deal-1490111514.
38. Representatives of the Korea Investment Corporation did not respond to inquiries by the author. A representative for Bernard Arnault said he would get back to a question about the pitch but did not. The Qatari consulate and embassy did not respond on behalf of Hamad bin Jassim Al-Thani. David Kocieniewski and Caleb Melby, "Kushners' China Deal Flop Was Part of Much Bigger Hunt for Cash."
39. Chris Christie, *Let Me Finish* (New York, NY: Hachette, 2019), 7.
40. Susanne Craig, Jo Becker, and Jesse Drucker "Jared Kushner, a Trump In-Law and Adviser, Chases a Chinese Deal," *New York Times,* January 7, 2017, https://www.nytimes .com/2017/01/07/us/politics/jared-kushner-trump-business.html.
41. Peter Grant, "Kushner Family Closes Deal to Unload 666 Fifth Avenue," *Wall Street Journal,* August 3, 2018, https://www.wsj.com/articles/kushner-family-close-to-deal-to -unload-666-fifth-avenue-1533322813.
42. Vornado Realty Trust, Form 10-K, Securities and Exchange Commission, Annual Report Pursuant to Section 13 or 15(d) of the Securities Exchange Act of 1934 for the Fiscal Year Ended December 31, 2012, 152.
43. Brookfield 2018 Annual Report, 150.
44. Brookfield Property Partners L.P., Form 20-F, Securities and Exchange Commission, Annual Report Pursuant to Section 13 or 15(d) of the Securities Exchange Act of 1934 for the Fiscal Year Ended December 31, 2017, 116, https://www.sec.gov/Archives/edgar/data /1545772/000154577218000003/bpy201720-f.htm; Qatar Investment Authority, "About Us," https://www.qia.qa/About/AboutUs.aspx.
45. Kerrie McHugh, email to author, May 12, 2020.
46. San Francisco Assessor-Recorder, Notice of Non-Responsibility, HWA 555 Owners LLC, Qatar Investment Authority Advisor (USA) Inc., August 30, 2018.
47. Kushner, "65 Bay St.," https://kushner.com/project/65-bay-street/.
48. "Trump Bay Street Jersey City," https://www.trumpbaystreet.com/apartments/nj/jersey -city/amenities.
49. 88 Kushner-KABR, EB-5 Project, Jersey City, U.S. Immigration Fund, https://visaeb-5 .com/project/88-kushner-kabr/; "Kushner Companies Closes on $200M from Citigroup for 65 Bay Street, A U.S. Immigration Fund Project," U.S. Immigration Fund, March 23, 2018, https://visaeb-5.com/kushner-companies-gets-200m-from-citigroup-for -65-bay-street/.
50. "EB-5 Immigrant Investor Program," https://www.uscis.gov/eb-5.
51. "Is the Investor Visa Program an Underperforming Asset?," *Hearing Before the Committee on the Judiciary House of Representatives,* 114th Cong., Second Session, February 11, 2016, https://www.govinfo.gov/content/pkg/CHRG-114hhrg98626/html/CHRG-114 hhrg98626.htm.
52. Report to Congressional Requesters, "Immigrant Investor Program, Additional Actions Needed to Better Assess Fraud Risks and Report Economic Benefits, U.S. Government Accountability Office, August 2015, https://www.gao.gov/assets/680/671940.pdf.
53. Shawn Boburg, "How Jared Kushner Built a Luxury Skyscraper Using Loans Meant for Job-Starved Areas," *Washington Post,* May 31, 2017, https://www.washingtonpost.com/in

vestigations/jared-kushner-and-his-partners-used-a-program-meant-for-job-starved-areas
-to-build-a-luxury-skyscraper/2017/05/31/9c81b52c-4225-11e7-9869-bac8b446820a
_story.html.

54. "Kushner Companies Closes on $200M."
55. "Trump Bay Street Jersey City."
56. Deed, January 5, 2015, Hudson County Register, One Journal Square Tower South, Urban Renewal Company LLC, Instrument Number 20150105010001280, https://acclaim .hcnj.us/AcclaimWeb/; Deed, January 5, 2015, Hudson County Register, One Journal Square Tower North, Urban Renewal Company LLC, Instrument Number: 20150105010001270, https://acclaim.hcnj.us/AcclaimWeb/; Deed, January 5, 2015, Hudson County Register, MEPT Journal Square Tower North, Urban Renewal Company LLC, Instrument Number: 20150105010001290, https://acclaim.hcnj.us/AcclaimWeb/.
57. "1 Journal Square," Kushner, https://kushner.com/project/1-journal-square/.
58. "Grassley Seeks Investigation of Companies' Promises of Green Cards," U.S. Senator Chuck Grassley, May 25, 2017, https://www.grassley.senate.gov/news/news-releases/grass ley-seeks-investigation-companies%E2%80%99-promises-green-cards.
59. Javier C. Hernández, Cao Li, and Jesse Drucker, "Jared Kushner's Sister Highlights Family Ties in Pitch to Chinese Investors," New York Times, May 6, 2017, https://www.nytimes .com/2017/05/06/world/asia/jared-kushner-sister-nicole-meyer-china-investors.html.
60. Emily Rauhala and William Wan, "In a Beijing Ballroom, Kushner Family Pushes $500,000 'Investor Visa' to Wealthy Chinese," Washington Post, May 6, 2017, https:// www.washingtonpost.com/world/in-a-beijing-ballroom-kushner-family-flogs-500000 -investor-visa-to-wealthy-chinese/2017/05/06/cf711e53-eb49-4f9a-8dea-3cd836fcf287 _story.html.
61. Javier C. Hernández, "Kushner Companies Backs Out of Chinese Investor Events After Furor," New York Times, May 12, 2017, https://www.nytimes.com/2017/05/12/business /kushner-china-real-estate.html.
62. Rauhala and Wan, "In a Beijing Ballroom."
63. Hernández, Li, and Drucker, "Jared Kushner's Sister Highlights Family Ties."
64. Jared Kushner, OGE Form 278e, March 31, 2017, 77.
65. Amy Brittain, "Days after Sister's Visa Pitch, Kushner Divested Asset Related to Jersey City Project," Washington Post, August 31, 2017, https://www.washingtonpost.com/inves tigations/days-after-sisters-visa-pitch-kushner-divested-asset-related-to-jersey-city-project /2017/08/31/0aa16284-8103-11e7-902a-2a9f2d808496_story.html.
66. Will Parker and Konrad Putzier, "Kushner, Unfiltered," The Real Deal, June 1, 2018, https://therealdeal.com/issues_articles/kushner-unfiltered/.
67. Analysis of New York City property records.
68. "Austin Nichols House," Kushner Companies, https://kushner.com/project/austin-nichols -house/; Charles V. Bagli, "Kushners Sought to Oust Rent-Regulated Tenants, Suit Says," New York Times, July 16, 2018, https://www.nytimes.com/2018/07/16/nyregion/kush ners-construction-tenants-lawsuit.html?module=inline.
69. Analysis of New York City property records.
70. Analysis of New York City property records.
71. Jared Kushner, OGE Form 278e, January 2019, https://s3.amazonaws.com/storage.citi zensforethics.org/wp-content/uploads/2019/06/14143054/KUSHNER-JARED_An nual-Report-2019Pending-WH-Action.pdf; Jared Kushner, OGE Form 278e, Septebmer 10, 2018.
72. Analysis of New York City property records.
73. NYC Department of Finance, Office of the City Register, Gellert Kent One LLC, August 25, 2017, https://a836-acris.nyc.gov/DS/DocumentSearch/DocumentImageView?doc

_id=2017083000592001; NYC Department of Finance, Office of the City Register, Gellert Kent Two LLC, August 25, 2017, https://a836-acris.nyc.gov/DS/Document-Search/DocumentImageView?doc_id=2017083000543001; NYC Department of Finance, Office of the City Register, Gellert Kent Three LLC, August 25, 2017, https://a836-acris.nyc.gov/DS/DocumentSearch/DocumentImageView?doc_id=2017083000575001.

74. Atalanta, "Careers," http://www.atalantacorp.com/join-our-team.php.

75. "President Donald J. Trump Announces Key Additions to his Administration," White House, January 4, 2018, https://www.whitehouse.gov/presidential-actions/president-donald-j-trump-announces-key-additions-administration-27/.

76. "UBS 2018-C5, Free Writing Prospectus, Collateral Term Sheet," Securities and Exchange Commission, December 6, 2018, https://www.sec.gov/Archives/edgar/data/1532799/000153949718001937/n1449_premktts-x2.htm.

77. "Gellert, Andrew Michael," U.S. Department of State, https://www.state.gov/gellert-andrew-michael-republic-of-chile-january-2018/.

78. Representatives for the Gellerts did not respond to requests for comment. "Nineteen Nominations and Two Withdrawals Sent to the Senate Today," White House, August 16, 2018, https://www.whitehouse.gov/presidential-actions/nineteen-nominations-two-withdrawals-sent-senate-today/.

79. Ryan M. Scoville, "Unqualified Ambassadors," Duke Law Journal, https://scholarship.law.duke.edu/cgi/viewcontent.cgi?referer=&httpsredir=1&article=3991&context=dlj.

80. Office of Government Ethics, "Public Financial Disclosure Guide, Liabilities," http://www.oge.gov/Web/278eGuide.nsf/Chapters/Liabilities?opendocument.

81. NYC Department of Finance, Notice of Property Value, Tax Year 2019–20, Document ID 2017090800269001, August 25, 2017, 80, https://a836-acris.nyc.gov/DS/Document Search/DocumentImageView?doc_id=2017090800269001.

82. NYC Department of Finance, Second Amended and Restated Mortgage, Document ID 2017090800269001, August 25, 2017, 53, 73, https://a836-acris.nyc.gov/DS/Document Search/DocumentImageView?doc_id=2017090800269001; Mega International Commercial Bank, Annual Report 2018, 41, https://www.megabank.com.tw/en-us/-/media/mega/files/bank/about/annul-report/2018/mega_annual_report_2018.pdf?la=zh-tw&hash=8FDF6EB95067AF32E151BBAD29FA317B; Mega Financial Holding Co., Annual Report 2018, 21, https://www.megaholdings.com.tw/upload/81/2019061716484339373.pdf; Jared Kushner, OGE Form 278e, May 15, 2019; Jared Kushner, OGE Form 278e, September 10, 2018; Jared Kushner, OGE Form 278e, March 31, 2017.

83. Mega Financial Holding Co., Annual Report 2018, 22–25, 291.

84. U.S. Department of State, "U.S. Relations with Taiwan," https://www.state.gov/u-s-relations-with-taiwan/.

85. NYC Department of Finance, Second Amended and Restated Mortgage, 37.

86. Jared Kushner, OGE Form 278e, May 15, 2019.

87. Benchmark 2018-B8 Mortgage Trust, J.P. Morgan Chase Commercial Mortgage Securities Corp., A-3-126, https://www.sec.gov/Archives/edgar/data/1013611/000153949718002076/n1444-x17_bmarkb8424b2.htm.

88. Benchmark 2018-B8 Mortgage Trust, J.P. Morgan Chase Commercial Mortgage Securities Corp., A-3-126.

89. Free Writing Prospectus, Structural and Collateral Term Sheet, Benchmark 2018-B8, November 29, 2018, 122, https://www.sec.gov/Archives/edgar/data/1013611/00015394 9718001894/n1444_x1-teaserts.htm.

90. NYC Department of Finance, Office of the City Register, 55 Prospect Owner LLC, October 2, 2013, https://a836-acris.nyc.gov/DS/DocumentSearch/DocumentImageView

?doc_id=2013101400498003; NYC Department of Finance, Office of the City Register, 81 Prospect Owner LLC, October 2, 2013, https://a836-acris.nyc.gov/DS/Document Search/DocumentImageView?doc_id=2013101400498001; NYC Department of Finance, Office of the City Register, 117 Adams Owner LLC, October 2, 2013, https://a836-acris .nyc.gov/DS/DocumentSearch/DocumentImageView?doc_id=2013101400498002; NYC Department of Finance, Office of the City Register, 77 Sands Owner LLC, October 2, 2013, https://a836-acris.nyc.gov/DS/DocumentSearch/DocumentImageView?doc_id=20 13101400498005; NYC Department of Finance, Office of the City Register, 175 Pearl Owner LLC, October 2, 2013, https://a836-acris.nyc.gov/DS/DocumentSearch/Docu mentImageView?doc_id=2013101400498004; Jared Kushner, OGE Form 278e, March 31, 2017, Annie Karni, "Kushner to Resign from Exec Posts, Divest Sizeable Assets," *Politico*, January 9, 2017.

91. Analysis of property records, NYC Department of Finance, Office of the City Register, Document ID 2013101400498006, October 2, 2013, https://a836-acris.nyc.gov/DS /DocumentSearch/DocumentImageView?doc_id=2013101400498006; NYC Department of Finance, Office of the City Register, Document ID 2013101400498007, October 2, 2013, 3, https://a836-acris.nyc.gov/DS/DocumentSearch/DocumentImageView?doc _id=2013101400498007; NYC Department of Finance, Office of the City Register, Document ID 2013101400498008, October 2, 2013, 3, https://a836-acris.nyc.gov/DS/Docu mentSearch/DocumentImageView?doc_id=2013101400498008; NYC Department of Finance, Office of the City Register, Document ID 2014120400677001, November 25, 2014, https://a836-acris.nyc.gov/DS/DocumentSearch/DocumentImageView?doc_id=20 14120400677001.

92. NYC Department of Finance, Office of the City Register, Document ID 20170404 00866001, April 6, 2017, https://a836-acris.nyc.gov/DS/DocumentSearch/Document ImageView?doc_id=2017040400866001; NYC Department of Finance, Office of the City Register, Document ID 20170407000290010, April 6, 2017, 4–5, 11, https://a836 -acris.nyc.gov/DS/DocumentSearch/DocumentImageView?doc_id=2017040700029001.

93. Don Fox telephone interview; Marilynn Glynn, telephone interview with the author, May 16, 2020; Scott Amey telephone interview.

94. Richard Painter telephone interview.

95. Free Writing Prospectus, Structural and Collateral Term Sheet, Benchmark 2018-B8, November 29, 2018, 7, 121, 125.

96. Free Writing Prospectus, Structural and Collateral Term Sheet, Benchmark 2018-B8, November 29, 2018, 121.

97. Analysis of Lobbying Disclosures, Office of the Clerk, United States House of Representatives, https://disclosurespreview.house.gov/?index=%22 lobbying-disclosures%22. For example: Q2 and Q3, 2017: Citibank lobbies Treasury, White House, and SEC on a range of financial issues and potential laws. Citibank also "met with administration on issues related to tax reform" and "met with House, Senate, and Administration on NAFTA." Q3 2017: Citibank lobbies Treasury, White House, SEC on range of financial issues and potential laws. They also "met with administration on issues related to tax reform." They also "met with House, Senate, and Administration on NAFTA."

98. "Remarks by President Trump at a Signing Ceremony for the United States-Mexico-Canada Trade Agreement," White House, January 29, 2020, https://www.whitehouse.gov/brief ings-statements/remarks-president-trump-signing-ceremony-united-states-mexico-canada -trade-agreement/.

99. "Press Briefing by Treasury Secretary Steven Mnuchin on North Korea Sanctions," White House, February 23, 2018, https://www.whitehouse.gov/briefings-statements/press-briefing -treasury-secretary-steven-mnuchin-north-korea-sanctions/.

100. Jim Acosta, "CNN Exclusive: At least 100 White House Officials Served with 'Interim' Security Clearances Until November," CNN Politics, February 15, 2018, https://www.cnn.com/2018/02/14/politics/security-clearances-white-house/index.html.

101. Free Writing Prospectus, Structural and Collateral Term Sheet, Benchmark 2018-B8, November 29, 2018, 6.

102. Choe Sang-Hun, "Computer Networks in South Korea Are Paralyzed in Cyberattacks," *New York Times*, March 20, 2013, https://www.nytimes.com/2013/03/21/world/asia/south-korea-computer-network-crashes.html.

103. U.S. Resolution Plan, Industrial and Commercial Bank of China, December 2018, https://www.fdic.gov/regulations/reform/resplans/plans/icbc-165-1812.pdf.

104. Norges Bank, "About," https://www.norges-bank.no/en/.

105. Shinhan Financial Group Co., Form 20-F, Securities and Exchange Commission, Annual Report Pursuant to Section 13 or 15(d) of the Securities Exchange Act of 1934 for the Fiscal Year Ended December 31, 2018, April 30, 2019, 250, https://www.sec.gov/Archives/edgar/data/1263043/000119312519127582/d669014d20f.htm.

CHAPTER TEN: FILL THE SWAMP

1. "Donald Trump Campaign Event in Green Bay, Wisconsin," C-SPAN, October 17, 2016, https://www.c-span.org/video/?417019-1/donald-trump-campaigns-green-bay-wisconsin.

2. "Presidential Candidate Donald Trump Campaign Event in Charlotte, North Carolina," C-SPAN, October 26, 2016, https://www.c-span.org/video/?417505-1/donald-trump-proposes-new-deal-urban-america.

3. Ben Schreckinger, "Inside Donald Trump's Election Night War Room," *GQ*, November 7, 2017, https://www.gq.com/story/inside-donald-trumps-election-night-war-room.

4. David Koch died on August 23, 2019. A spokesperson for Hamm did not respond to a request for comment. A spokesperson for Beal replied, "Mr. Beal does not dispute the *GQ* article's statement about his attendance at the event on the night of the 2016 election." Jim Chambless, email to author, May 13, 2020.

5. Representatives for Richard LeFrak and Carl Icahn did not respond to requests for comment. Phil Ruffin, interviewed by author, February 15, 2017.

6. Matthew J., Belvedere, "Wilbur Ross Gives Insider Account of How Icahn Left Trump's Victory Party and Made $1 Billion," CNBC, March 3, 2017, https://www.cnbc.com/2017/03/03/icahn-left-trumps-election-victory-party-to-buy-stocks-and-made-1-billion-says-wilbur-ross.html.

7. "Hearing on Nomination of Attorney General Scott Pruitt to be Administrator of the U.S. Environmental Protection Agency before the Committee on Environment and Public Works," 115th Cong., First Session, January 18, 2017, 56-57, 199-200, congress.gov/115/chrg/CHRG-115-shrg24034/CHRG-115shrg24034.pdf; Coral Davenport and Eric Lipton, "Trump Picks Scott Pruitt, Climate Change Denialist, to Lead E.P.A.," *New York Times*, December 7, 2017, https://www.nytimes.com/2016/12/07/us/politics/scott-pruitt-epa-trump.html.

8. "Icahn: Pruitt a Great Pick for EPA," *Bloomberg*, December 7, 2016, https://www.bloomberg.com/news/videos/2016-12-07/icahn-pruitt-a-great-pick-for-epa.

9. Icahn Enterprises LP, Investor Presentation, November 2016, 8; CVR Energy, Form 10-K, Securities and Exchange Commission, Annual Report Pursuant to Section 13 or 15(d) of the Securities Exchange Act of 1934 for the Fiscal Year Ended December 31, 2016, 61, https://www.sec.gov/Archives/edgar/data/1376139/000137613917000019/cvi2016form10-kx12312016.htm; analysis of stock price, CVR Energy, Yahoo Finance.

10. "Icahn: Pruitt a Great Pick for EPA."

11. "Carl Icahn on Trump's Cabinet Picks," Fox Business, YouTube, November 17, 2016, https://www.youtube.com/watch?v=ldp397wVpZg.

12. "Carl Icahn On Donald Trump's Approach to Regulatory Agencies, *Power Lunch,* CNBC," CNBC, YouTube, December 8, 2016, https://www.youtube.com/watch?v= 1YmpJPs-Dmc.

13. Dan Alexander, "Inside the $400 Million Fortune of Trump's Treasury Secretary Steve Mnuchin," *Forbes,* June 22, 2019, https://www.forbes.com/sites/danalexander/2019/07 /22/inside-the-400-million-fortune-of-trumps-treasury-secretary-steve-mnuchin /#2a7a22cd6333.

14. "Carl Icahn on Trump's Cabinet Picks."

15. Trump-Pence Transition Team, "President-Elect Donald J. Trump Names Carl Icahn Special Advisor to the President on Regulatory Reform," December 21, 2016, Wayback Machine, https://web.archive.org/web/20170317001315/greatagain.gov/icahn-advisor-regs -cd3c949af118.

16. Icahn Enterprises L.P., Form 10-K, Securities and Exchange Commission, Annual Report Pursuant to Section 13 or 15(d) of the Securities Exchange Act of 1934 for the Fiscal Year Ended December 31, 2016, 238, https://www.sec.gov/Archives/edgar/data /813762/000081376217000010/a10k-fy2016.htm#s462B417DD39057F3B79B11CA550 69E9A.

17. "Carl Icahn Talks Trump, EPA Rules, Asset Markets and AIG," *Bloomberg,* YouTube, August 17, 2016, https://www.youtube.com/watch?v=eWT-OG1sUy8&t=1s.

18. U.S. Office of Government Ethics, 18 U.S.C. § 208, Acts Affecting a Personal Financial Interest, https://www.oge.gov/Web/oge.nsf/Resources/18+U.S.C.+%C2%A7+208:+Acts+ affecting+a+personal+financial+interest.

19. Trump-Pence Transition Team, "President-Elect Donald J. Trump Names Carl Icahn."

20. Richard Painter, interviewed by author, August 2, 2019.

21. Analysis of Icahn Enterprises L.P. Schedule 13-D, Securities and Exchange Commission, September 19, 2016, https://www.sec.gov/Archives/edgar/data/813762/000092846416000226 /iepsch13damd42092116.htm; analysis of stock price on November 8, 2016, and December 22, 2016, Yahoo Finance, Icahn Enterprises L.P. https://finance.yahoo.com/quote/IEP/his tory?period1=1478476800&period2=1482624000&interval=1d&filter=history&frequency =1d; analysis of stock price on November 8, 2016, and December 22, 2016, Yahoo Finance, S&P 500, https://finance.yahoo.com/quote/%5EGSPC/history?period1=1478563200&pe riod2=1482451200&interval=1d&filter=history&frequency=1d.

22. Walter Shaub, interviewed by author, May 15, 2020.

23. Icahn Enterprises L.P. Form 10-K, Securities and Exchange Commission, Annual Report Pursuant to Section 13 or 15(d) of the Securities Exchange Act of 1934 for the Fiscal Year Ended December 31, 2019, 109, https://sec.gov/ix?doc=/archives/edgar/data/813762 /000081376220000008/iep-20191231.htm.

24. "Carl Icahn Issues Statement," August 18, 2017, https://carlicahn.com/carl-icahn-issues -statement/.

25. Scott Pruitt, Public Financial Disclosure, March 20, 2019, http://extapps2.oge.gov/201 /Presiden.nsf/PAS+Index/3973855AA50355BC852583C90027/E89D/$FILE/Edward-s -Pruitt-2018-278.pdf.

26. "U.S. Environmental Protection Agency—Installation of Soundproof Privacy Booth," U.S. Government Accountability Office, April 16, 2018, https://www.gao.gov/assets /700/691272.pdf.

27. Jennifer A. Dlouhy and Jennifer Jacobs, "EPA Chief's $50-a-Night Rental Raises White House Angst," *Bloomberg,* March 29, 2018, https://www.bloomberg.com/news/articles /2018-03-30/epa-chief-s-50-a-night-rental-said-to-raise-white-house-angst.

28. "Statements of Millan Hupp, director of scheduling and advance for EPA administrator Scott Pruitt, Before the Committee on Oversight and Government Reform, quoted in Elijah E. Cummings and Gerald E. Connolly to the Honorable Trey Gowdy," House Committee on Oversight and Reform, June 4, 2018, 5, https://oversight.house.gov/sites /democrats.oversight.house.gov/files/documents/2018-06-04.EEC%20Connolly%20 to%20Gowdy%20re.%20EPA%20Pruitt.pdf.

29. "EPA Head Scott Pruitt's Outreach to Chick-fil-A CEO on 'a Potential Business Opportunity,'" *Washington Post,* http://apps.washingtonpost.com/g/documents/national/epa -head-scott-pruitts-outreach-to-chick-fil-a-ceo-on-a-potential-business-opportunity /3006/.

30. Juliet Eilperin, Brady Dennis, and Josh Dawsey, "Scott Pruitt Enlisted an EPA Aide to Help His Wife Find a Job—With Chick-fil-A," *Washington Post,* June 5, 2018, https:// www.washingtonpost.com/national/health-science/scott-pruitt-enlisted-an-epa-aide -to-help-his-wife-find-a-job--at-chick-fil-a/2018/06/05/b798e4e4-5eac-11e8-9ee3-49d6 d4814c4c_story.html.

31. Scott Pruitt, email to author, May 11, 2020.

32. Donald J. Trump, Twitter, July 5, 2018, https://twitter.com/realDonaldTrump/status /1014956568129892352.

33. *Hearing on Nomination of Tom Price to Serve as Secretary of Health and Human Services, Before the Senate Committee on Health, Education, Labor and Pensions,* 115th Cong., First Session, January 18, 2017, https://www.congress.gov/115/chrg/CHRG-115shrg23749/CHRG -115shrg23749.htm.

34. Office of Inspector General, U.S. Department of Health and Human Services, "The Office of the Secretary of Health and Human Services Did Not Comply with Federal Regulations for Chartered Aircraft and Other Government Travel Related to Former Secretary Price," https://oig.hhs.gov/oas/reports/region12/A121700002.pdf.

35. Tom Price, telephone interview with author, May 12, 2020; "Statement from the Press Secretary," White House, September 29, 2017, https://www.whitehouse.gov/briefings -statements/statement-press-secretary-10/.

36. Juliet Eilperin and Josh Dawsey, "Zinke's Own Agency Watchdog Just Referred Him to the Justice Department," *Washington Post,* October 31, 2018, https://www.washington post.com/energy-environment/2018/10/30/zinkes-own-agency-watchdog-just-referred -him-justice-department/; Office of the Inspector General, U.S. Department of Interior, "Alleged Abuse of Position by Secretary Zinke," October 22, 2018, https://www.doioig .gov/reports/alleged-abuse-position-secretary-zinke; Office of the Inspector General, U.S. Department of Interior, "Investigative Report on Secretary Zinke's Use of Chartered and Military Aircraft Between March and September 2017," April 16, 2018, https://www .doioig.gov/reports/investigative-report-secretary-zinke%E2%80%99s-use-of-char tered-and-military-aircraft-between-march-and; Office of the Inspector General, U.S. Department of Interior, "Alleged Preferential Treatment in Grand Staircase-Escalante National Monument Boundary Decision," January 31, 2019, https://www.doioig.gov/re ports/alleged-preferential-treatment-grand-staircase-escalante-national-monument -boundary-decision; Office of the Inspector General, U.S. Department of Interior, letter relating to private email use, July 29, 2019, https://naturalresources.house.gov/imo /media/doc/Interior%20Inspector%20General%20Letter%20to%20Grijalva%20 and%20Cummings%20on%20Zinke%20Emails%20Investigation%20July%2029%20 2019.pdf; Office of the Inspector General, U.S. Department of Interior, letter relating to land developments in Whitefish, Montana, July 18, 2018, https://naturalresources.house .gov/imo/media/doc/Interior%20Department%20Inspector%20General%20Con firms%20Investigation%20of%20Zinke%20Halliburton%20Meeting%20July%20 18%202018.pdf.

37. U.S. Department of Interior, Planning, Analysis, & Competitiveness (PAC) Subcommittee, "Meeting Summary," December 21, 2018, https://www.doi.gov/sites/doi.gov/files/uploads/pac_meeting_summary_12.21.18_final_0.pdf.

38. Office of Inspector General, U.S. Department of Veterans Affairs, "Administrative Investigation—VA Secretary and Delegation Travel to Europe," February 14, 2018, https://www.va.gov/oig/publications/report-summary.asp?id=4034i.

39. Chase Peterson-Withorn and Jennifer Wang, "The $4.5 Billion Cabinet," *Forbes,* December 22, 2016.

40. "Remarks of Walter M. Shaub, Jr., Director, U.S. Office of Government Ethics, as Prepared for Delivery at 4:00 p.m. on January 11, 2017, at the Brookings Institution," https://www.oge.gov/web/oge.nsf/0/6E08189CF6AF742B852580A500799063/$FILE/Remarks%20of%20W%20M%20Shaub%20Jr%20(1).pdf.

41. "Virginia Military Institute Commencement Address," C-SPAN, May 16, 2018, https://www.c-span.org/video/?443252-1/rex-tillerson-warns-us-faces-growing-crisis-ethics-integrity.

42. *Hearing on the Nomination of Wilbur L. Ross, Jr., to Be Secretary of the Department of Commerce, Before the Senate Committee on Commerce, Science and Transportation,* 115th Cong., First Session, January 18, 2017 (statements of Wilbur Ross and Senator Richard Blumenthal), https://www.congress.gov/115/chrg/shrg25974/CHRG-115shrg25974.htm.

43. U.S. Senate, Roll Call Vote, 115th Cong., First Session, February 27, 2017, https://www.senate.gov/legislative/LIS/roll_call_lists/roll_call_vote_cfm.cfm?congress=115&session=1&vote=00073.

44. Dan Alexander, "The Case of Wilbur Ross' Phantom $2 Billion," *Forbes,* November 7, 2017, https://www.forbes.com/sites/danalexander/2017/11/07/the-case-of-wilbur-ross-phantom-2-billion/#7a8561327515.

45. Robert A. Taggart Jr., "The Growth of the 'Junk' Bond Market and Its Role in Financing Takeovers," in *Mergers and Acquisitions*, ed. Alan J. Auerbach (Chicago: University of Chicago Press, 1987), 5, https://www.nber.org/chapters/c5819.pdf.

46. Matthew Schifrin and Jason Zweig, "Dr. Feelgood," *Forbes,* March 4, 1991.

47. David Storper, interviewed by author, July 1, 2019.

48. Alexander, "The Case of Wilbur Ross' Phantom $2 Billion."

49. Laura Jereski and Jason Zweig, "Step Right Up, Folks," *Forbes,* March 4, 1991.

50. Alexander, "The Case of Wilbur Ross' Phantom $2 Billion."

51. WL Ross Holding Corp, Amendment No. 1 to Form S-1 Registration Under the Securities Act of 1933, May 30, 2014, 62, https://www.sec.gov/Archives/edgar/data/1604416/000114420414034367/v380025_s1a.htm.

52. Alexander, "The Case of Wilbur Ross' Phantom $2 Billion."

53. David Storper, interviewed by author, July 1, 2019.

54. Alexander, "The Case of Wilbur Ross' Phantom $2 Billion."

55. Paul W. Marshall and Todd H. Thedinga, "International Steel Group," Harvard Business School, January 20, 2004.

56. David Storper, interviewed by author, July 1, 2019.

57. The LTV Corporation, Form 11-K, Annual Report for the fiscal year ended December 31, 2002, Securities and Exchange Commission, July 2, 2003, https://www.sec.gov/Archives/edgar/vprr/0302/03025189.pdf.

58. Alexander, "The Case of Wilbur Ross' Phantom $2 Billion."

59. International Steel Group Inc., Amendment No. 4 to Form S-1, Registration Statement Under the Securities Act of 1933, December 10, 2003, 90, https://www.sec.gov/Archives/edgar/data/1231868/000095015203010219/l91798hsv1za.txt.

60. Alexander, "The Case of Wilbur Ross' Phantom $2 Billion."

61. Alexander, "The Case of Wilbur Ross' Phantom $2 Billion."

62. David Storper, interviewed by author, July 1, 2019.

63. Alexander, "The Case of Wilbur Ross' Phantom $2 Billion."

64. "The Forbes 400," *Forbes,* October 11, 2004.

65. Alison Leigh Cowan, "Hilary Geary and Wilbur Ross Jr," *New York Times*, Oct. 17, 2004, https://www.nytimes.com/2004/10/17/fashion/weddings/hilary-geary-and-wilbur-ross -jr.html.

66. David Storper, interviewed by author, July 1, 2019.

67. Alexander, "The Case of Wilbur Ross' Phantom $2 Billion."

68. Asher Edelman, interviewed by author, October 27, 2017.

69. Former WL Ross employee, interviewed by author, October 26, 2017; David Storper, interviewed by author, July 1, 2019; Analysis of Federal Election Commission, Individual Contributions, Rudy Giuliani Presidential Committee, ID: C00430512, March 19, 2007, https://www.fec.gov/data/receipts/individual-contributions/?committee_id=C0043 0512&contributor_employer=w.l.+ross&two_year_transaction_period=2008.

70. Alexander, "The Case of Wilbur Ross' Phantom $2 Billion"; property deed, Party 1: Dana Landry and William Moody. Party 2: Wilbur Ross, June 3, 2008. Palm Beach County Property Appraiser's Office.

71. TurboTax, "States with the Highest and Lowest Taxes," https://turbotax.intuit.com/tax -tips/fun-facts/states-with-the-highest-and-lowest-taxes/L6HPAVqSF; Florida Governor Ron DeSantis, "Governor Ron DeSantis' State of the State Address," January 14, 2020, https://www.flgov.com/2020/01/14/governor-ron-desantis-state-of-the-state-address/.

72. "AMVESCAP PLC to Acquire WL Ross & Co. LLC; Financial Restructuring Leader Joins Global Investment Manager," Business Wire, July 24, 2006, https://www.business wire.com/news/home/20060723005026/en/AMVESCAP-PLC-Acquire-WL-Ross-LLC -Financial.

73. *David Storper v. Invesco et al.*, NYSCEF Docket No. 298, Supreme Court of the State of New York, County of New York, https://iapps.courts.state.ny.us/fbem/DocumentDisplay /Servlet?documentId=yaYD0oBc214cP_PLUS_g15Gjt8g==&system=prod; Former WL Ross employee, interview with author, July 2018; former WL Ross employee, interview with author, June 2018; David Storper, interviewed by author, July 1, 2019.

74. Asher Edelman, interviewed by author, July 26, 2019.

75. "Asher Edelman on the State of the Art Market," Yahoo Finance, July 25, 2019, https:// finance.yahoo.com/video/asher-edelman-state-art-market-211426485.html.

76. Alexander, "The Case of Wilbur Ross' Phantom $2 Billion."

77. *Forbes* archives.

78. Brendan Coffey, "We're Cutting Our Calculation of Wilbur Ross's Net Worth to $860 Mil-lion," *Bloomberg,* November 5, 2017, https://www.bloomberg.com/news/articles/2017-11 -15/ross-s-net-worth-calculation-cut-to-860-million-by-bloomberg; *Forbes* archives.

79. Sam Green, interview with author, 2017.

80. "Oregon Public Employees Retirement Fund, Private Equity Portfolio" State of Oregon, December 31, 2016; "Private Equity Fund Adviser Settles with SEC for Failing to Dis-close Its Fee Allocation Practices," U.S. Securities and Exchange Commission, August 24, 2016, http://www.sec.gov/litigation/admin/2016/ia-4494-s.pdf; Alexander, "The Case of Wilbur Ross' Phantom $2 Billion."

81. Alexander, "The Case of Wilbur Ross' Phantom $2 Billion."

82. This and preceding two paragraphs: Dan Alexander, "New Details About Wilbur Ross' Business Point to Pattern of Grifting," *Forbes,* August 7, 2018, https://www.forbes.com /sites/danalexander/2018/08/06/new-details-about-wilbur-rosss-businesses-point-to -pattern-of-grifting/#6467ca2f1c33; Spokesperson for Commerce Department, email to author, August 1, 2018; Interviews with three former WL Ross employees in 2017;

"Verified amended complaint," Peter A Lusk v. Wilbur L. Ross et al., July 2, 2017, Supreme Court of the State of New York; "Second amended complaint and jury demand, "David H. Storper v. Invesco Ltd., WL Ross & Co. LLC, et al., July 21, 2015, Supreme Court of the State of New York; Defendants' memorandum of law in opposition to plaintiff's motion for leave to amend the complaint, David H. Storper v. Invesco, Ltd. WL Ross & Co. LLC, August 26, 2016, Supreme Court of the State of New York..

83. Complaint: Joseph E. Mullin v. WL Ross & Co. LLC et al., NYSCEF Doc. No. 2, Supreme Court of the State of New York, County of New York.

84. Alexander, "New Details About Wilbur Ross' Business"; Answer to the complaint: Joseph E. Mullin v. WL Ross & Co. LLC et al., NYSCEF Doc. No. 62, Supreme Court of the State of New York, County of New York; Order, Joseph E. Mullin v. WL Ross & Co. LLC, et al., February 23, 2018, Supreme Court of the State of New York.

85. Notice of Entry: Joseph E. Mullin v. WL Ross & Co. LLC et al., NYSCEF Doc. No. 61, Supreme Court of the State of New York County of New York; Stipulation - Discontinuance (Request to Do So Order): Joseph E. Mullin v. WL Ross & Co. LLC et al., NYSCEF Doc. No. 64, Supreme Court of the State of New York, County of New York.

86. Alexander, "New Details About Wilbur Ross' Business."

87. "Private Equity Fund Adviser Settles with SEC for Failing to Disclose Its Fee Allocation Practices," Securities and Exchange Commission.

88. Form 10-K, Invesco Ltd., Securities and Exchange Commission, February 19, 2016, http://www.sec.gov/Archives/edgar/data/914208/000091420816000846/a201510-k.htm.

89. Interviews with four former WL Ross employees in 2017.

90. Alexander, "New Details About Wilbur Ross' Business."

91. This and preceding two paragraphs: Alexander, "New Details About Wilbur Ross' Business"; "Order Instituting Cease-and-Desist Proceedings Pursuant to Section 203(K) of the Investment Advisers Act of 1940, Making Findings, and Imposing a Cease and-Desist Order," August 24, 2016, Securities and Exchange Commission, https://www.sec.gov/litigation/admin/2016/ia-4494.pdf.

92. David Storper, interviewed by author, July 1, 2019.

93. "Oregon Public Employees Retirement Fund, Private Equity Portfolio" State of Oregon, December 31, 2016; Private Equity Program Fund Performance Review, WL Ross, CalPers, http://www.calpers.ca/gov/page/investments/asset-classes/private-equity/pep-fund-performance; Alexander, "New Details About Wilbur Ross' Business."

94. Alexander, "The Case of Wilbur Ross' Phantom $2 Billion."

95. Wilbur Ross and Peter Navarro, "Why Trump Has a Better Economic Plan than Clinton," CNBC, August 16, 2016, https://www.cnbc.com/2016/08/15/why-trump-has-a-bett; Wilbur Ross donations to Donald J. Trump for President, Inc. and Trump Victory, July 17, 2016, Federal Election commission, http://www.fec.gov/data/receipts/individual-contributions/?committee_id=C00580100&committee_id=C00586826&committee_id=C00618871&committee_id=C00618389&committee_id=C00628396&contributor_name=ross+wilbur&two_year_transaction_period=2016.

96. Alexander, "The Case of Wilbur Ross' Phantom $2 Billion."

97. U.S. Office of Government Ethics, "Public Financial Disclosure Guide," https://www.oge.gov/Web/278eGuide.nsf/Content/For+Ethics+Officials+Document~1.06:+Failure+to+File+and+Falsification+Penalties.

98. Alexander, "The Case of Wilbur Ross' Phantom $2 Billion."

99. This and the following paragraph: Wilbur Ross interviewed by Dan Alexander, October 1, 2017, embedded in "The Case of Wilbur Ross' Phantom $2 Billion," *Forbes,* November 7, 2017, https://www.forbes.com/sites/danalexander/2017/11/07/the-case-of-wilbur-ross-phantom-2-billion/#7a8561327515.

100. Dan Alexander, "The Mystery of Wilbur Ross' Missing Billions," *Forbes,* October 16, 2017, https://www.forbes.com/sites/danalexander/2017/10/16/the-mystery-of-wilbur-ross -missing-billions/#66a8c3241c90.

101. "Donald Trump Cabinet Member Wilbur Ross Left $2B Off Reports, But Why?," NBC News, October 16, 2017, https://www.nbcnews.com/dateline/video/trump-cabinet-member -left-2b-off-reports-but-why-1074199107827.

102. Alexander, "The Mystery of Wilbur Ross' Missing Billions."

103. Alexander, "New Details About Wilbur Ross' Business."

104. David Storper, interviewed by author, July 1, 2019.

105. Wilbur Ross, Ethics Agreement Supplement to David Maggi, Alternate Designated Agency Ethics Official, January 31, 2017, https://extapps2.oge.gov/201/Presiden.nsf/PAS +Index/C4D33DB26307189E852580C8002C7A72/$FILE/Ross,%20Wilbur%20L %20finalAmendedEA.pdf.

106. Alexander, "The Case Of Wilbur Ross' Phantom $2 Billion."

107. This and preceding paragraph: Laura M. Holson, "A Palm Beach Power Hostess Prepares for Trump's Washington," *New York Times,* February 11, 2017, https://www.nytimes.com /2017/02/11/style/hilary-geary-ross-wilbur-ross-donald-trump-washington-society.html; Roll Call Vote, 115th Cong., First Session, Wilbur L. Ross, Jr., of Florida, to Be Secretary of Commerce, United States Senate, February 27, 2017, https://www.senate.gov/legislative /LIS/roll_call_lists/roll_call_vote_cfm.cfm?congress=115&session=1&vote=00073.

108. Wilbur Ross's calendar, January 20–December 31, 2017, 46, 903.

109. "White House Mess," White House, https://whitehouse.gov1.info/white-house-mess/.

110. "William A. Furman," Greenbrier Companies, https://www.gbrx.com/about-us/officers/.

111. Wilbur Ross, December 21, 2017, "Executive Branch Personnel Public Financial Disclosure Report: Periodic Transaction Report (OGE Form 278-T)," Office of Government Ethics, http://extapps2.oge/gov/201/Presiden.nsf/PAS+Index/F65307D0E7C6CA00852 582B000DEA10/$FILE/Wilber-L-Ross-12.21.17-278T.pdf.

112. Dan Alexander, "Wilbur Ross' Calendar Reveals Dozens of Meetings with Companies Tied to His Personal Fortune," *Forbes,* July 13, 2018, https://www.forbes.com/sites/for besdigitalcovers/2018/07/12/wilbur-ross-calendar-reveals-dozens-of-meetings-with -companies-tied-to-his-personal-fortune/#5e07a38f526a; U.S. Office of Government Ethics, "Analyzing Potential Conflicts of Interest," https://www.oge.gov/web/OGE.nsf/Resources /Analyzing+Potential+Conflicts+of+Interest; Campaign Legal Center, "Complaint regarding Commerce Secretary Wilbur L. Ross Jr. from the Campaign Legal Center to the Inspector General for the U.S. Department of Commerce," Aug. 13, 2018, https://cam-paignlegal.org/sites/default/files/2018-08/Hon%20Wilbur%20Ross%20Jr%20Com-plaint%202813%20Aug%20202018%29.pdf.

113. U.S. Department of Commerce spokesperson, email to author, January 27, 2020.

114. William A. Furman to Brad Botwin, May 30, 2017, https://www.bis.doc.gov/index.php /232-steel-public-comments/1798-greenbrier-companies-public-comment/file.

115. Alexander, "Wilbur Ross' Calendar Reveals Dozens."

116. U.S. Office of Government Ethics, "Analyzing Potential Conflicts of Interest."

117. Wilbur Ross, Periodic Transaction Report (OGE Form 278-T), May 23, 2017, https://ex-tapps2.oge.gov/201/Presiden.nsf/PAS+Index/1E5213DD0708E5898525812B0026F872/$ FILE/Wilbur-L-Ross-05.23.2017-278.pdf; Wilbur Ross, Periodic Transaction Report (OGE Form 278-T), May 23, 2017, https://extapps2.oge.gov/201/Presiden.nsf/PAS+Index /A2B1B7B55C19C8178525812D0026F7F3/$FILE/Wilbur-L-Ross-05.23.2017-278T(2). pdf; Office of Government Ethics, "Certificate of divestiture," Hilary R. Geary, April 14, 2017; Wilbur Ross's calendar, January 20–December 31, 2017, 204, 216–17.

118. Office of Government Ethics, "Certificate of divestiture," Hilary R. Geary, April 14, 2017.

119. U.S. Department of Commerce Inspector General Office Chief of Staff Robert Johnson, email to author, January 27, 2020; U.S Department of Commerce Inspector General Office Chief of Staff Robert Johnston, email to author, May 13, 2020.

120. Wilbur L. Ross, "Executive Branch Personnel Public Financial Disclosure Report: Periodic Transaction Report (OGE Form 278-T)," December 21, 2017, http://extapps2.oge .gov/201/President.nsf/PAS+Index/F65307D0E7C6CA00852582B000DEA10/$FILE /Wilber-L-Ross-12.21.17-278T.pdf.

121. Dan Alexander, "Lies, China and Putin: Solving the Mystery of Wilbur Ross' Missing Fortune," *Forbes*, June 18, 2018, https://www.forbes.com/sites/danalexander/2018/06 /18/lies-china-and-putin-solving-the-mystery-of-wilbur-ross-missing-fortune-trump -commerce-secretary-cabinet-conflicts-of-interest/#2f0797917e87; Form 20-F, Navigator Holdings, U.S. Securities and Exchange commission, 32; Sibur, "Changes in the Sibur Holdings' Shareholding Structure," April 28, 2017, http://investors.sibur.com/investor -news/2017/apr/8-04-2017-shareholders.aspx?sc_lang=en; U.S. Department of the Treasury, "Treasury Designates Russian Oligarchs, Officials, and Entities in Response to Worldwide Malign Activity," April 6, 2018, http://home.treasury.gov/news/press-releases /sm0338; U.S. Department of the Treasury, "Treasury Sanctions Russian Officials, Members of the Russian Leadership's Inner Circle, and An entity For Involvement in the Situation in Ukraine," March 20, 2014, https://www.treasury.gov/press-center/press-releases /Pages/jl23331.aspx.

122. Mike McIntire, Twitter, June 19, 2018, https://twitter.com/mmcintire/status/100918 2261068124171.

123. Wilbur Ross, Periodic Transaction Report (OGE Form 278-T), November 7, 2017, https://extapps2.oge.gov/201/Presiden.nsf/PAS+Index/7C998256034FCC3F852582B0006 DEA0B/$FILE/Wilber-L-Ross-11.07.17-278T.pdf.

124. Wilbur Ross, "Executive Branch Personnel Public Financial Disclosure Report; Periodic Transaction Report (OGE Form 278-T)," Office of Government Ethics, December 21, 2017, https://extapps2.oge/gov/201/Presiden.nsf/PAS+Index/F65307D0E7C6CA008525 2B00006DEA10/$FILE/Wilber-L-Ross-12.21.17-278T.pdf. Alexander, "Lies, China and Putin."

125. Dan Alexander, "Senators Ask SEC to Launch Insider Trading Investigation into Wilbur Ross," *Forbes*, June 28, 2018, https://www.forbes.com/sites/danalexander/2018/06 /28/senators-ask-sec-to-launch-insider-trading-investigation-into-wilbur-ross /#756fc9907eaa.

126. John Coffee Jr., email to author, June 27, 2018.

127. U.S. Office of Government Ethics, "Certification of Ethics Agreement Compliance," 2017, 3, https://extapps2.oge.gov/201/Presiden.nsf/PAS+Index/A0A1D4D7FB3BA22485 2581D0006CE4D5/$FILE/Ross,%20Wilbur%20EA%20Certification%20Combined %201-3.pdf; Wilbur Ross, Ethics Agreement Supplement to David Maggi, Alternate Designated Agency Ethics Official, January 31, 2017, 2, 8 and 9.

128. Alexander, "New Details About Wilbur Ross' Business."

129. Wilbur Ross, Periodic Transaction Report (OGE Form 278-T), December 21, 2017, 3, https://extapps2.oge.gov/201/Presiden.nsf/PAS+Index/F65307D0E7C6CA00852582B0 006DEA10/$FILE/Wilber-L-Ross-12.21.17-278T.pdf.

130. Wilbur Ross, Periodic Transaction Report (OGE Form 278-T), June 15, 2018, 2, https:// extapps2.oge.gov/201/Presiden.nsf/PAS+Index/7552585FF9FE4294852582C00027DC19 /$FILE/Wilbur-L-Ross-06.15.2018-278T.pdf.

131. Wilbur Ross, Periodic Transaction Report (OGE Form 278-T), October 1, 2018, 2, https://extapps2.oge.gov/201/Presiden.nsf/PAS+Index/1382897FDDC40D57852583A7 002D5BE3/$FILE/Wilbur-L-Ross-10.31.2018-278T.pdf

132. Alexander, "New Details About Wilbur Ross' Business."

133. Alexander, "Wilbur Ross' Calendar Reveals Dozens."

134. Wilbur L. Ross, "Ethics Agreement for Preclearance," January 15, 2017, https://extapps2 .oge.gov/201/President.nsf/PAS+Index/C4D33DB26307189E852580C8002C7A72/$F ILE/Ross%20Wilbur%20L%20finalAdmendedEA.pdf. Alexander, "Lies, China and Putin."

135. Wilbur Ross, Public Financial Disclosure, December 19, 2016, U.S. Office of Government Ethics, https://extapps2.oge.gov/201/Presiden.nsf/PAS+Index/88642A2CA81AA6 C2852580AB00618C/$FILE/Ross%Wilbur%20L%20Final%20278.pdf.

136. Alexander, "Lies, China and Putin."

137. National Public Radio, "Transcript of Wendy Teramoto's Deposition," August 24, 2018, https://apps.npr.org/documents/document.html?id=4829106-Pages-8-243-of-Transcript -of-Wendy-Teramoto-s; Alexander, "Wilbur Ross' Calendar Reveals Dozens."

138. Wendy Teramoto, Wendy Teramoto's Public Financial Disclosure, 2018, U.S. Office of Government Ethics.

139. Robert Profusek, email to author, November 1, 2018.

140. Toluse Olorunnipa and Dan Murtaugh, "U.S. Inks China Trade Deal Promoting Finance Services, Beef," Bloomberg, May 11, 2017, https://www.bloomberg.com/news/articles/2017 -05-12/u-s-reaches-deal-to-allow-exports-of natural gas-beef-to-china; Alexander, "Wilbur Ross' Calendar Reveals Dozens."

141. Gina Chon and Pete Sweeney, "China Surrenders Little to U.S. in First Round of Trade Talks," *New York Times*, May 12, 2017; Joshua P. Meltzer, "The U.S.-China Trade Agreement— A Huge Deal for China," Brookings.edu, May 15, 2017, https://www.brookings.edu/blog /order-from-chaos/2017/05/15/the-u-s-china-trade-agreement-a-huge-deal-for-china/.

142. Bob Woodward, *Fear: Trump in the White House* (New York: Simon & Schuster, 2018), 159, Kindle.

143. Woodward, *Fear*, 160.

144. "What Is the 2020 Census?," U.S. Census 2020, https://www.census.gov/about/who.html.

145. Andrew Reamer, "The Role of the 2020 Census in the Geographic Distribution of Federal Funds by County," GW Institute of Public Policy, June 13, 2019, https://gwipp.gwu.edu /sites/g/files/zaxdza2181/f/downloads/Reamer%20NACo%20Census%2006-13-19.pdf.

146. "Importance of the Data," U.S. Census 2020, https://2020census.gov/en/census-data .html.

147. "What Is the Electoral College?," National Archives, December 23, 2019, https://www .archives.gov/electoral-college/about.

148. Department of Commerce v. New York, 588 US _ (2019), June 27, 2019, Oyez, https:// www.oyez.org/cases/2018/18-966; "Department of Commerce et al. v. New York et al. Certiorari Before Judgment to the United States Court of Appeals for the Second Circuit." Department of Commerce et al. v. New York et al., 1, U.S. Supreme Court, https:// www.supremecourt.gov/opinions/18pdf/18-966_bq7c.pdf.

149. From "Six former Census Bureau directors" to here: "Administrative Record upon Which the Secretary of Commerce Based His Decision to Reinstate a Question Concerning Citizenship on the 2020 Decennial Census," U.S. Department of Commerce, June 8, 2018, 1069–70, 1289–95, 1303, http://osec.doc.gov/opog/foia/documents/ar%20-%20 final%20filed%20-%20all%20docs%20%5bcertification-index-documents%5d %206.8.18.pdf.

150. "Administrative Record upon Which the Secretary of Commerce," U.S. Department of Commerce, 1325.

151. "Administrative Record upon Which the Secretary of Commerce," U.S. Department of Commerce, 1331.

152. "Resolution Recommending That the House of Representatives Find William P. Barr, Attorney General of the United States, and Wilbur L. Ross, Jr., Secretary of Commerce, In Contempt of Congress for Refusal to Comply with Subpoenas Duly Issued by the Committee on Oversight and Reform," House of Representatives, June 24, 2019, 5, https://oversight.house.gov/sites/democrats.oversight.house.gov/files/census-contempt-report.pdf; Department of Commerce et al. v. New York et al., June 27, 2019, U.S. Supreme Court, 5, https://www.supremecourt.gov/opinions/18pdf/18-966_bq7c.pdf.

153. Hearing with Commerce Secretary Ross, Ways and Means committee Republicans, March 22, 2018, U.S. House of Representatives, http://www.youtube.com/watch?v=vylt-NTsT8I&feature=youtu.be&t=1h27m37s.

154. Hearing with Commerce Secretary Ross, Ways and Means committee Republicans, March 22, 2018.

155. "Resolution Recommending That the House of Representatives Find William P. Barr, Attorney General of the United States, and Wilbur L. Ross, Jr., Secretary of Commerce, in Contempt of Congress for Refusal to Comply with Subpoenas Duly Issued by the Committee on Oversight and Reform," House of Representatives, June 24, 2019, 5, https://oversight.house.gov/sites/democrats.oversight.house.gov/files/census-contempt-report.pdf.

156. "Hearing: FY19 Budget—Department of Commerce," U.S. House of Representatives Appropriations Committee, YouTube, March 20, 2018, https://www.youtube.com/watch?v=NDWiAiSWgNU&feature=youtu.be&t=4615; George Khoury, Esq, "What Are the Penalties for Lying to Congress?" FindLaw, March 2, 2017, https://blogs.findlaw.com/blotter/2017/03/what-are-the-penalties-for-lying-to-congress.html; "18 U.S. Code § 1621. Perjury Generally," Legal Information Institute, Cornell Law School, https://www.law|.cornell.edu/uscode/text/18/1621.

157. "Committee Approves Subpoenas in Security Clearance and Census Investigations," U.S. House of Representatives, April 2, 2019, https://oversight.house.gov/news/press-releases/committee-approves-subpoenas-in-security-clearance-and-census-investigations.

158. "Meet the Attorney General," U.S. Department of Justice, https://www.justice.gov/ag/staff-profile/meet-attorney-general.

159. "Resolution Recommending That the House of Representatives Find William P. Barr."

160. Andrew Desiderio, Twitter, July 24, 2019, https://twitter.com/AndrewDesiderio/status/1154132977829470212/photo/1.

161. "Resolution Recommending That the House of Representatives Find William P. Barr," 30, 31; "Findings of Fact and Conclusions of Law," State of New York et al. v. U.S. Department of Commerce, January 15, 2019, 8, https://assets.documentcloud.org/documents/5684706/Jan-15-2019-Ruling-by-U-S-District-Judge-Jesse.pdf; "Findings of Fact and Conclusions of Law," State of California et al. v. Wilbur Ross et al., 4, https://assets.documentcloud.org/documents/5760836/March-6-2019-Opinion-by-U-S-District-Judge.pdf; "Findings of Fact and Conclusions of Law," Robyn Kravitz, et al., v. United States Department of Commerce, et al., 8, https://assets.documentcloud.org/documents/5796349/April-5-2019-Opinion-by-U-S-District-Judge.pdf.

162. "Certiorari Before Judgment to the United States Court of Appeals for the Second Circuit," Department of Commerce et al. v. New York et al., June 27, 2019, U.S. Supreme Court, 5, https://www.supremecourt.gov/opinions/18pdf/18-966_bq7c.pdf.

163. David Storper, interviewed by author, July 1, 2019.

CHAPTER ELEVEN: 2020 MONEY

1. FEC Form 99, Donald J. Trump for President, Inc., January 20, 2017, docquery.fec.gov /pdf/569/201701209041436569/201701209041436569.pdf.

2. FEC Form 2 Statement of Candidacy, Obama, Barack, April 4, 2011, docquery.fec.gov /pdf/496/11930586496/11930586496.pdf; FEC Form 2 Statement of Candidacy, Bush, George W., May 15, 2003, docquery.fec.gov/pdf/753/23038081753/23038081753.pdf.

3. Federal Election Commission, Trump, Donald J. / Michael R. Pence, Candidate for President, ID: P80001571, Republican Party, Financial Summary, www.fec.gov/data/candi date/P80001571/?cycle=2016&election_full=true.

4. 13. FEC Form 3P, Report of Receipts and Disbursements, Donald J. Trump for President, Inc., filed June 20, 2016, docquery.fec.gov/cgi-bin/forms/C00580100/1079423/; FEC Form 3P Report of Receipts and Disbursements, Donald J. Trump for President, Inc., filed July 20, 2016, docquery.fec.gov/cgi-bin/forms/C00580100/1089674/.

5. Federal Election Commission, Trump, Donald J. / Michael R. Pence, Candidate for President, ID: P80001571, Republican Party, Financial Summary.

6. Form 990, 58th Presidential Inaugural Committee, Internal Revenue Service, https:// apps.irs.gov/pub/epostcard/cor/814463688_201710_990O_2018041215256354.pdf.

7. John Santucci, Matthew Mosk, Allison Pecorin, and Benjamin Siegel, "President Donald Trump's inaugural fund spent lavishly at his DC hotel, new docs show," ABC News, https:// abcnews.go.com/Politics/president-donald-trumps-inaugural-fund-spent-lavishly-dc /story?id=60361242; Maggie Haberman, Sharon LaFraniere, and Ben Protess, "At Trump's Inauguration, $10,000 for Makeup and Lots of Room Service, *The New York Times,* https:// www.nytimes.com/2019/01/14/us/politics/trump-inauguration-spending.html.

8. Analysis of FEC filings and Donald Trump's financial disclosure report. Donald Trump, OGE Form 278e, U.S. Office of Government Ethics 5C.F.R. art 2634, 05/15/2019.

9. Analysis of Donald Trump, OGE Form 278e; Trump International Hotel Liquor License Filings with Trust Info, ProPublica, January 26, 2017, 7, www.documentcloud.org /documents/3442581-Trump-International-Hotel-Liquor-License-Filings#document/p7.

10. Donald Trump, OGE Form 278e, U.S. Office of Government Ethics, 5 C.F.R. part 2634, May 15, 2019 (hereafter "Donald Trump, OGE Form 278e"), 10, 83, 63– 64, 65; Trump International Hotel Liquor License Filings with Trust Info, ProPublica, January 26, 2017, 7, www.documentcloud.org/documents/3442581-Trump-International-Hotel -Liquor-License-Filings#document/ p7.

11. Analysis of Federal Election Commission, Disbursements, Donald J. Trump for President, Inc.

12. Federal Election Commission, Schedule F, Itemized Coordinated Expenditures Made by Political Party Committees or Designated Agents on Behalf of Candidates for Federal Office, Filing FEC- 1192140, docquery.fec.gov/cgi-bin/forms/C00003418/1192140/sf; Federal Election Commission, Schedule F, Itemized Coordinated Expenditures Made by Political Party Committees or Designated Agents on Behalf of Candidates for Federal Office, Filing FEC- 1195108, docquery.fec.gov/cgi-bin/forms/C00003418/1194108/sf; Federal Election Commission, Schedule F, Itemized Coordinated Expenditures Made by Political Party Committees or Designated Agents on Behalf of Candidates for Federal Office, Filing FEC- 1210374, docquery.fec.gov/cgi-bin/forms/C00003418/1210374/sf; Federal Election Commission, Trump, Donald J., Candidate for President, ID: P80001571, Republican Party, Financial Summary.

13. Analysis of Federal Election Commission, Disbursements, Donald J. Trump for President, Inc.

14. Donald Trump, OGE Form 278e, May 15, 2019, 77; Trump International Hotel Liquor License Filings, 7.

15. Analysis of Federal Election Commission, Disbursements, Donald J. Trump for President, Inc.

16. Securities and Exchange Commission, WFRBS Commercial Mortgage Trust 2012 C7, Commercial Mortgage Pass- Through Certificates, Series C7, 97, www.sec.gov/Archives/edgar/data/1550120/000119312512254009/d350280dfwp.htm.

17. New York City public record; Securities and Exchange Commission, WFRBS Commercial Mortgage Trust 2012 C7, Commercial Mortgage Pass- Through Certificates, Series 2012 C7.

18. Dan Alexander, "How Donald Trump Shifted $11 Million of Campaign Donor Money into His Business," *Forbes*, December 6, 2018, www.forbes.com/sites/danalexander/2018/12/06/how-donald-trump-shifted-11mcampaign-donor-money-into-his-business/#a9a9e204d34c; author's audio recording, around November 20, 2018.

19. Author's audio recording, around November 20, 2018.

20. Alexander, "How Donald Trump Shifted $11 Million of Campaign Donor Money into His Business."

21. Analysis of Federal Election Commission, Donald J. Trump for President, Inc.

22. Analysis of Federal Election Commission, Donald J. Trump for President, Inc.

23. Analysis of restaurant space and Federal Election Commission, Disbursements, Donald J. Trump for President, Inc.

24. Analysis accounting for inflation of Prospectus Supplement, Wells Fargo Commercial Mortgage Trust 2012- LC5, Securities and Exchange Commission, July 20, 2012, 33, www.sec.gov/Archives/edgar/data/850779/000153949712000571/prospectus-supplement.htm.

25. Real estate expert, interviewed by author, March 15, 2019.

26. Eric Anton, telephone interview with author, March 2019; Dave Rodgers, telephone interview with author, March 15, 2019.

27. Donald Trump, OGE Form 278e, May 15, 2019, 55, and June 14, 2017, 28; Trump International Hotel Liquor License Filings, 7.

28. Federal Election Commission, Schedule B P, Itemized Disbursements, Tag Air, docquery.fec.gov/cgi-bin/fecimg/?201904159146326889.

29. Jerry Useem, "What Does Donald Trump Really Want?," Fortune, April 3, 2000, fortune.com/2000/04/03/what-does-donald-trump-really-want/.

30. "#1001 Donald Trump," *Forbes,* www.forbes.com/ profile/ donald- trump/#45afd82447bd.

31. Dan Alexander and Matt Drange, "Trump's Net Worth Tanks on New Forbes List of Richest Americans," Forbes, October 17, 2017, www.forbes.com/ sites/ danalexander/2017/10/17/the-poorer-president-donald-trumps-fortune-falls-600-million year/#6b91c2f3141b.

32. "#1001 Donald Trump."

33. Alexander and Drange, "Trump's Net Worth Tanks"; "Remarks by President Trump in Meeting with African American Leaders," White House, February 28, 2020, www.whitehouse.gov/briefings-statements/remarks-president-trump-meeting-african-american-leaders/.

34. "#1001 Donald Trump."

35. "Ross: Physically impossible for there to be a recession in 2020 with USMCA," Fox Business, January 30, 2020, https://www.youtube.com/watch?v=4qjxw8QWqfo.

36. Johns Hopkins University of Medicine, "Coronavirus Resource Center," https://coronavirus.jhu.edu/us-map.

37. Remarks by President Trump in Meeting with African American Leaders, February 28, 2020, https://www.whitehouse.gov/briefings-statements/remarks-president-trump-meeting-african-american-leaders/.

38. Dan Alexander, "Trump's Net Worth Drops, $1 Billion As Coronavirus Infects the President's Business," *Forbes*, April 2, 2020, https://www.forbes.com/sites/danalexander /#7c92f1a53c7a.

39. Matthew Galvin, telephone interview with author, March 24, 2020.

40. The White House, "President Donald J. Trump Is Providing Economic Relief to American Workers, Families, and Businesses Impacted by the Coronavirus," March 27, 2020, https://www.whitehouse.gov/briefings-statements/president-donald-j-trump-providing -economic-relief-american-workers-families-businesses-impacted-coronavirus/.

41. Department of the Treasury, "Paycheck Protection Program (PPP) Information Sheet: Borrowers," https://home.treasury.gov/system/files/136/PPP--Fact-Sheet.pdf.

42. "Sen. Schumer Breaks Down Massive Coronavirus Aid Package," MSNBC, March 25, 2020, https://www.youtube.com/watch?v=KbIy7zL74G0&t=625s

43. "H.R. 748 – Cares Act," U.S. Congress, https://www.congress.gov/bill/116th-congress /house-bill/748?q=%7B%22search%22%3A%5B%22cite%3APL116-136%22 %5D%7D&s=1&r=1.

44. Merrick Dresnin, interviewed by author, May 13, 2020.

45. New York Department of Labor, WARN notice, April 6, 2020, https://labor.ny.gov/app /warn/details.asp?id=7857; New York Department of Labor, WARN notice, March 25, 2020, https://labor.ny.gov/app/warn/details.asp?id=7825; Letter, Janine Gill to Steven Gustafon, Todd Wodraska, and Dave Kerner, April 3, 2020; State of California Employment Development Department, WARN report, July 1, 2019 to June 30, 2020, https:// edd.ca.gov/Jobs_and_Training/warn/WARN-Report-for-7-1-2019-to-6-30-2020.pdf; Letter, Janine Gill to Steven Gustafon, Gail Coniglio, and Dave Kerner, March 27, 2020; Letter, Al Linares to Steven Gustafon, Juan Carlos Bermudez, and Carlos A. Gimenez, March 27, 2020; Letter, LaDawndre Stinson to Carolyn Goodman and Marilyn Kirkpatrick, April 3, 2020; Washington, D.C., Department of Employment Services, WARN notifications, https://does.dc.gov/page/industry-closings-and-layoffs-warn-notifications -2020; Illinois Department of Commerce and Economic Opportunity, WARN report, March 31, 2020; Virginia Employment Commission, WARN notice, April 2, 2020, https://www.vec.virginia.gov/warn-notice-detail/11787; Letter, Scott Ingwers to Scott Murakami and Kirk Caldwell, March 31, 2020.

46. Frankie Ortiz, interview with author, June 10, 2020.

47. Donald Trump, OGE Form 278e, 7.

48. Eric Trump, Twitter, June 10, 2020, https://twitter.com/EricTrump/status/12709067 67300603904.

49. Donald J. Trump, Twitter, June 10, 2020, https://twitter.com/realDonaldTrump/status /1270907701472747520.

50. "Florida Coronavirus Map and Case Count," *The New York Times*, https://www.nytimes .com/interactive/2020/us/florida-coronavirus-cases.html.

51. The White House, "Remarks by President Trump, Vice President Pence, and Members of the Coronavirus Task Force in Press Briefing," March 21, 2020, https://www.whitehouse .gov/briefings-statements/remarks-president-trump-vice-president-pence-members-coro navirus-task-force-press-briefing-7/.

52. Mortgage, Assignment of Leases and Rents, Fixture Filing and Security Agreement, Trump Endeavor 12 LLC, Deutsche Bank Trust Company Americas, August 7, 2015 and June 11, 2012.

53. Analysis of financial disclosure, interest rate benchmarks, and property records; Donald Trump, OGE Form 278e, May 15, 2019; Valuation Adjustment Board, Miami-Dade County, records related to property tax appeals for Trump National Doral, 227; 1 Month London Interbank Offered Rate (LIBOR), based on U.S. Dollar (USD1MTD156N),

https:// fred.stlouisfed.org/series/USD1MTD156N; 3 Month London Interbank Offered Rate (LIBOR), based on U.S. Dollar (USD3MTD156N), https:// fred.stlouisfed.org /series/ USD3MTD156N; 6 Month London Interbank Offered Rate (LIBOR), based on U.S. Dollar (USD6MTD156N), https:// fred.stlouisfed.org/series/ USD6MTD156N; 12 Month London Interbank Offered Rate (LIBOR), based on U.S. Dollar (USD-12MD156N), https:// fred.stlouisfed.org/series/ USD12MD156N; Bank Prime Loan Rate (DPRIME), https:// fred.stlouisfed.org/series/ DPRIME; Mortgage, Assignment of Leases and Rents, Fixture Filing and Security Agreement, Trump Endeavor 12 LLC, Deutsche Bank Trust Company Americas, August 7, 2015, and June 11, 2012.

54. Valuation Adjustment Board, Miami-Dade County, records related to property tax appeals for Trump National Doral, 227.

55. Spokesperson for the Trump Organization, email to author, March 12, 2020.

56. Analysis of financial disclosure, interest rate benchmarks, and property records; Donald Trump, OGE Form 278e, May 15, 2019; 1 Month London Interbank Offered Rate (LIBOR), based on U.S. Dollar (USD1MTD156N), https:// fred.stlouisfed.org/series /USD1MTD156N; 3 Month London Interbank Offered Rate (LIBOR), based on U.S. Dollar (USD3MTD156N), https:// fred.stlouisfed.org/series/ USD3MTD156N; 6 Month London Interbank Offered Rate (LIBOR), based on U.S. Dollar (USD6M-TD156N), https:// fred.stlouisfed.org/series/ USD6MTD156N; 12 Month London Interbank Offered Rate (LIBOR), based on U.S. Dollar (USD12MD156N), https:// fred .stlouisfed.org/series/ USD12MD156N; Bank Prime Loan Rate (DPRIME), https:// fred .stlouisfed.org/series/ DPRIME; Mortgage, Assignment of Leases and Rents, Fixture Filing and Security Agreement, Trump Endeavor 12 LLC, Deutsche Bank Trust Company Americas, August 7, 2015, and June 11, 2012.

57. Leasehold deed of Trust, Assignment of Leases and Rents, Fixture Filing and Security Agreement, Trump Old Post Office LLC and Deutsche Bank Trust Company Americas, Washington, D.C., Recorder of Deeds, Doc No. 2014073616, August 12, 2014.

58. Analysis of financial documents released by the *Washington Post,* report published by CNN, President Trump's 2019 financial disclosure report, Ivanka Trump's 2019 financial disclosure report, interest rate benchmarks, and property records.

59. David Enrich, Ben Protess, and Eric Lipton, "Trump's Company Seeks to Ease Financial Crunch as Coronavirus Takes Toll," *New York Times,* April 2, 2020, www.nytimes .com/2020/04/02/business/economy/coronavirus-trump-company-finances.html; Leasehold Deed of Trust, Assignment of Leases and Rents, Fixture Filing and Security Agreement, Trump Old Post Office LLC and Deutsche Bank Trust Company Americas, Washington, D.C., Recorder of Deeds, Doc. No. 2014073616, August 12, 2014. Mortgage, Assignment of leases and rents, fixture filing and security agreement, Trump Endeavor 12 LLC, Deutsche Bank Trust Company Americas, August 7, 2015; Mortgage, Assignment of leases and rents, fixture filing and security agreement, Trump Endeavor 12 LLC, Deutsche Bank Trust Company Americas, June 11, 2012.

60. Analysis of Wells Fargo Commercial Mortgage Trust 2012- LC5, Prospectus Supplement; analysis of Nike lease, November 30, 1995, 7, New York City Department of Finance, Office of the City Register, a836-acris.nyc.gov/DS/DocumentSearch/DocumentImage View?doc_id=FT_1180004945118.

61. Don Fox, interviewed by the author, May 12, 2020; Virginia Canter, interviewed by the author, May 13, 2020; Richard Painter, interviewed by the author, May 11, 2020; Marilyn Glynn, interviewed by the author, May 16, 2020; Walter Shaub, interviewed by the author, May 15, 2020.

62. Analysis of *Forbes* research.